OXFORD MONOGRAPHS ON
LABOUR LAW

General Editors: Paul Davies,
Keith Ewing, Mark Freedland

JUSTICE IN DISMISSAL

Oxford Monographs on Labour Law

General Editors: Paul Davies, Fellow of Balliol College, Oxford and Reader in Law at Oxford University; Keith Ewing, Professor of Public Law at King's College, London; and Mark Freedland, Fellow and Tutor in Law at St. John's College, Oxford.

This series is the first new development in the literature dealing with labour law for many years. The series recognizes the arrival not only of a renewed interest in labour law generally, but also the need for a fresh approach to the study of labour law following a decade of momentous change in the UK and Europe. The series is concerned with all aspects of labour law, including traditional subjects of study such as industrial relations law and individual employment law, but it will also include books which examine the law and economics of the labour market and the impact of social security law upon patterns of employment and the employment contract.

Titles already published in this series

The Right to Strike
K. D. EWING

Legislating for Conflict
SIMON AUERBACH

Justice in Dismissal

The Law of Termination of Employment

HUGH COLLINS

CLARENDON PRESS · OXFORD
1992

Oxford University Press, Walton Street, Oxford OX2 6DP
Oxford New York Toronto
Delhi Bombay Calcutta Madras Karachi
Petaling Jaya Singapore Hong Kong Tokyo
Nairobi Dar es Salaam Cape Town
Melbourne Auckland
and associated companies in
Berlin Ibadan

Oxford is a trade mark of Oxford University Press

Published in the United States
by Oxford University Press, New York

British Library Cataloguing in Publication Data
Data available

Library of Congress Cataloging in Publication Data
Collins, Hugh, 1953–
Justice in dismissal : the law of termination of employment /
Hugh Collins.
(Oxford monographs on labour law)
Includes bibliographical references and index.
1. Employees, Dismissal of—Law and legislation—Great Britain.
I. Title II. Series.
KD3110.C65   1992   344.41'012596—dc20   [344.10412596]   91–35922
ISBN 0–19–825435–0

Typeset by Cambridge Composing (UK) Ltd
Printed in Great Britain by
Biddles Ltd
Guildford & King's Lynn

To
Katrina and Allegra

Editor's Preface

It is our aim as editors of this series to promote the publication of books which will make a distinctive contribution to the study of labour law. For this purpose, we have adopted a deliberately open-ended view of the subject. Consequently we expect to deal with topics which straddle the frontiers between labour law and other areas of law, whether it be social security law, pensions law, or company law. We expect that books in the series will not necessarily adopt a formal or legalistic approach, for we would wish to encourage authors to draw upon the contributions made by other disciplines, whether it be industrial relations, political science or economics. And we expect, finally, that books in the series will not concentrate exclusively on legal developments in Britain. We are conscious of the importance of EEC law, and aware of the growing interest in the labour laws of EEC member states, as well as in comparative labour law generally.

We feel that this third title to appear in the series amply sustains the level of intellectual inquiry which the series has sought to attain. Hugh Collins is among the most persistent and effective challengers to existing orthodoxies, whether substantive or methodological, working in the area of labour law. It must constitute a major event in this field of scholarship that he has decided to offer a fundamental evaluation of the extent to which the law concerning termination of employment can claim to have realized any ideal of industrial justice. His further decision to relate that evaluation to theories of moral and political philosophy, and his rejection of the possibility of value-free interpretation of the law as it stands, make the editors optimistic that this work will indicate the wider jurisprudential significance of the law about unfair dismissal and about redundancy, as well as enriching the literature in a central part of labour law itself.

P.L.D.
K.D.E.
M.R.F.

5 November 1991

Preface

DISMISSAL is the popular term used to describe an employer's action of terminating a contract of employment with a particular employee. This book examines the law of termination of employment in the United Kingdom (except Northern Ireland) with a view to assessing the justice achieved for employees by its provisions and social effects. It is a critical assessment, one which both challenges some of the basic principles of the law and points to misconceived interpretations and unsatisfactory applications of the law to particular cases. The source of these criticisms springs in part from detailed examination of the effects of the law and selective comparisons with other legal systems, but primarily the critique engages with perspectives derived from moral and political philosophy. This is a work, therefore, which combines legal analysis with deeper reflections about the demands of social justice. I hope that this book will prove of interest not only to labour lawyers but also to philosophers and anyone interested in the social justice achieved by the institutions of modern industrial societies.

During many years working in this field in Oxford I benefited from the advice, criticisms, but above all from the encouragement of Mark Freedland. Without his enthusiasm I doubt whether this work could have been finished, or, rather, separated from everything else which interests me. I am also particularly grateful to the Fellows of Brasenose College who granted me exceptional leave, and the American Council of Learned Societies which funded research for a broader project, of which this book evidently forms a part, on workplace justice as a whole. The other editors of this series, Paul Davies and Keith Ewing, gave me the benefit of their detailed comments on the essays which comprise this book. In addition, Emily Jackson saved me from many obscurities and Arabella Tait provided most efficient research assistance.

H.C.

London School of Economics
1 May 1991

Contents

x   Contents

Abbreviations

AC	Law Reports Appeal Cases
ACAS	Advisory, Conciliation, and Arbitration Service
BJIR	*British Journal of Industrial Relations*
CA	Court of Appeal
Ch.	Law Reports Chancery Division
Ch. D.	High Court Chancery Division
Ct. Sess.	Court of Session
Div. Ct.	Divisional Court of the Queen's Bench
EAT	Employment Appeal Tribunal
ECHR	European Court of Human Rights
ECJ	European Court of Justice
EPCA	Employment Protection (Consolidation) Act
HL	House of Lords
ICR	Industrial Cases Reports
ILJ	*Industrial Law Journal*
ILO	International Labour Organization
IRLR	Industrial Relations Law Reports
IT	Industrial Tribunal
ITR	Industrial Tribunal Reports
KIR	Knight's Industrial Reports
LQR	*Law Quarterly Review*
MSPB	Merit Systems Protection Board
NIRC	National Industrial Relations Court
QB	Law Reports Queen's Bench
RTDC	*Revue Trimestrielle Droit Civil*
S. Ct.	Supreme Court
SI	Statutory Instrument
USCA	United States Court of Appeals
WLR	Weekly Law Reports

Table of Cases

France

Table of Statutes

United States

France

European Community

Introduction

WE frequently demand justice from the State and in our relations with others. This desire for justice encompasses demands with respect to both the distribution of wealth and power in society and the manner in which individuals and institutions conduct themselves towards us. Debates about justice usually focus upon the question of how the institutions of the State and law should be arranged in order to satisfy such ends as promoting the common good and the protection of individual rights. But here our interest lies in a microcosm of those questions of justice, namely justice in the workplace.

But what is justice in the workplace? At its core, no doubt, lies the principle of a fair day's work for a fair day's pay. Since work and pay are allocated in market economies through contracts of employment, the central question of workplace justice becomes the fairness of this exchange relation. There can be few more hotly contested issues in modern industrial societies than whether bargains between employers and individual employees achieve a fair exchange, or whether the bargaining position of the employee needs to be improved by either state intervention or the promotion of collective bargaining. Despite the importance of this issue for general schemes of social justice, we should not overlook the fact that the workplace provides the site for other significant dimensions of justice such as physical safety, equality of opportunity, and personal fulfilment.

In particular, the nature of the relations established in the typical workplace raise the issue of whether the distribution of power between employer and worker can satisfy acceptable criteria of justice. It is widely recognized that employees, on taking a job, enter into a relation of subordination to their employers, though the causes and exact dimensions of this power relation remain controversial. The employer normally acquires the right to direct production and manage the workforce to serve the goals of the business. The workforce assumes a correlative obligation to comply with lawful instructions, with disobedience being deterred by the threat of disciplinary sanctions. This relation of subordination should also be subjected to scrutiny in order to determine the justice of its arrangements. We can ask such questions as whether this inequality of power serves worthwhile general interests in collective welfare and whether the disciplinary power is exercised fairly and with due regard for the interests of individual employees.

The essays comprising this book examine these issues of justice in connection with the fiercest sanction which backs up managerial authority to direct the workforce, the power of dismissal. By terminating the contract of employment, the employer deprives individual workers of their major source of income. The dismissal may also deprive workers of membership of the most significant community in their life and jeopardize their status in society more generally. Although the harm caused to the employee by dismissal will depend heavily on how quickly and in what capacity he or she regains employment elsewhere, there can be little doubt that in many instances the disciplinary power of an employer is equivalent or greater in its effects to that exercised by the criminal courts. In the same way as state punishment must be critically examined in all its aspects to discover whether it rests upon sound and acceptable principles of justice, so too the disciplinary practices of employers should be tested against ideals of justice.

In Britain these disciplinary practices were regarded as sufficiently unsatisfactory by the conventional standards of justice for legislation to control the abuse of managerial power to be introduced in Parliament in 1971. The law of unfair dismissal, now contained in the Employment Protection (Consolidation) Act 1978, permits workers to contest the reasonableness of their dismissals before specialist Industrial Tribunals, and, if they succeed in demonstrating the unfairness of the dismissal, they may be reinstated to their jobs or receive compensation. These Industrial Tribunals therefore have the task of determining the fairness of dismissals, and in so doing they must articulate a conception of justice in the workplace with respect to the power of dismissal.

The availability of these decisions, and those of higher appeal courts, for scrutiny makes it possible here in this book to consider the issue of justice in workplace discipline, not only at the highest abstract levels of social and political theory, but also in the concrete context of a multitude of reported cases. This opportunity is vital to the success of my enterprise, for without the constant juxtaposition of the general and the particular, without the need to discover a principled basis for particular decisions, and without the need to explain the precise application of abstract ideals, a theory of justice in the workplace would dissolve into either anodyne abstractions or chaotic particularity.

Even though this material appears promising for a thorough examination of one aspect of workplace justice, it has to be admitted that popular perceptions of justice differ markedly in this everyday context. Any view of the appropriate principles and their application to particular cases may appear little more than an arbitrary choice between a wide range of available standards. These standards for the fairness of dismissals range from the impractical stance that employees should always keep their jobs, to the other extreme view, which would undermine the legislation completely, that employers should enjoy an unlimited discretionary power to terminate employment at will. To overcome this problem of diversity of perceptions of justice in dismissal, we must devise a method for ascertaining in a systematic and convincing fashion the appropriate principles of justice. Before identifying this method, we should highlight some of the factors which prevent the adoption of any simple principle of justice in dismissal.

We should realize from the outset that termination of employment may occur in a wide range of cases, from deliberate sex and race discrimination, to a strict insistence upon demanding performance standards, to the simple insolvency of the business. Each of these reasons for dismissal demands a separate principled response. Even where the reason for dismissal is similar, such as theft from the employer, we should recognize that the variety of jobs, each with its traditional standards of conduct and particular disciplinary standards, may compel separate and distinct treatment of each case. Some employees will be dismissed for taking trivial amounts, such as stationary worth 50p or a hamburger from the canteen, whereas others who use the office telephone for private calls costing hundreds of pounds will merely be reprimanded. We must anticipate, therefore, that not only will the relevant principles of justice be controversial, but also that they must be exceedingly complex in order to cope with the variety of contexts surrounding dismissals.

For these reasons, readers will not discover in the following pages some brief set of principles of justice which can be applied to all cases of dismissal. Nor will they discover a comprehensive treatment of every type of case which might arise before a tribunal. Nor will they even discover a unified style of moral and political reasoning which points to the appropriate principles of justice. Instead they will discover eight essays organized around particular problems of justice raised by cases of termination of employment and the law governing them. Each essay adopts methods which seem to me to be the most appropriate to find useful and constructive solutions to the questions of justice raised in these contexts. Since the methodology and aims of this work may prove unfamiliar and puzzling, in this introduction it seems helpful to provide an initial explanation of my general approach.

The central method of the book for articulating the appropriate principles of justice involves an interpretative stance. We examine both the legislation and the decided cases with a view to discovering the underlying principles which best explain the political and legal decisions behind them. Such an interpretation commences by seeking general principles which are broadly consistent with the legal materials. But then a further choice must be made between the range of principles which might account for the law, for each principle represents differing conceptions of justice in dismissal. This choice necessarily involves a moral decision. This decision must be informed by reflection upon the consequences for the employer's power of dismissal of the adoption of one amongst many competing principles. It must also be informed both by a sense of historical development and a knowledge of the powers and limitations of the legal institutions engaged in the application of the law. These dimensions contribute to the persuasive force of the interpretation of the appropriate principles of justice. But, in the final analysis, the selection of a particular interpretation must be grounded in moral evaluation.

A simple example of this interpretation method should make it appear less confusing. When an employer decides to dismiss an employee for redundancy, that is, when, because of changing market circumstances, the employer no longer has any need for his or her services through no fault of his or her own, the question arises whether in fairness the employer ought to consult the employee. Some tribunals have viewed such discussions with the individual as an essential element of fair treatment, whereas others have tended to view such an exercise as a futile waste of time. An interpretative approach examines these differing views in order to discern the underlying principles of justice at stake. The former view probably rests on an ideal of respect for the dignity of the individual employee, whereas the latter emphasizes the need to ensure the efficiency of personnel practices. We must then choose between these principles to discover the best interpretation of the law. We must ask which principle best accounts for the details of the legislation and decisions of the tribunals in this matter and related issues such as disciplinary procedures in other kinds of dismissals. But if this examination of the legal materials reveals diversity and inconsistency, as I suggest it often will, then ultimately the interpretative method requires a moral choice between the competing principles. Although this choice inescapably depends upon moral considerations, we should also consider the consequence of a selection of a particular principle for industrial relations, manpower policies, employers' personnel practices, and other general welfare considerations, and then temper the choice of principle in order to avoid potential adverse consequences in these fields. With all these factors in mind, we may conclude that the principle of efficiency best accounts for the law and suggests the best interpretation of it, provided that it is recognized that efficiency actually points strongly in favour of consultation with the employee on certain aspects of the dismissal and his or her future prospects for employment.

This interpretative approach necessarily breaks with the tradition of legal scholarship which seeks to provide an accurate and comprehensive statement of the current law. Other books have assayed this task and no doubt prove invaluable to legal practitioners in the field. But I believe that any scrupulous account could only reveal inconsistencies in the legislative provisions and the decisions of the tribunals, and in these inconsistencies I detect rival conceptions of justice in dismissal. By articulating these rival conceptions in this book, we should be in a better position to select between them, and thus discover the predominant line of authoritative decisions about the content of the current law.

But of course my ultimate aim does not lie simply in providing a useful description of the law. What interests me most is the moral evaluation of the rival conceptions of justice in dismissal revealed in the legislative provisions and the tribunals' decisions. The best interpretation of the law thus becomes a critical interpretation. It rejects as morally unacceptable some aspects of law and the principles on which those legal provisions rest.

[1]

Harsh But Fair

MR MATHEWSON probably now regrets taking a lunch break. On 10 December 1987 he left his work as a chrome finisher responsible for polishing metal dentures, a job which he had held for five and a half years, to go to the bank to cash his pay cheque. By chance he met a friend waiting at a bus stop, from whom he purchased a small amount of cannabis for his personal use. He decided to take his little stash home, but on the way he saw a fellow employee having his lunch in the park, so he stopped for a chat. Two police officers then approached and with apparent clairvoyance arrested him on suspicion of being in possession of drugs. They took him to the police office and charged him. Eventually he returned to work an hour late. One of the directors of the company asked him for an explanation, and he confessed that he had been arrested for possession of cannabis. The director discussed the matter with another senior employee, then summarily dismissed Mr Mathewson. Feeling that he had been treated unjustly, Mr Mathewson brought a claim for unfair dismissal before an Industrial Tribunal, a specialist court comprising a legally qualified chairman and two wingmen representing each side of industry.

The tribunal noted that the employers had not discussed the issue with Mr Mathewson, therefore giving him no chance to explain himself or point to any mitigating factors in his favour. Nor had they given him the company personnel handbook, which stated that an employee would be dismissed, 'should he or she be convicted by a court of an offence such as theft, indecent behaviour or assault, which, although not connected with the company, gives reasonable doubt as to the individual suitability for employment in our type of business'. Nor was there any evidence either at the time of the dismissal or at the hearing before the tribunal to suggest that the employee had ever used or been in possession of drugs at work. Mr Mathewson explained to the tribunal that he enjoyed a spliff at weekends and in the evenings at home because it helped him to relax. Nevertheless, a majority of the tribunal (the legally qualified chairman dissenting) decided that the dismissal was fair. They came to the conclusion that it could not be said, on the information before the employers at the time of the dismissal, that their reaction in dismissing the employee summarily, although harsh, was outwith the band of reasonable responses, and so the dismissal was fair. The employee's appeal was subsequently dismissed, because the Employment

Appeal Tribunal could not find that the lower tribunal had misdirected itself in law or had reached a perverse conclusion on the facts.[1]

Harsh but fair: the adjectival apposition reveals the true colours of the law of unfair dismissal. The tribunal regarded the director's decision as a severe punishment, one which the tribunal itself, if it had been charged with making the decision, would not have reached. For being an hour late back for work, Mr Mathewson lost his source of income, probably resulting in economic hardship, and the ensuing harm to his reputation probably made it difficult for him to regain employment where he could exercise his skills. Yet the test of fairness under the legislation, as it has been interpreted by the courts, does not permit the tribunal to substitute its own judgment on the facts of the case; it is limited to the question whether the employer's decision was so unreasonable that it fell outside the boundaries of any possible reasonable response to the employee's misconduct. Only when the employer's decision steps outside this charmed and manipulable circle will an Industrial Tribunal regard the dismissal as unreasonable and unfair.

How has this happened? How has the law of unfair dismissal, which was heralded as protecting employees' job security, as even giving workers property rights in their jobs,[2] become sterilized to such an extent that it endorses and legitimizes harsh disciplinary treatment of employees and only deters wholly unreasonable, irrational, and arbitrary dismissals? This chapter examines the forces which have contributed to this gap between high expectations of improvements in job security and the actual application of the law to ordinary cases such as the claim presented by Mr Mathewson.

This enquiry focuses upon the attitude of the courts and tribunals to the legislation. We seek an explanation of why they adopted interpretations of the concept of fairness at the heart of the law of unfair dismissal which created merely a small improvement in the job security of employees. Before tackling this central question, however, we should reflect more systematically upon the aims of the legislation itself. Was it really intended to grant workers a property right in their jobs? To what extent and in what respects did Parliament aim to grant employees job security? In section 1, I suggest an interpretation of the concept of job security, the general aim of the legislation, which best fits the broad scheme of the legislation. In section 2,

[1] *Mathewson* v. *R. B. Wilson Dental Laboratories* [1988] IRLR 512 (EAT).
[2] For references to this rhetoric, see P. J. White, 'Unfair Dismissal Legislation and Property Rights: Some Reflections' (1985), 16(4), *Industrial Relations Journal*, 98, at p. 104 n. 10; R. J. Sutherland, 'Redundancy: Perspectives and Policies' (1980), 11(4), *Industrial Relations Journal*, 17. For similar rhetoric in the USA, see D. J. Harmann and Y. S. Sor, 'Property Rights in One's Job: The Case for Limiting Employment-At-Will' (1982), 24, *Arizona Law Review*, 763; W. Gould, 'The Idea of the Job as Property in Contemporary America: The Legal and Collective Bargaining Framework' (1986), *Brigham Young University Law Review*, 885; G. Minda, 'The Common Law of Employment At-Will in New York: The Paralysis of Nineteenth Century Doctrine' (1985), 36, *Syracuse Law Review*, 939; M. Glendon and G. Lev, 'Changes in the Bonding of the Employment Relationship: An Essay on the New Property' (1979), 20, *Boston College Law Review*, 457.

I examine from a historical point of view the immediate political motives for the 1971 legislation which instituted the law of unfair dismissal. This combination of interpretation and historical understanding should permit a firmer grasp upon the true expectations with respect to job security which the legislation engendered. We can then match these expectations against the courts' and tribunals' interpretation of the concept of fairness, with the ultimate aim of discovering the extent to which, and the reasons why, they proceeded to frustrate the aims of the legislation in its application to individual cases.

1. GENERAL AIMS

What conception of job security lies behind the law of unfair dismissal? We should bear in mind that the legislation shows evidence both of a desire to establish a measure of job security and an acknowledgement that the protection should be confined, because the law envisages the possibility of a fair dismissal. When interpreting the general principles on which this legislation rests, it is important to commence with some brief reflections on the question why the law makes no attempt to establish an absolute entitlement to job security, a form of property right in a job.

HATS AND JOBS

What can I own? The law says that I can own my hat, but not the cold wind which makes it necessary. Ownership normally implies many different rights, duties, and other incidents, and, depending on the precise mix of legal attributes of a relation, we may properly differentiate between degrees and types of ownership.[3] In its primary meaning, however, ownership, conceived as absolute private ownership, comprises the core features of legal protection for secure possession of the thing and the right to control its sale or alienation; no one can take my hat without fear of punishment for theft, and no one (except the State) can compel me to lend or sell my hat unless I so choose. Taking ownership in this primary sense and deferring till later conceptions of job property which have reduced legal incidents,[4] we must observe that legal systems differ in their itemization of the things which may be privately owned: all include hats; none includes the wind. What about jobs?

When committing itself to a list of objects susceptible of private ownership, every legal system embodies certain political principles. These princi-

[3] A. M. Honoré, 'Ownership', in A. G. Guest (ed.), *Oxford Essays in Jurisprudence* (Oxford, 1961), Ch. 5.
[4] The arguments for and against recognition of a property right in a job are considered in greater detail in Ch. 5; see also S. Rottenburg, 'Property in Work' (1961–2), 15, *Industrial and Labor Relations Review*, 402.

ples may concern general welfare considerations, such as maximizing the wealth and happiness of the society by recognizing property rights, or they may focus on the way ownership satisfies the needs of individuals for dignity, liberty, and self-development.[5] The balance between these principles may be struck in a host of ways, and the precise interpretation and application of each principle may differ markedly. Consider, for example, the aim of maximizing the general welfare: what objects should this goal regard as suitable for private ownership? In capitalist societies, general welfare considerations such as utility and efficiency are used to justify not only private ownership of personal effects such as hats but also capital in its many forms such as land, factories, machinery, and technical knowledge.[6] In contrast, visions of an ideal communist society usually differentiate between capital, which should be controlled by the community to ensure its most beneficial use, and personal effects which may be privately owned for the sake of general welfare.[7]

Neither system, however, endorses private ownership of a job by the worker. He enjoys neither secure possession nor absolute control over its alienation. Under the centralized economic planning of an ideal communist society, the plan must also direct workers to the tasks required to be performed and so workers cannot be permitted to disrupt the plan by an insistence upon staying at the same job. Similarly, under a market economy where demand for labour directs workers to jobs, the market would cease to function efficiently if employers were not permitted to enter and to terminate contracts of employment at their discretion in the light of market conditions.

The stark antithesis between ownership of jobs and the exigencies of a market economy is revealed in the legal principles governing the contract of employment developed in Europe and the United States of America during the nineteenth century. Under these rules, which share many common principles, an employer can normally terminate the contract at any time for any reason at all. The employer enjoys the freedom to substitute another, perhaps more productive worker, at will. The employer's sole obligation towards the employee consists in the payment of any outstanding wages due under the contract, or compensatory damages for breach of that obligation. The employee cannot insist on remaining at his or her work and receiving remuneration until he or she chooses to resign.[8] Nor, of course, can an employee sell his or her job to another worker. A concierge of an apartment building in France purported to sell his position to a successor, only to

[5] Alan Ryan, *Property and Political Theory* (Oxford, 1984), 7–13.

[6] Jeremy Bentham, *The Theory of Legislation* ed. C. K. Ogden, (London, 1931), 111–23; Harold Demsetz, 'Towards a Theory of Property Rights' (1976), 57, *American Economic Review*, 347; Richard A. Posner, *Economic Analysis of Law* (3rd edn., Boston Mass., 1988), Ch. 3.

[7] Bertolt Brecht, '*The Caucasian Chalk Circle*', in John Willett and Ralph Manheim (eds.), *Bertolt Brecht Collected Plays*, (London, 1976), vii.

[8] This statement of the law may now have to be qualified in the light of recent decisions such as *Powell* v. *London Borough of Brent* [1987] IRLR 466 (CA); see Ch. 7.

discover that the court regarded the transaction as void.[9] In contrast, the employer can defend his or her private ownership of the means of production from compulsory alienation. The workers cannot acquire legal title to the plant and tools by either force or reliance upon general welfare considerations, even supposing that they could demonstrate that they could run the factory more efficiently as a workers' co-operative. Why do modern legal systems universally reject the idea of granting workers property rights in their jobs?

The underlying reason for the rejection of ownership of jobs by all types of economic system consists in an appeal to general welfare considerations. Such considerations include reference to the wealth, happiness, and satisfaction of preferences of all the members of a society. These factors suggest strongly that employers or managers of capital investments should enjoy the freedom to allocate jobs to the most productive workers.

In the first instance, this freedom permits the business to be run as efficiently as possible, maximizing production for the same labour costs. The employer can weed out the idlers and the incompetent and replace them with a skilled, committed workforce. In the longer term, such efficient businesses should survive and prosper in competitive markets, leading to high levels of employment and satisfactory levels of remuneration for the workforce. These benefits to the community as a whole would be severely impeded if each worker could insist upon retention of his or her job, regardless of competence or effort.

As well as harming productive efficiency, ownership of jobs would create friction in the labour market, by preventing reductions in the workforce to meet declining demand and by discouraging workers from seeking new jobs. This would exacerbate the problem of wage-stickiness, that is, the tendency of wages not to fall in money terms despite reduction of demand, and might therefore fuel the fires of inflation and eventually increase levels of unemployment.[10] Moreover, the question whether work is serving any productive use at all must be a matter of business judgement. By granting a worker the right to remain in possession of a particular job, regardless of whether useful work remains to be done, a property right in a job would block necessary adjustments to market conditions in the productive activities of a community.

In the light of these general welfare considerations connected with productive efficiency and the material benefits provided by a competitive economy, whether it be run on the basis of planning, markets, or some form

[9] Cass. civ. 20.2.1973 (Caillet c. Dame Nivesse), DS 1974. 34, note Malaurie.

[10] See R. A. Epstein, 'Agency Costs, Employment Contracts, and Labor Unions', in John W. Pratt and Richard J. Zeckhauser, *Principals and Agents: The Structure of Business* (Boston, Mass., 1985), 127; id. 'In Defense of the Contract at Will' (1984), 57, *University of Chicago Law Review*, 947; Jeffrey L. Harrison, 'The "New" Terminable-at-Will Employment Contract: An Interest and Cost Incidence Analysis' (1984), 69, *Iowa Law Review*, 327.

of mixed economy, it seems that a legal entitlement to absolute job security could not be justified because it poses a serious threat to general welfare. But this argument does not rule out the possibility of some limited protection for job security being consistent with general welfare considerations. We must next consider, therefore, whether the law of unfair dismissal could be justified by those same general welfare considerations which decisively rule out ownership of jobs.

GENERAL WELFARE

General welfare considerations do not point unambiguously towards granting employers the freedom to hire and fire workers at will. A general welfare calculus should include the consideration that employees may prefer a measure of job security and be prepared to sacrifice some other benefits such as higher wages for the sake of it. We should also remember the possibility that a sense of job security may encourage a worker to commit his or her efforts more wholeheartedly to the business aims of the enterprise. The Japanese system of lifetime employment in large firms is often admired and sometimes emulated because of its contribution of the efficiency of the workforce. Similarly, some firms offer informal guarantees of job security to core groups of workers in the belief that this will improve the efficiency of these groups at the expense of a relatively small additional cost.[11] In addition, legal protection from dismissal may encourage workers to voice objections to management directions rather than to quit and to impose the costs of hiring and training a new worker on the employer. It is difficult, however, to derive a justification for compulsory legal controls over an employer's power of dismissal from such general welfare considerations.[12]

One way to measure general welfare is to regard freely chosen agreements as likely to represent bargains which maximize the preferences of people. Each person selects upon an idiosyncratic scale of values what he wants most and the trade-offs he is prepared to accept. He then seeks bargains through markets which maximize the sum of those values. If everyone is permitted this freedom, then it seems likely that the outcome of all these market transactions will tend to maximize the general welfare viewed as the sum of preference satisfaction. This approach to the measurement of general welfare tends inexorably to favour the adoption of freedom of contract and to reject compulsory terms which might interfere with choices. It follows that, on this

---

[11] For examples, see J. F. Bolt, 'Job Security: Its Time has Come' (1983), 61, *Harvard Business Review*, pt. 6, p. 115.

[12] For a detailed examination of such attempts, see Note, 'Protecting At-Will Employees against Wrongful Discharge: The Duty to Terminate Only in Good Faith' (1980), 93, *Harvard Law Review*, 1816; A. S. Leonard, 'A New Common Law of Employment Termination' (1987), 66, *North Caroline Law Review*, 632, at p. 677; Note, 'Employer Opportunism and the Need for a Just Cause Standard' (1989), 103, *Harvard Law Review*, 510.

assessment of general welfare, the law should at most facilitate the creation of contracts which provide enhanced job security, by, for example, providing a remedy of an injunction to prevent the employer from going back on his or her promise, but that a mandatory prohibition against unfair dismissals should not be permitted on the ground that it is likely to detract from general welfare.

One possible challenge to this simple model relies upon the possibility of distorted preferences. It may be argued, for instance, that workers do not appreciate the value which they really place upon job security, or that although they realize its value, do not foresee either the extent to which job security will be at risk under a new employer or how this preference might be realized through contractual agreements. Similarly, employers may by reason of tradition or through fear of loss of power be reluctant to relinquish disciplinary power over the workforce, even though this concession would in fact improve productivity and reduce labour costs. If so, then, consistently with the standard of general welfare, the law might supply the terms of the agreement which would have been reached but for the presence of distorted preferences, and these terms might incorporate provisions against unfair dismissal.

This argument for justifying a law of unfair dismissal on the basis of general welfare considerations encounters several difficulties. The assumption that preferences have been distorted in the past may be hard for many to swallow, but it can be supported by observation of collective agreements. These agreements between employers and unions frequently make provision for improvements in job security through grievance procedures. It may be alleged that the combination of an improved bargaining position and greater sophistication in bargaining skills acquired through collective strength permits expression of the true preferences of workers.

Much more troublesome for the argument based on general welfare is the observation that, even if preferences are distorted, the correct remedy is not to force the parties to contract on any particular set of terms, such a compulsory term against unfair dismissal, but rather to alert them to such a possibility and facilitate such transactions if the parties so wish. On this reasoning the law should not impose a law of unfair dismissal, but rather make it possible through its recognition of the effectiveness of certain standard terms and the provision of appropriate remedies to enable the parties to select job security as a feature of their relationship if they so wish. One way in which this might be achieved would be through an implied term providing for a measure of job security in every contract of employment, which could then be excluded by contrary agreement. The implied term would function as a signal to the parties that their best interests may well lie in an agreed measure of job security, so that any detraction from job security would have to be derived from an express and articulated preference. It is clear, however, that the law of unfair dismissal constitutes more than an implied term of the contract of employment. For most employees covered by the legislation, it is a mandatory term, and any agreement which purports to exclude its effect will be void.[13] As long as this provision persists, it presents a serious obstacle to reconciling the legislation with general welfare considerations.

The preceding analysis of justifications for the legislation on the ground of general welfare assumed that the satisfaction of preferences through freely chosen contracts was the best means for maximizing welfare. This assumption is itself questionable. The defect of this measurement is that it limits preference satisfaction to the ability to pay for it in the market. It seems likely, however, that some redistribution of wealth outside market transactions, by, for instance, the tax and social security systems, will improve general overall welfare. Can this redistributive approach to general welfare be used in order to justify the mandatory imposition of the law of unfair dismissal?

We could certainly imagine that the aim of the legislation was to redistribute wealth from employers to workers. By giving workers an additional right, the right not to be unfairly dismissed, we have rewritten contracts to their advantage and imposed potentially greater labour costs on employers. The prohibition on employees of giving up this right could then be explicable on the basis of the fear that employers would buy this right back so cheaply because of their superior bargaining position that the redistributive aim would become imperilled.

In recent years, such redistributive motives for compulsory terms in contracts have been subjected to much adverse criticism.[14] The major concern is that the redistributive aim can either be thwarted or lead to unintended undesirable effects. One possibility is that employers will simply reduce wages in order to pay for their increased labour costs resulting from legal regulation, so that no effective redistribution of wealth will be achieved. Another possibility must be that employers will reduce the numbers of workers employed in order to compensate for increased labour costs, so that the improved job security for some is paid for not by the employer but by other workers who are unemployed. It is far from certain whether these methods for subverting the redistributive aim occur in the context of the law of unfair dismissal. There may be sufficient wage rigidity and friction in the labour market for the cost of such legal rights to remain upon the employer, at least in the short term.[15] Nevertheless, the risk of frustration of the redistributive aim presents a real danger.

We must conclude that, at best, general welfare considerations provide a

---

[13] EPCA 1978, s. 140.

[14] For an acute review and assessment of these debates, see A. T. Kronman, 'Contract Law and Distributive Justice' (1980), 89, *Yale Law Journal*, 472.

[15] See Ch. 8; and also S. L. Willborn, 'Individual Employment Rights and the Standard Economic Objection: Theory and Empiricism' (1988), 67, *Nebraska Law Review*, 101.

flimsy basis for an inalienable right to claim unfair dismissal. General welfare considerations both support measures to augment the total sum of preference satisfaction as well as justify redistribution to the poorer sections of the community. Redistributive principles tending towards general welfare may support some limited intervention in the form of an implied term, but it must remain uncertain whether they justify within the general welfare calculus any compulsory restrictions on maximizing the productive efficiency of labour through the use of the power of dismissal. These conclusions suggest that we should look elsewhere for firmer foundations of principle to explain the general aim of the unfair dismissal legislation.

RIGHTS

I believe that we can discover these principles through a closer examination of the types of hardship caused to employees who have been dismissed. By switching the focus from the possible goals being pursued by the law to the interests which it is designed to protect, we look for principles of justification which imagine the law of unfair dismissal as protecting an existing, if poorly realized, political and social order, rather than seeking to transform the workplace for the sake of new social priorities.

The employee who loses his or her job in an economy which uses market exchanges to direct labour towards remunerative employment is immediately deprived of his or her major source of wealth, and will possibly suffer long-term impoverishment as a result of unemployment. At the same time the worker is excluded from the workplace which is likely to constitute a significant community in his or her life. It may be through this community, for instance, that the worker derives his or her social status and self-esteem. The workplace community may also provide the principal source of friendships and social engagements. Dismissal may also prevent a worker from exploring any fulfilling intellectual, artistic, or physical challenges posed by the job, unless similar work is found shortly. The manner of the dismissal may also cause harm to the worker's reputation in the local community and contribute to the worker's sense of disgrace and rejection. Together, these various factors resulting from dismissal and exclusion from the workplace may contribute to a loss of self-esteem and a psychological experience of 'anomie'.

Although the concern for the poverty of the dismissed employee can be remedied by the law of unfair dismissal through an award of compensation, this is clearly not the best mechanism. Poverty may afflict those who have been fairly dismissed as well. Furthermore, economic hardship may be relieved by more straightforward mechanisms. Poverty may be relieved by the social security system. Alternatively, the cost may be imposed initially upon the employer, either by requiring a lump sum severance payment in all cases of dismissal, or by extending the required period of notice before a termination of the contract is effective. If the relief of poverty seems unlikely to be the motive for the legislation, then what about the other types of hardship caused to the employee?

I suggest that these other types of potential hardship should be regarded as providing the key to explaining the principles on which the legislation was constructed. The recognition of these diverse, largely non-economic forms of hardship reflects both a concern for the dignity of individuals as persons of independent moral worth and a respect for each person's attempt to bring meaning to his or her life through work. These two values or principles— the dignity and autonomy of individuals—provide together the best justification for the compulsory protection of job security even at the expense of risking a diminution of general welfare.

The principles of dignity and autonomy embody a notion of individual rights, and these rights serve to override the uncertain implications of general welfare considerations in so far as they cast doubt on justifications for intervention in contracts of employment. These rights, if not 'trumps' which overwhelm general welfare considerations, as in Dworkin's metaphor,[16] at least tip the balance decisively in favour of a particular measure of legal regulation. Moreover, it is because individual rights are at stake in dismissal that we cannot countenance their alienability. Just as we would not wish someone to sell his vote or trade away his right to freedom of speech, so too the law is unwilling to permit workers to give up their right to claim unfair dismissal whatever the price offered by the employer.

DIGNITY

Invasions of the right to dignity consist in acts and omissions which fail to treat individuals with concern and respect.[17] Discrimination against an individual on the ground of his or her colour or sex provides a simple illustration. An employer who dismisses a worker on the basis of such an unalterable characteristic, because the employer regards such a characteristic as diminishing the worth of the individual, involves a denial of respect for the individual. Similarly, an employer who summarily dismisses a worker after hearing allegations of misconduct, without either investigating the matter properly or giving the employee an opportunity to rebut any charges, also treats the employee with disrespect. By failing to comply with standards of procedural fairness, the employer reveals a lack of concern for the interests of the employee, treating him or her as a commodity to be bought and sold rather than a person to be treated with respect.[18]

---

[16] Ronald Dworkin, *A Matter of Principle* (Oxford, 1986), 259–72.

[17] This interpretation of the right to dignity mirrors its interpretation, also under the nomenclature of a right to moral independence, in Ronald Dworkin, *Taking Rights Seriously* (London, 1977), ch. 9; see also id., *A Matter of Principle*, ch. 14.

[18] See Ch. 4.

But why are all dismissals not invasions of the right to dignity? The abrupt termination of employment might be viewed in every case as evidencing a lack of concern for the individual. If so, then the right to dignity would support a legal entitlement tantamount to ownership of the job, so that employees could never lose their jobs against their will.

This argument fails to notice that the employer's reason for dismissal must be closely examined in order to determine whether it involves disrespect for the individual. An employer may exercise disciplinary power in a rational manner in pursuit of his or her business purposes without derogating from the employee's right to dignity. He or she may dismiss an employee who is idle or incompetent, for example, because this fits into a rational exercise of the disciplinary power which exists to support the co-ordination of efficient production. Such a dismissal involves no disrespect for the individual. The dismissal of the incompetent worker is not grounded in disrespect for the individual in himself or herself, but in a legitimate concern to promote the general welfare achieved by efficient production.

The key to understanding the extent to which respect for the dignity of the individual should control an employer's disciplinary power rests in the concept of rationality. Where a dismissal can be fitted into a rational pursuit of business objectives, then the dismissal will involve no disrespect for the individual even though the dismissal may tarnish the employee's reputation. The exact nature of this rationality remains controversial and provides the focus of the discussion in Chapter 3. For present purposes it suffices to adopt Unger's insight that forms of work organization enact and embody a particular conception of reason.[19] The right to dignity requires management to adopt a rational manpower policy consonant with the ends and methods of the business under which decisions to terminate employment are grounded in relevant and sufficient reasons.

Within this conception of the right to dignity, therefore, dismissal for good cause involves no disrespect towards the individual. If the employee has been shown to be incompetent or disruptive, then a rational exercise of management's discretionary power of dismissal will not violate the right. Where, however, the dismissal is based upon irrelevant considerations, such as conduct wholly unconnected to the employee's performance at work, or the employee's characteristics such as sex or race which the employer views as reasons for treating the employee with less than equal respect, then the dismissal does involve a violation of the right to dignity and so justice requires that it should be prohibited or penalized.

The right to dignity therefore does not support a degree of job security equivalent to ownership of jobs, but it does require legal protection against unfair dismissal. Because an individual right is at stake, the uncertain

[19]   Roberto M. Unger, *False Necessity* (Cambridge, 1987), 145.

implications of general welfare considerations may be ignored in order to secure respect for the right.

The second strand of justification for the law of unfair dismissal concerns each person's attempt to bring meaning to his or her life through work. Although the workplace does not provide the sole means for choosing a way of life, and indeed should not be permitted to dominate other opportunities,[20] for a majority of the adult population economic necessity combines with intellectual and physical challenge to render work a focal point of meaning. At social gatherings the question 'What do you do?' ranks alongside enquiries into marital status and church attendance as important to character and interests. It may be true, of course, that many people find their work dissatisfying or boring, viewing it simply as an instrument for acquiring wealth. But this sense of dissatisfaction itself reveals a wish that their work could contribute more substantially to their attempts to establish meaning for their lives.

As Joseph Raz argues,[21] a liberal society should foster worthwhile opportunities for people to pursue their personal goals in order to augment their autonomy. We should distinguish between this idea of autonomy and a negative conception of freedom. The value of autonomy cannot be satisfied by a State which merely maximizes the freedom of individuals to do whatever they want. This negative notion of freedom is used to justify the freedom to make contracts of employment on any terms which the parties choose. It therefore rules out the possibility of mandatory law of unfair dismissal. The idea of autonomy, though an interpretation of the concept of freedom, often warrants legal restriction and regulation. It is a positive and perfectionist notion of freedom, one which requires regulation of social life in order to ensure fair access to worthwhile experiences in life. The key requirement of the idea of autonomy is that a society's institutions and rules should be organized in such a way so as to multiply as far as possible the diversity of real opportunities for its members to construct meaning for their lives.

Many such opportunities depend upon the establishment of social structures and economic conditions before they can be readily available. For this reason a policy of full employment, that is, jobs available for all who wish to take them up, comprises an important element in a society which endorses the value of autonomy. But the nature of those jobs also colours the degree of autonomy achieved by a society. A workplace governed by harsh rules and brutal conditions detracts from autonomy almost as much as the unavailability of work altogether. The idea of autonomy therefore suggests a

---

[20] See Ch. 7.
[21] Joseph Raz, *The Morality of Freedom* (Oxford, 1986).

role for the law to promote social structures at work through which the opportunities for people to bring meaning to their lives through work are enhanced.[22]

Job structures which satisfy such a goal are those likely to offer relatively secure tenure, with opportunities for promotion, diversity of challenges, and the exercise of initiative. Ruthless subordination to the direction of owners' or managers' wishes renders work merely a relinquishment of autonomy rather than an opportunity to enhance it. Within this framework the law of unfair dismissal finds its justification in its imposition upon employers of standards for the exercise of disciplinary power. These standards aspire to establish workplaces which offer better opportunities for the individual to be, in Joseph Raz's memorable phrase, the author of his or her own life.[23]

To understand the sense in which the value of autonomy aims to improve the quality of job structure at work, it is helpful to view the internal management of the firm as a form of bureaucratic organization.[24] Management directs the enterprise through a system of rules which differentiate between jobs by specifying the tasks involved in each and by organizing them in a rank order of hierarchy. Further rules determine payment and promotion systems which function as an administrative alternative to market forces and are commonly known as the internal labour-market.[25] Finally, a disciplinary code attaches sanctions to breaches of any of the rules. The concern for the autonomy of the individual demands that this bureaucratic organizational structure should accommodate as far as possible opportunities for individuals to become the author of their own lives.

At first blush this concern for autonomy might suggest that the law should prevent any discipline at work, and instead compel employers to permit employees to select any kind of work of their choice and to be free to enjoy leisure at any time. Again this verges on the vesting in employees of property

---

[22] For a similar argument see D. M. Beatty, 'Industrial Democracy: A Liberal View of Labour Relations' (1984–5), 19, *Valparaiso University Law Review*, 37.

[23] Raz, *Morality of Freedom*, 369–73, 417.

[24] For the development of this bureaucratic analysis, see Max Weber, *Economy and Society* ed. G. Roth and C. Wittich (Berkeley, Calif. 1978), 988; Alvin W. Gouldner, *Patterns of Industrial Bureaucracy* (London, 1955); Reinhard Bendix, *Work and Authority in Industry* (New York, 1956); Elliott Jacques, *A General Theory of Bureaucracy* (London, 1976); Richard Edwards, *Contested Terrain* (New York, 1979); Dan Clawson, *Bureaucracy and the Labor Process* (New York, 1980); D. Loshak, 'Le Pouvoir Heirarchique dans l'entreprise privée et dans l'administration' (1982), *Driot Social*, 22; Sanford M. Jacoby, *Employing Bureaucracy* (New York, 1985); H. Collins, 'Market Power, Bureaucratic Power and the Contract of Employment' (1986), 15, *ILJ* 1.

[25] Paul Osterman (ed.), *Internal Labor Markets* (Cambridge, Mass., 1984); J. M. Malcolmson, 'Work Incentives, Hierarchy, and Internal Labor Markets' (1984), 92, *Journal of Political Economy*, 486; H. I. Hartmann, 'Internal Labor Markets and Gender: A Case Study of Promotion', in Clair Brown and Joseph A. Pechman (eds.), *Gender in the Workplace* (Washington, DC, 1987), 59; J. L. Medoff and K. G. Abraham, 'Experience, Performance, and Earnings' (1980), 95, *Quarterly Journal of Economics*, 703; Claus Offe, *Industry and Inequality*, trans. J. Wickham (New York, 1977).

rights in their jobs. But this interpretation of the argument misunderstands the strength and province of the value of autonomy.

The ideal of autonomy accepts that individuals must be constrained by the technical demands of efficient production, so that the bureaucratic framework at work must co-ordinate production and integrate the division of labour. The opportunity to work is itself an important dimension of autonomy, but, for these jobs to exist at all, they must fit into the economic and technical constraints of the dominant mode of production in a society. What the value of autonomy suggests is that the job structures should preserve as many opportunities to discover meaningful employment as possible consistent with the necessity of work organization.

For example, efficient organization of work normally requires a disciplinary code to deter disruption of production, but the value of autonomy insists that such a code be published for employees and applied impartially so that employees can guide their behaviour according to its lights. The value of autonomy thus introduces the principles of the Rule of Law into the workplace disciplinary code, for just as a citizen must be able to discover the law or else live in constant fear of unexpected punishment by the State, so too the employee must know the disciplinary code or else work in fear of sudden loss of employment.[26] For this reason it would be unjust to permit the employer of Mr Mathewson to rely upon an uncommunicated disciplinary code in order to justify the dismissal.

But the value of autonomy goes beyond the principles of the Rule of Law, for it requires further restrictions on managerial disciplinary power. It provides a ground for questioning the necessity of particular disciplinary rules. Since all these rules restrict the freedom of individuals at work, they must be shown to be reasonably necessary for the efficient co-ordination of work or they will comprise an unjust restriction upon autonomy. The value of autonomy also demands a narrow province for the legitimate exercise of managerial authority. Attempts by employers to regulate the lives of employees outside work must usually comprise an unjustified invasion of freedom. Teasing out the requirements of autonomy in this way, we can gradually build up a picture of a disciplinary code, or more generally a scheme of job structures, which satisfies the demands of autonomy of the maximum extent, yet which remains compatible with the demands of an efficient and competitive business organization.

This justification for the law of unfair dismissal relies upon a particular interpretation of the value of freedom in the concept of autonomy. In order to foster this value, the law is warranted in overriding any countervailing welfare considerations which may point to the wealth-maximizing potential of a regime of termination of employment at will. Once again, however, this justification cannot support a property right in the job. A dismissal may be

---

[26] Joseph Raz, *The Authority of Law* (Oxford, 1979), ch. 11.

perfectly justified because it does not infringe autonomy at all, where for example the worker lacks the skills to take up the available opportunity. The value of autonomy sets an ideal for the social structures of the disciplinary code and for job structures at work; it does not propose a justification for ownership of a job by a particular worker.

THE INTEREST IN JOB SECURITY

Together, these two strands of justification for the law of unfair dismissal—a respect for the dignity of the individual and an improvement in the conditions of work which are conducive to autonomy—amount to a defence of an employee's interest in job security, but not to a property right in a job. In this book, we will define and calculate the employee's interest in job security by reference to these two arguments for its protection.

This interpretation of the underlying justification of legislation against unfair dismissal suggests both why many legal systems have passed legislation which improves a worker's job security, and why none of these laws goes so far as to grant the employee a property right in his or her job. The interest in job security cannot warrant a complete defence of an employee's possession of a job. Nor can it support automatic compensation on termination of employment, without regard to fault of the parties,[27] for either this would deter all dismissals if the sum was set at a high amount, or provide no incentive for employers to alter disciplinary practices if the sum was pitched at a low level. Legislation based upon employees' interest in job security should seek rather to discourage dismissals where the employer lacks relevant and substantial reasons for terminating the relationship.

I will defer detailed consideration of the appropriate remedy for the protection of employees' interest in job security till Chapter 7. But at this point it is worth observing that the rejection of the idea that the law of unfair dismissal is based upon a strong conception of a property right in a job tends to undermine the idea that the appropriate remedy should be restoration of the property, that is, reinstatement in the job. Instead, the question becomes what remedy is best likely to protect the dignity of workers and to promote work structures compatible with the ideal of autonomy. I shall argue later that liability to pay compensation for unfair dismissals will best achieve these ends in the normal run of dismissals.[28]

By neither granting a property right in the job nor leaving the employer with unfettered power is dismiss employees at will, the legislation forges a

---

[27] C. R. Gullett and G. D. Greenwade, 'Employment at Will: The No Fault Alternative' (1988), 39, Labor Law Journal, 372.

[28] In other words, the legislation establishes liability rather than property rules: G. Calibresi and D. Melamed, 'Property Rules, Liability Rules, and Inalienability: One View of the Cathedral' (1972), 85, Harvard Law Review, 1089; Jules L. Coleman, Markets, Morals and the Law (Cambridge, 1988), ch. 2.

compromise between, on the one hand, the economic efficiency and general welfare considerations which push generally, though not unambiguously, towards employment relations terminable at will by the employer, and on the other, the protection of the individual employee's interest in security of employment to the extent necessary to respect the right to dignity and to promote autonomy.

Exactly how this compromise should be forged remains the central difficulty of these laws. The legislature can rarely dictate the precise outcomes for particular cases through specific rules. The variety of circumstances in which employers dismiss workers and the need to draw boundaries on the basis of the degree of the employee's fault prevents the adoption of crisp rules of guidance. An employee's misconduct in, for instance, arriving late for work may appear much more important in one sort of job such as a football referee than another such as a solicitor. Moreover, one minute's tardiness must appear much less grave than a couple of hours. The justice of a dismissal must also depend upon the reasons given by the employee for his or her late arrival: did the train break down or did sleepy-head simply roll over when the alarm clock buzzed? In practice, therefore, the legislature must delegate the task of elaborating and implementing a conception of fairness or justice in dismissals to the adjudicators. At most the legislature can only indicate that the court should examine whether the employer had 'just cause' for a discharge,[29] or genuine and serious reasons,[30] or, in the verbose test of reasonableness contained in the British unfair dismissal legislation:

the determination of the question whether the dismissal was fair or unfair, having regard to the reason shown by the employer, shall depend on whether in the circumstances including the size and administrative resources of the employer's undertaking the employer acted reasonably or unreasonably in treating it as a sufficient reason for dismissing the employee; and that question shall be determined in accordance with equity and the substantial merits of the case.[31]

For the courts and tribunals vested with the jurisdiction to apply the vague standards of fairness and reasonableness which constitute the tests of whether the dismissal was justifiable, there lurks the unresolved dilemma of balancing the general welfare considerations against the individual interest in job security. Consider, for example, the case where an employer seeks to replace a satisfactory worker with one recommended as outstanding. Here the general welfare considerations indicate that the dismissal is justifiable, but against this argument the court must balance the interest of the satisfactory worker in keeping his or her job. (The calculus becomes further

---

[29] Wrongful Discharge From Employment Act 1987 (Ch. 641), Montana Code 39-2-901 to 39-2-914.
[30] French Code du Travail, art. L. 122-14-3.
[31] EPCA 1978, s. 57(3).

complicated if one recognizes that the outstanding worker has an interest from the perspective of enhancing autonomy in obtaining the job to which he or she is well suited.) To say that the employer must have acted fairly or reasonably for the dismissal to be justified does not begin to provide a court with a practicable set of scales for balancing these independent considerations of general welfare and individual interest.

The essays which comprise this book examine this question, of what constitutes justice in dismissals, from a variety of angles. I will consider how the legislature, the courts, and specialist tribunals have in fact sought to strike the balance between these competing considerations. Their approaches will be critically assessed for their coherence; their judgments will be evaluated for the justice of their results. But before tackling this central issue of justice in dismissals, we should reflect further on the origins and motives of the legislation and the nature of the dilemmas confronting courts or tribunals; for although we may have succeeded in identifying the general principles on which the legislation rests, we should be alert to the point that parliament, in enacting the legislation, may have also been pursuing a narrower and more pragmatic political agenda, whilst the courts and tribunals, when interpreting the legislation, may also have been concerned to defend their own political ideals which may clash at points with those underlying the legislation.

2. ORIGINS OF THE LEGISLATION

The legislation on unfair dismissal was instituted in Britain in 1971,[32] perhaps two centuries after wage labour became the principal source of income for the majority of the population. In some other European countries such as Germany the legislation occurred early in this century;[33] and elsewhere, as in France, the courts developed in the nineteenth century some circumscribed limitations upon the employer's power to dismiss a worker.[34] In the United States only one state legislature, Montana,[35] has enacted a just cause statute, though once again the courts have developed on their own some limitations upon the employer's power to terminate the contract at will.[36]

---

[32] Industrial Relations Act 1971, s. 22.

[33] T. Ramm, 'Labor Courts and Grievance Settlement in W. Germany', in Benjamin Aaron (ed.), *Labor Courts and Grievance Settlement in Western Europe* (Berkeley, Calif., 1971); Otto Kahn-Freud, *Labour Law and Politics in the Weimar Republic* (Oxford, 1981); A. Döse-Digenopoulos and A. Höland, 'Dismissal of Employees in the Federal Republic of Germany' (1985), 48, *Modern Law Review*, 539.

[34] M. M. Plasencia, 'Employment-At-Will: The French Experience as a Basis for Reform' (1988), 9, *Comparative Labor Law Journal*, 294.

[35] Wrongful Discharge From Employment Act 1987 (Ch. 641), Montana Code 39-2-901 to 39-2-914. A. S. Leonard, 'A New Common Law of Employment Termination' (1987), 66, *North Carolina Law Review*, 632.

[36] Note, 'Protecting At Will Employees against Wrongful Discharge: The Duty to Terminate

The late arrival of these laws compared to the spread of the contract of employment must be explained in large part by reference to the patterns of political representation in the legislatures, with employers or their sympathizers effectively retaining power until this century. Yet this political explanation can only account in part for the delay in attempts to regulate dismissal from employment. The British unfair dismissal legislation occurred long after comparable regulation of such matters as the relation between landlord and tenant and the development of a social security system to assist those out of work. Moreover, many other aspects of the contract of employment such as minimum wages and maximum hours had been regulated from as far back as the Truck Acts of 1848 and even earlier.[37] Even in 1946 when a Labour Government swept to power in Britain and inaugurated the fundamental institutions of the welfare state such as free secondary education and health care, still no steps were taken to safeguard an individual employee's interest in job security. The enactment of a statute against unfair dismissal was evidently not regarded as part of the agenda of those representing the labour interest until much later. Indeed, strange as it may seem, the statute was eventually passed by a Conservative Government, at a time when a consensus had emerged concerning the need for such a law. How, then, may we account for the apparently late arrival of this legislation and its enactment at the beginning of the 1970s?

The beginning of an understanding of the origins and the apparent tardiness of this legislation lies in an appreciation of how it conflicts with the dominant labour law policy of successive governments during this century. The nature of this policy has been described as industrial pluralism.[38] Its key feature consists in the belief that the best and fairest way to resolve disputes between capital and labour is to leave the parties to hammer out their own bargains. Industrial pluralism holds that collective bargaining between management and unions should determine the terms and conditions

---

only in Good Faith' (1980), 93, *Harvard Law Review*, 1816; Note, 'Protecting Employees At Will against Wrongful Discharge: The Public Policy Exception' (1983), 96, *Harvard Law Review*, 1931; C. W. Summers, 'The Contract of Employment and the Rights of Individual Employees: Fair Representation and Employment at Will' (1984), 52, *Fordham Law Review*, 1082. For similar judicial developments in Japan, see Y. Matsuda, 'Japan' (1980), 11, *Bulletin of Comparative Labour Relations*, 133, at p. 142.

[37] e.g. Health and Morals of Apprentices Act, George III, c. 73 (1802) regulates morality in cotton and woollen mills and incidentally restricts hours of work to 12.

[38] Alan Fox, *Beyond Contract: Work Power and Trust Relations* (London, 1974), 260–70; H. A. Clegg, 'Pluralism in Industrial Relations' (1975), 13, *British Journal of Industrial Relations*, 309; K. Stone, 'The Post-War Paradigm in American Labour Law' (1981), 90, *Yale Law Journal*, 1509; H. Collins, 'Against Abstentionism in Labour Law', in John Eekelaar and John Bell (eds.), *Oxford Essays in Jurisprudence Third Series* (Oxford, 1987), 79; K. E. Klare, 'Labor Law as Ideology: Toward a New Historiography of Collective Bargaining Law (1981), 4, *Industrial Relations Law Journal*, 450; W. Korpi, 'Industrial Relations and Industrial Conflict: The Case of Sweden', in Bensam Martin and Everett M. Kassalow, *Labour Relations in Advanced Industrial Societies: Issues and Problems* (Washington, DC, 1980), 89.

of employment. The principal role of government and law is the minimal one of permitting such collective bargaining to take place, a policy aptly described by Kahn-Freund as 'collective *laissez-faire*'.[39] The law is not absent altogether, for in some instances it may channel, promote, and control the practices of collective bargaining. But the law should remit to the parties themselves the choice of terms or substantive outcomes of bargaining.

Many considerations probably led to the adoption of this abstentionism of industrial pluralism as a central feature of labour law policy. In a period of full employment in the post-war boom of the 1950s and 1960s, the unions were often sufficiently strong to insist upon recognition and collective bargaining. So to some extent government policy made a virtue out of the inevitable. But, in addition, industrial pluralism appears attractive to philosophers of a market economy. The practice of collective bargaining leaves the parties with considerable autonomy to determine their own interests and to strike their own bargains. The *laissez-faire* aspect of the policy appeals to those seeking to avoid regulation of the economy by the State. Furthermore, if it is accepted that individual employees lack equality of bargaining power with employers, then collective bargaining can be presented as an ordinary market transaction where the problem of inequality has been avoided. The continuing abstention of the State even after 1945 appealed both to employers who wanted to return to a free market economy after the war, and to unions, which, confident of their bargaining power, sought autonomy and independence so that they could gain through vigorous negotiations a substantial share of the increase in material propserity for their members.[40] In short, collective bargaining was a private market mechanism which suited both sides of industry at the time.

Unfair dismissal legislation runs against the grain of this policy of industrial pluralism. It involves direct mandatory regulation of the workplace. It removes from the parties the freedom to settle their own terms and substitutes independent legal standards. Furthermore, its application requires intervention by the courts, a prospect which appealed neither to management, who preferred to retain as much of their prerogative as could be preserved through collective bargaining, nor to unions, who suspected the courts of systematic bias in favour of employers. It is true, of course, that some regulation of employment in respect of safety, wages, and hours already existed alongside the general policy of abstentionism. But the unfair dismissal legislation involves a qualitative leap in the nature of legal regulation of the workplace.

Existing regulation of employment essentially settled basic conditions

---

[39] Otto Kahn-Freund, *Selected Writings* (London, 1978), at p. 8 (an essay originally published in 1959).
[40] A. Flanders, 'The Tradition of Voluntarism' (1974), 12, *British Journal of Industrial Relations*, 352; M. Rogin, 'Voluntarism: The Political Functions of an Antipolitical Doctrine' (1962), 15, *Industrial and Labor Relations Review*, 521.

below which no worker should be permitted to fall. This 'floor of rights', as Wedderburn dubbed this legislation,[41] scarcely affected the vast majority of the workforce after 1945, for terms and conditions of employment normally exceeded these basic conditions. In contrast, the law of unfair dismissal, by regulating the disciplinary power of management, goes right to the heart of every employment relation. Its standards in effect constitute the nature of every employment relation. The policy of 'collective *laissez-faire*' could be reconciled with the existence of minimum standards in the labour market as a safety net for those lacking effective collective bargaining at all. But the policy could not tolerate the deep penetration into the practices of management and the mandatory security of employment envisaged in an unfair dismissal law. In these circumstances, it is hardly surprising that the legislation was not on the political agenda as part of the post-war settlement.

Why, therefore, did the policy change so radically as the 1960s came to a close? The policy of 'collective *laissez-faire*' had increasingly become suspect during those years.[42] The worry became that full employment gave unions such strong bargaining power that they could demand levels of wages which had begun to fuel an inflationary spiral and had destroyed the competitiveness of British industry. Proposed restraints upon free collective bargaining became increasingly significant in political programmes, eventually resulting in statutory incomes policies which limited wage rises, and attempts to weaken the power of unions by restricting the right to strike. Against this background of a declining faith in the policy of 'collective *laissez-faire*', there emerged a secondary problem which a 1960s Royal Commission into industrial relations (the Donovan Commission) addressed.

Despite the strong bargaining power of unions, their local representatives at plant level, often called shop stewards, had not always succeeded in establishing regular practices of collective bargaining with management. The result was serious disruption to production from industrial action whenever a dispute arose at plant level. Disputes over dismissals were an important illustration of this. Only a few employers had agreed a grievance procedure with the union at plant level,[43] so that when the workforce regarded a dismissal as unjustified, its only recourse was to take industrial action. The press was full of stories of the follies resulting from the absence of appropriate dispute-settlement procedures, such as the case where the dismissal of a 61-year-old man caught with a flask of tea in his hand provoked a week's strike of 1,000 men.[44] In the view of the Donovan Commission the principal

---

[41] Lord Wedderburn, *The Worker and the Law* (3rd edn., Harmondsworth, 1986), at p. 6.

[42] Paul Davies and Mark Freedland, *Kahn-Freund's Labour and the Law* (3rd edn., London, 1983), editors' introduction.

[43] For an examination of the contradictory evidence of the extent of grievance procedures prior to 1971, see Ch. 8.

[44] Meyers, *Ownership of Jobs: A Comparative Study* (Los Angeles, 1964), at p. 29; Royal Commission on Trade Unions and Employers' Association, Cmnd. 3623 (1965–8), paras. 409–15, 526–34.

solution to this problem lay in the formalization of plant-level collective bargaining procedures.[45] This approach was clearly heavily influenced by the philosophy of industrial pluralism. Yet strangely the Donovan Commission also proposed the enactment of a statute on unfair dismissal,[46] thereby apparently endorsing a radically different approach to the regulation of labour relations.

Two factors probably led to this change of direction in the Donovan Commission, whose recommendations were accepted on this point by all major political parties. In the first place, the strike problem was regarded as so urgent that immediate action seemed preferable to waiting until the slow processes of formalization of plant-level bargaining emerged. As Kahn-Freund observed at the time, 'Our collective bargaining machinery has stalled and legislation has to take its place'.[47] Since strikes over dismissals constituted about a third of the total, a statute diverting these disputes into the peaceful forum of a court or tribunal seemed suddenly a necessary measure.[48] We can perceive here elements of a 'corporatist' approach to problems of industrial conflict, one which seeks to channel conflict into an organizational framework of negotiation between employers, unions, and government.[49] But what ultimately seems to have turned the tide was a deeper philsophical debate about labour law policy.

At first glance this philosophical debate is not apparent in the Donovan Commission. The report describes a conflict between quality versus quantity in the protection of job security.[50] The Commission acknowledges that voluntarily agreed disciplinary procedures are likely to provide the best safeguard for job security, but it expresses its concern that it seemed likely that a substantial proportion of the workforce would not receive protection from unfair dismissal because these groups would continue to lack any collective bargaining arrangements at all. British law would therefore not comply with the new international standards promulgated by the International Labour Organization in its Termination of Employment Recommendation 1963 (No. 119) which had been accepted by the United Kingdom Government in 1964.[51] This concern for the plight of workers

---

[45] Ibid., paras. 532, 534.

[46] Ibid., paras. 453, 528.

[47] Otto Kahn-Freund, *Labour Law: Old Traditions and New Developments* (Toronto, 1968), at pp. 40–1.

[48] Royal Commission on Trade Unions and Employers' Associations, Cmnd. 3623 (1965–8), paras. 409–15; Industrial Relations Bill Consultative Document, para. 52 (5/10/70) quoted in Steven D. Anderman, *Unfair Dismissal* (2nd edn., London, 1985), at pp. 4–5.

[49] Keith Middlemas, *Politics in Industrial Society* (London, 1979, ch. 13; C. Crouch, 'The State, Capital, and Liberal Democracy', in id. (ed.), *State and Economy in Contemporary Capitalism* (London, 1979); H. Collins, 'Capitalist Discipline and Corporatist Law' (1982), 11, *ILJ* 78.

[50] Royal Commission on Trade Unions and Employers' Associations, Cmnd, 3623 (1965–8), paras. 533–44.

[51] Ibid., paras. 525, 545; B. Napier, 'Dismissals: The New ILO Standards' (1983), 12, *ILJ* 17.

outside the scope of collective bargaining arrangements marks a change in philosophical orientation. Instead of the commitment to the abstentionism of industrial pluralism, we begin to see a new concern for the protection of the individual rights of workers regardless of whether they can establish and defend those rights through collective bargaining and grievance procedures.[52] Such a commitment to individual rights necessarily involves the introduction of legal regulation of the workplace to enforce those rights. In turn this legal regulation represents the antithesis of 'collective *laissez-faire*'.

Three vital contrasts between the orientation of industrial pluralism and that of individual employment rights should be stressed.

1. The philosophy of individual rights rejects the collectivism of collective bargaining and stresses instead the importance of the individual's interests in justice in the workplace.

2. The philosophy of individual rights withdraws respect for private market relations and prefers the imposition of public standards.

3. The philosophy of individual rights requires legal intervention rather than private dispute settlement through grievance procedures.

In the case of dismissals, the individual right concerned was often described as a property right in a job, though, as we have seen, the employee's interest in job security is better conceived as a right to dignity combined with the establishment of conditions for autonomy or freedom.

This combination of a subtle but fundamental reorientation in the philosophy relating to labour policy with the perceived urgency of the strike problem accounts for the sudden rise of the law of unfair dismissal to the top of the political agenda as the 1960s drew to a close. The Industrial Relations Act 1971 established a right not to be unfairly dismissed and vested jurisdiction to hear complaints in specialist courts called Industrial Tribunals,[53] with appeals on points of law to the National Industrial Relations Court (NIRC), later reconstituted as the Employment Appeal Tribunal (EAT),[54] and thence to higher appeal courts on points of law.[55] Despite subsequent modifications, the principal features of this legislation have remained unchanged. The task of determining the relevant standards of fairness or justice in dismissals is therefore allocated in the first instance to Industrial Tribunals, subject to oversight by the appeal courts. In order to understand how this task has been approached, the first step consists in an appreciation

---

[52] Cf. Bob Hepple, 'A Right to Work?' (1982), 10, *ILJ* 65.

[53] Section 22, now EPCA 1978, ss. 54, 67. For the history of these Industrial Tribunals and the reason for their selection to have jurisdiction in cases of unfair dismissal, see P. Davies and M. Freedland, 'Labour Courts and the Reform of Labour Law in Great Britain', in *In Memoriam Zvi Bar-Niv: Collection of Essays on Labour Law* (Tel Aviv, 1987).

[54] Employment Protection Act 1975, ss. 87–8, now EPCA 1978, ss. 135–6.

[55] For an examination of the scope of error of law in this context, see Sir John Wood, 'The Employment Appeal Tribunal as it Enters the 1990s' (1990), 19 *ILJ* 133, at pp. 135–7.

of the predicament in which courts and tribunals found themselves when called upon to apply the statute.

3. THE COMMON LAW OF WRONGFUL DISMISSAL

I commence from the premiss that judges interpret statutes primarily according to the background values and assumptions of the common law. The likely consequences of their decisions will not be entirely absent from the judges' minds either, but my contention is that their preliminary understanding of the import of a statutory rule or phrase will be grounded in the context of the existing doctrinal fabric of the law. It would therefore be wrong to approach the judicial interpretation of the unfair dismissal legislation from the perspective of an instrumentalist analysis which suggests that the judges systematically favour one set of values such as a strong managerial prerogative power to dismiss workers. This may be the effect of their decisions, but not the reason or values guiding their interpretation of the law. In order to grasp the nature of these values we need to study briefly the background rules of the common law governing termination of employment which the statute sought to supervene.

The key feature of the common law of termination of contracts of employment is the abnegation of the law. Broadly speaking, the courts decline to adjudicate over the rights and wrongs of dismissals. Since the beginning of the nineteenth century,[56] there has in fact been a cause of action available to employees, the action for wrongful dismissal, and in some instances the courts grant employees a remedy in damages for breach of contract. But the availability of this cause of action should not obscure the fundamental point that the common law courts effectively decline to review the exercise of managerial power to dismiss. The action for wrongful dismissal only constitutes a small chip in an otherwise clear message of the common law which endorses managerial prerogative power over disciplinary issues.

The reason why the action for wrongful dismissal at common law provides scant assistance to dismissed employees is that it rarely applies and then normally only offers insignificant remedies. The action for wrongful dismissal arises where a dismissal occurs without due notice. British courts imply into contracts of employment a requirement that both parties should give reasonable notice prior to termination. But the notice period became normally the same as the period governing payment of wages in arrears, subject to contrary agreement or custom.[57] Thus if a worker is paid by the day or the week, then the required notice period at common law is merely a

[56] M. R. Freedland, *The Contract of Employment* (Oxford, 1976), 21.
[57] Ibid. 153.

day or a week respectively. This position has been slightly improved by statute so that broadly speaking employees are entitled to one week's notice for each year of employment up to a maximum of twelve.[58]

Assuming, however, that an employer has dismissed a worker without giving due notice, or pay in lieu of notice, then an action for wrongful dismissal still fails if the employee has committed a serious breach of the contract meriting summary dismissal. Courts imply many terms into contracts of employment, such as the employee's duties to be loyal, competent, careful, and obedient.

Without attempting an exhaustive enumeration of the duties imposed in this way upon a servant, I may mention: (1) the duty to give reasonable notice in the absence of custom or express agreement; (2) the duty to obey the lawful orders of the master; (3) the duty to be honest and diligent in the master's service; (4) the duty to take reasonable care of his master's property entrusted to him and generally in the performance of his duties; (5) to account to his master for any secret commission or remuneration received by him; (6) not to abuse his master's confidence in matters pertaining to his services . . .[59]

Breach of these terms usually suffices to warrant summary dismissal.

In the rare case where the employer has both failed to give reasonable notice of termination and lacks a sufficient reason to justify summary dismissal, then the action for wrongful dismissal succeeds, but rarely is the remedy worth the trouble.[60] In the first place, the courts limit the measure of damages to the payment due under the contract of employment if due notice had been given.[61] Thus if a worker entitled to a week's notice was wrongfully dismissed, then he or she is entitled to the balance of his or her wages for the remainder of the week. This technique of quantification effectively denies both full expectation and reliance damages to dismissed employees, and restricts the remedy to the level of an action for an agreed sum in debt.[62]

Yet at the same time, and perhaps anomalously, the courts apply all the normal rules governing the limitation of damages such as mitigation and set-off. Thus an employee is under a duty to mitigate his or her loss by seeking a job forthwith. If he or she succeeds in finding work promptly, the pay he or she receives from the new employer during the expiration of the notice

---

[58] EPCA 1978, ss. 49–51 (as amended by The Employment Act 1982) originating from the Contracts of Employment Act 1972 and the Contracts of Employment Act 1963.

[59] *Lister* v. *Romford Ice and Cold Storage Co. Ltd.* [1957] AC 555, per Lord Tucker at p. 594.

[60] The principles governing damages for wrongful dismissal are set out clearly in *Gunton* v. *Richmond-upon-Thames London Borough Council* [1980] ICR 755 (CA).

[61] Freedland, *Contract of Employment* 250.

[62] In a sense, of course, the wages are the employee's expectation, but the employee may have other expectations such as bonus payments which, in the absence of clear contractual entitlement, seem irrecoverable: *Laverack* v. *Woods of Colchester Ltd.* [1967] 1 QB 278. For a sustained attempt to reconcile the cases with the expectation measure, see Freedland, *Contract of Employment*, 246–61.

period due from the former employer is deducted from the measure of damages; and if the employee fails to find work the damages may still be reduced on the ground that he or she has failed to make reasonable efforts to mitigate his or her loss. As well as mitigation, the courts reduce the measure of damages by the amount of any state benefits received by the unemployment worker and any tax liability saved by dismissal. This deduction even includes those benefits derived from the compulsory National Insurance scheme,[63] though of course normally ordinary insurance payments are not deducted from the measure of damages for breach of contract. In effect, the courts encourage the State to subsidize the dismissal of workers by reducing the cost to employers.

At the end of the day, therefore, few employees are likely to gain substantial sums from a successful action for wrongful dismissal. Only in the case of highly paid employees benefiting from contracts specifying lengthy notice periods will an action for wrongful dismissal be worth pursuing. The general effect of the common law is to remove any legal supervision of dismissals. The employer is left to manage and discipline the workforce without serious risk of incurring a substantial legal challenge. It is for this reason that we can say that the common law abnegated control over termination of contracts of employment.

This leaves an unregulated power relation at the heart of the employment relation. The power of the employer stems primarily from ownership of the means of production, buttressed no doubt by the extensive implied duties imposed upon employees which have the effect of licensing summary dismissal in a wide range of instances. In US law, where the common law does not even recognize a requirement upon the employer to give due notice of termination of employment, this position is aptly described as termination at will, thus emphasizing the unfettered discretion of the employer. Although in theory English law grants damages to compensate for breach of the term granting reasonable notice prior to dismissal, this hardly suffices to diminish the general discretion enjoyed by employers over disciplinary matters.

The factory code is the visible embodiment of this power relation: a set of rules and punishments issued unilaterally by the employer which regulates employees' behaviour in the workplace. The common law licenses the exercise of the power and does little to restrain it, except in the case of well-paid employees. The common law seems to appropriate the medieval idea of the master being able to rule his own private household without the State's supervision, and then applies it to the modern factory of the Industrial Revolution. The legal mechanism to achieve this domination comprises the contract of employment, which, as developed by the courts, reinterprets the

---

[63] *Westwood* v. *Secretary of State for Employment* [1985] AC 20 (HL); *Parsons* v. *B. N. M. Laboratories Ltd.* [1964] 1 QB 95 (CA); J. McMullen, 'Statutory Periods of Notice and the Duty to Account for Benefits Received' (1984), 13, *ILJ* 259.

diffuse and reciprocal bonds of loyalty and support between master and servant in the household as implied terms imposing duties upon an employee, breach of which entitles the employer to dismiss summarily without any compensation.[64]

4. THE IDEOLOGY OF THE COMMON LAW

It is against this background that the law of unfair dismissal was enacted. How did this colour judges' appreciation of the new law? The key to an understanding of their disposition towards the new law lies in an appreciation of how the abstentionist position at common law was justified. It might be thought that the justification is self-evident: it clearly suits employers very well to be left to regulate their own disciplinary matters as they wish, and the judges simply complied with this wish out of class loyalty. Alternatively, it might be alleged that the judges appreciate intuitively the general welfare considerations adumbrated earlier which support the maximum freedom to terminate contracts of employment. Recall the example where the employer substitutes an outstanding worker for one who is merely satisfactory, thus improving productive efficiency, with possible gains in profits to the employer and higher wages to the employee, and long-term benefits for the economy as a whole in succouring competitive business. But if we examine the reasons given for the development of the common law, we discover neither expressions of class allegiance nor affirmations of the necessity of pursuing the goal of wealth maximization at all costs to individuals. One finds instead a complex moral argument which is concerned to delineate an appropriate role for the courts in this sphere of economic life together with affirmations of the fairness or justice of the common law to the parties.

Supporters of the common law to this day emphasize these virtues which can be summarized under three headings:

1. Respect for the autonomy of the private sphere;
2. Neutrality between conflicting interests;
3. Equality of treatment of the parties.

Having elaborated these three perceived virtues of the common law, we can begin to see how these values and assumptions behind the common law were calculated to stifle the impact of the unfair dismissal legislation.

PRIVACY

Respect for private autonomy demands that limits be set to the State's intervention in relations between individuals. This value of privacy calls for abstentionism by the State. Both sides of industry have frequently appealed

---

[64] Alan Fox, *Beyond Contract: Work, Power and Trust Relations* (London, 1974), 175–90.

to this value in order to resist legislative control over labour relations. For example, unions have constantly asserted the value of voluntarism in their internal organization, thereby expressing a preference for unions to be regarded as private self-governing contractual associations rather than public bodies subject to the community's rules and standards.[65] Similarly, supporters of the termination-at-will position of the common law have defended it in terms of the appropriateness and desirability of keeping the State out of private contractual relations.[66]

Some of the persuasive force of this characterization of employment as a private relation springs from the legal tradition of regarding master and servant law as a branch of the law of persons and private households.[67] In its modern form, this argument stresses the personal and private nature of the employment relation, one unsuited to coercive regulation and control by the State.[68] The whole emphasis on privacy taps into the broader libertarian sentiment of setting strict limits to state power.

From these perspectives, the abnegation of the common law, far from being a failure to respect the interests of individuals, becomes instead the ultimate form of respect for private autonomy by leaving the parties to their own devices. The fact that this abnegation in general leads to unbridled disciplinary power at the disposal of the employer no more weakened lawyers' faith in the appropriateness of abnegation than did the similar effect of abnegation in the household which tended to reinforce the man's physical and economic domination of the woman.[69]

NEUTRALITY

The common law's weak protection for workers also proved attractive to the courts, because it avoided the minefield of expressing any direct preference between capital and labour. By declining to adjudicate whether the employer had good reasons for dismissal, the courts were able to duck highly charged political questions such as whether it was improper to dismiss a worker on account of his or her membership of a union. The common law maintains a stance of neutrality on such questions, leaving it to the parties to fix the terms of their agreement, which will then be enforced.

Underlying this preference for neutrality, of course, stands the courts' quest for legitimacy. Through the stance of neutrality, they could avoid the

---

[65] A. Flanders, 'The Tradition of Voluntarism' (1974), 12, *British Journal of Industrial Relations*, 352.

[66] R. A. Epstein, 'In Defense of the Contract at Will' (1984), 57, *University of Chicago Law Review*, 947.

[67] O. Kahn-Freund, 'Blackstone's Neglected Child: The Contract of Employment' (1977), 93, *LQR* 508.

[68] R. W. Power, 'A Defence of the Employment at Will Rule' (1983), 27, *Saint Louis University Law Journal*, 881.

[69] Katherine O'Donovan, *Sexual Divisions in Law* (London, 1985), 10–19.

appearance of favouring either side in the struggle between classes or the contests between opposing interest groups, presenting themselves as neutral arbiters over the terms of contractual agreements.

EQUALITY

Finally, advocates of the common law position emphasize the formal equality or mutuality of the rules.[70] Since no one proposes that the employee should be denied his or her general liberty to leave his or her job on the spot, because this would represent too great an invasion of the freedom of the worker, it is argued that for reasons of equality and mutuality the employer should also have the right to terminate the employment at will.

Like any standard of formal equality, this principle is vulnerable to the criticism that the real needs and interests of the parties differ so substantially that formal equality effectively masks and legitimizes substantive inequality.[71] To meet this objection, it must be asserted that employees benefit an equal amount from the rule by alleging, for example, that the right to resign from one's job discourages the employer from imposing harsh and extortionate demands upon employees. It may also be alleged that the costs to the employer of protest resignations in terms of harm to any reputation for being a good employer and the additional expense for personnel administration are considerable, and so normally they will be avoided by recognizing a degree of job security.[72]

Many will regard these alleged virtues of the common law of dismissal as little more than mystifictions of the real class interests at stake. But whether or not these sceptics are right, it should be recognized that the common law functions behind the veil of these ideologies, and that legal reasoning uses these justifications to elaborate the principles of the relevant law. My aim here lies not in demystification, but rather in examining the gravitational pull of these values and assumptions on the judicial interpretation of the unfair dismissal legislation.

5. JURIDIFICATION OF MANAGERIAL PREROGATIVE

My thesis is that this unfair dismissal legislation runs against the grain of these background assumptions and values of the common law. A law of

---

[70] For the use of this argument by the courts, see S. Jacoby, 'The Duration of Indefinite Employment Contracts in the United States and England: A Historical Analysis' (1982), 5, *Comparative Labor Law*, 85, at pp. 122–6.

[71] K. Marx, 'Critique of the Gotha Programme', in Karl Marx and Frederick Engels, *Selected Works* (International Publishers edn., New York, 1968), 315–35.

[72] Epstein, 'In Defense of the Contract at Will'.

unfair dismissal requires the courts to abandon all three underlying justifications for their stance of abnegation.

The legislation demands an investigation of the propriety of the exercise of managerial discretion, hitherto a largely unregulated sphere of private autonomy. It requires the courts to favour the interests of employees in job security, thereby abandoning the legitimizing stance of neutrality between capital and labour. Finally, the formal legal equality is shattered, for whilst employees remain free to terminate the employment relation for any reason abruptly, the employer has to follow certain procedures and give acceptable reasons for dismissals.

This deep penetration into the management rights terrain involves nothing short of a reorientation of the relation between State and civil society, or between the courts and the management of business. Instead of deferring to the business judgement of the management, the traditional stance of corporate and labour law, the unfair dismissal legislation applies a regulatory framework to the practices of disciplining labour. It imposes mandatory standards of behaviour in a sphere of social life hitherto regarded in law as an unregulated private arrangement of exchange. In this sense the legislation inaugurates a juridification of managerial prerogative and it is this proposed juridification which runs deeply contrary to the settled values and background assumptions of the common law.

The term juridification has been used in several senses in the context of labour law. Sometimes it means little more than an increase in the quantity of law—more statutes, precedents, and administrative regulations. In the work of Simitis, juridification means more precisely the substitution of mandatory public regulation of terms of the employment relation in place of private freedom of contract.[73] On the other hand, Teubner,[74] following Weber to a considerable extent,[75] regards a central aspect of juridification as the process of replacing the formal general private law such as ordinary contract law with specific regulation aimed at social goals such as the improvement of working conditions. The law of unfair dismissal apparently provides a good example of this modern form of law which is particularistic, discretionary, and heavily dependent for its interpretation on references to other moral and economic norms. But none of these meanings for juridification is intended here.

Not that any of them would make much sense. Although the common law

---

[73] S. Simitis, 'The Juridification of Labor Relations' (1985), 7, *Comparative Labor Law*, 93; id. 'Juridification of Labor Relations', in Gunther Teubner (ed.), *Juridification of Social Spheres: A Comparative Analysis in the Areas of Labor, Corporate, Antitrust and Social Welfare Law* (Berlin, 1987), 113. Cf. J. Clark, 'The Juridification of Industrial Relations: A Review Article' (1985), 14, *ILJ* 69.

[74] G. Teubner, 'Juridification: Concepts, Aspects, Limits, Solutions', in id. (ed.), *Juridification of Social Spheres*, 3, at pp. 10–19.

[75] Max Weber, *Economy and Society*, ed. G. Roth and C. Wittich (Berkeley Calif., 1978), ii. 880–900.

formulated its support for managerial power in the form of implied terms, that is, directory rather than mandatory norms as Simitis suggests, employees stood little chance of rebutting these implied terms on the ground that they had not wished to assent to them. To defeat employees' claims that they had not assented to implied terms granting disciplinary powers, the courts relied upon the employer's custom of discipline to assert that it was implied into the contractual arrangement.[76] Teubner's concept of juridification cannot assist us to contrast the general common law of contract with the specific legislation on unfair dismissal, for I have been at pains to demonstrate the idiosyncratic nature of the common law's regulation of termination of employment, with its reluctance to intervene in contractual disputes and its unprincipled assessment of damages. So we merely see the replacement of one highly specific regime by another, albeit one created by the judges and the other by the legislature.

What I seek to stress by my use of the term juridification is that this legislative intervention tackles a field hitherto unregulated by law to any significant extent. The term juridification therefore denotes the advent of legal regulation in an area of social life previously left to private power, which, though indirectly constituted by laws such as those establishing private ownership of the means of production and the province of legitimate industrial action, was not itself directly colonized and moulded by law.

In sum, by requiring the juridification of managerial disciplinary powers, the legislation presents the courts with a task which they have previously sought to avoid altogether for the reasons connected with the respect for individual autonomy and the need to legitimize their position outlined above. In these circumstances we cannot expect an avid endorsement of the principles of the legislation and a fervent pursuit of employees' interest in job security. On the contrary, what we may expect is a reluctance to intervene in disciplinary matters except in the most egregious cases of unfair dismissal.

This abstentionist position stands quite independently of any sympathies which the judiciary might share with the immediate aims of the legislation to reduce strikes over dismissals and to provide a peaceful mechanism for the resolution of labour disputes. In fact, as we shall see in Chapters 4 and 8, the courts shared the aims of the Donovan Commission and early decisions assisted to a considerable extent in bringing them to fruition by insisting that employers should follow basic procedural standards of fairness.[77] Yet this sympathy for the immediate aims of the legislation should not be permitted to obscure the more fundamental antagonistic relation between the courts and the role assigned to them by the law. It is this reluctance to introduce

---

[76] *Sagar* v. *Ridehalgh & Sons Ltd.* [1931] 1 Ch. 310 (CA).
[77] *Earl* v. *Slater & Wheeler (Airlyne) Ltd.* [1972] ICR 508 (NIRC); *James* v. *Waltham Holy Cross Urban District Council* [1973] ICR 398 (NIRC).

juridification of managerial prerogative over discipline which supplies the undercurrent of the crucial decisions interpreting the legislation. The early emphasis upon the procedural dimension of fairness betrays this reluctance, for attention to procedural standards was perceived by the courts as presenting a less serious threat to managerial discretion than a full-scale review of the substantive merits of the management's decision to dismiss an employee.[78]

All these themes underlying the judicial interpretation of the unfair dismissal legislation are amply illustrated by the first case to reach the highest appeal court. In *Devis (W.) & Sons Ltd.* v. *Atkins*,[79] the employer dismissed the employee without giving a fair warning that disobedience to a particular instruction would result in dismissal. A week later the employer discovered evidence pointing to fraudulent misconduct of the employee. Before the House of Lords, the employee's claim for unfair dismissal was upheld on the ground that the employer had failed to adopt a fair procedure prior to dismissal. But the employee was denied any compensation on the ground that in view of his fraudulent conduct it would not be just and equitable to make an award. This denial of compensation mirrored exactly the stance of the common law of wrongful dismissal, under which no damages would be awarded if the employer could demonstrate that grounds warranting summary dismissal existed even though undiscovered at the time of the dismissal.[80] This strange combination of a finding of unfair dismissal with a denial of compensation reveals clearly both the judicial sympathy towards the aim of the legislation, to introduce more orderly procedures to industrial relations, and a simultaneous reluctance to depart from the traditional attitude of the common law, to respect the private autonomy of managerial prerogative. The court drew directly upon the standards of the common law of wrongful dismissal in order to determine what was just and equitable in an award of compensation under the new legislation. In subsequent decisions, even that concept of fairness which emphasized procedural regularity as the minimum and least invasive form of control over managerial prerogative compatible with the existence of the unfair dismissal legislation gave way to the court's more profound antipathy to the juridification of managerial disciplinary powers.

6. THE RANGE OF REASONABLE RESPONSES TEST

This investigation of the origins of the legislation and the background framework from which the courts and tribunals approached the question of

---

[78] H. Collins, 'Capitalist Discipline and Corporatist Law' (1982), 11, *ILJ* 78, at pp. 87–8.
[79] [1977] ICR 662 (HL).
[80] *Boston Deep Sea Fishing and Ice Co.* v. *Ansell* (1899) 39 Ch. D. 339; *Cyril Leonard & Co.* v. *Simo Securities Trust Ltd.* [1972] 1 WLR 80 (CA).

fairness in unfair dismissal accounts in large measure for the failure of Mr Mathewson's claim. The dominant approach to the question of fairness preserves the managerial prerogative to determine when dismissal is the appropriate punishment. In this way the tribunals continue the common law's respect for the autonomy of managerial prerogative, refusing to impose independent standards of just conduct. The courts handle the problem of juridification posed by the novel legislation by persisting in their stance of declining to interfere with the exercise of managerial disciplinary power. But the common law's pattern of abnegation reveals itself in a new guise under the statutory jurisdiction.

Instead of professing the employer's right to terminate the contract of employment for any reason, under the legislation the courts must accommodate the legal requirement that the dismissal must be shown to be fair. The courts perform this task by demanding that the employer should demonstrate that a dismissal was within the range of reasonable responses to the employee's behaviour. The range of reasonable responses test of fairness replaces a more or less complete refusal to enter into the private sphere of managerial prerogative with a qualified refusal. The employer's decision is fair provided that it is not so unreasonable that no reasonable employer could have reached such a decision. But this formula provides few occasions for justified interference with managerial prerogative, for dismissals may prove harsh but fair as Mr Mathewson discovered.

The range of reasonable responses test replaces the statutory test of fairness in terms of the reasonableness of the employer's decision with a negative, but not identical, formula of whether the employer's conduct was unreasonable. The statute, it will be recalled, poses the question whether 'the employer acted reasonably or unreasonably in treating it [i.e. his reason for dismissal] as a sufficient reason for dismissing the employee'.[81] But the tribunals in practice impose the subtly different formulation that the employer's decision should be shown to fall outside the range of reasonable responses to the circumstances. This reformulation of the reasonableness test involves a double shift in the linguistic construction.

First, the insertion of the word 'range' qualifies what may be regarded as reasonable. The idea of a range of reasonable conduct broadens the scope for legitimate disciplinary action by denying implicitly that a fixed standard of reasonableness should be applied. For example, if we ask whether it was reasonable for an employer to permit an employee to remove a safety guard from a machine in order to improve access, we might conclude in the light of a subsequent injury that permission was unreasonable since it subverted the purpose of the guard. But by emphasizing the possibility of a range of reasonable responses to the situation, we introduce by implication a host of other factors such as efficiency in production and the willingness of the

---

[81] EPCA 1978, s. 57(3).

employee to accept the risk of injury, all of which tend to weaken criticism of the employer's conduct by pointing to relevant considerations other than the risk of injury to the employee. Similarly, in Mr Mathewson's case, the insertion of the idea of a range of reasonableness opened the gate to allow the employer to rely heavily on his disapproval of drugs as a factor relevant to the reasonableness of his decision, which could then be set off against the weakness of the employer's justification for dismissal in its other aspects such as the absence of proper hearing and the triviality of the employee being an hour late for work.

A second shift away from the statutory formulation in the linguistic construction involves an emphasis upon the question of the 'unreasonableness' of the employer's decision rather than its 'reasonableness'. This again has the effect of broadening the scope of legitimate disciplinary action. For example, if we ask whether a knife is sharp, then we might expect a negative reply if the knife's edge falls anywhere between completely blunt and slightly dull. If, on the other hand, we ask whether the knife is blunt, then we receive a negative answer provided that the knife has some cutting edge. In the middle range the knife is neither sharp nor blunt, but depending on how the question is posed, either answer can be prompted. The same presumptions may be created by the alternative formulations of the test of reasonableness. In the middle range of cases, where the dismissal was neither clearly fair nor unfair, if the tribunal asks whether the employer's decision was reasonable, the question tends to lead to a negative response and a finding of unfairness. If, on the other hand, the tribunal asks whether the employer's decision was unreasonable, the question tends to shift the middle ground into the realm of fair dismissals. A decision may not be a reasonable one, but neither will it be wholly unreasonable. In Mr Mathewson's case, the Industrial Tribunal probably did not regard the employer's decision as reasonable, but they could not say that it was unreasonable, so a finding of fair dismissal was prompted by the way in which the question was posed.

In short, the effect of the courts' and tribunals' double reformulation of the statutory test is to create a presumption of fairness and an excuse for non-intervention. The tribunal will not make its own decision about the question whether dismissal was merited for fear of the problem of juridification. It simply endorses the practices of management in all but the most unreasonable and irrational instances of abuse of managerial disciplinary power.[82] Thus Mr Mathewson's dismissal could be harsh but fair, not

---

[82] For a predictable and parallel response to the problem of juridification elsewhere, see the way in which the US Merit System Protection Board, a tribunal vested with jurisdication to hear grievances of federal employees, tends to uphold dismissal in cases of allegations of poor performance provided that a 'reasonable person could agree' with the decision: *Parker* v. *Defense Logistics Agency*, 1 MSPB 489, 492 (1980); and see Note, 'Developments in the Law: Public Employment' (1984), 97, *Harvard Law Review*, 1611, at p. 1639; P. A. Price, 'Dismissals of Civil Service Employees for Unacceptable Performance' (1986), 29, *Howard Law Journal* 387.

reasonable but not unreasonable, and certainly not outside the range of reasonable responses so as to render it wholly unreasonable.

Although the common law's pattern of abnegation with respect to managerial prerogative persists through these subtle shifts of interpretation, the legislation nevertheless does introduce some qualified controls. Tribunals find some dismissals unfair because they fall outside the range of reasonable responses appropriate for employers. We should therefore turn to the question of what principles of justice or fairness determine the setting of this boundary for intervention. But an answer to this question requires an investigation of the relevance and impact of many aspects of justice.

Mr Mathewson's case illustrates well the variety of issues which may be raised in even a run-of-the-mill decision. First comes the substantive issue of fairness of whether Mr Mathewson's hour's lateness for work as a result of his arrest merited dismissal. Should such misconduct provide a sufficient reason for dismissal? Should the employer's personnel handbook be relevant to this question, whether or not its contents were communicated to the employee? We must also consider, secondly, whether the employer initiated sufficient enquiries and provided sufficient opportunity for the employee to explain himself in order to satisfy standards of procedural fairness. The detailed standards of substantive and procedural justice applied by the tribunals will be considered in Chapters 3 and 4 respectively. But this case raises a third dimension of justice as well, for Mr Mathewson believed that how he conducted himself outside work and outside working hours was none of the employer's business. The dismissal therefore interfered with his privacy and liberty, as well as causing him the economic hardship of unemployment. The threat to civil liberties posed by the exercise of managerial disciplinary powers will be explored in Chapter 6.

But no single case can illustrate by itself the host of questions of justice raised by dismissals, because they may occur in a wide variety of circumstances and for differing motives. Some dismissals may prove the inevitable result of the employer's insolvency, others may be inspired by discriminatory or anti-union sentiments, and the appropriate response from the law of dismissal to these situations should be quite distinct. Similarly, dismissals during strikes pose important social and political questions about the fair balance of economic power between capital and labour during collective bargaining, whereas dismissals of individuals for incompetence raise completely different issues including the adequacy of an employer's training and supervision of workers.

Despite this diversity of the issues of justice which dismissals pose, in the next chapter I will suggest that, with the aid of a clear taxonomy of the different types of dismissals, it is possible to approach the substantive and procedural questions of justice in a much more systematic and coherent manner than has so far been achieved by the British legislature, the courts, and the tribunals.

[2]

A Taxonomy of Dismissals

THE enormous variety of circumstances in which dismissals take place inevitably pushes regulatory legislation towards the enactment of general standards. The core provision of the British legislation, as we have seen, insists that the tribunal should assess the employer's reason for dismissal for its reasonableness in the light of the circumstances and the justice and equity of the case. This broad standard leaves to the courts and tribunals the task of elaborating the concept of fairness in the run-of-the-mill case. Yet the legislature does offer more precise guidance both in structuring the tribunal's inquiry and in foreclosing issues of fairness by predetermining the outcome in cases with particular characteristics. A closer inspection of these specific provisions which effectively restrict a tribunal's discretion suggests a relatively coherent though differentiated scheme of principles of fairness with respect to the diversity of dismissals. The aim of this chapter is to distil from the apparently chaotic statutory provisions a coherent scheme of principles of fairness in dismissals which presents the legislation in its best light.

1. THE STRUCTURE OF THE FAIRNESS INQUIRY

In order to comprehend how and when the legislation tends to foreclose the fairness inquiry, we must briefly review the general structure of the legal questions which a tribunal has to address. Most of the relevant provisions are located in Part V of the Employment Protection (Consolidation) Act 1978 (EPCA). This part commences with the enactment of the general right to claim unfair dismissal:

S. 54(1) In every employment to which this section applies every employee shall have the right not to be unfairly dismissed.

We shall examine later how the ambit of this right is severely curtailed by the restrictive conditions precedent to an employee being entitled to advance a claim.[1] The legislation then divides the fairness inquiry into three stages.

Stage one requires the employee to demonstrate to the tribunal that he or she has been dismissed by his or her employer. Here the fundamental question is whether the employee resigned or was dismissed, whether he or

---

[1] See Ch. 8.

she was pushed or jumped of his or her own free will. The second stage of the fairness inquiry requires the employer to prove to the tribunal what was the principal reason for the dismissal and that this reason amounts to a substantial reason of a kind such as to justify the dismissal of an employee holding the position which that employee held.[2] The final stage consists of the general test of reasonableness in EPCA 1978, s. 57(3), which, as we saw in the previous chapter, the tribunals have interpreted as a test which poses the question whether the employer's response to the circumstances was outside the range of reasonable responses of employers. We need to examine a little more fully the first and second stages of the fairness inquiry in order to appreciate the mechanisms by which the legislation forecloses the results.

DISMISSAL

The statute provides for the purpose of distinguishing dismissals from resignations an exhaustive definition of the concept of dismissal:

[A]n employee shall be treated as dismissed by his employer if, but only if,—
(a) the contract under which he is employed by the employer is terminated by the employer, whether it is so terminated by notice or without notice, or
(b) where under that contract he is employed for a fixed term, that term expires without being renewed under the same contract, or
(c) the employee terminates that contract, with or without notice, in circumstances such that he is entitled to terminate it without notice by reason of the employer's conduct.[3]

Proof of dismissal in the first stage of the inquiry rarely presents a problem to employees, especially since the employee has the right to a written statement of the reasons for dismissal on request.[4] The statutory definition clearly encompasses all the normal instances of dismissals with notice and summary dismissals. But that is not to say that the statutory concept of dismissal cannot provoke considerable technical difficulties for employees.

The most unsatisfactory omission from the statute concerns agreed terminations of the contract of employment. Although many of these agreements will be caught by paragraph (b) concerning the expiration of a fixed term, *ad hoc* agreements to end the employment relationship must be placed in a category to which they are not properly suited, that is, either

---

[2] EPCA 1978, s. 57(1).
[3] EPCA 1978, s. 55(2). For detailed examination of the application of these provisions, see Steven D. Anderman, *The Law of Unfair Dismissal* (2nd edn., London, 1985), ch. 3; P. Elias, 'Unravelling the Concept of Dismissal' (1978), 7, *ILJ* 16 and 100. In addition, the statute provides in cases of a woman returning to work after confinement (s. 56) and strikers being victimized by not being offered re-engagement (s. 62(3)) that the failure to re-engage should be regarded as a dismissal.
[4] EPCA 1978, s. 53.

dismissal by the employer or resignation by the employee. The courts have ruled that termination by mutual agreement will not count as a dismissal, provided that the employee's consent was genuine.[5] For example, in *Birch* v. *University of Liverpool*,[6] the employer, faced by cuts in government funding, invited staff to take advantage of an early retirement scheme which was intended to reduce the workforce by 300 posts. The employee applied for early retirement, the application was approved by the university, which then formally requested his retirement on a particular date. In the context of the employee's claim for a redundancy payment, where the same statutory definition of dismissal applies,[7] on the preliminary point of whether the employee had been dismissed, the Court of Appeal ruled that such a termination of employment by mutual agreement could not amount in law to a dismissal. The fact that the employer had reserved the ultimate power of control over selection for early retirement, no doubt for reasons of sensible manpower planning, did not prevent the case from falling into the category of termination by mutual agreement.

One wonders whether the employee realized that by accepting the carrot of early retirement he was also agreeing by implication to give up statutory rights under the law of dismissal. To accept that such agreements are even possible runs the risk of undermining the safeguards of EPCA 1978, s. 140, which invalidate express agreements to exclude or limit statutory rights. The whole legal construct of termination by mutual agreement should be regarded as an unwarranted fabrication by the courts. It makes no sense in terms of legal analysis, for every employer's termination by notice is also a termination by agreement under the notice provisions included in the contract, yet these must count as a dismissal for otherwise only summary dismissals would be caught by the statute. Moreover, this invention by the courts produces injustice, for it permits employers by contractual arrangements which contain no express warning to induce employees to relinquish their statutory rights, when if such renunciations were explicit they might be void. At the very least the courts should restore the presumption articulated by Lord Denning, MR in *Lees* v. *Arthur Greaves (Lees) Ltd.*

If the employment is terminated by agreement, then he gets no compensation. So the tribunal and the court should not find an agreement unless it is proved that he really did agree with full knowledge of the implications which it held for him.[8]

---

[5] *Lees* v. *Arthur Greaves (Lees) Ltd.* [1974] ICR 501 (CA); *Igbo* v. *Johnson Matthey Chemicals Ltd.*[1986] ICR 505 (CA).

[6] [1985] ICR 470 (CA), noted M. R. Freedland, 'Premature Retirement and Normal Retirement; Freedom versus Expectation in the Appellate Courts' (1985) 14, *ILJ* 243.

[7] EPCA 1978, s. 83.

[8] [1974] ICR 501 (CA), at p. 505; see also the significance of bad faith and failure to disclose information in *Caledonian Mining Co. Ltd.* v. *Bassett and Steel* [1987] ICR 425 (EAT), noted J. Holland, 'Bad Faith Dismissals' (1987), 16, *ILJ* 252.

Further difficulties for employees arise from the courts' interpretation of paragraph (c), the statutory provision for constructive dismissal. When an employee resigns in protest against the employer's conduct, he or she must claim that he or she has been constructively dismissed in order to comply with the requirement of dismissal. Unless the employee can point to an important term of the contract which the employer has broken by his or her conduct, such as a failure to pay the agreed wages,[9] or an unjustified insistence upon performance of jobs outside the terms of the employment,[10] then a tribunal will deny that the employee was entitled to resign and claim constructive dismissal. The emphasis upon the requirement of a fundamental breach of an express or implied term of the contract of employment, introduced by *Western Excavating (ECC) Ltd.* v. *Sharp*,[11] does pose, however, the not inconsiderable obstacle for employees without the benefit of legal advice of presenting their claims to have been constructively dismissed in the technical language of repudiatory breach of contract.

This linkage between the statutory concept of dismissal and the common law of implied terms also seems likely to restrict the circumstances when an employee is entitled to resign in protest at the employer's conduct, because the common law traditionally placed few obligations on employers other than the express terms of the contract. Although the courts and tribunals have recognized that the old common law must be brought up to date to include an obligation upon employers to be 'good and considerate' towards employees,[12] and not to conduct themselves in a manner likely to destroy or seriously damage the relationship of confidence and trust between employer and employee,[13] the employee cannot succeed in a claim of constructive dismissal without demonstrating a fundamental breach of such obligations.

The height of this hurdle for employees may be illustrated by *Woods* v. *W. M. Car Services (Peterborough) Ltd.*,[14] where, following a sale of the business, the new employers reorganized the business which involved changing the employee's duties both as to title and as to the work she was expected to do, and they tried unsuccessfully to persuade her to accept a reduction in pay. As a result of these proposed changes and many other incidents, the relations between the parties became severely strained, so that the employee clearly lost all trust and confidence in her new employers. Nevertheless the Industrial Tribunal decided that she was not entitled to

[9] *R. F. Hill Ltd.* v. *Mooney* [1981] IRLR 258 (EAT) (unilateral change in the method of calculating sales commission).
[10] *Pedersen* v. *Camden London Borough Council* [1981] ICR 674, [1981] IRLR 173 (CA) (change of work from bar steward to catering duties).
[11] [1978] QB 761; [1978] ICR 221; [1978] IRLR 27 (CA).
[12] *Woods* v. *W. M. Car Services (Peterborough) Ltd.* [1982] ICR 692 (CA) per Lord Denning, MR at p. 698.
[13] *Courtaulds Northern Textiles Ltd.* v. *Andrew* [1979] IRLR 84 (EAT); *Post Office* v. *Roberts* [1980] IRLR 347 (EAT); *Lewis* v. *Motorworld Garages Ltd.* [1986] ICR 157 (CA).
[14] [1982] ICR 692 (CA).

resign and claim constructive dismissal, for the employers were held not to be in fundamental breach of the implied terms of the contract. Treating the issue as a question of fact,[15] the Court of Appeal declined to intervene and so upheld the tribunal's decision. This reveals that, even though in fact the employer's actions may have destroyed trust and confidence, the tribunal will only find a fundamental breach of this term where it believes that the employer acted either maliciously or extraordinarily unpleasantly.

The legalism of this stage of the inquiry, which works to the considerable disadvantage of the employee, has been further accentuated by the wholly unjustified introduction of arcane concepts from the common law such as the doctrine of frustration. In cases involving absence from work due to long-term illness,[16] or imprisonment,[17] employers have often, but not always,[18] successfully argued that the contract has been automatically terminated by operation of law under the doctrine of frustration, thereby removing the case from the exclusive statutory definition of dismissal. By accepting this device, the tribunals permit employers to evade the duty to demonstrate that the termination of employment was reasonable in all the circumstances under the general test of fairness. Not only is this manipulative evasion of statutory duty unjust, but it also seems clearly bad in law, for contracts, like the contract of employment, which are terminable on reasonable notice, should never be frustrated,[19] since contractual terms making provision for a contingency prevent the application of the doctrine.[20]

SUBSTANTIAL REASON

The employer's burden of establishing a substantial reason for dismissal at the second stage turns out to be light in practice. The statute identifies potential substantial reasons as lack of capability or qualifications, miscon-

---

[15] For criticism of this paradox that the legalistic approach to the question of constructive dismissal in tribunals is treated as an unreviewable question of fact by the appeal courts, see H. Collins, 'Judicial Review of Tribunal Decisions in Cases of Unfair Dismissal' (1981), 10, *ILJ* 256. A slightly more interventionist stance appears in *Lewis* v. *Motorworld Garages Ltd.* [1986] ICR 157 (CA).

[16] *Marshall* v. *Harland & Wolff Ltd.* [1972] ICR 101 (NIRC); *Egg Stores (Stamford Hill) Ltd.* v. *Leibovici* [1977] ICR 260 (EAT); *Hart* v. *A. R. Marshall & Sons (Bulwell) Ltd.* [1977] ICR 539 (EAT). See also *Notcutt* v. *Universal Equipment Co. (London) Ltd.* [1986] ICR 414 (CA).

[17] *Hare* v. *Murphy Bros. Ltd.* [1974] ICR 603 (CA) (Lord Denning); *Shepherd (F. C.) & Co. Ltd.* v. *Jerrom* [1986] ICR 802 (CA).

[18] *Marshall* v. *Harland & Wolff Ltd.* [1972] ICR 101 (NIRC); *Converform (Darwen) Ltd.* v. *Bell* [1981] IRLR 195 (EAT); *Harman* v. *Flexible Lamps Ltd.* [1982] IRLR 418 (EAT); *Chakki* v. *United Yeast Co. Ltd.* [1982] ICR 140 (EAT); *Norris* v. *Southampton City Council* [1982] ICR 177 (EAT); *Williams* v. *Watsons Luxury Coaches Ltd.* [1990] ICR 536 (EAT).

[19] *Harman* v. *Flexible Lamps Ltd.* [1982] IRLR 418 (EAT); doubted in *Notcutt* v. *Universal Equipment Co. (London) Ltd.* [1986] ICR 414 (CA) by Dillion, LJ (at p. 420) on surely the perverse ground that unless frustration applied then employers would be faced with claims for unfair dismissal.

[20] *Tarnesby* v. *Kensington and Chelsea and Westminster Area Health Authority* [1981] ICR 615 (HL).

duct, redundancy, and illegality, but this list is only indicative, so employers may put forward any type of reason as a substantial one. The courts have demonstrated a willingness to regard almost any reason put forward by the employer as such a substantial reason, thereby setting a low threshold.[21] In particular, a substantial reason need not comprise either a breach of contract or a threat to proper performance of the job:

> The hurdle over which the employer has to jump at this stage of an inquiry into an unfair dismissal complaint is designed to deter employers from dismissing employees for some trivial or unworthy reason. If he does so, the dismissal is deemed unfair without the need to look further into its merits. But if on the face of it the reason *could* justify the dismissal, then it passes as a substantial reason, and the inquiry moves on to s. 57(3), and the question of reasonableness.[22]

Only when the employer fails to establish any reason at all will the employer's defence normally fail at this stage.

But since the burden of proof to establish a substantial reason lies on the employer, he must take care to produce evidence before the tribunal in support of the alleged principal reason for dismissal. In *Smith* v. *City of Glasgow District Council*,[23] the House of Lords insisted that if an employer was unable to prove the principal reason for dismissal, or part of it, then the dismissal was necessarily unfair. The employers in this case had conducted a thorough inquiry which reached the conclusion that the employee had misconducted himself by failing to respond adequately to requests for information. But the Industrial Tribunal subsequently rejected this finding by the employer's inquiry as either untrue or at least unproven. In these circumstances the House of Lords concluded that the employers had failed to establish a substantial reason by merely referring to the conclusions of the internal inquiry, so the dismissal was unfair. Although this robust decision restores some teeth to the second stage of the fairness inquiry, its effect must be limited provided that employers rely upon reasons for dismissal which they can support from the available evidence.

FAIRNESS AND REMEDIES

In practice, therefore, the question of fairness tends to develop to the third stage of the inquiry with its general test of reasonableness. The burden of proof under EPCA 1978, s. 57(3), is neutral,[24] so that both employer and employee must lead argument and evidence in order to convince the tribunal of the reasonableness or otherwise of the dismissal.

---

[21] J. Bowers and A. Clarke, 'Unfair Dismissal and Managerial Prerogative: A Study of "Other Substantial Reason"' (1981) 10, *ILJ* 34.

[22] *Gilham* v. *Kent County Council (No. 2)* [1985] ICR 233 (CA) per Griffiths, LJ at p. 239.

[23] [1987] IRLR 326 (HL).

[24] As a result of amendment by the Employment Act 1980, s. 6, which restored the position under s. 24(6), Industrial Relations Act 1971.

If the tribunal determines that the employer acted outside the range of reasonable responses to the employee's conduct, then the normal remedy will be an award of compensation under two headings.[25] A basic award provides a sum calculated on the basis of the three variables of normal weekly pay, length of service for the employer, and the age of the employee.[26] In addition, a compensatory award permits a tribunal to award a lump sum which approximates to the employee's likely economic losses resulting from dismissal.[27]

2. FORECLOSURE OF THE FAIRNESS INQUIRY

In the light of this structure for the fairness inquiry, we can discern two possible routes by which the legislation may foreclose the issue. On the one hand, it may determine whether or not a particular reason for dismissal should count as a substantial reason for dismissal, and, on the other, it may deem dismissals for a particular reason to be automatically reasonable or unreasonable. The legislation adopts both these techniques.

SUBSTANTIAL REASONS

Certain reasons for dismissal are regarded as substantial reasons, thereby relieving the employer of the light burden of convincing the tribunal that the reason for the dismissal is one which might potentially justify it. We have already noted that the statute lists capability, qualifications, misconduct, redundancy, and illegality as substantial reasons.[28]

From the point of view of foreclosure of the fairness inquiry, the most significant of these itemized substantial reasons concerns dismissals for redundancy, as defined in Part VI of EPCA 1978. This normally includes dismissals in the event of business closure and reductions in the workforce to cut labour costs. In addition, dismissals for an economic, technical, or organizational reason in connection with the sale of a business are also deemed to count as dismissals for a substantial reason.[29] As well as resolving the question whether a reason for dismissal unconnected to fault on the part of the employee could count as a substantial reason for dismissal, these provisions tend to foreclose the fairness inquiry in one vital dimension.

---

[25] EPCA 1978, s. 72. On the practice of using compensation rather than the available remedy of reinstatement, see Ch. 7.

[26] EPCA 1978, s. 73.

[27] Ibid., s. 74.

[28] Ibid., s. 57(2). See, also, dismissal of a replacement worker on the return of an employee from maternity leave, ibid., s. 61.

[29] Transfer of Undertakings Regulations 1981, Regulation 8; H. Collins, 'Dismissals on Transfer of a Business' (1986), 15, *ILJ* 244; id., 'Transfer of Undertakings and Insolvency' (1989), 18, *ILJ* 144; P. L. Davies, 'Acquired Rights, Creditors' Rights, Freedom of Contract, and Industrial Democracy' (1989), 9, *Yearbook of European Law*, 21.

Having demonstrated the fact of a reduced demand for labour, the employer has established a substantial reason for dismissal. The tribunals then quickly conclude in most instances that it was reasonable to dismiss for this economic reason of redundancy. The tribunals need not assess the reasonableness of the employer's initial decision to reduce the workforce. Instead they are directed to award the employee a limited measure of compensation in the form of a redundancy payment. This constitutes a lump sum based upon the three variables of weekly pay, length of service, and age,[30] equivalent to the basic award of compensation for unfair dismissal.

The effect of this structure of the legislation is to withdraw one crucial area of managerial prerogative from inspection by the tribunals. The implicit reason for this exemption appears to be that business judgements with respect to manpower requirements are not, and should not be, susceptible to evaluation by an external tribunal. We can detect here, therefore, a special impact of the problem of juridification, this time on the face of the legislation itself. Respect for the autonomy of business judgements goes so far as to relieve the employer from having to justify the reasonableness of his or her policy of reducing the size of the workforce.

These rules governing dismissals for reasons of redundancy therefore normally exempt employers from the inquiry into the fairness of the dismissal. Indeed, it is possible that the legislators of 1971 intended that proof of redundancy should suffice to exclude the application of the fairness standard altogether, except where the principles of selection violated a collective agreement, in which case the dismissal was automatically unfair under EPCA 1978, s. 59. This reading of legislative intent may explain why so little was done to integrate the new unfair dismissal legislation with the preceding law of redundancy payments and why breach of collectively agreed procedures was singled out for special treatment in s. 59. Nevertheless, the Court of Appeal rejected this interpretation of the legislation decisively in *Bessenden Properties Ltd.* v. *Corness*.[31] Here the employee was selected for redundancy in preference to two other workers performing the same job, even though she had greater seniority and was head of the department, the reason being that she was married and the others single so that her husband could support her.[32] The court upheld an award of compenstion for unfair dismissal in addition to a redundancy payment, holding that the general fairness standard could apply to the grounds for selection for redundancy. Subsequent decisions have confirmed that a redundant employee may claim that a dismissal was unfair under the third stage as a result of lack of consultation,[33] or selection on arbitrary or irrational grounds.[34]

---

[30] EPCA 1978, s. 81 and Schedule 4.
[31] Note (1974) [1977] ICR 821 (CA).
[32] This ground for selection would now contravene the Sex Discrimination Act 1975, s. 3.
[33] *Polkey* v. *A. E. Dayton Services Ltd.* [1988] ICR 142 (HL).
[34] *Williams* v. *Compair Maxam Ltd.* [1982] ICR 156 (EAT).

Nevertheless, in practice, most redundancy dismissals will be regarded as fair and so the fairness inquiry will be truncated. The employer's grounds for selection and procedural steps are likely to fall within the range of reasonable responses to the redundancy situation. Indeed, many of the decisions which gave birth to the range of reasonable responses test were concerned with relieving employers from close scrutiny of their manpower decisions in cases of redundancy.[35] In practice, therefore, the redundancy situation normally provides the employer with a strong defence to a claim for unfair dismissal, so that he or she avoids liability for the compensatory award at the price of acknowledging liability to pay the lesser sum of the basic award. The absence of fault on the part of the employee here in the context of redundancy dismissals does not entitle him or her to greater compensation, but rather confines him or her to a smaller severance payment.

AUTOMATIC UNFAIRNESS

An even more significant foreclosure of the fairness inquiry occurs when the statute determines that dismissal for a particular reason should be regarded as automatically unfair. This technique applies most notably to dismissals relating to trade union membership and to some dismissals on the ground of the pregnancy of the employee.[36] These isolated occasions when the legislature has spoken unequivocally regarding the fairness or unfairness of the dismissals deserve close attention, for they reveal certain underlying principles of fairness embedded, though not properly developed, within the legislation.

The current law provides for the automatic unfairness of a dismissal if the principal reason was connected to the employee's membership of a trade union.[37] This applies not only to anti-union discrimination by an employer, but also to dismissals in support of a closed shop, so that dismissals for non-membership of a trade union are equally unfair. This parity of protection for the right to belong and not to belong to a trade union has not always been the case. Provisions relating to dismissals in support of a closed shop have a chequered career, varying from the automatic fairness of such dismissals (subject to an exception for genuine religious beliefs),[38] to their fairness contingent upon the satisfaction of numerous statutory conditions such as an affirmative ballot in support of the closed shop by 80 per cent of the workforce.[39] In view of the requirement to respect the freedom not to

---

[35] e.g. *Vickers Ltd.* v. *Smith* [1977] IRLR 11 (EAT).

[36] Other examples include: dismissal of a redundant employee in contravention of a customary arrangement or agreed procedure in the absence of special reasons, EPCA 1978, s. 59(*b*); dismissal in connection with the transfer of an undertaking which is not for an economic, technical, or organizational reason, Transfer of Undertakings Regulations 1981, Reg. 8(1).

[37] EPCA 1978, s. 58.

[38] Trade Union and Labour Relations Act 1974, Sched. 1, para. 6.

[39] Employment Act 1982, s. 3.

associate with a trade union, endorsed albeit equivocally, by the European Court of Human Rights,[40] it seems likely that the present position of parity of protection for both the positive and negative aspects of the rights will prevail in the future.

Apart from the automatic unfairness of dismissals in connection with trade union membership, the striking feature of these provisions concerns the unique set of remedies afforded to a successful claimant. Not only will the dismissed employee be entitled to claim the normal measure of compensation for unfair dismissal, but also the basic award is fixed at a generous minimum level,[41] and the employee can claim a special award,[42] which in essence amounts to punitive damages, for it is likely to amount to as much as twenty times the normal measure of compensation for unfair dismissal. Where a trade union may be thought to be in part responsible for provoking the dismissal by industrial pressure, the employer or employee may join the union to the proceedings and then the tribunal may distribute the liability to pay the punitive damages between the employer and the union in the proportions which it considers just and equitable.[43]

This legislative scheme provides dramatic protection for the right to freedom of association in the context of trade union membership. The risk of punitive damages should deter any employer from deliberately discriminating against an employee on the ground or his or her membership or non-membership of a trade union. In effect the worker receives a substantial guarantee of job security, not just compensation, with respect to his or her membership of a trade union. Although this technique remains restricted to one aspect of the civil liberty of freedom of association, albeit a crucial one in the context of industrial relations and the philosophy of industrial pluralism, it points towards a more general approach to the safeguarding of civil liberties from the exercise of managerial power.

The Sex Discrimination Act 1975 and Race Relations Act 1976 provide financial remedies for employees who suffer any intentional detriment including dismissal on grounds of sex, marital status, race, and ethnic origins. Where these statutes apply to a dismissal, the employee may use them or the unfair dismissal legislation, but any compensation awarded under one claim must be set off against an award of compensation under the other to prevent double recovery for loss.[44] None of this legislation provides for the automatic unfairness of the dismissal under the law of unfair dismissal, though of course tribunals will invariably find a dismissal unfair

---

[40] *Young, James and Webster* v. *United Kingdom* [1981] IRLR 408 (ECHR); M. Forde, 'The "Closed Shop" Case' (1982), 11, *ILJ* 1; see Paul Davies and Mark Freedland, *Labour Law: Text and Materials* (2nd edn., London, 1984), at pp. 664–7 on the inconclusive nature of the decision.
[41] EPCA 1978, s. 73(4A), as amended by Employment Act 1982, s. 4.
[42] Ibid., s. 75A, as amended by Employment Act 1982, s. 5.
[43] Ibid., s. 76A, as amended by Employment Act 1982, s. 7.
[44] Ibid., s. 76.

once a discriminatory motive has been established. In practice, however, because the burden of proof and the measure of compensation is probably more favourable to the employee under the discrimination legislation,[45] dismissals tainted by discrimination are unlikely to be considered under the unfair dismissal legislation.

In one aspect of sex discrimination, however, the unfair dismissal legislation makes special provision. A dismissal for a reason connected with pregnancy is automatically unfair, unless the woman is incapable of adequately doing the work, or continued employment of her would contravene some law.[46] The exception does not apply where the employer has a suitable available vacancy of work for the pregnant woman pending the commencement of her maternity leave. The ordinary remedy of compensation for unfair dismissal applies to these cases. The courts and tribunals have interpreted the scope of this provision broadly, so that selection amongst a group of workers for redundancy on the ground that the employee would shortly take maternity leave is automatically unfair,[47] and so too is dismissal during maternity leave because the employer cannot find a temporary replacement and so has been compelled to engage a permanent replacement.[48]

The automatic unfairness of dismissal on grounds of pregnancy is slightly illusory, however, because of the breadth of the potential justifying exception available to employers. Although the legislation rules out the simple prejudice that pregnant women should not work, the employer may escape the automatic unfairness of the dismissal by pointing to aspects of the job which a pregnant woman is incapable of doing adequately. Even more damaging to the general principle, if the woman experiences the medical problems often associated with pregnancy, such as swelling of the veins, hypertension, depression, which cause her to be absent from work, then the employer may justify the dismissal on the ground of incapacity within the exception.[49] The breadth of this exception may have to be revised to bring it into conformity with the Equal Treatment Directive of the European Community, for this prohibits adverse discrimination on the ground of financial consequences flowing from pregnancy.[50] Even with the current exception, however, the protection afforded to pregnant women by a foreclosure of the fairness inquiry indicates the seeds of a more general principle of automatic unfairness for discriminatory dismissals.

Is it too far-fetched to discern in these diverse provisions which foreclose

[45] *North West Thames Regional Health Authority* v. *Noone* [1988] ICR 813 (CA).

[46] EPCA 1978, s. 60.

[47] *Stockton-on-Tees Borough Council* v. *Brown* [1988] ICR 410 (HL).

[48] *Clayton* v. *Vigers* [1989] ICR 713 (EAT).

[49] *Grimsby Carpet Co. Ltd.* v. *Bedford* [1987] ICR 975 (EAT); see S. Bailey, 'The Wording of Section 60 of EPCA 1978' (1988), 17, *ILJ* 191.

[50] Directive 76/207; *Dekker* v. *Stichting Vormingscentrum Voor Jonge Volwassen*, Case No. 177/88 [1991] IRLR 27 (ECJ).

the fairness inquiry in whole or in part some underlying principles of fairness? Against this possibility, it should be acknowledged that the EPCA 1978 comprises in an important sense a 'checkerboard statute',[51] that is, a collection of rules promulgated by different authors at different times reflecting the changing balance of forces of political opinion. In addition, we cannot view this statute in isolation. Other legislation governing termination of employment such as the sex and race discrimination legislation reveals important dimensions of fairness as well. Nevertheless, what I shall suggest is that sifting through this legislation, and using comparative perspectives, it is possible to see lurking behind this rather pragmatic and disorganized set of statutory materials, some guiding themes or principles through which the law distinguishes three types of dismissals on the ground that different considerations of fairness apply in each case and that the remedy provided by the law should differ according to what response is appropriate. Having outlined this taxonomy of principles of fairness in relation to dismissals, we can then consider the extent to which the current law falls short of enacting such a coherent scheme. My contention will be that it is precisely when the law fails to remain faithful to this implicit set of underlying principles that it creates the opportunity for injustice.

3. THREE TYPES OF DISMISSAL

The legislation makes no attempt to foreclose the unfairness inquiry in cases involving the misconduct or incompetence of employees. These are the paradigm cases envisaged by the structure of the legislation, so a tribunal must proceed through the three stages of the inquiry to reach a determination of the case. This category we may call disciplinary dismissals.

The legislation makes special provision for cases where the motive for dismissal relates to the employer's manpower requirements generally, as opposed to the behaviour of a particular employee. The remedy for these economic dismissals, as I shall call them, is normally one of severance pay under the redundancy payments legislation rather than the broader compensatory provisions of unfair dismissal. To achieve this distinction between disciplinary and economic dismissals, Part VI of the EPCA 1978 enacts a general right to claim a redundancy payment in the event of economic dismissal. Then s. 57(2)(c) of the EPCA 1978 states that redundancy should count as a substantial reason for dismissal at the second stage of the fairness inquiry. This leaves open the possibility that an economic dismissal might also be an unfair one under the third stage of the fairness inquiry, but this is unlikely since the tribunals will normally regard redundancy as a reasonable ground for dismissal. Unfair redundancies may arise, however, where the principles of selection for dismissal amongst the workforce are regarded as

[51] Ronald Dworkin, *Law's Empire* (Cambridge, Mass., 1986), at pp. 178–86.

unreasonable or where the procedure adopted by the employer is unfair. Indeed, EPCA 1978, s. 59(*b*), provides for the automatic unfairness of economic dismissals at the third stage of the fairness inquiry if the selection violated an agreed procedure unless special reasons justified a departure from the arrangement. But these possibilities for a simultaneous claim for a redundancy payment and compensation for unfair dismissal based on the unfairness of the dismissal procedure should not be permitted to obscure the general emphasis of the legislation, which, by its detailed and separate handling of redundancies in Part VI, makes it evident that these economic dismissals should be subject to a different regime from that applicable to disciplinary dismissals.

Where the legislation forecloses the fairness inquiry at the third stage by determining that dismissals connected with trade union membership and pregnancy are automatically unfair, we can discern yet a third set of principles in operation. Here the employer's motive for the dismissal is regarded as a contaminated reason, or, as the statutes used to say, an 'inadmissible reason'.[52] Not only is this justification for dismissal completely unacceptable, but also the employer will be penalized by the higher level of damages of the special award in the case of dismissals connected with trade union membership. These provisions seem to take a stand on the importance of the employer's respect for certain basic rights of workers, the freedom to join a trade union and the right to be treated as an equal. The invasion of these rights is not simply unfair but an affront to the State, deserving a punitive response. Although the example of trade union membership seems rather isolated, it can be represented as an instance of a third category of dismissal, which we may term a public rights dismissal, in which the employer's reason for dismissal involves the denial or subversion of a basic right or civil liberty of an employee, for which the law's response must go beyond economic compensation to a specific and forceful defence of the right itself.

This analysis therefore suggests that the dismissal legislation should be interpreted as distinguishing three types of dismissal. These are united by their general aim to improve the job security of employees, as discussed in the previous chapter, but dissimilar in the policies and principles which they promote. Disciplinary dismissals concern ordinary cases of misconduct and incompetence on the part of the employee. Economic dismissals result from business factors independently of the possible fault of the employee. Public rights dismissals identify cases where the employer's motive for dismissal involves an attack on the basic rights or civil liberties of the worker. In the remainder of this section, I elaborate upon this tripartite distinction, paying special attention to the appropriate principles of justice applicable to each type of dismissal.

---

[52] Trade Union and Labour Relations Act 1974, Sched. 1, para. 6(6).

DISCIPLINARY DISMISSALS

The governing idea of disciplinary dismissal concerns the attribution of fault. Before the tribunal both employer and employee seek to demonstrate the fault of the other party. The employer tries to persuade the tribunal that the dismissal was for a substantial reason connected to the voluntary behaviour of the employee, such as misconduct or incompetence. In response, the employee insists that either he or she was blameless or that the employer acted improperly in dismissing him or her.

Ordinary dismissals for misconduct and incompetence initiate a suprisingly complex form of fault inquiry. The employer has to demonstrate that the dismissal was for a substantial reason, and then the Industrial Tribunal decides whether in the circumstances the dismissal fell within the range of reasonable responses to the employee's behaviour. The reasonableness of the employer's conduct hinges upon the degree of fault on the part of the employee: the graver the misconduct of the employee, the more likely that the employer was not at fault in dismissing him or her.

A close analogy to the structure of this fault inquiry occurs in the criminal law relating to defences of justification. Where a person relies upon a defence of self-defence to a criminal charge, the law asks whether indeed the victim posed a threat to the life or limb of the accused and whether the accused's response of committing a criminal offence was reasonable in all the circumstances. Here the deliberate criminal act of the accused is presumptively wrong, but if it was a reasonable response to a situation created by the victim which threatened the life or limb of the accused, then the victim's misconduct may justify the accused's wrong. Similarly, the structure of the unfairness inquiry in disciplinary dismissals raises the presumption that the dismissal was a wrongful act, so that the employer must justify the dismissal as a proportionate response to the fault of the victim, the dismissed worker. This structure of the fault inquiry is of course reflected in the tribunal's formula governing the test of fairness, the range of reasonable responses test.

These justification defences thus pose the complex fault inquiry of simultaneously judging the degree of blame to be attached to the victim and the reasonableness of the response of the accused. A tribunal must examine both sides of the equation, the fault of the employee and the reasonableness of the employer's response. The greater the fault of the employee, the broader will be the range of responses available to the employer. Equally a venial fault of the employee reduces the scope of reasonable responses, thereby rendering the severe disciplinary action of dismissal almost certainly an unreasonable response.

Yet the criminal law analogy should not be pushed too far, for the remedy for unfair disciplinary dismissals emphasizes compensation rather than punishment. The type of wrong committed by the employer is a civil wrong, like torts concerning personal injury or damage to property. The remedy is designed to rectify the unfair infliction of a wrong as between the two parties concerned. The aim is corrective justice, to compensate the employee for the economic loss caused by an unjustified civil wrong.

Corrective justice implies, and the law of unfair dismissal adopts this implication, that the measure of compensation should reflect the extent to which the wrongdoer is responsible for the harm caused. In the law of tort, the contributory negligence of the victim reduces an award of damages since he or she is to some extent to blame for the loss as well. Similarly, an award of compensation for unfair dismissal may be reduced by a tribunal to reflect the degree to which the employee is to blame for his or her misfortune—the provisions on contributory fault which reduce the measure of compensation,[53] and the extent to which the employee might have reduced his or her economic loss by, for example, accepting another job—the provisions on mitigation of loss.[54]

ECONOMIC DISMISSALS

Here the employer justifies the prime-facie wrongful act of dismissal not by reference to the fault of the employee, but rather by reference to market forces. These market forces usually consist either in downward fluctuation of product markets which force reductions in the workforce (reduction of labour demand), or in competitive pressures which compel an employer to make more efficient use of labour (reduction of labour costs) by, for example, making one person do the work of two or eliminating restrictive working practices and introducing flexibility with the desired effect of reducing the necessary level of manpower. An employer may rely upon such market forces to justify the fairness of a dismissal.

Yet this justification is only a partial justification for the wrong, for it remains true that the worker has lost his or her job through no fault of his or her own. Although the defence of redundancy or economic cause evades full liability for dismissal, it still raises the question of how the social costs arising from the consequent unemployment should be distributed. These social costs may comprise income support for the worker and his or her dependants during the ensuing period of unemployment, health care, the cost of retraining the worker for the available jobs, and support for geographical mobility to enable the worker to find a job. These social costs of economic support for unemployed workers could be picked up by the state, or be allocated to the employer, or left to lie where they fall—on the worker.

Three arguments for compelling an employer to contribute to the social costs arising from economic dismissals should be considered. Forcing the employer to internalize some of these externalities in his or her costs

---

[53] EPCA 1978, ss. 73(7B), 74(6).
[54] Ibid., s. 74(4), and, to a limited extent, s. 73(7A).

calculation of the efficiency of making economic dismissals will place a brake on the number of economic dismissals which take place. If the employer has to fork out a substantial measure of severance pay for each dismissed worker, then this additional cost may make it more economical to avoid redundancies and to keep on more workers. This argument deliberately sacrifices the efficiency of the business for the sake of maximizing levels of employment in the economy and of heightening workers' job security. It may be combined with, but is not dependent on, a second argument which suggests that a long-serving employee acquires a kind of property right in his or her job, for deprivation of which he or she should receive a measure of compensation. A third argument justifies the allocation of part of the social cost on to employers on the ground that employers are in some instances the most efficient avoiders of social cost. For example, an employer may be able to retrain a worker for an available job at less expense than the State or the worker, so, by compelling the employer to do so, the social costs of economic dismissals are reduced.

These three arguments will be assessed in greater depth in Chapter 5. Here it suffices to note that the second argument differs radically from the other two, for the idea of compensation for a property right envisages a form of corrective justice, whereas the others rely explicitly on considerations of distributive justice. It is these distributive considerations concerning the allocation of social cost which, I shall argue more fully later, mark out economic dismissals for distinct treatment. The principles of justice which determine whether and to what extent the employer should be required to pay compensation to the dismissed worker should and do reflect these distributive considerations. Accordingly, what basically distinguishes economic from disciplinary dismissals is that only in the former category should distributive considerations regarding social cost govern the determination of the appropriate circumstances in which an employer should be required to pay compensation.

In short, economic dismissals do not pose a question of fault and blame as between the parties, but rather initiate an inquiry into what amounts to a fair distribution of the burden of social cost as between the employee, the employer, and the State. For this reason, we must take into account as part of the law's response to economic dismissals the extent to which the State, through its social security payments, active manpower policies, and subsidies to the employer to offset the cost of severance payments, assumes the burden of these social costs as well. The justice of the law's handling of economic dismissals depends upon the allocation of the burden between all three players.

PUBLIC RIGHTS DISMISSALS

The final type of dismissal requires a foreclosure of the fairness inquiry because the employer adopts an inadmissible reason for dismissal. Having ascertained that the employer's principal reason for dismissal at the second stage of the inquiry involves a violation of the public rights or civil liberties of the worker, the tribunal eschews the third stage of the inquiry applicable to ordinary disciplinary dismissals and proceeds to an immediate determination of unfairness. The fault of the employer in detracting from such public rights warrants the award of a remedy without any further need to balance the competing interests.

The remedy goes beyond compensation between the parties on the principles of corrective justice. The remedy must also symbolically affirm society's commitment to respect for civil liberties. Suitable remedies for this purpose might include punitive damages, criminal penalties, and reinstatement backed up by punitive threats. The current law regarding dismissal on the ground of trade union membership favours punitive damages, which may be increased by an employer's refusal to reinstate the worker. Whatever technique seems appropriate, however, the aim of the remedy should not be to grant the dismissed worker a windfall but to deter those exercises of managerial prerogative which detract from the civil liberties and fundamental rights of employees. This category of dismissals recognizes that an employer's economic power over employees presents an equal threat to the liberty and equality of citizens as the potential abuse of State power.

A CRITICAL INTERPRETATION

This tripartite division of dismissals, if enacted conscientiously, would bring a structure and coherent rationale to the handling of dismissals and it would shape the relevant criteria of fairness. But of course the current state of the law only approximate loosely to this scheme. The legislature's deviations from the standard pattern applicable to disciplinary dismissals point to the presence of the distinct categories of economic and public rights dismissals, but neither has been fully realized. The three categories represent a constructive interpretation of the law, drawing out features and distinctions which present the law of dismissal in its best light. The recognition of these categories and an understanding of their respective principles of justice or fairness enables us to adopt a critical stance towards the law, one which challenges the coherence and consistency of the current statutory provisions for their failure to enact in a thoroughgoing manner such a tripartite scheme.

Although I shall insist that this scheme underlies the legislation, it should be pointed out that not every instance of dismissal falls conveniently under one or other heading. Consider, for instance, a case where dismissal results from prolonged absence from work due to illness. Tribunals handle such cases as disciplinary dismissals on the ground of incapacity, being understandably reluctant to treat this absenteeism as misconduct. But we can also find signs in their decisions which reflect the insight that to some extent the case involves an economic dismissal, for the employee is not to blame for his misfortune and the employer's reason for dismissal is usually connected to the exigencies of production and the need to have a full complement of staff. One such sign is a greater disposition in such cases to require the employer to consider the possibility of finding the employee alternative work which he is fit to perform, a requirement of reasonableness which betrays elements of the search for an active manpower policy.[55] But these examples of particular cases which do not fit squarely with the legislative tripartite scheme do not detract from the value of elucidating and pressing for a more complete realization of it.

In the remainder of this chapter we will consider the extent to which the current law departs from this scheme and see the undesirable and unsatisfactory results which occur as a result of such deviation. Since the current law is organized by making disciplinary dismissals the residual category, carving out economic and public rights dismissals from this norm, then the inadequacies of the current law can be demonstrated by showing that too many cases fall into the residual category of disciplinary dismissals as a result of the inadequate scope given to the other two types of dismissals.

4. THE CONCEPT OF REDUNDANCY

The special regime applicable to economic dismissals is defined by reference to the concept of redundancy. Where a court or tribunal discovers that a worker is not redundant, the case falls to be decided under the ordinary principles of unfair dismissal suitable for disciplinary dismissals. The employer then relies upon the residual category of 'other substantial reason' rather than misconduct or incompetence as the principal reason for dismissal.

STATUTORY DEFINITION

The concept of redundancy is defined in EPCA 1978, s. 81(2):

For the purposes of this Act an employee who is dismissed shall be taken to be dismissed by reason of redundancy if the dismissal is attributable wholly or mainly to—

(a) the fact that his employer has ceased, or intends to cease, to carry on the business for the purposes of which the employee was employed by him, or has ceased, or intends to cease, to carry on that business in the place where the employee was so employed, or
(b) the fact that the requirements of that business for employees to carry out work of a particular kind, or for employees to carry out work of a particular kind in the place where he was so employed, have ceased or diminished or are expected to cease or diminish.

---

[55] *Garricks (Caterers) Ltd.* v. *Nolan* [1980] IRLR 259 (EAT); *Spencer* v. *Paragon Wallpapers Ltd.* [1977] ICR 301 (EAT), at p. 304.

Part (a) of this definition plainly encompasses plant closure, and this rarely causes a problem of interpretation. More difficult are the cases under (b) where the business remains alive but management decides to shed some of the labour force or reorganize the relations of production by redirecting labour to new tasks. The question here is whether the statutory phrase applies: have the requirements of the business for employees to carry out work of a particular kind diminished?

The first thing to notice about this statutory definition of redundancy is that it does not take the simple course of triggering the special regime applicable to economic dismissals whenever the employer's justification for termination consists in a reference to diminishing labour requirements. This creates immediately the possibility that not every instance where the principles governing economic dismissals would appear appropriate will be included by the concept of redundancy. It is far from clear why the legislature opted for this convoluted and restrictive conception of economic dismissals.

Part of the explanation for this failure to achieve a coherent treatment of economic dismissals may lie in this historical origin of the concept of redundancy. The Redundancy Payments Act 1965 preceded the law of unfair dismissal, so that, at the time of its inception, it provided the first and only means by which employees could bring a substantial claim for compensation for dismissal against their employers. In seeking to introduce compensation for economic dismissals alone, clearly the legislation needed to distinguish redundancies from cases of disciplinary dismissals, and perhaps it sought to achieve this differentiation by referring to the employer's diminishing requirements for work of a particular kind to be performed rather than the employer's lack of need for a particular employee since the latter phrase could conceivably refer to incompetent employees as well. But this is surely a cumbersome way of excluding disciplinary dismissals, which could have been exempted by some simple statement that the dismissal must not be motivated by some particular fault of the worker arising from misconduct or incompetence. Perhaps, therefore, Parliament had an additional motive for adopting this strange statutory formulation.

Parliament may have been concerned to target a particular kind of economic dismissal for redistribution of social costs, but not every kind. This possible rationale for the definition of redundancy has of course long since lost its point as a result of the introduction of the law of unfair dismissal. Now a narrow concept of redundancy merely serves to throw the employee's claim back into the category of disciplinary dismissals, to which it will often be wholly unsuited. Assuming, however, that in 1965 Parliament did seek to target a particular kind of economic dismissal, what could this be in the light of the statutory definition?

The phrases of the statutory definition of the redundancy seem to encompass three types of targeted economic dismissal:

Case (1): business or plant closure leading to dismissals;
Case (2): dismissals resulting from changes in technology or processes of production so that the skills used and tasks performed by particular workers are no longer required;
Case (3): the shifting of production to a new location.

If these three types of economic dismissal represent the limits of the concept of redundancy, then at least two other types will be excluded:

Case (4): workforce reductions short of plant closure resulting from a decline in product demand.

These dismissals might be excluded if the statutory provision was read to refer solely to Case (2) and not to the more general case of dismissals across the board regardless of the particular skills or tasks performed by workers. In practice, however, the courts have regarded Case (4) as falling within the concept of redundancy, reasoning that the requirements of the employer for employees has diminished and ignoring the intervening phrase referring to work of a particular kind.[56] This interpretation clearly makes sense, for if it is right to redistribute the social costs of dismissals resulting from total plant closure under Case (1), then it must also be right to apply the same principles to partial shut-downs.

Case (5): reorganizations of the workforce designed to reduce labour costs through greater flexibility to working practices, with a consequent reduction in staffing levels.

In this example two kinds of employees might be seeking a redundancy payment: those dismissed because of the reduction in staffing levels, and those required to accept new terms and conditions of employment reflecting the requirement of flexible working practices. The former group fall squarely within the statutory formulation, for their services are no longer required to perform work of a particular kind. The second group who have retained jobs, though with new demands placed upon them, fit less easily under the statute. Although the imposition of new terms and conditions will normally be regarded as a constructive dismissal by the employer, since the employer still offers these employees work, it is more difficult to argue that the employer's demand for their work has diminished.

Yet it is hard to see what worthwhile redistributive policy might be represented by a concept of redundancy which excludes this second group of workers in Case (5). A good case can be made for providing incentives for the workforce to agree to dismissals in order to introduce new technology and production processes under Case (2), but surely an equally strong case can be made for incentives for better use of the labour force under Case (5). Indeed the desire to promote better productivity by dismantling restrictive labour practices was a frequently expressed ambition of governments at the

---

[56] *Lesney Products & Co. Ltd.* v. *Nolan* [1977] ICR 235 (CA).

time of enactment and ever since.[57] So in this respect one is forced to conclude that on the face of it, the statutory concept of redundancy displays neither clear labour market policies nor any coherent redistributive scheme for the social costs of economic dismissals. To the extent that the concept of redundancy excludes the second group of workers under Case (5), then it thwarts the achievement of a coherent and principled resolution of the problems presented by economic dismissals.

JUDICIAL INTERPRETATION

For a quarter of a century, however, the courts have placed their own interpretations upon the statutory concept of redundancy. This complicates the current legal position because the courts have produced results which are both hard to square with the words of the statute and which appear to defeat the aim of a coherent and principled response to economic dismissals.

Early interpretations of the statute tended to reduce the province of Case (2) to vanishing-point. In *North Riding Garages* v. *Butterwick*,[58] the employee had been the workshop manager of car repairs for a garage for thirty years. New employers who took over the business required him to adapt to new working methods including increased paperwork, to undertake new duties including the giving of estimates of repair costs to customers, and to achieve higher standards of efficiency. On his failure to do so satisfactorily, he was dismissed and replaced. The Divisional Court, which had the power of review over industrial tribunals until 1971, reversed the tribunal's award of a redundancy payment. It held that an employee who continued in the same kind of work was not redundant if he failed to adapt to new working methods and techniques and to achieve higher standards of efficiency. This decision represents the facts as relating to the employee's incompetence rather than a change in the employer's business requirements, by describing the failure to adapt to new techniques as incompetence rather than a change in the nature of the work to be performed. Because the employers still required a workshop manager, albeit one with different skills, the court denied that the requirements of the business had changed. This interpretation of the phrase 'work of a particular kind' introduces the gloss that the work may remain constant despite changed methods, additional duties, and demands for new skills. This removes from the category of economic dismissals those employees who cannot adjust to new technologies and an expansion of their duties. But surely those employees should be handled within the framework of economic dismissals rather than introducing the fault inquiry of disciplinary dismissals, for the underlying cause of the

---

[57] S. R. Parker, C. G. Thomas, N. D. Ellis, and W. E. J. McCarthy, *Effects of the Redundancy Payments Act* (London, 1971), at p. 3.
[58] [1967] 2 QB 56 (Div. Ct.).

dismissal springs from the employer's worthwhile attempts to improve efficiency by introducing new working methods, and the employee is the victim of these competitive pressures. The appropriate response from the law is not to allocate blame but rather to pursue the policy of a fair redistribution of the social cost of adjustment to new economic conditions.

The decision in *Butterwick* left rather obscure what the meaning of the phrase 'work of a particular kind' might be once new working methods and additional duties were excluded. The answer given in *Vaux and Associated Breweries* v. *Ward*[59] was that the nature of the tasks performed by the employee would have to alter fundamentally. In this case the brewery dismissed a middle-aged woman from the position of barmaid which she had held for seventeen years at the Star and Garter Hotel and replaced her with a younger more glamorous barmaid to attract new customers to the recently refurbished bar. Because the work remained essentially the same, however, namely serving beer and other drinks to customers from behind the bar, the claim for redundancy failed, there being no diminution in the requirements of the business for this sort of work. The court indicated that the result would have been different if the new job involved a substantial change of tasks, such as mixing cocktails or waiting at tables. Again this narrows the category of economic dismissals unduly, for, despite the inherent sexism of the employer's decision, presumably they knew the business sufficiently well to reach a reasonable calculation that they would increase turnover by engaging attractive staff. But, if so, then the motive for the dismissal rests securely in the category of a business requirement, a response to market forces, over which the employee has no control. The appropriate response from the law of dismissal should be framed in terms of a redistribution of the social cost generated by the employer's reaction to market conditions.[60]

These early decisions under the Redundancy Payments Act effectively reduced the scope of Case (2) envisaged by the statute to situations where the job had disappeared altogether. This excluded from the province of economic dismissals both significant changes in the skills or qualities of the worker required by the employer, as well as the requirement to adapt to new working methods and technologies. Recent court decisions, however, cast some doubt on the validity of the reasoning in those early cases.

Instead of defining the work of the employee by reference to the tasks performed, the Court of Appeal has indicated that the correct test should comprise a combination of the terms and conditions of employment as well as the tasks actually performed by the employee. In *Cowan* v. *Haden Ltd.*,[61] the employee was promoted from regional surveyor to divisional contracts surveyor, but because of a downturn in the business, he was subsequently

---

[59] (1969) 7 KIR 308 (Div. Ct.).

[60] There is also an argument for including this case within the category of public rights dismissals.

[61] [1983] ICR 1 (EAT); (CA).

dismissed. The Industrial Tribunal found that he had been dismissed for redundancy because the employers no longer required anyone to perform his current job of divisional contracts surveyor. The EAT allowed an appeal against this conclusion on the ground that the tribunal had misdirected itself in law. Under a flexibility clause in the contract of employment, the employee could still have been required to perform the work of a regional surveyor, for which the employer had a continuing need and which in fact the employee had continued to perform after his promotion. The EAT decided that the tribunal had applied incorrect law by failing to ask the question whether the employer's requirements for employees who could be required under their contracts of employment to perform the work of regional surveyors had diminished. The Court of Appeal finally allowed the employer's appeal and restored the finding of redundancy. The court argued that the flexibility clause should be interpreted and confined in the light of the employee's job title, so that the Industrial Tribunal's finding that the employer ceased to require a divisional contracts surveyor sufficed to bring the case within the statutory concept of redundancy. This reasoning in the Court of Appeal emphasizes the importance of the terms of the contract of employment, especially the title of the post, as the principal tool for identifying the work performed by the employee. This differs markedly from the detailed examination of the precise tasks performed by the employee in the earlier Divisional Court's decisions. We should infer that the reasoning though not the result in *Vaux and Associated Breweries* v. *Ward* was incorrect: the particular work performed by the employee should be defined by reference primarily by reference to the job title and specification and not by a minute examination of the tasks performed.

This subtle shift in the interpretation of the concept of work of a particular kind opens up the possibility of bringing the law much closer into line with the imputed purpose of the legislation so that it encompasses Case (2). When the technology or production processes alter so that the employer requires employees with new skills, it seems likely that the job specification will change and probably the job title as well, so that the old job will disappear and the dismissed employee be regarded as redundant. For example, when secretarial staff have to work with word processors instead of typewriters, it seems likely that the job specification will change for the employer will have to be explicit in his or her requirement of the new skill if useful staff are to be recruited. Although the new secretary may still be producing dictated letters on a machine, his or her new skills will be acknowledged in the job specification, so that it will be clear to the tribunal that the old job has disappeared and that a redundancy payment is due.

Case (3) under the statute, which envisages the relocation of work, makes sense as a form of economic dismissal, for it recognizes that geographical mobility can present considerable difficulties to workers with a home and dependants. From the perspective of a fair distribution of social cost, it is efficient to provide the worker with financial assistance to move or to compensate him or her for the economic loss caused by dismissal if the costs of mobility appear too great. This aim can be defeated, however, if the courts acknowledge the force of express or implied mobility clauses in the contract of employment. By recognizing that the employer acts under such a clause when directing an employee to a new place of work, the court places the social cost of geographical mobility back on to the employee, for the place of work is now deemed to be any place in which the employer directs the employee to work under the clause of the contract.

Although the courts have resisted the implication of geographical mobility clauses which demand travel beyond locations within a reasonable daily reach of home,[62] they nevertheless operate a presumption that all contracts of employment contain a mobility clause.[63] When faced with an express mobility clause of wider geographical scope, however, they permit the relocation of work not to count as a redundancy. Here the policy behind the redundancy payments legislation is subordinated to the court's respect for the autonomy of the parties to the contract of employment, a central plank of the ideology of the common law.[64] In *Nelson* v. *British Broadcasting Corporation*,[65] the employee's contract of employment as a producer entitled the BBC to direct him to any place of work in the organization. When the BBC closed the Caribbean Service where the employee worked and offered him a job elsewhere, the Court of Appeal decided that he was not redundant because there was work for producers elsewhere in the Corporation, thereby taking the case out of the category of economic dismissals and into the framework of the fairness inquiry of disciplinary dismissals. From the perspective of handling problems of geographical mobility as one of social cost to be redistributed between the parties without any allocation of fault or blame, then this decision makes no sense at all. The employee in fact receives a windfall of the compensatory award for unfair dismissal instead of the law finding the most efficient way to reduce the social costs engendered by plant closure.[66] It would be better to regard cases such as this as economic dismissals, with the employer's offer of suitable alternative employment being a defence to a claim for compensation if unreasonably refused, as envisaged by EPCA 1978, s. 82(5).

Case (5) has caused considerable difficulty, for the courts became committed to the idea that some reorganizations for reasons of efficiency were not redundancy situations, but that other reorganizations forced upon the employer because of the pressure of business conditions were. This untenable

---

[62] *O'Brien* v. *Associated Fire Alarms Ltd.* [1968] 1 WLR 1916 (CA); *Jones* v. *Associated Tunnelling Co. Ltd.* [1981] IRLR 477 (EAT).

[63] *Courtaulds Northern Spinning Ltd.* v. *Sibson* [1988] ICR 451 (CA); see J. Holland and A. Chandler, 'Implied Mobility Clauses' (1988), 17, *ILJ* 253.

[64] See above, p. 32.

[65] [1977] ICR 649 (CA).

[66] In the next chapter we will see how the court subsequently deprived the employee of most of this windfall under the contributory fault provisions.

distinction was championed by Lord Denning, MR. For example, in *Johnson
v. Nottinghamshire Combined Police Authority*,[67] the Court of Appeal found
that two women clerks were not redundant when they refused to change
from normal working hours and a five-day week to a shift system and a six-
day week. Lord Denning distinguished between cases where on the one
hand the employer insists upon a change in the terms of conditions of
employment to improve efficiency, which do not count as redundancy, and
on the other where the reason for change is the decline in profitability and/
or overstaffing, which are redundancy situations. The tribunals follow this
distinction on the whole, so that dismissals to avoid overstaffing will be
regarded as instances of redundancy,[68] but reorganizations of work not
entailing dismissals but simply major changes in the terms and conditions of
employment will not count as redundancies.

Lord Denning revealed the policy behind this interpretation of the statute
in a later case. In *Lesney Products ' Co. Ltd.* v. *Nolan*, he insisted that,

it is important that nothing should be done to impair the ability of employers to
reorganize their workforce and their terms and conditions of work so as to improve
efficiency.[69]

What Lord Denning fails to appreciate in such remarks is that economic
dismissals pose the question of how should the social costs resulting from
economic dislocation be distributed between the workers and their employer.
The substantial change in the terms and conditions of employment for the
two clerical workers in *Johnson* v. *Nottinghamshire Combined Police Authority*
could clearly make it difficult for them to continue working depending on
their personal circumstances. The question then arises from these constructive economic dismissals whether the employer should contribute to the
social costs which arise from unemployment. The law of redundancy does
not contemplate restricting the employer's power to reorganize the workforce
to achieve better use of labour power. What it seeks to do is to prevent the
employer from regarding the social costs which arise as a pure externality,
for which he or she bears no responsibility. For these reasons, dismissals
resulting from reorganization of the workplace and the substitution of new
terms and conditions for workers should be handled within the framework
of the law governing economic dismissals.

OTHER SUBSTANTIAL REASON

The upshot of this treatment of instances of Case (5) is that many cases
where the redistributive policies of the category of economic dismissals

---

[67] [1974] ICR 170 (CA).

[68] *Sutton* v. *Revlon Overseas Corporation Ltd.* [1973] IRLR 173 (NIRC); *Robinson* v. *British
Island Airways Ltd.* [1978] ICR 304 (EAT); *Carry All Motors Ltd.* v. *Pennington* [1980] ICR 806
(EAT).   [69] [1977] ICR 235 (CA).

would seem to be appropriate, such as a major change in the employee's terms and conditions of employment in order to improve labour efficiency, are excluded. This creates the absurd consequence that these employees are excluded from the most appropriate response of the law, and then find themselves in a position to bring a claim under the disciplinary dismissal provisions, with potentially a higher level of compensation. Although this avenue looks promising from the point of view of employees, despite its subversion of a coherent approach to the law's treatment of economic dismissals, in practice this route seems to have been closed off.

In a typical case, *Hollister* v. *National Farmers Union*,[70] the employee refused the new terms and conditions resulting from a reorganization of the business and was dismissed. The employer defeated the claim for unfair dismissal, not on the ground of redundancy for presumably the facts fell within the ruling of *Johnson* v. *Nottinghamshire Combined Police Authority*, but rather on the ground that there was a substantial reason for dismissing the employee, namely the need to reorganize the business and that it was reasonable to dismiss the worker in these circumstances. In other words, the employer has an easy ride to justify the dismissal under the rubric of other substantial reason as soon as the employer appeals to business considerations, for the courts will not in general look behind the business reasons and assess their merits. So Mr Hollister fell between two stools: neither redundant because his claim fell outside those instances of Case (5) which the courts regard as redundancy situations; nor unfairly dismissed because the employer could justify the reorganization by reference to business considerations and treat the employee's refusal of new terms and conditions as a fault for the purpose of a disciplinary dismissal.

It is certainly arguable that the extension of the category of other substantial reason to considerations not directly connected with the employee's fault is an improper move by the courts, and that they should have limited their interpretation of meaning of substantial reason to misconduct, incompetence, and analogous instances of fault on the part of the employee. The tensions within this strained interpretation stand out when one realizes that the employee's refusal to accept the employer's repudiatory breach of contract by a unilateral change in the terms of employment becomes characterized in the framework of disciplinary dismissals as a fault on the part of the employee meriting dismissal. But against this criticism it may be said that given the restrictive statutory definition of redundancy, it is hard to see where else the courts could pigeon-hole this sort of case, and it is worth noting that Parliament has since indirectly endorsed this practice with the Transfer of Undertakings Regulations 1981, Regulation 8(2).

In conclusion, what is needed is a statutory redefinition of the concept of redundancy which serves the function of triggering the exemption from the

---

[70] [1979] ICR 542 (CA).

ordinary law of disciplinary dismissals wherever the social policy of redistribution of the social costs of unemployment seems appropriate. At least all five instances described above should be included. This could be achieved simply be redefining the concept of redundancy to comprise all dismissals (including constructive dismissals) for business reasons or reasons of efficiency unconnected with fault on the part of the dismissed employee.

5. PUBLIC RIGHTS DISMISSALS

If we can say that the law's approach to economic dismissals slightly misfires, then we must acknowledge that the handling of public rights dismissals explodes into chaos. In truth only the special provision relating to dismissals in connection with trade union membership comes close to the special degree of protection required for the symbolic and effective affirmation of these fundamental rights.

At the outset, however, we should admit that the list of fundamental rights deserving of equivalent protection is controversial. Consider, for example, the right to strike. Although embraced by many constitutions in Europe, it has never been included in the Anglo-American tradition as one of the fundamental rights on a par with other civil liberties. Indeed the handling of dismissals during industrial action under the unfair dismissal legislation has the effect of severely impairing the exercise of this right. The general principle governing the fairness of dismissals during strikes, lock-outs, and other forms of industrial action holds that Industrial Tribunals should not entertain claims for unfair dismissal, but dismiss the case unless the employee can demonstrate that he or she was victimized in comparison to other workers who were locked-out or who were taking official industrial action at the date of his or her dismissal.[71] Where victimization during an official strike is demonstrated, the ordinary reasonableness test of fairness applies to the case. Strictly speaking these provisions do not state that dismissals during industrial conflict are automatically fair. They merely remove the jurisdiction of the Industrial Tribunals, the underlying reason being that tribunals should not be required to judge the merits of collective disputes between employers and workers. But, in its effects, this removal of jurisdiction amounts to the automatic fairness of such dismissals. Far from providing protection for the right to strike, the law of unfair dismissal treats industrial action as conduct which entirely removes a worker from the province of the legislation.

As well as raising the question of the list of appropriate rights, the development of a category of public rights dismissals poses the question of the precise scope of these rights. Consider the idea of freedom of speech. Should this civil liberty be permitted to extend to the workplace with full

---

[71] EPCA 1978, ss. 62, 62A, as amended by Employment Act 1990, s. 9.

effect so that the employer cannot use disciplinary powers to restrict any form of speech or communication by employees? This would seem too strong, for the employer may have a legitimate interest in matters such as trade secrets which he or she will not want his or her employees disclosing to all the world. A more difficult case concerns the position of an employee who criticizes the conduct of management in a letter to the local newspaper. In these circumstances dismissal would clearly subvert the employee's freedom of speech, but can the employer justify the dismissal by appealing to the need to preserve order and discipline in the workplace and thus not to permit anyone to sound off whenever and wherever he or she likes?

These are difficult issues to which we shall return in Chapter 6. Our present concern is to examine the extent to which the law of unfair dismissal adequately establishes a framework which gives due protection to those rights which are recognized. With respect to this question, we should note that even where certain rights have been acknowledged by legislation to be applicable to the workplace, such as the right to be treated as an equal under the sex and race discrimination legislation, the law of unfair dismissal fails to respond by creating a special regime of automatic unfairness buttressed by punitive sanctions.

With the partial exception of pregnancy dismissals, described above, the claimant for compensation for unfair dismissal in a case where the grounds for dismissal are alleged to be connected with sex or race must in theory persuade the tribunal that it was unreasonable for the employer to dismiss for that reason. Similarly, the right to return to work after maternity leave is not buttressed by an automatic finding of unfair dismissal if the employer refuses to re-engage the woman,[72] but again she has to persuade the tribunal that the employer was at fault in failing to do so. The tribunals, of course, readily accept the point, but the result is not automatic in law.

Nor does the law of unfair dismissal provide additional compensation in such cases of discriminatory dismissals. But this omission from the unfair dismissal legislation has been indirectly remedied by awards of compensation under the sex and race discrimination legislation itself. On proof of direct discrimination under that legislation, the courts may award aggravated and exemplary damages for injury to feelings and insulting treatment.[73] These measures of damages may far exceed any compensation for economic losses resulting from a dismissal. They are subject, however, to the same upper limit as that applicable to ordinary cases of unfair dismissal,[74] so the punitive element in these awards may not prove substantial.[75] It seems strange that

---

[72] EPCA 1978, s. 56. On the contrary, EPCA 1978, s. 56A, gives the employer numerous defences which permit him or her to deny that the woman was dismissed at all.

[73] *Alexander* v. *Home Office* [1988] 685 (CA); *City of Bradford Metropolitan Council* v. *Arora* [1991] IRLR 165 (CA).

[74] Sex Discrimination Act 1975, s. 65(2); Race Relations Act 1976, s. 56(2), both as amended by EPCA 1978.

[75] e.g. *North West Thames Regional Health Authority* v. *Noone* [1988] ICR 813 (CA).

an employee who is dismissed because he or she is a member of a trade union has considerably more generous rights to compensation than one dismissed because he or she is black.

Beyond these cases where the legislation already provides a remedy, albeit incomplete, there lie many cases where no legislation assists a worker to defend his or her civil rights at all. Here we can mention, for example, discrimination on grounds of sexual preference. The dismissal or a homosexual on that ground alone is not necessarily regarded by the law of unfair dismissal as unfair. The question falls to be decided under the range of reasonable responses test. If the employer can persuade the tribunal that it was within the range of an employer's reasonable responses to the employee's homosexuality that he should be dismissed, then the dismissal will be fair. Many tribunals have upheld such dismissals as fair.[76] In effect this permits the general discriminatory attitudes of employers with respect to homosexuals to legitimize dismissals. The reasoning fails to grasp the point that a civil liberty of the worker is gravely threatened. Although the criminal law no longer regards the majority's prejudices against homosexuality to warrant punishment, the law of dismissal permits reliance upon those prejudices to justify private economic sanctions.

The failure of the law of unfair dismissal to develop a category of public rights dismissals tarnishes its attempt to introduce workplace justice. The possibility of such a framework is revealed by its handling of dismissals connected with one aspect of the right to freedom of association. The legislature's omission to realize more broadly this third type of dismissal, even in matters already receiving special treatment such as sex and race discrimination, seriously detracts from its vision of fairness.

[76] e.g. *Saunders* v. *Scottish National Camps Association Ltd.* [1980] IRLR 174 (EAT); [1981] IRLR 277 (Ct. Sess.); *Gardiner* v. *Newport County Borough Council* [1974] IRLR 262 (IT).

[3]

Substantive Fairness in Disciplinary Dismissals

AT the heart of the dismissal legislation lies the standard of fairness in the context of disciplinary dismissals. The structure of this fairness standard has been described by analogy with the criminal law of self-defence. The legislation renders a dismissal unfair unless the employer can justify it, much like the wrongfulness of a killing unless a justification such as self-defence can be relied upon. The justification which the employer must produce in disciplinary dismissals takes the form of demonstrating fault attributable to the employee.

It should be noted, however, that even when the employer successfully proves substantive fault, a tribunal must still consider whether the employer acted according to an unfair procedure, and, if so, then this may render the dismissal unfair. In practice the standards of procedural and substantive fairness cannot be strictly separated, and indeed their precise interaction supplies a key to understanding how the tribunals have developed the concept of fairness. Nevertheless, in this chapter we shall focus upon the standard of substantive fault and defer to Chapter 4 an examination of procedural standards and how they relate to substantive conceptions of fault.

This chapter seeks the best interpretation of the substantive fairness standard in relation to disciplinary dismissals. Such an interpretation does not limit itself to a description of the decisions of the courts and tribunals. Even if such a description were thought desirable, the wealth of material from reported and unreported decisions would render the task both unmanageable and fruitless, for all that such a survey would reveal is inconsistency and diversity unless each decision is confined to its particular facts. My interpretation, however, tries to abstract the principles on which the courts and tribunals act, and then seeks to fit these principles into a coherent moral and political vision of justice in dismissal. This interpretation presents the best, in the sense of morally the best, account of the principles embedded in the case law, according to a method analogous to that described by Professor Dworkin.[1] My interpretation of these decisions imagines that a number of competing conceptions of fault, with their derivative principles for applica-

---

[1] Ronald Dworkin, *Law's Empire* (Cambridge, Mass., 1986).

tion to particular cases, struggle for supremacy in the decisions of the courts and tribunals. Although each of these conceptions of fault has influenced the development of the law, I suggest that one conception ultimately predominates in the sense that it both fits most closely the current practice of the courts and tribunals and at the same time presents an attractive ideal of justice in disciplinary dismissals.

1. THE CHALLENGE OF INTERPRETATION

In composing such an interpretation of judicial application of statutory provisions, one course to take would be to examine the preceding principles of the common law to discover competing conceptions of fault, and then try to identify which of these conceptions the courts have favoured in their interpretation of the statute. Yet, in this instance, it would surely be a serious mistake to rely upon the general principles of the common law to provide the moral standard for refining an interpretation of the standard of fairness. We noted in Chapter 1 that the statute on unfair dismissal set out to reverse the principles of the common law which in effect grant an employer a discretion to terminate the contract at will. To attempt to interpret and present in its best light the standard of fairness embedded in the tribunals' decisions from the perspective of the prior institutional morality of the common law would be a perverse exercise, one which would deliberately ignore the aim of the statute to replace those earlier moral standards. Yet we cannot, unfortunately, rely upon the general aim of the legislation as an adequate guide for the desired form of interpretation.

GENERAL AIM AND CRITERIA OF FAULT

The key to ascertaining the principles governing the fairness standard must relate more specifically to the criteria of fault by which the employer must justify the dismissal. It is important to realize that these fault criteria may have only a distant relation to the underlying goals of the legislation. The general aim of the law of unfair dismissal, be it to improve general welfare, efficiency, or, as I have argued, to secure respect for the dignity of workers and to promote conditions for autonomy, does not determine the conception of fault which justifies dismissal.

The same divergence of principles emerges in relation to other analogous protective legislation. The general aim of laws protecting the security of tenure of tenants in rented accommodation may be to satisfy a desire for security and a permanent home, but the conditions of forfeiture of the right to tenure, such as a failure to pay rent, find their underlying source and justification in other social policies such as support for the fairness of contractual exchanges or the preservation of an adequate supply of accommodation on the market. Similarly, the conception of fault in the law of unfair dismissal appears to derive at least in part from principles of justice which are independent of those which justified the enactment of the law originally.

Consider, for example, a case where a dismissal is provoked by late arrival at work. The employer has promulgated a clear rule requiring prompt attendance, and has carried out an investigation which elicits the information that the lateness was due to the breakdown of the employee's car, but nevertheless the employer decides to dismiss. Can we determine from the ideas of dignity and autonomy which justify the legislation whether the employee's fault suffices to warrant dismissal? I suggest that they are insufficiently determinate to require any particular result in a case such as this, so these values must be supplemented by further standards.

Respect for the dignity of the individual employee requires the employer not to act for reasons or in a manner which involves disrespect for the individual in himself or herself. In the absence of some invidious form of discrimination or an unfair procedure, however, it remains far from clear whether the employer's insistence upon punctuality involves any disrespect to the individual. Some further assistance in assessing whether such disrespect exists may be gleaned by asking whether the employer's action can be fitted into a rational pursuit of his or her business objectives. The employer's desire to keep production on time may be regarded as a legitimate business objective, but this still leaves open the possibility that the employer's insistence upon such a strict rule may be unreasonable in the circumstances of this case and that the employer's policy could entail disrespect for individuals by treating them as commodities to be manipulated according to the demands of the production process. Respect for the dignity of the individual serves to exclude certain reasons for dismissal as unjust, but it does not appear useful when a court must engage in subtle assessments of the degree of the employee's fault and the reasonableness of the employer's response.

For similar reasons, the justification for the legislation in terms of promoting conditions for autonomy cannot supply adequate criteria for assessing the fault of the employee. The value of autonomy suggests that the rules concerning attendance at work should preserve as much individual freedom as possible to the extent consistent with the technical and economic necessities of work organization. From this perspective, it cannot be determined in advance whether strict rules concerning punctuality invade or satisfy the value of autonomy. We would need to investigate more fully the employer's reasons for the policy of strict punctuality and to consider whether any exceptions might be made out of deference to the autonomy of individuals. But even if this conception of autonomy were fully elucidated in the context of this particular employer's business, we would still not have brought into the picture the mitigating circumstance that the employee's car broke down. To introduce this element into the scales of fairness, we require a more subtle process which balances the degree of fault on the part of the employee against the exigencies of the employer's production process.

The values of dignity and autonomy therefore supply important, but ultimately incomplete, guides to the examination of the question of the employee's fault. They certainly offer a better starting-point than the principles of the common law for an interpretation of the moral standard underlying the tribunal's conception of fairness. But we must go beyond these fundamental values of the legislation if we wish to pin down precisely how the standard of fairness is constructed. The materials for such an interpretation must lie in the decisions of the tribunals and courts themselves. But these materials present several obstacles to any such interpretation.

A POVERTY OF PRINCIPLE

The first and apparently paradoxical obstacle in the way of generating such an interpretation springs from a difficulty in discovering any suitable materials in the decisions of the tribunals against which to check the accuracy of the interpretation. The problem of juridification described in Chapter 1 hinders any attempt to adopt an interpretative stance towards the practice of tribunals. It leads to the approach towards the fairness standard summarized in these words by Browne-Wilkinson, J.:

the function of the industrial tribunal, as an industrial jury, is to determine whether in the particular circumstances of each case the decision to dismiss the employee fell within the band of reasonable responses which a reasonable employer might have adopted. If the dismissal falls within the band the dismissal is fair: if the dismissal falls outside the band it is unfair.[2]

This approach severely circumscribes the degree to which the tribunals can challenge the exercise of managerial disciplinary powers. It prevents a tribunal from replacing management's decision in a particular case with a decision of its own. A tribunal need not explicate its own standard of fault, but merely assess whether the employer's standard was unreasonable. It therefore relieves the tribunal of the task of formulating principles of fairness. The frequent analogy drawn between the Industrial Tribunal and a jury[3] not only signifies that the court should be reluctant to review its appreciation of the facts, but also suggests that the tribunal's task is not to formulate principles of adjudication but merely to reach a decision on the facts presented. In the absence of such statements of principle, the task of interpreting the implicit standard of fairness becomes very difficult indeed.

But it does not become impossible. The range of reasonable responses test

---

[2] *Iceland Frozen Foods Ltd.* v. *Jones* [1983] ICR 17 (EAT), at p. 25.
[3] e.g. *Bessenden Properties Ltd.* v. *Corness* (1974) [1977] ICR 821 (CA); *Williams* v. *Compair Maxam Ltd.* [1982] ICR 156 (EAT).

still requires management to pass some standard of legitimate behaviour, since the test envisages that some dismissals will fall outside the band of fairness. The law sets a boundary of rationality around the employer's discretion, and dismissals outside this boundary will be regarded as unfair or insufficiently justified. Indeed, unless some boundary had been set, there would be no possibility of any dismissals being found to have been unfair on substantive grounds. The subject for interpretation becomes the principles which establish this boundary. Thus the abstentionism caused by the problem of juridification does not preclude the possibility of an interpretation of the fairness standard which presents it in its best light, but it does explain the absence of clearly accessible moral criteria advocated by the tribunals.

Further relief from the poverty of discussion of principle may be afforded by careful scrutiny of the tribunals' application of the legislative provisions regarding contributory fault:

Where the tribunal finds that the dismissal was to any extent caused or contributed to by any action of the complainant it shall reduce the amount of the compensatory award by such proportion as it considers just and equitable having regard to that finding.[4]

Under this provision tribunals must go further towards articulating the kinds of conduct which should be regarded as constituting fault on the part of the employee. By examining such decisions, both in respect to the types of conduct regarded as being at fault and in respect to the severity of the fault as revealed by the proportion by which the compensation is reduced, our interpretation of the tribunals' view of fairness can be further tested and refined.

The available evidence to support or falsify any potential interpretation of the principles governing the substantive criteria of fairness is therefore sparse but not impossible to obtain. The clues gained from these materials can be tested against some paradigm moral standards which might inform the tribunals' interpretation of the fairness standard. Even minor confirmations or dissonances between each paradigm and the practice of the tribunals may substantially assist to pin down which paradigm best fits their idea of fairness. Before articulating these paradigms, however, we must consider a potentially even greater obstacle to the task of interpretation.

CONVENTIONS AND NORMS

The question here is whether the legal materials are susceptible to any kind of interpretation at all. Not every social practice can be interpreted in the sense of discovering its underlying moral vision. Some practices may be merely matters of convention, like the way we use words to signify particular

---

[4] EPCA 1978, s. 74(6).

things. It makes little sense to ask why the word tree is used to refer to certain types of plant life and not others; it is just a convention of the language. Is the practice of the tribunals in determining the fairness standard similarly a practice which is not susceptible to interpretation?

A boundary of reasonable behaviour may be set by reference to either a normative or a conventional standard. A normative standard originates from the tribunal's own perceptions of justice; it imposes an ideal of behaviour which derives from a conception of justice. Although no doubt this normative conception of fault will be coloured by the tribunal's own sense of conventional standards justifying dismissal, in principle it does not invariably defer to those standards and may seek to improve them. In contrast, a conventional standard permits the actual practice of employers when setting the requisite degree of fault to justify dismissal to govern the fault standard of the legislation.

A conventional approach to the concept of fault may be formulated in differing degrees of generality. The conventional standard may be derived from the particular employer in question, the industrial sector of the employer's business, the geographical region, or, at the other end of the spectrum, the practice of all employers. But whatever the source of the conventional standard, because it rests upon practice rather than reasoned principles, it impedes the discovery of the principles governing the fault criterion. Indeed, if the boundary is merely a matter of convention, like the meaning of particular words, then the practice will not be susceptible to interpretation at all.[5]

To what extent, if any, do the tribunals establish the fairness standard by reference to conventional practice? Consider first the extreme test of permitting the particular employer's own standard of fault to govern the range of reasonable responses. On this approach to the concept of fault, the employer lays down the standard of deviance in advance, and, provided that the employer conforms to his or her own announced standard, then the dismissal will be justified. In *Hadjioannou* v. *Coral Casinos Ltd.*,[6] a blackjack inspector in a casino broke the employer's rule against socializing with members of the club. The tribunal found that the employee knew of this rule, so the dismissal was fair. At first sight it may seen absurd that the courts should permit an employer to determine what standard of justification should be applicable to his or her business. This would surely deprive the legislation of any significant impact on managerial prerogative. This worry is indubitably

[5] M. Dummett, 'A Nice Derangement of Epitaphs: Some Comments on Davidson and Hacking', in E. Lepore (ed.), *Truth and Interpretation: Perspectives on the Philosophy of Donald Davidson* (Oxford, 1986), 459; L. Wittgenstein, *Philosophical Investigations* (2nd edn., trans. G. E. M. Anscombe, Oxford, 1958), s. 201; K. Krees, 'The Interpretative Turn' (1987), 97, *Ethics*, 834; M. Moore, 'The Interpretative Turn in Legal Theory' (1989), 41, *Stanford Law Review*, 871.
[6] [1981] IRLR 352 (EAT).

well grounded, but in view of the variety of circumstances in which dismissals take place and the different techniques of production which may render the requirements of employers for obedience or competence rather different, it will be tempting for a tribunal to fine tune its standard of fairness by reference to the employer's own disciplinary rules. In the case of casinos, for example, it may be of the utmost importance that employers should be able to rely on the unimpeachable integrity of inspectors. Furthermore, the employee seems in a weak position when he or she asserts that despite disobedience to a promulgated rule, he or she should nevertheless be regarded as having been unfairly dismissed. In practice, therefore, the employer's rule book plays an important role in the determination of the fairness of a dismissal.

As a result, the quest for an interpretation of the fairness standard may seem doomed from the start. The standard may prove no more and no less than what each employer deems it to be for his or her particular workplace. The question for the tribunal would be confined to whether the employer had conformed to his or her own rules and customary practices relating to discipline.

This issue of consistency is certainly a relevant question for tribunals to consider, for if it can be demonstrated that a dismissal for a particular sort of misconduct such as a minor assault was not the regular practice of the employer and that employees in similar situations had not been dismissed before, then a tribunal will most likely find the dismissal unfair on the ground that it is unreasonable or inequitable.

The word 'equity' in the phrase 'having regard to equity and the substantial merits of the case' in 57(3) comprehends the concept that employees who behave in much the same way should have meted out to them much the same punishment.[7]

Of course, the tribunal will not be driven to a finding of unfairness on this ground of inconsistency, if it discovers a material difference between the two cases, such as the fact that one employee was in a position of greater responsibility;[8] or, as occurred in Hadjioannou's case, that the dismissed employee had not co-operated and admitted fault whereas another had done so; or if management had announced in advance that its disciplinary practice in relation to a particular offence would be altered. Nevertheless, the deference shown by tribunals to the employer's own standard of fault does raise the question whether any principled interpretation of the fault standard is possible.

This obstacle to interpretation is relieved, once it is realized that an employer's conformity with his or her own disciplinary practices is a necessary but not a sufficient condition to satisfy the fault standard. Even

---

[7] *Post Office* v. *Fennell* [1981] IRLR 221 (CA).
[8] *G. S. Packaging Ltd.* v. *Sealy* (1983) EAT 396/82.

where the employer has acted consistently in following a promulgated rule or customary practice, the tribunal may still find the employer's conduct unreasonable. In *Watling & Co. Ltd.* v. *Richardson*,[9] the EAT insisted that the employers in the electrical contractors business were not entitled to engage workers for work on particular contracts and then dismiss them immediately upon completion of the job without considering whether they might be transferred to a new job. Strictly speaking, the employers were regarding this case as one of an economic dismissal, and their failure to establish the economic need for dismissal left them with little ground to stand on. But the general point of the case with respect to disciplinary dismissals is plain: that even though a tribunal must not substitute its own views for that of an employer, but rather inspect the facts to determine whether the employer acted within the range of actions which reasonable, fair, and prudent employers might have taken, it is still possible to find cases where the employer's conduct, though a consistent practice, is so harsh or arbitrary that it cannot be regarded as falling within the range of reasonable responses. In this case, the failure to consider the possibility of a transfer between jobs, despite being the standard practice of the employers and perhaps being also a common practice in the industrial sector, was regarded by the court as self-evidently outside the range of reasonable responses.

One thing however is clear, and that is that the claim that employers in this field have the right to 'hire and fire' regardless of the obligations imposed by the modern law can be rejected out of hand . . . the most that can be said is that in its application it is right, as it is in every case, to take account of the circumstances of the particular business or trade. But it should be realized that if in the past a particular business or trade has been carried on in a manner which is incompatible with those obligations it is the manner of carrying on the business which will have to change and not the obligations disregarded.[10]

But even though the tribunals reject consistent practice by a particular employer as a sufficient reason for dismissal, this last case raises the question whether or not the fairness standard still remains conventional in the sense that, although it cannot be completely determined by a particular employer, it will be determined by the standard practice of employers in general. In *Watling & Co. Ltd.* v. *Richardson* the tribunal was prepared to reject the standard of fairness adopted by the pool of employers in the electrical contracting business as a whole, not just the particular employer's standard practice in the case. On the other hand, in *Saunders* v. *Scottish National Camps Association Ltd.*,[11] where the caretaker of a children's summer camp was dismissed because he was a homosexual, the tribunal relied upon the standard set by employers in general to conclude that the dismissal was

[9] [1978] ICR 1049 (EAT).
[10] Ibid., per Phillips, J., at p. 1052.
[11] [1980] IRLR 174 (EAT); affirmed [1981] IRLR 277 (Ct. Sess.).

reasonable. Because the tribunal believed that employers in general would think it undesirable that homosexuals should work in proximity to children, then this provided sufficient justification for the dismissal. This case indicates that the standard of fairness will be drawn from the practices of employers in general, not the particular sector of industry. But it remains a conventional standard of fault, one which reflects the practices of employers, rather than one imposed normatively in the interests of justice by the tribunals. As a conventional standard, it appears to comprise a matter of social practice, not susceptible to interpretation but merely to description.

Yet I think that ultimately we should resist the conclusion that the reliance upon the standard of fault generally accepted by employers is merely a matter of convention. The tribunals do not carry out an empirical examination of the practice of employers in order to determine whether or not most employers would regard the employee's conduct as a sufficient reason for dismissal. By denoting the Industrial Tribunal as an industrial jury, the courts make it plain that the tribunal can rely upon its own general knowledge and common sense in order to formulate the fairness standard. The members of the Industrial Tribunal draw upon their experience of the standards of employers, but then interpret that experience to set the boundary of the range of reasonable responses. The boundary line draws upon conventional practices, but represents an interpretation of those practices, viewing them in the light which the members of the tribunal regard as most fair and reasonable. The approach is neither wholly conventional nor normative, neither merely standard-reflecting nor standard-imposing.[12] The tribunal adopts an interpretative approach itself, taking its own view of industrial practice viewed in its best light. Because this fairness standard is an interpretation of practice, not just a description of conventional standards, it therefore becomes susceptible to an interpretation itself.

GOOD INDUSTRIAL PRACTICE

Two significant considerations influence Industrial Tribunals in their interpretation of employers' practices. The first is the tribunals' sense of what counts as a good industrial practice, and the second comprises the Codes of Practice which amount to an official view of how industrial relations should be conducted.

Because the lay members of both Industrial Tribunals and the EAT represent both sides of industry, both union and management, their opinions about appropriate standards of conduct may represent a negotiated compro-

[12] Paul Davies and Mark Freedland, *Labour Law: Text and Materials* (2nd edn., London, 1984), 471 ff.; P. Elias, 'Fairness in Unfair Dismissal: Trends and Tensions' (1981), 10, *ILJ* 201, 212–13.

mise of interests which represent the considered views of both sides on what good industrial relations demands.[13]

The Industrial Tribunal is an industrial jury which brings to its task a knowledge of industrial relations both from the view point of the employer and the employee. Matters of good industrial relations practice are not proved before an Industrial Tribunal as they would be proved before an ordinary court; the lay members are taken to know them. The lay members of the Industrial Tribunal bring to their task their expertise in a field where conventions and practices are of the greatest importance.[14]

This represents a rather ideal view of the function of the lay members of the tribunals. In practice they must perform the dual and incompatible roles of being both representatives of a particular side of industry and at the same time neutral and impartial judges. The tension is heightened in the EAT where the jurisdiction is limited to questions of law, which appears to leave no province of relevant expertise for the lay members. The composition of these tribunals probably represents a corporatist theme in the origins of the legislation, that is, the search for mechanisms to resolve social disputes through agreements between collective organizations and the State.[15] Given the aims of the legislation as I have described them in terms of respect for the dignity and autonomy of the individual, however, it might make better sense to staff the tribunals with lawyers who have been specially trained in industrial relations and the objectives of the legislation. It was, after all, the lay members of the Industrial Tribunal who decided that Mr Mathewson's dismissal was 'harsh but fair', and the legally qualified chairman who proved more sensitive to the issues of fair procedure and respect for the private life of the employee.

Nevertheless, ideals of good industrial practice do serve to filter out oppressive or harsh disciplinary practices of employers as components of the standards of fault applied by the tribunals. Although the tribunals may not always articulate these ideals fully, they provide the basis for rejecting the conventional practice of employers as the basis for the standard of fault. The ideal of good industrial practice, the 'collective wisdom' of the Industrial Tribunal acting as an industrial jury, provides the touchstone for determining how a reasonable employer should conduct disciplinary matters in phrases such as the following taken from *Watling (N. C.)& Co. Ltd.* v. *Richardson*:

---

[13] Sir John Wood, 'The Employment Appeal Tribunal as it Enters the 1990s' (1990), 19, *ILJ* 133, at p. 139; The Hon. Mr Justice Browne-Wilkinson, 'The Role of the Employment Appeal Tribunal in the 1980s' (1982), 11, *ILJ* 69; The Hon. Mr Justice Phillips, 'Some Notes on the Employment Appeal Tribunal' (1978), 7, *ILJ* 137, at p. 140.

[14] *Williams* v. *Compair Maxam Ltd.* [1982] ICR 156 (EAT) per Browne-Wilkinson, J., at pp. 160–1.

[15] See T. Ramm, 'Labor Courts and Grievance Settlement in West Germany', in Benjamin Aaron (ed.), *Labor Courts and Grievance Settlement in Western Europe* (Berkeley, Calif., 1971), 83, at p. 149.

the industrial tribunal, while using its collective wisdom is to apply the standard of the reasonable employer; that is to say, the fairness or the unfairness of the dismissal is to be judged not by the hunch of the particular industrial tribunal, which (though rarely) may be whimsical or eccentric, but by the objective standard of the way in which a reasonable employer in those circumstances, in that line of business, would have behaved.[16]

A second, rather weaker, influence upon the tribunals' interpretation of the conventional practices of employers comes from the Codes of Practice issued by the official advisory body on industrial relations, the Advisory Conciliation, and Arbitration Service (ACAS).[17] Tribunals are under a duty to take relevant provisions of these Codes into account when considering the question of the fairness of a dismissal.[18] The Code of Practice on Disciplinary Practice and Procedures in Employment,[19] emphasizes primarily the importance of formal, written procedures for discipline and grievances. These influence significantly the standards of procedural fairness to be considered in the next chapter by supplying a standard of good industrial relations practice against which the practices of employers may be judged.

On substantive issues, however, the Code says little except to point out that criminal offences outside employment should not be treated as automatic reasons for dismissal, but rather the employer should consider whether the offence is one which makes the individual unsuitable for his or her type of work or unacceptable to other employees.[20] Instead the Code hastily delegates the task of formulating appropriate standards to the employer.

5. Management is responsible for maintaining discipline within the organization and for ensuring that there are adequate disciplinary rules and procedures. The initiative for establishing these will normally lie with management.

Even where the standard has not been delegated, as in connection with criminal offences, it seems to carry little weight in such cases as *Mathewson* v. *R. B. Wilson Dental Laboratories*,[21] where, it will be recalled, the drugs offence outside working hours was accepted by the tribunals as a reasonable ground for dismissal without any other. Perhaps stronger assistance for employees in some instances could be gleaned from the seldom cited Industrial Relations Code of Practice,[22] which requires management to

[16] [1978] ICR 1049 (EAT), per Phillips, J., at p. 1056.
[17] Established by Employment Protection Act 1975, s. 1.
[18] Employment Protection Act 1975, s. 6(11). The Codes may be amended or withdrawn under the procedure laid down in Employment Act 1990, s. 12.
[19] Employment Protection Code of Practice (Disciplinary Practice and Procedures) Order 1977, SI 1977, No. 867.
[20] Code of Practice, para. 15(c).
[21] [1988] IRLR 512 (EAT).
[22] Enacted under Industrial Relations Act, ss. 2–4, and continued in force by EPA 1975, Sched. 17, para. 4.

ensure such matters as adequate training for the job, to observe minimum standards about working conditions, and to provide the employee with all relevant information about the job.[23]

Even so, although the Codes of Practice are not a powerful determinant of the fault standard applied by the tribunals, they do colour the tribunals' interpretations of good industrial practice, which in turn set limits to the extent to which they are prepared to endorse the conventional disciplinary practices of employers as reasonable and fair. The tribunals' appeals to good industrial practice and their collective wisdom reveal that despite reliance upon the conventional disciplinary standards adopted by employers ultimately their conception of fault is a selective and normative interpretation of those practices, which itself is susceptible to further interpretation.

The question thus becomes what moral conception of justice in disciplinary dismissal underlies the courts' and tribunals' interpretation of good industrial practice. Since what should count as 'good' and 'bad' disciplinary practices requires a normative judgment, one which sets standards rather than merely reflecting them, it must rest upon an unarticulated moral conception which establishes the criteria of justice in disciplinary dismissals.

The next two sections of this chapter elucidate a number of paradigm conceptions of fault which have probably influenced the tribunals. These conceptions of fault are divided between rights-based and goal-based perspectives,[24] a distinction explained immediately below. But we should note an extremely important feature of all these paradigms of justice in disciplinary dismissals before proceeding any further.

The structure of the fairness inquiry in disciplinary dismissals, I have argued, gravitates towards an investigation of the fault of the employee. This focus upon the individual and the merits of this particular claim invites the tribunals, in articulating the normative standards of good industrial practice, to focus upon the individual interests of the employer and the employee rather than broader public interests. For example, it is possible to argue for a public interest in the establishment of collective bargaining practices to regulate industrial relations in the workplace. Alternatively, we can discern a public interest in promoting training of workers in general (as opposed to firm-specific) skills in the workplace. Conceptions of good industrial practice could include these public interest dimensions, so that the tribunals would place considerable weight on the effects of collective bargaining and training in their determinations of fairness. Yet the focus of the legislation on the question of the fault of the employee steers the tribunals away from these considerations of public interest when formulating normative conceptions of good industrial practice. The paradigms of fault which we will consider all

[23] See cases cited in Steven D. Anderman, *The Law of Unfair Dismissal* (2nd edn., London, 1985), 192–3.
[24] This follows the terminology of R. M. Dworkin, *Taking Rights Seriously* (London, 1977), at p. 169.

share a reluctance to incorporate broader public interest concerns. To some extent my suggestion in Chapter 2 that a distinct category of public-rights dismissals should be recognized goes some way towards remedying this potential defect, for, as I shall argue in Chapter 6, protection of these rights should be supported on the basis of their improvement of the common good. But the fundamental weakness of all the standards of substantive fairness which compete for dominance in the decisions of the tribunals remains that they lack a dimension of respect for the public interest because of their focus upon individualized questions of fault, blame, and desert.

RIGHTS AND GOALS

In a rights-based frame of reference, the conception of fault starts with the premiss that the employee enjoys a right to his or her job. To establish fault, the employer must demonstrate that the employee's conduct has been such as to forfeit that right. On a goal-based perspective, the fault lies in deviance from behaviour consonant with the goals of the business. For example, if we regard the goal of the business as providing an efficient service to the public, then conduct which undermines the efficiency of that service would be regarded as deviant behaviour attracting the label of fault sufficient to justify dismissal.

It is worth observing from the outset, that a rights-based approach seems to set a higher standard for the criteria of fault. The rhetoric of forfeiture of rights suggests a grave delinquency, whereas deviance from standards of behaviour consonant with the goals of the enterprise indicates a lesser degree of culpability. For example, if we imagine the case of a barely competent employee, we may not be able to say that his or her relatively poor work amounts to blameworthiness and forfeiture of a right, whereas it may certainly be characterized as behaviour inconsistent with the pursuit of the business goal of maximizing profits. Similarly, an employee absent from work through illness may not be regarded as having been sufficiently blameworthy to deserve loss of his or her job, although a prolonged absence could prove disruptive and costly to an employer and require, for good business reasons, the replacement of the employee.

This difference in the weight attached to job security between rights-based and goal-based conceptions of fault corresponds to their social origins in rival ideologies of good industrial relations.[25] The rights-based paradigms mostly articulate a pluralist frame of reference, which recognizes a legitimate divergence of interest between capital and labour and seeks through social institutions such as collective bargaining and law to achieve a peaceful and fair compromise between those conflicting interests. In contrast, goal-based paradigms fit closely into a unitary frame of reference, which stresses the

[25] Alan Fox, *Beyond Contract: Work Power and Trust Relations* (London, 1974), Ch. 6.

common interest of workers and employers in efficient production, and consequently tends to deny the validity of interests such as job security which might obstruct the pursuit of that goal.[26]

The next two sections consider the types of justification which can be put forward in these two categories of rights-based and goal-based justifications. The forms of justification of dismissal are set out in the form of paradigms, so that their strengths and weaknesses as possible conceptions of fairness may be clearly appreciated. Here I am assessing these paradigms by reference to moral criteria, noting what consequences for the job security of employees will follow from their adoption. I am also concerned to assess whether they do in reality establish a normative standard for informing the idea of good industrial practice rather than one which merely reflects the conventional practices of employers. Following this discussion of paradigm forms of justification, the next section considers the predominant approach which the courts and tribunals have adopted, that is, we answer the question of which paradigm best fits the legal decisions. My concluding section ventures an interpretation of the substantive concept of fairness in disciplinary dismissals. It suggests that a particular variant of the paradigm which most closely fits the practice of the courts and tribunals should be regarded as the best interpretation of their practice because of its moral attractiveness in the light of its consequences for job security.

2. RIGHTS-BASED JUSTIFICATIONS

Two types of rights-based justification of dismissal have influenced the courts. The first mirrors the common law of wrongful dismissal by suggesting that employees forfeit their right to their jobs when they commit serious breaches of their contracts of employment. The second picks up the theme of a property right in a job and holds that employees forfeit their property rights in their jobs by blameworthy behaviour.

BREACH OF CONTRACT

Here, in order to justify the dismissal, the employer asserts that the employee committed a fundamental breach of contract and that this fault is sufficient to disentitle the employee of his or her right to keep his or her job. Under the common law, this reasoning provides the employer with a complete defence to a claim for damages for wrongful dismissal. The process of reasoning first requires the employer to point to a term of the contract which has been broken by the employee. Then the employer must assert either that breach of this term is inevitably a serious breach of contract, or that, in the

[26] Cf. H. Forrest, 'Political Values in Individual Employment Law' (1980), 43, *Modern Law Review*, 361.

circumstances, breach of this term was sufficiently serious in the light of the consequences of the breach so as to deprive the employee of his or her right to job security.

As will be evident from the outline of this form of justification, the employer's case depends heavily on the establishment of a suitable term in the contract of employment. Yet the source of these terms are sufficiently numerous and fertile that rarely does this present a serious obstacle. As well as the express terms of the contract agreed between the parties, the law will imply certain standard terms into contracts of employment and will incorporate other documents into the contract such as works rules, personnel handbooks, and collective agreements. At first sight this form of justification adopts a sensible approach, since the court establishes the fault of the employee by reference to a serious breach of an obligation under the contract of employment which the employee has undertaken voluntarily. Yet on further examination, we will see that on this contractual approach an employer will seldom be unable to demonstrate breach of contract, and thus rarely will a dismissal be regarded as unfair.

The first warning signal about this approach occurs when we consider the nature of the terms which the courts routinely imply into contracts of employment. Here we can observe a long tradition of the courts imposing numerous duties upon employees to behave loyally, obediently, carefully, and co-operatively.[27] These terms bolster managerial authority to such an extent that any conduct on the part of the employee which falls short of complete subordination to the employer's wishes is likely to constitute a breach of an implied term. If so, then proof of breach of an implied term provides employers with a ready justification for disciplinary dismissals in nearly every case. Although the implied terms apparently establish an objective standard, that is, one imposed by the law, in practice their deference to managerial authority ensures that any conduct of the employee which an employer dislikes sufficiently to treat as grounds for dismissal will constitute a breach of contract. This has the effect that on the contractual approach to the issue of fault, the law of unfair dismissal endorses management's subjective or conventional appreciation of what should count as a sufficient justification for dismissal.

The same flaw applies to the use of works rules and personnel handbooks as the source of terms of the contract of employment. Because the employer initiates these documents, using them as an administrative device to organize and regulate the workplace, they represent the employer's own subjective view of his or her disciplinary requirements. Accordingly, if the court then decides that the rules have become incorporated into the contract of employment as terms of that agreement, which is the normal interpretation

---

[27] See Ch. 1.

of their legal significance,[28] then in effect the employer's own views of fault and justification are merely reinforced by the courts, rather than an independent normative standard applied to judge his or her conduct.[29]

This flaw in the contractual approach towards the identification of fault justifying dismissal may perhaps be ameliorated when the terms of the contract of employment have been set by collective agreement. In these circumstances we may assume that the union has bargained for some limits upon the managerial discretion to dismiss employees. The empirical studies reveal unfortunately that union officials have normally been willing only to negotiate disciplinary procedures rather than to agree substantive standards which determine when dismissal is warranted.[30] But in those rare cases when the union is prepared to support publicly the idea that some dismissals are justified and fix disciplinary standards by collective agreement, then management would not be able to rely upon its own conception of fault in order to justify a dismissal, but would have to satisfy collectively agreed standards.

This collective contractual approach colours the US system of arbitration. Labour arbitrators chosen jointly by the collective parties use the collective agreement as a guide in determining whether dismissal was for 'just cause'. Arbitration decisions have often been presented as a dynamic interpretation and elaboration of the code established by the collective agreement.[31] But of course this just cause standard, unless clarified by custom and precedent in the workplace, cannot avoid the risk that arbitrators will continue to respect management's subjective appreciation of what should count as a sufficient reason for dismissal. A recent study of arbitrators' interpretations of the just cause standard indicates that one ground for dismissal which is often accepted is the employer's desire to avoid conduct that would interfere with

---

[28] e.g. R. v. East Berkshire Area Health Authority, ex parte Walsh [1984] IRLR 278 (CA); Financial Techniques Ltd. v. Hughes [1981] IRLR 32 (CA); contra: Secretary of State for Employment v. ASLEF (No. 2) [1972] ICR 19 (CA). For detailed discussion, see H. Collins, 'Market Power, Bureaucratic Power, and the Contract of Employment' (1986), 15, ILJ 1, 4–6.

[29] We discover a clear comparative illustration of this delegation of the fault standard to management by reference to the personnel handbooks in the context of the US Federal Civil Service internal personnel practices. An employee can appeal to the Merit Systems Protection Board against unjust disciplinary action, but in the case of allegations of incompetence the legislation requires the Board to judge the employee's behaviour by reference to the rules laid down by the Office of Personnel Management, the general managerial administrative agency. Hence in cases of incompetence the Board merely rubber stamps management's own views about the relevant standards of competence required for the job. Parker v. Defense Logistics Agency, 1 MSPB 489 (1980); Note, 'Developments in the Law: Public Employment' (1984), 97, Harvard Law Review, 1611, at pp. 1639–41; P. A. Price, 'Dismissals of Civil Service Employees for Unacceptable Performance' (1986), 29, Howard Law Journal, 387.

[30] Linda Dickens et al., Dismissed (Oxford, 1985), at p. 241. To some extent agreements which provide for an external neutral party to adjudicate may envisage that such an arbitrator will attempt to formulate disciplinary rules which the collective parties might have been prepared to accept.

[31] B. Aaron, 'Some Procedural Problems in Arbitration' (1957), 10, Vanderbilt Law Review, 733; J. G. Getman, 'Labor Arbitration and Dispute Resolution' (1979), 88, Yale Law Journal, 916.

the employer's ability to operate the business successfully.[32] Such a broad principle runs counter to the idea that arbitrators elaborate the collective agreement, for it looks solely to the interests of the business. This suggests that adherence to collectively agreed standards for dismissal can only be secured by more detailed rules than a simple just cause standard.

In applying the British law of unfair dismissal, the courts seem to have paid scant attention to the rules established by collective agreements. Nor does the statute require them to do so except in connection with economic dismissals, in which case EPCA 1978, s. 59(b), renders dismissals automatically unfair if the employer fails to comply with a customary arrangement or collective agreement in the absence of special reasons justifying a departure from those arrangements. The tribunals have interpreted this provision for automatic unfairness extremely narrowly, so that it applies only to agreements concerning the substantive criteria for selection, such as the common rule of 'Last In—First Out', but not procedural agreements requiring consultation and negotiation with the union.[33]

The normal approach of the tribunals to the relevance of collective agreements to standards of fairness in disciplinary dismissals appears to be that laid down in *Gilham* v. *Kent County Council (No. 2)*.[34] Following cuts in central government funding for local authorities, the employer proposed to reduce labour costs in its provision of school meals by departing from the national level collective agreement which set minimum levels of remuneration for catering staff. The local union officials were not prepared to discuss the dramatic cuts in pay, but insisted that these nationally agreed minima would have to be renegotiated at national level, if at all. The employer then terminated the existing contracts of employment and offered new contracts to all staff at lower rates of pay. The Industrial Tribunal held that the dismissal was unfair. The Court of Appeal dismissed the employer's appeal, but made it clear that it would have been an error of law for the Industrial Tribunal to have treated the council's breach of the collective agreement as determinative. A breach of collective agreement should be treated only as a factor to be balanced against others in determining the question of fairness. Notice what pains the court takes to deny the relevance of any public interest in supporting observance of collective agreements in formulating its conception of fault. In this case a substantive standard was involved, but the same balancing approach appears in cases where the employer breaches an agreed disciplinary procedure. In *Bailey* v. *BP Oil (Kent Refinery) Ltd.*,[35] the employer omitted to inform the appropriate trade union official as soon as

[32] R. I. Abrams and D. R. Nolan, 'Toward a Theory of "Just Cause" in Employee Discipline Cases' (1985), *Duke Law Journal*, 594.

[33] *McDowell* v. *Eastern British Road Services Ltd.* [1981] IRLR 482 (EAT). See C. Grunfeld, *The Law of Redundancy* (3rd edn., London, 1989), at pp. 303–10.

[34] [1985] ICR 233 (CA).

[35] [1980] ICR 642 (CA).

possible that dismissal was contemplated, as provided for in the agreed disciplinary procedure. Although the EAT allowed the employee's appeal against the tribunal's finding of fair dismissal, the Court of Appeal insisted that the employer's failure to comply with a disciplinary procedure agreement was only a factor to be taken into account, so the tribunal's approach was correct and its decision should stand.[36] Once again a public interest in supporting collectively agreed procedures is discounted in favour of emphasizing questions of individual fault and blame.

These cases reveal that the courts reject a strict contractual approach, believing that management must retain a degree of flexibility in exercising its power of dismissal which can override collective agreements. The conventional practices of management can determine ultimately the precise content of disciplinary standards, even where more objective standards have been collectively agreed. Even if the tribunals were to draw upon collective agreements to establish rigorous guidelines for determining fault, this approach would be incomplete, for it would not assist the majority of workers who lack the benefit of collective agreements. Indeed, as we noted in Chapter 1, one of the principal purposes of the legislation was to improve the job security of unorganized workers, so it would defeat this purpose to limit the conception of fault to that established by any applicable collective agreement.

For these reasons, a contractual approach to the substantive concept of fairness appears profoundly unsatisfactory. It would in effect delegate to management the determination of the relevant standards of fault rather than provide an independent normative conception of fault. This paradigm could be given more substance if the courts adopted a new approach towards implied terms which limited managerial disciplinary powers. Although we noted in Chapter 2 some limited signs of such a development,[37] to take this process any further would demand from the common law a fundamental reorientation of its perception of the employment relation. In view of the problem of juridification discussed in Chapter 1, which suggests that the common law background deeply influences the courts' approach towards this legislation, we should not stake the success of this legislation upon such a remote eventuality occurring. It would also be possible to weaken the employer's control over the standard of fault by preventing the works rules and personnel handbooks from becoming terms of the contract of employment. Indeed in some cases courts have acknowledged that these rules comprise regulations for the exercise of administrative discretion rather than strict contractual rights.[38] But this would leave a void, which would only be filled by the implied terms of the common law, so the consequence of

---

[36] The court's exact approach to the question of procedural fairness was flawed because of its adherence to *British Labour Pump Co. Ltd.* v. *Byrne* [1979] ICR 347 (EAT): see Ch. 4.

[37] See p. 44.

[38] e.g. *Secretary of State for Employment* v. *ASLEF (No. 2)* [1972] ICR 19 (CA).

delegating the definition of fault to the employer would simply reappear in a novel form. Finally, the contractual approach could be improved by requiring the tribunals to respect the terms of collective agreements, but this could not provide a complete guide to the standard of fairness because of both the normal absence of clear disciplinary criteria in collective agreements and the incomplete coverage of collective bargaining over the nation's workforce.

FORFEITURE OF PROPERTY RIGHT

In the opening chapter we noted that the common law has never recognized the existence of a property right in a job and that this position is intrinsic to a market economy and probably any other type of viable industrial economy. Nevertheless we should recognize that the rhetoric of property rights remains a popular way of expressing the idea that employees should enjoy greater job security than accorded to them by the common law's doctrine of termination at will.

The nearest approach to a general realization of job property yet achieved in Britain occurred in the form of the unfair dismissal legislation first introduced by the Industrial Relations Act 1971. In its conception this legislation made substantial steps in the direction of job property, a trend even more prominent in the reforms in the unfair dismissal legislation made by the Employment Protection Act 1975.[39]

Is it possible, therefore, to conceive a special type of property right suitable to express the idea of job security, and then elaborate an idea of fault which specifies those cases where the employee's fault amounts to a forfeiture of that right?

The potential advantage to employees of this theoretical approach lies in its strong presumption in favour of job security. The main point of alleging a property right in a job would be to suggest that certain compulsory alienations of the right by dismissal should be regarded as void, thereby rendering the appropriate remedy one of restoration of the property or job by reinstatement. A second implication of the property right analogy is that it creates two heads of liability: compensation for the forceful taking of the right, and compensation for the loss of economic value represented by the right.[40] These two heads of liability might well be represented by the division in the current law of compensation for unfair dismissal between the basic and compensatory awards. The recognition of a property right might also justify and trigger independent requirements of fair procedure or due process, violation of which would constitute a separate and additional ground

---

[39] Paul Davies and Mark Freedland, *Labour Law: Text and Materials* (2nd edn., London, 1984), at p. 431. See also P. J. White, 'Unfair Dismissal Legislation and Property Rights: Some Reflections' (1985), 16(4), *Industrial Relations Journal*, 98.

[40] G. Calibresi and A. D. Melamed, 'Property Rules, Liability Rules and Inalienability: One View of the Cathedral' (1972), *Harvard Law Review*, 85; J. L. Coleman and J. Kraus, 'Rethinking Legal Rights' (1986), *Yale Law Journal*, 95.

for complaint. The presumption of greater job security also arises in part because a property right, unlike a contractual right, has its legal incidents determined by the law. The recognition of a property right would therefore escape the employer's power to determine in advance the standard of fault, so it would offer a truly objective normative standard of justification. The legal conception of the property right would fix the conditions under which there might be compulsory alienation as part of the rules defining the entitlement.

The first hurdle in establishing a workable paradigm for fairness along these lines consists of the numerous conceptual problems which lawyers would have to resolve. Unless the normal remedy for unfair dismissal became one of reinstatement as opposed to compensation, the form of property right would have to be unusual, for it would lack the conventional incident of property rights that it cannot be alienated without the owner's consent.[41] The acceptance of the possibility of a fair dismissal for misconduct or incompetence immediately prevents a precise analogy with a typical property right over which the employee enjoys control over possession and alienation.

One way of formulating the nature of this property right would be to draw an analogy with compulsory acquisition of land by the State for some public purpose such as building a road. Here a general welfare criterion justifies the compulsory deprivation of a property right. This analogy cannot be exact, however, for it is generally recognized that the State must pay compensation to the landowner despite the general welfare justification, whereas under the law of unfair dismissal the employer need pay no compensation for a fair dismissal. But a deeper problem with the analogy is that it transforms the concept of fairness back into some form of goal-based justification, the weaknesses of which will be considered below. In effect the property right drops out of the inquiry and is replaced by an assessment of general welfare.

Perhaps a closer analogy from the law of property can be discovered in those equitable interests in land established by proprietary estoppel. Where a landowner stands by and watches another improve the value of his or her land by building a house on it, then a court will extract from the landowner some equitable compensation, which in some cases may amount to a deprivation of the property right entirely.[42] The courts assert in these instances that it would be inequitable or unconscionable for the landowner to insist upon his or her strict property rights. This analogy suggests that to constitute the degree of fault meriting dismissal the employee's conduct must have been sufficiently unconscionable to deprive him or her of his or her property rights in the job. The advantages of this analogy consist both in the recognition that it is the misconduct of the property right holder, the

---

[41] S. Rottenburg, 'Property in Work' (1961–2), 15, *Industrial and Labor Relations Review*, 402; R. H. Fryer, 'The Myths of the Redundancy Payments Act' (1973), s, *ILJ* 1, at p. 5.

[42] *Crabb* v. *Arun District Council* [1976] Ch. 179 (CA); *Pascoe* v. *Turner* [1979] 2 All ER 945 (CA).

employee, which justifies the appropriation, and that the misconduct may prove of sufficient gravity to deprive the owner of his or her right without compensation. On the other hand, the analogy provides only a vague guide through the concept of unconscionable conduct to the criterion of fault by which the employee forfeits his or her right. The analogy tends therefore to restate the problem rather than to provide a solution.

Another conceptual problem is posed by the date of the inception of the right. Does the property right vest immediately in the employee upon hiring, or does it only arise by dint of lengthy service? Similarly, does the right increase in strength as a result of length of service? Yet a further conceptual problem is raised by the question whether the right refers to a particular job or whether it is a more general right against the employer to suitable employment within the organization. The latter seems a better view, for otherwise there is the risk that the promotion of an employee to a higher grade might be regarded as deprivation of a property right in the earlier job without fault on the part of the employee and therefore a case of unfair dismissal.

Despite these puzzling conceptual problems, it may prove possible to explore the flexibility and subtlety of the conceptions of property rights in the common law in order to give practicable sustance to the idea of a property right in a job. We should not rule out the possibility at this stage that the property right notion could inform an interpretation of the fairness standard which could provide the key to an interpretation of how the tribunals set the boundary of reasonable responses.

3. GOAL-BASED JUSTIFICATIONS

The general form of goal-based justifications is that the employee's conduct interferes with the pursuit of a goal and this interference constitutes the fault justifying dismissal. We should consider two forms of this justification. A narrow form identifies the relevant goal as that of the employer's interest in the productive efficiency of each member of the workforce. A broad form envisages the goal as the interests of the firm, which encompasses, as well as the efficient use of labour, such matters as product market success, reputation, and customer loyalty.

PRODUCTIVE EFFICIENCY

At first sight it may appear strange to attempt to derive the concept of fairness from the notion of efficiency in the light of the discussion in Chapter 1 of how the legislation probably interferes with efficiency. But we should notice that the concept of efficiency has altered in these two contexts. In the earlier discussion, the argument was that the parties to a contract of employment would not normally agree to a restriction upon the employer's power to terminate the contract of employment at will, because employees would not wish to accept a commensurate reduction in wages to take into account the increased cost of labour to employers. Although we subjected this theory to some criticism, it remains probable that this standard of efficiency known as Pareto optimality would not be satisfied by the legislation itself. In the context of attempting to define a concept of substantive fairness, however, we can shift the focus towards the standard of productive efficiency. Here the test of justification consists in the employer proving that he or she can improve productive output by replacing one worker with another, holding the rate of pay constant, and taking into account all relevant costs including training and transaction costs such as hiring. The focus has shifted from the institutional arrangements, that is, the terms of the economic relation of employment, to the efficiency of employing one particular worker compared to another as a basis for the fault standard. The law of unfair dismissal may still be inefficient, but the employer's decision to dismiss in a particular case may be justified by reference to the marginal productivity of two comparable workers.

A preliminary worry about this standard of productive efficiency is that it has the potential of rendering every dismissal fair, provided that an employer can persuade the court that he or she will be able to find a more productive employee. Given that some superman or superwoman may always be round the corner, the employer may be able to justify the dismissal of even competent and obedient workers. Alternatively, the employer could justify the dismissal on the ground of productive efficiency if he or she could find a satisfactory replacement prepared to work for a lower wage. The employer's task of justifying dismissals of employees absent from work through illness would also become trivial, since he or she can easily defend the proposition that a healthy worker with good attendance improves productive efficiency.

But this worry that the standard of productive efficiency places little constraint upon employers can be overstated for two reasons. In the first place, the test of productive efficiency must take into account the costs of replacing one worker with another. Here the costs include the search costs such as advertising and interviewing, and then the training costs of teaching an outside worker the new job. We might also include as a cost the harm to an employer's reputation with his or her employees if he or she is seen to dismiss too readily, with a consequent decline in the loyalty and commitment of the remainder of the workforce to productive efficiency. In the second place, where the incumbent worker possesses firm-specific skills or knowledge, then it seems unlikely that even the most gifted outsider will be able to achieve equivalent productive output in a short space of time. It is for these reasons, amongst others, of course, that, even in legal regimes such as the USA where termination at will remains the legal rule, most employees have a reasonable expectation of holding on to their jobs as long as they perform competently.[43] The standard of productive efficiency would therefore be rarely met unless the worker was seriously underperforming or disruptive to the business.

The standard of productive efficiency would constrain the employer in the types of allegations of fault which might be put forward in order to justify dismissal. For example, where a customer expresses a dislike of a particular worker, this would not be sufficient to warrant dismissal unless it could be shown that this dislike was interfering with the worker's productivity. It would also rule out dismissals based upon considerations unrelated to productivity in the job, such as the employer's dislike of the worker's characteristics or behaviour outside working hours. The standard would also place limits upon the employer's right to dismiss for misconduct, for the employer would have to demonstrate that the act of disobedience or insubordination actually harmed the productive efficiency of the worker. An isolated instance of misconduct might well fail to satisfy this test.

The vital weakness of the standard of productive efficiency lies not so much in the principle, but in its application. Since the test depends heavily upon matters within management's control, such as measurement of output and the costs of replacement, a tribunal would be hard pressed to provide its own objective assessment of whether the productive efficiency standard had been satisfied. Like the perhaps apocryphal magistrate who asked an accused how could he be innocent as he had been arrested and charged by the police, the tribunal might be tempted into the pattern of reasoning which asks why would the employer dismiss someone unless he or she thought it worth while?

One should also question whether this standard of fault, like other goal-based standards, undervalues the job security of an incumbent employee? Although the costs of dismissals should place a brake upon replacement of employees, the strength of the incumbent's position would depend critically upon his or her acquisition of firm-specific skills and knowledge. In jobs requiring little of these special attributes, where the work required is unskilled and the labour market is oversupplied with unskilled workers, there would be little brake on fair dismissals of incumbents. This would be true for employees with considerable length of service or seniority, unless their jobs required these firm-specific skills. It seems wrong in principle that the job security of employees should differ according to this attribute which is beyond their control.

[43] E. Sehgal, 'Occupational Mobility and Job Tenure in 1983' (Oct. 1984), *Monthly Labour Review*, 18; Robert E. Hall, 'The Importance of Lifetime Jobs in the US Economy' (1982), 72, *American Economic Review*, 716; John T. Addison and Alberto C. Castro, 'The Importance of Lifetime Jobs: Differences between Union and Nonunion Workers' (1987), 40, *Industrial and Labor Relations Review*, 393.

HARM TO INTERESTS OF THE FIRM

In this broader version of the goal-based approach to the definition of fault, the employee's fault lies in his or her conduct being harmful to the interests of the firm more generally. This would include not only productive efficiency, but also any other interests of the employer such as administrative efficiency and success in the product market. For example, an employer might believe that continued employment of a particular individual would harm the reputation of the business, and use this as the justification for dismissal even though the employer cannot demonstrate that a replacement would be more productive. Similarly, an employer might be able to assert more easily that an isolated act of disobedience, if left unremedied, would undermine managerial authority, and would therefore be harmful to the interests of the firm. By changing the frame of reference of the fault inquiry to harm to the interests of the firm, the complex economic analysis of the productive efficiency standard would be short-circuited, and all that an employer would be required to demonstrate is that the dismissed worker had harmed the interests of the business, not that a hypothetical replacement would be more productive.

One major problem posed by this approach is that it tends to delegate to management the task of setting the fault standard by leaving management to determine where the interests of the business lie. A tribunal is unlikely to question management's assertion that it has an interest in such matters as efficiency and a trustworthy and reliable workforce. It is then but a short step to take to accept management's interpretation of the demands of this interest in the context of a particular firm. The interest in a reliable workforce becomes concretized into the need for strict timekeeping on pain of dismissal; or the interest of the managers of a casino in the integrity of inspectors becomes concretized into an absolute rule against socializing with customers. If the tribunals are to avoid such subjectivism in the standard with its concomitant abandonment of independent normative control over managerial prerogative, some further qualification must be imposed to test the legitimacy of the application of the interest claimed by the employer.

Such a qualification might be supplied by comparison with the conventional practice of other employers in the same line of business. If the managers of the casino could demonstrate that other owners of casinos had found it necessary to impose a strict rule against fraternizing with customers to ensure the integrity of inspectors, then this would satisfy the requirement that the precise interpretation of the employer's interest was appropriate in this case. But this broader conventional approach still identifies good disciplinary practice with the practice of employers rather than articulating a moral conception of fault. Alternatively, therefore, the tribunals could rely upon their own experience and their appreciation of the risks of the harm involved to determine whether the employer's assessment of harm was accurate. The tribunal could simply assert that the risk of serious harm was minimal from their experience, so the employee was not at fault in the required sense to justify dismissal.

Even if such a brake upon subjectivism were effective, this fourth approach remains vulnerable to the objection that it focuses exclusively upon the interests of the firm and ignores those of the employee. It lacks a balancing factor which would weigh up the interest of the employee in job security against the risk of harm to the business. For example, where a customer with strong bargaining power insists upon the dismissal of a particular employee, the harm to the interests of the business approach to questions of fairness would invariably permit such a dismissal. In similar circumstances the Court of Appeal in *Dobie* v. *Burns International Security Services (UK) Ltd.*[44] overturned a tribunal decision that the dismissal was fair and remitted the case for a further hearing. The court insisted that the tribunal should have had regard to the question whether the employer had acted unreasonably by failing sufficiently to take into account the extent of the injustice to the employee. It should be pointed out, however, that the Court of Appeal certainly contemplates the possibility that customer insistence may justify a dismissal provided that the employer has no other reasonable course of action open to him or her. Yet the tribunal's decision illustrates precisely the danger of focusing exclusively upon the employer's interests when setting the standard of fault.

Another significant effect of this exclusive focus upon the interests of the employer is the absence of a test of proportionality. Unlike the other three approaches, which assess the gravity of the employee's fault to discover whether either dismissal or some lesser disciplinary sanction may be warranted, this fourth approach seems to permit any harm to the interests of the firm to justify dismissal. Some minor misconduct or some small degree of incompetence may suffice to count as harm to the interests of the firm sufficient to justify dismissal. Again this objection might be overcome if dismissal were only justified where the employee's conduct posed a risk of substantial harm to the interests of the firm. The function of the requirement of substantial harm would be to reflect in the test of fault the interest of the employee in job security, the central aim of the legislation, without which any substantive test of fairness is likely to deprive the law of any significant impact.

It is not clear, however, whether such a requirement of substantial harm suffices to achieve a desirable balance between the competing interests of employer and employee. Consider a not infrequent type of case where the employer knows after careful investigation that one of a small number of employees has been guilty of serious misconduct, but cannot discover which individual is the true culprit. The employer may successfully argue that the

---

[44] [1984] ICR 812 (CA).

continued employment of all members of the group poses a sufficiently serious risk that the dismissal of everyone is warranted. Yet all bar one of the dismissed workers are completely innocent of wrongdoing. This goal-based approach of assessing the harm to the interests of the firm seems to justify riding roughshod over the interests of individual employees in job security.

4. THE PRACTICE OF THE TRIBUNALS

Having considered the moral strengths and weaknesses of these four paradigms for justifications of dismissals and their potential to provide independent normative guides to good industrial practice, can we say that any one of them fits the practice of the courts and tribunals in determining questions of fairness under the statute? The question cannot be answered easily, as we have seen, because so many cases turn on the 'range of reasonable responses' test. For the bulk of dismissals, the tribunal can simply say, having heard the evidence, that the dismissal was within the band of reasonable conduct open to the employer, without needing to specify exactly how the tribunal would set the parameters of that band. Many other cases raise problems of proof of the facts, and, once the tribunal's decision about the truth of the matter has been reached, the question of the reasonableness of the dismissal is discussed summarily. In addition, because of the problem of juridification noted in Chapter 1,[45] the courts prefer to decide a case on grounds of procedural unfairness rather than to address directly the substantive question of fairness. But relying on the slender evidence of the remaining cases, what conception of fault lies at the heart of the courts' decisions?

I will suggest that the last approach to the question of fault predominates in the tribunals. The tribunals will find sufficient fault to justify dismissal on a broad range of facts where the employer asserts that the employee's conduct has caused harm to the interests of the business, or the risk of harm. A dismissal falls within the 'range of reasonable responses' if the employer demonstrates that the employee's conduct harmed the interests of the business or posed a risk of harm. But we have noted that this test may be formulated in crucially different ways. The employee's interest in job security may be considerably improved if the tribunals demand that the harm to the employer's business should be substantial in order to count as the requisite degree of fault. I shall argue further that the interpretation of the practice of the tribunals which presents it in its best light does encompass this additional requirement that the harm should be substantial.

Industrial Tribunals generally reject the contractual approach on the grounds that it is both too broad and too narrow. The test is too broad because it would permit an employer to insist upon a harsh and unreasonable

[45] See p. 34.

disciplinary code. In contrast, under the British law of unfair dismissal, the courts have insisted that an employer cannot simply rely upon a disciplinary rule which states that instant dismissal will be the punishment, but the employer must demonstrate that he or she has had regard to all the circumstances. In *Ladbroke Racing Ltd.* v. *Arnott*,[46] the employees had admittedly broken the rule against placing bets at the betting shop where they worked on behalf of customers, but the court argued that the dismissals were unreasonable because the cases concerned relatively minor infringements of the rule, there was no personal advantage to the claimants, and the claimants were under the impression that their immediate supervisor had given his permission. This rejection of strict enforcement by an employer of his disciplinary code indicates a divergence between the concept of fault developed by the tribunals and the contractual approach precisely because of this defect in the contractual approach that it delegates to the employer the power to determine the relevant criteria of fault.

The tribunals also regard the contractual approach as too narrow, because in some instances they believe that it may be reasonable to dismiss an employee even where the employee has conformed to all the contractual requirements and so no breach of contract can be found.[47] It is not unusal, for instance, for the tribunals to decide that a dismissal was fair on the ground that the employee behaved unreasonably by insisting upon his or her strict contractual rights.[48] Even if the dismissal is held to be unfair in those circumstances, the tribunal will certainly reduce the measure of compensation on the ground of contributory fault.[49] For these reasons, as well as the tribunal's lack of deference to collective agreements described earlier, the contractual approach cannot provide the conceptual framework for an interpretation of the practice of the tribunals.

The forfeiture of a property right approach to the issue of fault cannot be discerned in the reasoning of the tribunals in disciplinary dismissals. We shall see in Chapter 5 that the idea of the job as property has influenced the tribunals in their approach to the handling of economic dismissals, though, even in that context, as we noted in Chapter 2, the analogy carries little weight in determining the scope of the concept of redundancy and the award of redundancy payments. This should not surprise us, for even though the analogy with property rights has played an important part in rhetorical justifications for the introduction of the unfair dismissal legislation, the principal question under discussion in this chapter is when such a property right may be forfeited by the fault of its possessor. Since this idea of

---

[46] [1983] IRLR 154 (Ct. Sess.).
[47] *London Borough of Redbridge* v. *Fishman* [1978] IRLR 69 (EAT).
[48] *Hollister* v. *National Farmers' Union* [1979] ICR 542 (CA); *Richmond Precision Engineering Ltd.* v. *Pearce* [1985] IRLR 179 (EAT).
[49] *Nelson* v. *BBC (No. 2)* [1980] ICR 110 (CA).

forfeiture by fault is an extremely uncommon phenomenon in the general law of property, the analogy tends to provide scant guidance to the tribunals.

Nor does the approach of productive efficiency appear in the reasoning of the tribunals. In part this may be due to the complexity of the economic formula. But more decisively the approach seems too narrow to explain many of the tribunals' decisions where the misconduct does not seem to have affected the employee's performance at work, but simply weakened the employer's trust in the employee. There is no doubt that tribunals regard such matters as the employee's conduct outside working hours and customer preferences as potentially fair grounds for dismissals, but neither of these considerations could be justified by reference to the standard of productive efficiency.

In addition, the standard of productive efficiency cannot account for the importance which the tribunals attach to protecting the position of incumbent employees. An employer will not be able to justify a dismissal simply on the ground that he or she has discovered a better or a cheaper worker to perform the same job. The fault standard requires the employer to point to misconduct or lack of capacity falling below the average employee before the dismissal can fall within the range of reasonable responses.

In fact, the evidence from the reported decisions points overwhelmingly to the adoption by the tribunals of the harm to the interests of the business approach described above. Many of the key indicators that this approach is being used can be detected in the regular practices of the tribunals. Furthermore, the fundamental criticism of this approach, namely, that it defers too easily to employers' perceptions of their own interest, seems to be confirmed by these same decisions.

In cases in which the employer tries to justify the dismissal by reference to events which take place away from work and outside working hours, the tribunals demonstrate a persistent willingness to regard the dismissals as within the range of reasonable responses. Thus in *Saunders* v. *Scottish National Camps Association Ltd.*,[50] where it will be recalled the employee was a homosexual, the employers expressed the worry that their customers, parents of the children at the summer camp, might be put off sending their children to the camp, and in these circumstances it was regarded as within the range of reasonable responses of the employer to dismiss the employee. Here the employer's perception of the risk of harm goes unchallenged, with the effect that the tribunal delegates the criteria of fault to the employer. The same analysis applies to *Mathewson* v. *R. B. Wilson Dental Laboratories*,[51] the case of dismissal for an arrest outside work for possession of cannabis.

Another indication of the dominance of the harm to interests approach

---

[50] [1980] IRLR 174 (EAT); [1981] IRLR 277 (Ct. Sess.).
[51] [1988] IRLR 512 (EAT).

can be found in the absence of a test of proportionality of disciplinary measures. In *British Leyland UK Ltd*. v. *Swift*,[52] an employee was dismissed after eighteen years' service after a car's tax disc belonging to the employers was discovered on his own vehicle. He was subsequently convicted after pleading guilty to fraudulent use of the licence. The Industrial Tribunal found that there was abundant evidence for an employer to reach the conclusion that the applicant had been guilty of gross misconduct, but it found the dismissal unfair on the ground that dismissal was too severe a penalty for a relatively minor offence after many years of satisfactory service. The Court of Appeal overturned this decision, insisting that the tribunal had misapplied the range of reasonable responses test.

The first question that arises is whether the Industrial Tribunal applied the wrong test . . . They said: '. . . a reasonable employer would, in our opinion, have considered that a lesser penalty was appropriate'. I do not think that that is the right test. The correct test is: Was it reasonable for the employers to dismiss him? If no reasonable employer would have dismissed him, then the dismissal was unfair. But if a reasonable employer might reasonably have dismissed him, then the dismissal was fair. It must be remembered that in all these cases there is a band of reasonableness, within which one employer might reasonably take one view: another quite reasonably take a different view. One would quite reasonably dismiss the man. The other would quite reasonably keep him on. Both views may be quite reasonable. If it is quite reasonable to dismiss him, then the dismissal must be upheld as fair: even though some other employers may not have dismissed him.

Lord Denning, MR, makes it clear in this passage that no fine judgments of proportionality can be rendered in assessing the fairness of a dismissal. This is surely correct, for the tribunals cannot be expected to measure in millimetres the just measure of the sanction. In France, where the tribunals (*conseils de prud'hommes*) do accept the principle of proportionality, they nevertheless restrict intervention to cases where the disciplinary sanction is clearly disproportionate to the employee's fault.[53] Yet Lord Denning goes much further to deny any effective test of proportionality at all. The range of reasonable responses test sets boundaries, not standards, and those boundaries stretch as far as the reasonable employer sees fit. The harm to the business of dishonest conduct was evident, and it could not be said that no reasonable employer would have dismissed the employee in such circumstances.

Yet another indication that the harm to interests approach predominates in judgments of fault can be discovered in those cases where a group of employees are all dismissed because the employer, after careful investigation, cannot discover which individual is culpable. Here, subject to the fairness of

---

[52] [1981] IRLR 91 (CA).
[53] Code du Travail L. 122–43; J. E. Ray, 'Contrôle minimum ou contrôle normal du juge judiciaire en matière disciplinaire' (1987), *Droit Social*, 365.

the employer's investigatory procedures, the dismissal will be fair despite the evident injustice to innocent members of the group.[54] The tribunals regard the risk of unfairness to innocent employees as requiring the employer to carry out extremely careful investigations, but not to prevent the employer from dismissing all members of the group, for the risk of harm to the business suffices to justify the dismissals.

One final and striking illustration of the adoption of the harm to the interests of the business approach to the question of fault may be gleaned from decisions which focus on the question of contributory fault. In Chapter 7 we will examine in greater detail how the tribunals reduce the measure of compensation by reference to the idea that the employee was the author, to some extent, of his or her own misfortune. At this point, however, it should be observed that the harm to interests approach justifies a finding of fair dismissal in cases where the employee lacks the talents or skills to measure up to the employer's standard of required competence in performance of the job, even though the employee is doing his or her best. In *Kraft Foods Ltd.* v. *Fox*,[55] the employee was appointed to the position of clerk manager, but was subsequently dismissed for the principal reason that he was unable to perform the job up to the high standards expected by the employer. The Industrial Tribunal permitted the claim for unfair dismissal, though reduced the measure of compensation by 50 per cent to take account of the employee's incompetence. On appeal, however, the EAT set aside the finding of unfair dismissal on the understanding that the employer would make some *ex gratia* payment. The EAT seems to have taken the view that the harm to the business from the employee's incompetence must count as a good reason for dismissal. On the other hand, the EAT was unwilling to reduce the measure of compensation for contributory fault unless the incompetence was wilful. This decision reveals that the exclusive focus on the interests of the business makes it possible to determine that the employee is at fault for the purpose of deciding whether or not the dismissal was unfair, even though the tribunal cannot attribute any blameworthy behaviour to the employee at all. No clearer indication exists that the fault inquiry for substantive fairness depends almost exclusively upon the employer's determination of whether the interests of his business have been harmed.

5. THE BEST INTERPRETATION

The above analysis of the standard of substantive fairness adopted by the tribunals suggests some conclusions which may point the way forward towards a more satisfactory approach. It is clear that even under the 'range

---

[54] *Monie* v. *Coral Racing Ltd.* [1981] ICR 109 (CA); *Whitbread PLC* v. *Thomas* [1988] ICR 135 (EAT); *Parr* v. *Whitbread & Co.* [1990] ICR 427 (EAT).
[55] [1978] ICR 311 (EAT).

of reasonable responses' test the tribunals must set normative standards in determining the boundaries of reasonableness. By pitching those standards of fault by reference to the criterion of harm to the interests of the firm, however, the tribunals present only a weak challenge to the free exercise of managerial prerogative. The exclusive emphasis on the interests of the firm in settling the gravity and types of conduct which will be regarded as constituting sufficient fault to justify dismissal has the tendency to discount systematically any conflicting interests of the employee and the public.

On the other hand, the three alternative approaches seem either equally unattractive or too obscure to provide practical guidance. In some respects the narrow test of productive efficiency yields the most appealing conception of fault, for it compels employers to adopt reasons for dismissal which are both closely tied to performance at work and give substantial weight to the interests of the incumbent employee in job security. Nevertheless the obstacles to the adoption of this approach seem considerable. Not only would the tribunals have to engage in an unfamiliar economic analysis where their assessments would be vulnerable to misleading information provided by the employer, but also the tribunals would have to abandon their settled approach which recognizes that valid reasons for dismissal include matters such as customer preferences which do not impinge directly on the productive efficiency of the individual.

Consistent with my stated aim of providing the best interpretation of the tribunals' practice, it seems better to propose an interpretation of the settled harm to the interests of the business approach which takes into account the twin dangers of that approach, that is, its lapses from setting normative standards into mere endorsement of conventional managerial disciplinary practices, and its exclusive focus on the interests of employers. These dangers may be reduced, but not excluded altogether, by requiring tribunals to test the alleged harm against two further qualifications: first, that the harm to the business should be recognized and acted upon by other employers in the same line of business, and secondly, that the harm should be substantial. Decisions which explicitly or implicitly adopt such qualifications should be emphasized as representing the best practice of the tribunals. Both qualifications combat the inherent danger of the harm to interests standard that it merely endorses management's own view as to the appropriate disciplinary standards. The requirement of substantial harm introduces in addition an element of proportionality in order to ensure that the employee's interest in job security is placed in the balance.

But can it be plausibly argued that the tribunals in fact adopt such an approach to the question of substantive fairness? Is this interpretation compatible with the reasoning which holds that dismissals may be 'harsh but fair'? Perhaps not, but the practice of the tribunals is not uniform at this level of detail in the application of the harm to the interests of the business approach.

We have certainly encountered many instances where the tribunals refer to the practices of other reasonable employers or, what amounts to the same thing, the standards of good industrial practice, to provide guidance on the question of sufficiency of the reason for dismissal. For example, in *Watling (N. C.) & Co. Ltd.* v. *Richardson*, the EAT insisted that dismissal of construction workers on the completion of a particular project was unreasonable because it was not consistent with 'the objective standard of the way in which a reasonable employer in those circumstances, in that line of business, would have behaved'.[56] Often the ground for criticism of a decision of an Industrial Tribunal has not been that it failed to judge the fairness of the dismissal by reference to the standards of other reasonable employers, but rather, as in *Saunders* v. *Scottish National Camps Association Ltd.*,[57] that other employers seem to behave unfairly or in a prejudiced manner yet regard this as reasonable.

Similarly, we have encountered many instances where the employer's reason for dismissal, though a relevant one under the harm to interests approach, was insufficient to justify dismissal. Almost all cases where the tribunal makes a finding of unfair dismissal but then reduces the measure of compensation by reference to the contributory fault of the employee fall into this category.

Further support for this interpretation may be found in cases such as *Dobie* v. *Burns International Security Services (UK) Ltd.*, where the Court of Appeal remitted the case back to the Industrial Tribunal on the ground that the tribunal had failed to consider the factor of injustice to the employee when he was dismissed at the request of an important customer:

In deciding whether the employer acted reasonably or unreasonably, a very important factor of which he has to take account, on the facts known to him at that time, is whether there will or will not be injustice to the employee and the extent of that injustice. For example, he will clearly have to take account of the length of time during which the employee has been employed by him, the satisfactoriness or otherwise of the employee's service, the difficulties which may face the employee in obtaining other employment, and matters of that sort.[58]

In this passage, the emphasis upon the issue of the justice to the employee, and in other passages the emphasis on the closing words of EPCA 1978, s. 57(3), that the tribunal must have regard to 'equity and the substantial merits of the case', should be regarded as techniques which place a brake upon the employer's assertion that the dismissal is justified because of the harm to the business. This harm must be balanced against the injustice to the employee, and, where the harm is slight or transitory, then the dismissal may not be justified.

---

[56] [1978] ICR 1049 (EAT), per Phillips, J., at p. 1056.
[57] [1980] IRLR 174 (EAT); [1981] IRLR 277 (Ct. Sess.).
[58] [1984] ICR 812 (CA) per Lord Donaldson, MR, at p. 817.

Cases concerning the illness of employees also provide support for the view that the employer should demonstrate a substantial harm to the interests of the business. Most cases of illness lead to the absence of the employee from work.[59] This absence normally provides grounds for the employer to assert that his or her business has been harmed by a reduction in productive efficiency, though the precise cost to the employer depends upon the system of payment, the amount of any contractual entitlement to sick pay, and the extent to which the employer may recoup the cost of Statutory Sick Pay from the State.[60] Despite the obvious harm to the interests of the business from absenteeism, the tribunals demonstrate a reluctance to treat dismissal as a reasonable response to illness. This reluctance depends upon a sense that the employee cannot be held to be to blame for his or her misfortune. In addition, sometimes the illness may prove the result of working conditions, so in a way it may be regarded as the employer's responsibility. But instead of this absence of fault preventing the dismissal from being fair, as it might for instance on the forfeiture of property right approach, the tribunals respond by insisting that employers should demonstrate that the harm to the business has reached a degree of gravity that it is no longer practicable to retain the employee and keep his or her job open. For example, Wood, J., in the EAT indicated many of the factors to which a reasonable employer should have regard in a case of intermittent absences through ill health:

the nature of the illness; the likelihood of recurring or some other illness arising; the length of the various absences and the spaces of good health between them; the need of the employer for the work done by the particular employee; the impact of the absences on others who work with the employee; the adoption and the exercise carrying out of the policy; the important emphasis on a personal assessment in the ultimate decision and of course, the extent to which the difficulty of the situation and the position of the employer has been made clear to the employee so that the employee realises that the point of no return, the moment when the decision was ultimately being made may be approaching.[61]

Most of these considerations tend towards requiring the employer to demonstrate that the employee's absences from work have reached the point where they seriously damage the productivity of the business.[62] In the case of a long-term illness, again the tribunals emphasize that the employer must demonstrate a compelling business need to replace the employee:

---

[59] But see *Harper* v. *National Coal Board* [1980] IRLR 260 (EAT), where the employee's epileptic fits presented a danger of physical violence to other workers, and the dismissal was fair; see also *Pascoe* v. *Hallen and Medway* [1975] IRLR 116 (EAT).

[60] Under the Social Security and Housing Benefits Act 1982 the employer must generally pay the employee sick pay at the relatively low statutory sums, but then may deduct these payments from the National Insurance Contributions he would otherwise have made. These deductions cannot be made in all instances, however, as in the case of the first 3 days of lost work. See Richard Lewis, 'The Privatisation of Sickness Benefit' (1982), 11, *ILJ* 245.

[61] *Lynock* v. *Cereal Packaging Ltd.* [1988] IRLR 510 (EAT), at p. 512.

[62] See also *Tan* v. *Berry Bros. & Rudd Ltd.* [1974] ICR 586 (NIRC), and cases discussed in Steven D. Anderman, *The Law of Unfair Dismissal* (2nd edn., London, 1985), at pp. 182–5.

The basic question which has to be determined in every case is whether, in all the circumstances, the employer can be expected to wait any longer and, if so, how much longer?[63]

What is crucial in determining the reasonableness of the employer's decision to dismiss in cases of illness is the urgency of the need to replace the employee, a consideration which stresses a requirement to demonstrate substantial harm to the business, so it will not usually suffice merely to prove that the employee has been absent from work.

If, therefore, it is possible to present such an interpretation of the harm to the interests of the business approach to the question of fault in disciplinary dismissals as being consistent with much of the practice of the tribunals, then it is to be recommended as providing also the best interpretation of this practice, because it counters the twin dangers of this approach described above. This conclusion leads to the proposal that tribunals should more explicitly and routinely determine whether dismissal falls outside the 'range of reasonable responses' of employers by asking three questions:

1. What harm or risk of harm to the business resulted from the employee's conduct?
2. Was that harm a type recognized by other employers in that line of business as calling for disciplinary measures?
3. Was the harm substantial or likely to be so, so that the extent of the harm outweighs the potential injustice to the employee?

The limited scope of this interpretation of the fairness standard should be stressed before concluding. It covers only the category of disciplinary dismissals, and within these it excludes criteria of procedural fairness to be considered in the next chapter. Most significantly, this interpretation has little to say about the standard of fairness applicable to cases involving infringements of civil liberties or public rights, where such balancing of interests may appear less appropriate because of the importance of the rights at stake. We are left, therefore, with a relatively small group of cases where the employee disputes that his or her conduct merited dismissal, and for these the range of reasonable responses test should be interpreted along the lines of the three questions suggested above.

[63] *Spencer* v. *Paragon Wallpapers Ltd.* [1977] ICR 301 (EAT), per Phillips, J., at p. 307.

[4]

Procedural Fairness

WE can view the procedure by which a dismissal is tested for its fairness as a series of interactive stages. At the beginning the employer decides either unilaterally or by collective agreement to institute a procedure for handling dismissals and grievances. Next the employer dismisses an employee either by following the agreed procedure or failing to do so. In most cases where the employee contests the fairness of the dismissal a conciliation officer appointed by ACAS then encourages the parties to settle their dispute without further litigation. If the claim reaches an Industrial Tribunal without being settled, the tribunal conducts a pre-hearing review when, if it decides that the employee has no reasonable chance of success, it may ask for a deposit and make an order for costs. Finally, the case presented by each side to the dispute will be heard by the tribunal and it will determine whether or not the dismissal was unfair.

One of the purposes of this chapter is to reveal how these different procedural stages interact with each other. Although the central question before the Industrial Tribunal is whether or not the employer handled the case fairly, the likelihood of the employee in fact receiving a fair procedure depends critically on other stages of the procedural process. In particular, we will note the significance of the agreed contractual procedure, if any, for if an employee can enforce this agreed procedure by way of an injunction in the ordinary courts, then, as we shall see, this is much more likely to ensure observance of a fair procedure than any threat of a determination of unfair dismissal. In addition, we will pay close attention to the conciliation stage, for its emphasis upon monetary settlements rather than strict procedural regularity seems calculated to undermine any legal support for the idea that employers should be required to adopt fair disciplinary procedures. Questions about the fairness of the procedures before Industrial Tribunals themselves will be considered in Chapter 8 in the broader context of an assessment of the merits of this institution for adjudication. We shall begin where the previous chapter left off, that is, by examining the interpretation placed by Industrial Tribunals on the concept of fair dismissal procedures, deferring until later in the chapter a consideration of the significance of agreed disciplinary procedures and conciliation.

Although the unfair dismissal legislation scarcely mentions fair procedures, since its inception the courts and tribunals have emphasized that the fairness of the employer's procedures surrounding the dismissal comprises an important element in the general test of reasonableness under EPCA 1978, s. 57(3). Not only must the employer demonstrate a substantial reason for dismissal and the reasonableness of dismissal for that reason, but must also persuade the tribunal that he or she conducted the process of making the dismissal fairly. Lord Bridge summarized this requirement of fairness in the leading case, *Polkey* v. *A. E. Dayton Services Ltd.*, in the following terms:

Thus, in the case of incapacity, the employer will normally not act reasonably unless he gives the employee fair warning and an opportunity to mend his ways and show that he can do the job; in the case of misconduct, the employer will normally not act reasonably unless he investigates the complaint of misconduct fully and fairly and hears whatever the employee wishes to say in his defence or in explanation or mitigation; in the case of redundancy, the employer will normally not act reasonably unless he warns and consults any employees affected or their representative, adopts a fair basis on which to select for redundancy and takes such steps as may be reasonable to avoid or minimise redundancy by redeployment within his own organisation.[1]

In this chapter we shall ascertain the principles on which the requirements of procedural fairness are based. This demands an interpretation of the practice of the courts and tribunals which identifies the underlying conception of fairness from which the procedural standards originate. Once again we should attempt the best interpretation of this practice, that is, an interpretation presenting the practice of the tribunals in its best light.

Lord Bridge's survey of the law highlights two particular features vital to any such interpretation. First, he affirms that procedural standards apply to all types of dismissals, but indicates clearly that the precise requirements vary according to the grounds for the dismissal. Secondly, he is also careful to qualify the generality of his statement by indicating that the procedural standards apply only in the normal case. He leaves open the possibility that in abnormal cases an employer need not conform to the normal standards. An interpretation of the principles governing procedural fairness which fits the law of unfair dismissal must therefore accommodate both the diverstiy of standards and their flexibility in particular contexts.

1. THREE MODELS OF PROCEDURAL FAIRNESS

In order to grasp the moral significance of possible interpretations of the law, we should identify at the outset three paradigms of procedural fairness. These abstract models reflect different moral justifications for conformity to standards of procedural fairness. These differing justifications lead to a diversity in the precise requirements on a person seeking to comply with the demands of procedural fairness. Moreover, the differing justifications suggest

[1] [1988] ICR 142 (HL), at pp. 162–3.

opposing reasons which might be put forward for the relaxation of their procedural requirements. These models thus contribute to a formulation of the best interpretation of the practice of the tribunals by simultaneously illuminating potential moral justifications and pointing to relevant reasons for diversity and flexibility in procedural standards.

RESPECT FOR DIGNITY

One justification for procedural fairness which predominates in criminal law and public law is grounded in the idea of respect for the dignity of the individual. It holds that the State should observe the rules of natural justice or due process before any deprivation of liberty or property, or any denial of some important legitimate expection, for the sake of demonstrating respect for the individual affected by the decision.[2] The rules of natural justice focus on the right to an impartial hearing, because decision-makers have a duty to show that they are considering and taking into account the interests of the individual. Important elements of the right to an impartial hearing include an unbiased tribunal, the right to know the charges or allegations, and the oppportunity to rebut them.

Because these requirements are demanded out of respect for the individual, a basic right of every citizen, then, outside conditions of national emergency or security, they should rarely admit of any derogation or exception. Even when a criminal has been caught red-handed, he or she is still entitled to all his or her procedural rights under the law of criminal procedure. Nevertheless, in the context of challenges to public administrative action, the courts are prepared to derogate from the strict rules of natural justice. Lapses from these strict rules can only be justified, however, when there has been no risk of unfairness nor any possible appearance of unfairness.[3] For the sake of developing a clear paradigm, here we will ignore these qualifications to the strict rules of natural justice recognized in public law.

These strict standards of natural justice could be applied without substantial modification to disciplinary dismissals. An employer could be required before making a dismissal for misconduct or incompetence to inform the employee of the reasons for dismissal, to carry out a thorough investigation of the facts, and to give the employee the opportunity at a hearing before an independent person or committee to rebut the charges or explain mitigating circumstances. Any breach of these procedural requirements would then

---

[2] For examples of this justification, see G. Maher, 'Natural Justice as Fairness', in Neil MacCormick and Peter Birks, *The Legal Mind* (Oxford, 1986), ch. 6; F. Michelman, 'Formal and Associational Aims in Procedural Due Process', in John W. Chapman and J. Roland Pennock (eds.), *Due Process* (New York, 1977), ch. 4.

[3] R. v. *Chief Constable of Thames Valley Police, ex parte Cotton* [1990] IRLR 344 (CA); M. R. Freedland, 'Status and Contract in the Law of Public Employment' (1991), 20, *ILJ* 72.

render the dismissal unfair. In some legal systems such as France, the legislation provides expressly for mandatory procedural steps such as written notice of the grounds for dismissal and the opportunity for a hearing,[4] but this strict approach based upon principles of natural justice is out of tune with the flexibility of British law as indicated by Lord Bridge. This model of procedural fairness, based on respect for the dignity of the individual, therefore may serve only as an aspiration rather than a precise interpretation of the principles of procedural fairness adopted by the courts for disciplinary dismissals.

Another sticking-point for this model of procedural fairness arises from its insistence upon the impartiality of the ultimate decision-maker. An employer is unlikely to find it acceptable to relinquish the ultimate power of senior management to make dismissals, even though higher management acting as agent for the employer cannot satisfy the requirement of natural justice that it be seen to be impartial. Evidence to support such a reluctance to relinquish power to an independent body can be found in the fact that, although the legislation permits employers and unions to contract out of the unfair dismissal legislation, provided that they adopt an approved scheme of grievance arbitration culminating in a hearing before an independent body,[5] only one employer has agreed to such a procedural model to gain exemption from the legislation.[6]

It is harder to transpose this model to economic dismissals. The natural justice requirements presuppose the existence of some charge being levelled against an individual or some disputed question of fact to be resolved by a tribunal. Where management decides as a result of market considerations to reduce the size of the workforce, however, the dismissals are not justified by reference to the fault of the employee, so a formal hearing is an inappropriate standard of procedural justice. Only if management were required by law to justify its decision to reduce the size of the workforce by reference to economic considerations would it make sense to demand a formal hearing to ascertain the facts and to ensure the rationality of the decision. As we shall see in Chapter 5, the law eschews such a requirement, so there is no place for natural justice requirements in economic dismissals. But that is not to say that no procedural standards should be required; merely that the adversary model contained in the criminal law and expressed in the principles of natural justice is inappropriate.

These problems with the natural justice model, based upon respect for individual dignity, suggest that it probably lacks the diversity and flexibility to provide the basis for a satisfactory interpretation of the principles of fair

---

[4] Code du Travail, arts. L. 122-12–122-14.
[5] EPCA 1978, ss. 65–6.
[6] C. Bourn, 'Statutory Exemptions for Collective Agreements' (1979) 8, *ILJ* 85; Linda Dickens, Michael Jones, Brian Weekes, and Moira Hart, *Dismissed: A Study of Unfair Dismissal and the Industrial Tribunal System* (Oxford, 1985), at pp. 238–40.

procedures in the context of unfair dismissal. The natural justice model seems inappropriate for economic dismissals. In addition, the strict standards derived from the right to respect imply both a degree of formality and a degree of independent control over managerial power which the law is unlikely to require.

DEMOCRATIC PARTICIPATION

The model of democratic participation suggests that fair procedures should try to maximize the opportunity for consultation and expression of differing opinions before a decision is reached. The aim is to allow those likely to be affected by a decision an equal chance to have their views considered. The focus here is not so much on individual rights, though respect for the individual plays a part of the justification for democracy, but on the maximization of democratic participation in decisions affecting people's lives to the extent consistent with effective government.[7] Participation contributes to open decision-making, which in turn is conducive to results which are generally morally acceptable. At the same time participation requires those involved to develop and refine their own moral viewpoints.[8] This justification admits the possibility of derogation from procedural standards when further consultation would impede to an unacceptable extent any decision from being reached at all.

In the context of dismissals, this model suggests that the workforce and the individuals concerned should be consulted prior to dismissals. Consultation with the workforce could be through representative machinery established under collective bargaining arrangements or by specially created Works Councils as in West Germany.[9] Management would also have to conduct individual consultation with workers likely to be dismissed. This justification for procedural fairness therefore regards an impartial hearing as insufficient, for it demands an opportunity for workers to be consulted and to participate in decisions at every stage of the procedures leading to dismissals.

This model could fit economic dismissals without too much difficulty. It would require the employer to consult a recognized trade union and the individual workers concerned about the decision to make redundancies. These requirements are in fact to a large extent already mandated by current

---

[7] R. A. Macdonald, 'Judicial Review and Procedural Fairness in Administrative Law: II' (1980), 26, *McGill Law Journal*, 1; R. B. Stewart, 'The Reformation of American Administrative Law' (1975), 88, *Harvard Law Review*, 1667.

[8] D. J. Galligan, *Discretionary Powers* (Oxford, 1986), 355.

[9] M. Weiss, 'Individual Employment Rights: Focusing on Job Security in the Federal Republic of Germany' (1988), 67, *Nebraska Law Review*, 82; A. Döse-Digenopoulos and A. Höland, 'Dismissal of Employees in the Federal Republic of Germany' (1985), 48, *Modern Law Review*, 539. For a wider comparative perspective, see B. A. Hepple, 'Some Comparative Reflections' (1980), 11, *Bulletin of Comparative Labour Relations*, 231, at pp. 240–3.

legislation. The Employment Protection Act 1975, Part IV, imposes a duty upon employers to consult a recognized trade union prior to redundancies, and failure to do so results in compensation to the affected workers known as the protective award.[10] Under the ordinary test of fairness for unfair dismissal, individual consultation in cases of economic dismissals has also been consistently demanded by the courts, as in *Polkey* v. *A. E. Dayton Services Ltd.* itself.[11]

The precise scope and time allowed for such collective and individual consultation are potentially important limitations on the degree of democratic participation. The legislation requires collective consultation, not collective bargaining, so the employer need do no more than inform a recognized union of redundancy plans and listen to the union's objections and counter-proposals. The employer need not ultimately allow the consultations to affect his or her original plans in the slightest degree, let alone seek an agreement with the union. Individual consultation seems equally a futile gesture, for the employer need not put forward any constructive proposals to assist the employee in searching for new work or retraining, but simply explain the harsh reality of the impending redundancy. Even so, the current law clearly envisages to some extent an element of democratic participation in decisions to make economic dismissals.

The element of democratic participation fits less easily into the framework of disciplinary dismissals. It implies both that the employer and workforce should jointly set the disciplinary standards of conduct and that the final decision to dismiss should be made with the participation of representatives of the workforce. Management may be unwilling to concede such an impairment of its powers and the consequent risk of its disciplinary authority breaking down through obstruction by the workforce. The introduction of procedural standards based on the justification of democractic participation runs headlong into the very notion that management should have the power to dismiss workers. At the same time, union officials normally do not wish to place themselves in the position of participating in disciplinary decisions, thereby endorsing and legitimizing the exercise of managerial prerogative.

Judging this model by reference to the criteria of diversity and flexibility, it appears to fall short in important respects. The standard of participation does offer some degree of flexibility, especially if it is recognized that some limits must be placed upon consultation in order to ensure that decisions are reached. Unfortunately it lacks diversity, for though the democratic participation idea fits well into the framework of economic dismissals, its fundamental challenge to the disciplinary authority of management renders it implausible as an interpretation of fair procedures in cases of misconduct and incompetence.

[10] M. R. Freedland, 'Employment Protection: Redundancy Procedures and the EEC' (1976), 5, *ILJ* 24.
[11] [1988] ICR 142 (HL).

EFFICIENCY

A third model of procedural fairness recognizes that careful decisions are often the best ones. It therefore demands that the employer's procedure prior to dismissals should be designed to ensure so far as possible that the decision is based on the best information available at reasonable cost concerning the facts and the likely consequences. In addition, efficiency considerations require, within reasonable bounds of administrative cost, careful consideration of the facts ascertained in order to ensure that all relevant factors are considered and irrelevant ones ignored. This model combines the aim of achieving the best results from the point of view of the aims of the decision-maker, whilst at the same time it is recognized that considerations of costs must place limits upon the scope of any investigation and hearing prior to a decision being reached.

In applying this efficiency model of procedural fairness to dismissals, the key idea is that thorough procedures avoid costs to employers arising from erroneous dismissals. By dismissing only those workers who are either disruptive to production, seriously incompetent, or genuinely no longer needed, and no others, the employer achieves the most efficient use of his labour force. Erroneous dismissals of satisfactory employees may incur unnecessary costs with respect to search, hiring, and training for firm-specific skills, as well as the possible deleterious effects of the replacement workers being less efficient and a general sense of grievance arising among the workforce which would undermine the authority of management. But against these advantages of ensuring that only efficient dismissals are made should be weighed the administrative burden of a sophisticated disciplinary and selection process which generates the best information available and acts on it carefully.

These efficiency considerations can account well for both the diversity and flexibility of procedural standards. With the governing principle of establishing an efficient procedure at the forefront, the detailed requirements can be adjusted to the precise reason for the dismissal, the administrative structure of the employer, and the likely difficulties of proof of facts and assessment of alternatives. In disciplinary dismissals, for example, the employer would be required to check the fact of the employee's fault, but not to the extent of imposing an exorbitant administrative expense. Similarly, in the context of economic dismissals, the employer would be required to consider whether alternatives to dismissal might be possible, such as redeployment, and whether his selection of particular employees for dismissal will be in the best interests of the business; but the point of such enquiries would be to ensure that the employer reaches the best decision, not to prevent a prompt decision from being reached.

It may appear strange at a superficial level that procedural requirements, which ostensibly are designed to benefit employees, should derive their justification from their benefit to the employer. If the best interests of employers lie in adopting procedures prior to dismissal, then one might have thought that they could safely be left to develop those procedures themselves out of self-interest. To this objection to the efficiency model two observations should be made. In the first place, we should recall that at the time of the inception of the legislation there was public concern that the absence of procedures was creating chaos in industrial relations. Although it was believed that employers would eventually adopt procedures of their own accord, in the public interest it was judged necessary to hasten this process through legislation if at all possible. Secondly, we should remember that these abstract models of procedural fairness are designed to elucidate the conception of fairness which shapes the courts' and tribunals' decisions with respect to the required standards of procedural fairness. It seems entirely possible that this conception of procedural fairness has been developed from a managerial perspective, that is, one which sets procedural requirements by reference to the long-term interests of good management rather than by reference to the interest of workers.

For these reasons we should not be surprised to discover a paternalist and managerialist orientation in the conception of procedural fairness in the law of unfair dismissal. The underlying moral principle, here supporting procedures required by efficiency, is one of maximizing general welfare. The general welfare standard is interpreted primarily as requiring support for the profitability and efficiency of business, though benefits to welfare are increased also by the satisfaction of employees' desire for fair procedures.

At first sight, therefore, this third efficiency model of procedural fairness appears to offer an interpretation of the law which best fits the practice of the tribunal. It provides a general principle applicable to the whole range of dismissals, yet it is also sensitive to the need to accommodate both the diversity and flexibility of procedural standards. In order to examine whether this efficiency model of procedural fairness does indeed supply the best interpretation of legal practice, we must now consider the evidence from the cases.

2. THE SHIFTING COURSE OF THE TRIBUNALS

Even a brief perusal of the tribunals' decisions reveals unfortunately that they have not adopted a consistent approach towards setting standards of procedural fairness. Many commentators have detected divergencies between different courts and tribunals, and changes of emphasis within the same court over a period of time. But the cases do fall into an intelligible pattern when viewed in a historical perspective. This section divides the development of procedural standards chronologically into three broad periods. It should be admitted that one finds traces of all three approaches in each period, so the divisions reflect changes of emphasis rather than decisive breaks with previous practice. Nevertheless, this division into periods permits a clearer appreciation of the details and ramifications of the current legal position.

This job of clarifying the current legal position with respect to standards of procedural fairness serves as a necessary preliminary step to returning to the main focus of our enquiry. In the following section we will be in a position to answer the question, which model of procedural fairness offers the best interpretation of the current practice of the courts and tribunals. I shall argue that it imitates almost precisely the efficiency model of procedural fairness.

SYMBOLIC AFFIRMATION: 1971–1977

Despite the almost complete absence of reference to the procedural dimension of fairness in the original legislation, the courts immediately emphasized the importance of fair procedures. They demanded scrupulous attention to detailed procedural guidelines. For example, the National Industrial Relations Court insisted that not only was a warning necessary, but also that a warning was inadequate unless it stated that the next offence would certainly lead to dismissal.[12] The court maintained that an unfair procedure alone could render a dismissal unfair. Where an employee whose job was as an estimating and planning engineer returned from sick leave only to be presented with a letter of summary dismissal because the employers had discovered certain inadequacies in his work during his absence, the court held the dismissal unfair because the employee had been given no opportunity to rebut the charges of incompetence even though the tribunal concluded that the charges were in fact well founded and were a sufficient reason for dismissal.[13] In another case two employees were summarily dismissed for misconduct during their lunch break and the court affirmed the need for a hearing:

The employees' conduct certainly merited a warning that it must not occur again. It certainly merited censure. It could never justify summary dismissal without opportunity for explanation.[14]

This statement left open the possibility that in cases of very serious misconduct no hearing was necessary, but even this exception was rejected in some cases!

Whatever the circumstances, whatever the employee is alleged to have done, and however serious it may be, it is, in our judgment, always necessary that he should be

---

[12] *Hewittson* v. *Anderton Springs* [1972] IRLR 56 (NIRC).
[13] *Earl* v. *Slater & Wheeler (Airlyne) Ltd.* [1972] ICR 508 (NIRC).
[14] *Shipside (Ruthin) Ltd.* v. *Transport and General Workers' Union* [1973] ICR 503, per Sir John Donaldson at p. 510.

afforded some opportunity of explaining himself to those persons in management who will in the first instance take the decision whether or not he is to be dismissed.[15]

Two motives probably lay behind this emphasis upon procedural standards. One aim was to reduce industrial conflict by encouraging employers to handle dismissals more carefully. Under the governing legislation at that time, the courts were instructed to interpret the law in such a way as to develop and maintain orderly procedures in industry.[16] This was reinforced by the Code of Practice which emphasized the need for formal procedures.[17] Behind the Code and the judgments of the NIRC probably lay the belief that British management needed to become more professional in its handling of personnel issues, which translated into an emphasis upon bureaucratic procedures which permitted all grievances to be aired in line with the Human Relations School of management theory.[18] The employer was required to adopt formal disciplinary procedures on pain of a finding of unfair dismissal.

One suspects also that the emphasis upon procedures was a way of avoiding the more difficult substantive questions of unfairness, which, for the reasons described in Chapter 1 as the problem of juridification, were less easy for the courts to resolve. By determining that a dismissal had been unfair on the ground of a bad procedure, the courts could avoid direct second-guessing of management's substantive disciplinary decisions with a consequent reduction of the threat to managerial prerogative.[19]

Yet despite the importance attached to procedures, the courts were not willing to allow the pursuit of this policy and strategy to undermine the corrective justice basis of the law of unfair dismissal. A way to reconcile these competing considerations was discovered in following a finding of unfairness based upon a defect in procedure by a denial of a compensatory award in cases where an employee was at fault. At this time the sole monetary remedy for unfair dismissal lay in a compensatory award which was supposed to reflect the justice and equity of the case. Where the courts perceived that the employer had good grounds for dismissal, then, despite the finding of unfairness, compensation would be reduced, in some cases to nil. Thus in the case of the planning and estimating engineer, although the employee won his claim for unfair dismissal, he was not entitled to any compensation because the unfairness of the dismissal had caused him no loss since the employers by adopting a different procedure could have dismissed him fairly.[20] Similarly, a failure to consult a worker before making him redundant rendered the dismissal unfair, but since this unfairness had not added to the

---

[15] *Budgen & Co.* v. *Thomas* [1976] ICR 344 (EAT), per Phillips, J., at p. 348.
[16] Industrial Relations Act 1971, s. 1.
[17] Industrial Relations Code of Practice (1972), paras, 130–3.
[18] See K. Stone, 'The Post-War Paradigm in American Labor Law' (1981), 90, *Yale Law Journal*, 1509, at pp. 1566–71.
[19] H. Collins, 'Capitalist Discipline and Corporatist Law' (1982), 11, *ILJ* 78, at p. 88.
[20] *Earl* v. *Slater & Wheeler (Airlyne) Ltd.* [1972] ICR 508 (NIRC).

claimant's loss, he received no compensatory award. As the court observed: 'the purpose of assessing compensation is not to express disapproval of industrial relations policy. It is to compensate for financial loss.'[21]

This rather perplexing practice achieved the result of a symbolic affirmation of importance of procedures whilst preserving the corrective justice principle of unfair dismissal legislation. A wrong had been committed, but since no loss had been caused, there was no need to order compensation.

This approach to procedural fairness received endorsement by the House of Lords at the close of this period in its first decision on the legislation in *Devis & Sons Ltd.* v. *Atkins.*[22] In that case the employers ordered the employee, as manager of an abattoir, to purchase cattle directly from farmers rather than dealers. Following persistent disobedience to this instruction, the employers decided to dismiss him and offer him six weeks' salary in lieu of notice and a further substantial sum as compensation for loss of office. This offer was withdrawn a week after the dismissal when facts came to the knowledge of the employers which indicated that the employee had been guilty of gross misconduct. The Industrial Tribunal found the dismissal unfair because of the lack of sufficient warning of the risk of dismissal, and it further ruled that evidence of misconduct discovered subsequent to dismissal was irrelevant to the question of the fairness of the dismissal. The House of Lords dismissed the employer's appeal, on the prinicple that under the reasonableness test of the legislation the conduct of the employer must be judged by reference to the facts known to him at the time of the dismissal. On those facts, the tribunal was entitled to find that the employer had acted unfairly because of the lack of sufficient warning. Nevertheless, the House of Lords supported the view that the compensatory award should be reduced to nil in order to reflect all the considerations of corrective justice:

the award must be just and equitable in all the circumstances, and it cannot be just and equitable that a sum should be awarded in compensation when in fact the employee has suffered no injustice by being dismissed.[23]

By this device the courts achieved the aim of compelling employers to tighten up on procedures without undermining their perception of the ultimate corrective justice aim of the legislation. Yet at the same time as approving the approach of symbolic affirmation, the House of Lords laid the ground for a dramatic reversal of the policy.

PROCEDURE AS SUBSTANCE: 1977–1986

The second period was triggered by the introduction of the basic award. Under the Employment Protection Act 1975, ss. 73–5, the measure of

---

[21] *Clarkson International Tools Ltd.* v. *Short* [1973] ICR 191 (NIRC), per Sir John Donaldson, at p. 196.
[22] [1977] ICR 662; [1977] AC 931 (HL).   [23] Per Viscount Dilhorne [1977] ICR 679.

compensation for unfair dismissal was increased to include not only the compensatory award but also the basic award, calculated in the same way as a redundancy payment largely on the basis of the length of service. The Labour Government intended that an employee who had been unfairly dismissed should normally receive the basic award as a minimum entitlement, leaving to the courts a discretion over the quantum of the compensatory reward to reflect the degree of fault on the part of the employee. In the event of contributory fault by the employee the basic award could be reduced,[24] but not below a minimum of two weeks' pay.[25] The House of Lords in *Devis & Sons Ltd.* v. *Atkins* expressed alarm at a potential threat posed by the basic award to its conception of corrective justice. Their Lordships observed with horror that they would not in future be able to achieve the same just result of nil compensation in a case like *Devis & Sons Ltd.* v. *Atkins*, because there was no power to reduce the basic award in the light of fault of the employee unknown to the employer at the time of the dismissal. Lord Diplock viewed this situation as a 'veritable rogue's charter'.[26]

The same concern emerged much more significantly in cases where the finding of unfairness rested largely on the employer's failure to follow reasonable procedural steps. Since the basic award could not be reduced even on proof of contributory fault on the part of the employee below the minimum of two weeks' pay, the policy of symbolic affirmation was no longer fully available. Once a tribunal had decided that the dismissal was unfair for bad procedure, then it was bound to award the employee a minimum basic award even if it could reduce the compensatory award to nil. The EAT began to resist this conclusion, suggesting that the tribunal could decide alternatively that the dismissal was fair if the proper procedure would not have made any difference to the result. Thus a failure to consult the employee in a dismissal for redundancy would not necessarily render the dismissal unfair if consultation would not have made the slightest difference.[27] Similarly the Court of Appeal dropped the necessity of a prior warning in cases of misconduct.[28]

With this spectre of corrective injustice before their eyes, the courts and tribunals began to withdraw from the strict insistence upon procedural propriety which marked the first period. A fair procedure ceased to count as an independent requirement for a fair dismissal; it was treated instead as merely one aspect of the whole case. The Court of Appeal decided that the absence of consultation with employees about a proposed business reorganization resulting in major changes in terms and conditions was only one factor

[24] Employment Protection Act 1975, s. 75(7).
[25] Ibid., s. 74(2).
[26] [1977] ICR 672.
[27] *British United Shoe Machinery Co. Ltd.* v. *Clarke* [1978] ICR 70 (EAT).
[28] *Retarded Children's Aid Society Ltd.* v. *Day* [1978] ICR 437 (CA).

to be considered in the general question of fairness, not an independent requirement of fairness.[29] Where the employer had good substantive reasons for a dismissal, having for example caught the employee red-handed stealing company property, the need for procedural steps could be eliminated by trading them off against the strong substantive reasons for dismissal. The more compelling the employer's case based on the employee's fault, the less he or she needed to worry about following any procedural standards. As a result, those cases largely disappeared where the tribunal had found that the dismissal was unfair because of the absence of procedural fairness, despite the employer having a good reason for dismissal.

This phenomenon of substantive considerations overwhelming procedural requirements received a particularly unfortunate expression in *British Labour Pump Co. Ltd.* v. *Byrne*. In this case of alleged dishonesty, the EAT upheld the tribunal's findings that the dismissal was unfair because the employer had failed to investigate the facts in sufficient depth. But in resisting the employer's appeal, the EAT ventured a general test for when bad procedures should not lead to a finding of unfairness:

It seems to us that the right approach is to ask two questions. In the first place, have the employers shown on the balance of probabilities that they would have taken the same course had they held an inquiry, and had they received the information which that inquiry would have produced? Secondly, have the employers shown—the burden is on them—that in the light of the information which they would have had, had they gone through the proper procedure, they would have been behaving reasonably in still deciding to dismiss?[30]

In other words, a dismissal would not be unfair for improper procedure, if the employer could show on a balance of probabilities that such a failure would not have affected the reasonableness of the decision to dismiss. In the context of this case, where the issue was whether the employer's investigation and hearing were sufficient, this test was appropriate, for it demonstrated the inadequacy of the procedure because it had failed to reveal important facts. But when applied across the board to any claim of improper procedure, as the *British Labour Pump* test was quite frequently in such cases as a failure to consult the employee and his or her medical adviser before a dismissal for absence caused by illness,[31] then it tended to reduce procedural requirements to vanishing-point. A poor procedure could only render a dismissal unfair if a correct procedure would have made a difference to the result in the sense that it would then plainly have been unreasonable for the employer to dismiss the employee. This permits the substantive considerations to overwhelm the procedural aspects of the case in all but the rare instance where

[29]   *Hollister* v. *National Farmers' Union* [1979] ICR 542 (CA).
[30]   [1979] ICR 347 (EAT) per Slynn, J., at pp. 353–4.
[31]   *Taylorplan Catering (Scotland) Ltd.* v. *McInally* [1980] IRLR 53 (EAT).

the employer has made a major error in his assessment of the facts which would have been revealed by further inquiry or a hearing.

The demise of the independent importance of procedural standards in this middle period is well illustrated by the decision of the Court of Appeal in *Wass Ltd.* v. *Binns*.[32] The employee had worked as a heavy goods vehicle driver for the employer for thirteen years. One Monday morning the manager asked him to check the roadworthiness of a small lorry because he might have to take it to London. The employee erupted, shouting that 'There is no way I am taking that f——ing four wheeler to London', and he stormed off giving what was described as a 'V' sign Harvey Smith style. Later that day the employee visited his doctor who certified that he was unfit to work owing to exhaustion and a rib injury. In the meantime the employers ignored their own disciplinary code which provided for warnings and a hearing and summarily dismissed the employee. Despite the complete absence of any procedural steps, the Industrial Tribunal held that the dismissal was fair, relying on the approach in *British Labour Pump Co. Ltd.* v. *Byrne*. The absence of the hearing had not ultimately prejudiced the employee, for even if the employer had discovered the employee's poor health, it would still have been reasonable for the employer to dismiss him for his misconduct. The Court of Appeal, by a majority, declined to interfere with this decision. The implication of this case is that where an employer has good substantive reasons for dismissal, then procedural steps may be ignored with impunity, quite the opposite message to that conveyed by the courts in the early years of the legislation. What happened in effect was that procedural considerations were treated as a subsidiary element of substance rather then enjoying independent weight as necessary elements of fairness. In short, the aim of corrective justice finally overwhelmed the original concern for promoting fair procedures.

THE REVIVAL OF PROCEDURAL STANDARDS: 1986 ONWARDS

The third period had its origins in part in changes to the basic award introduced by the Employment Act 1980.[33] The courts were empowered to reduce the basic award in the light of any conduct of the employee prior to the dismissal. This removed the spectre foreseen in *Devis & Sons Ltd.* v. *Atkins* of an employee winning a substantial basic award even though he had been secretly guilty of grave misconduct. In addition, the Employment Act 1980 abolished the minimum basic award of two weeks' pay.[34] This made it possible once again to reach a decision that the dismissal was procedurally unfair but decline to award any compensation.

---

[32] [1982] ICR 486; [1982] IRLR 283 (CA).
[33] S. 9(4), substituting new s. 73(7B) EPCA 1978; H. McLean, 'Fair Procedure and Contribution' (1986), 15, *ILJ* 205.
[34] S. 9(5).

Shortly afterwards, the EAT under the Presidency of Browne-Wilkinson, J., began to reassert the importance of fair procedures,[35] though this received little support from the Court of Appeal. The turning-point came when in two cases the House of Lords reaffirmed their earlier approach in *Devis & Sons Ltd.* v. *Atkins* and restored the independent importance of procedural standards to the test of fairness. In *West Midlands Co-operative Society Ltd.* v. *Tipton*,[36] the House of Lords upheld a decision of an Industrial Tribunal that a dismissal could be unfair on the ground that an employer had refused to allow an employee to exercise his right under the company's disciplinary procedures to appeal against his dismissal for absenteeism. More decisively, in *Polkey* v. *A. E. Dayton Services Ltd.* the House of Lords affirmed that an economic dismissal without warning or consultation could be unfair even though such procedural steps might not have made any difference to the outcome.[37] Yet this revival of procedural standards did not accomplish a complete return to an insistence on procedural rectitude in accordance with tribunal practice in the early years.[38]

Whilst reasserting the importance of procedural standards, the House of Lords in *Polkey* v. *A. E. Dayton Services Ltd.* made it clear that these standards should not be regarded as mandatory. When applying the range of reasonable responses test under EPCA 1978, s. 57(3), courts and tribunals should assume that a reasonable employer would normally carry out a fair procedure according to the ACAS Code of Practice. As Lord Bridge noted in his remarks quoted at the beginning of this chapter, this entails, in disciplinary dismissals, giving an employee an opportunity to give an explanation and to rebut charges, and, in economic dismissals, an opportunity for consultation. But a failure to comply with these normal procedures will not necessarily result in a finding of unfair dismissal. Lord Mackay, LC, states that:

If the employer could reasonably have concluded in the light of the circumstances known to him at the time of the dismissal that consultation or warning would be utterly useless he might well act reasonably even if he did not observe the provisions of the code. Failure to observe the requirement of the code relating to consultation or warning will not necessarily render a dismissal unfair.[39]

This decision overrules the line of authorities originating in *British Labour Pump Co. Ltd.* v. *Byrne.* The employer who fails to follow a fair procedure can avoid a finding of unfairness, not when the result would have been the same in any case on a balance of probabilities as under the test in *British*

---

[35] e.g. *Williams* v. *Compair Maxam Ltd.* [1982] ICR 156 (EAT); *Sillifant* v. *Powell Duffryn Timber Ltd.* [1983] IRLR 91 (EAT); *Freud* v. *Bentalls Ltd.* [1983] ICR 77 (EAT).
[36] [1986] ICR 192; [1986] AC 536 (HL).
[37] [1988] ICR 142 (HL); R. W. Rideout, 'Clogging the Labour Pump: Will "Equity" Find Another Outlet?' (1988), 17, *ILJ* 41.
[38] H. Collins, 'Procedural Fairness after Polkey' (1990), 19, *ILJ* 39.
[39] [1988] ICR 142 (HL) per Lord Mackay, at p. 153.

Labour Pump Co. Ltd. v. *Byrne*, but where on the facts known to the employer at the time of the dismissal he or she could reasonably conclude that no explanation or consultation could suffice either to mitigate or alter his or her decision. The House of Lords accepted the argument that to permit an employer to rely upon hypothetical events which would have taken place after the dismissal would be inconsistent with the principle in *Devis & Sons Ltd.* v. *Atkins* that the fairness of the dismissal should be judged on the basis of facts known to the employer at the time of the dismissal alone.

More importantly, this decision stiffens the procedural requirements compared to the second period, but it does not restore them to the almost mandatory level of the first period. The House of Lords envisages a modification of procedural requirements in abnormal cases. These exceptional cases are not defined by reference to the gravity of the employee's misconduct, for that would be to permit substantive considerations to overwhelm procedural fairness. Instead, the exceptional cases comprise those where procedural steps are unnecessary because employers reasonably suppose that they already have all the facts of the matter before them. The duty of employers consists not in running through a fair procedure, but in taking all reasonable steps to ensure that they have ascertained all the relevant facts including mitigating circumstances. In this vein in *West Midlands Co-operative Society* v. *Tipton*, Lord Bridge pointed out that the employer was not under a strict duty to permit the employee's appeal under the domestic disciplinary procedure in every case.

There may, of course, be cases where, on the undisputed facts, the dismissal was inevitable, as for example where a trusted employee, before dismissal, was charged with, and pleaded guilty to, a serious offence of dishonesty committed in the course of his employment. In such a case the employer could reasonably refuse to entertain a domestic appeal on the ground that it could not affect the outcome.[40]

The statement of Lord Mackay, LC, in *Polkey* v. *A. E. Dayton Services Ltd.* quoted above is to the same effect. Relaxation of procedural requirements is permissible where the employer reasonably concludes that further inquiry would be 'futile'.[41]

The governing principles on procedural fairness under the current law thus take their starting-point from the range of reasonable responses test. The employer must act at all times within the range of reasonable responses to the events, and in the normal case this means that an employer should follow the steps set out in the ACAS Code of Practice. The extent of the procedural steps necessary before a dismissal can be fair depends upon whether a reasonable employer would consider that his or her knowledge of the facts of the matter were sufficient so that further procedural steps would serve no useful purpose. Following this approach in *Mathewson* v. *R. B.*

[40] [1986] ICR 192, at p. 204.
[41] Per Lord Bridge [1988] ICR 142, at p. 163.

Wilson Dental Laboratory,[42] the case concerning dismissal for arrest for possession of cannabis during a lunch break considered in Chapter 1, the EAT had no trouble in upholding the tribunal's decision that the dismissal was fair despite the absence of warning or a hearing, because the employee had admitted his offence so the employer had reasonable grounds for deciding that further inquiries would serve no useful purpose. This was not a case of substantive considerations overwhelming the standards of procedural fairness, for the tribunal regarded the dismissal for this minor offence outside work as harsh. Rather the range of reasonable responses test operated simultaneously to reduce both substantive and procedural standards. The duty upon the employer to follow fair procedures diminishes upon a sliding scale according to the likelihood that he or she can make the correct decision without further procedural steps.

Despite this relaxation of procedure compared to the first period, however, the House of Lords in *Polkey* v. *A. E. Dayton Services Ltd.* preserved the doctrine that it is possible to reduce the measure of compensation to nil where the facts before the tribunal reveal that the employee suffered no injustice, because the employer would have been entitled to dismiss him or her fairly if he or she had known the true facts of the case. The reduction in compensation should be assessed according to the likelihood that the employee would have kept his or her job if the true facts had been known.[43]

3. AN INTERPRETATION OF PROCEDURAL FAIRNESS

To which of the three models of procedural justice described above does the current practice of the courts and tribunals most closely conform?

The practice deliberately avoids the strict attention to procedure envisaged by the theory of respect for the dignity of the individual. On this model the employee should be entitled to the rules of natural justice without exception. No doubt this strict model rarely applies in its entirety to public authorities outside the criminal process, but here I seek to test the strength of this model as an interpretation of the current practice of the tribunals, not to examine at this stage whether the adoption of the more flexible approach to the rules of natural justice used by the courts in the context of judicial review of administrative bodies would provide superior protection to that currently enjoyed by employees under the law of unfair dismissal.

The reluctance of the tribunals to adopt the strict rules of natural justice demanded by respect for the dignity of individuals is revealed in many of their decisions. It is frequently stated that considerations of natural justice

---

[42] [1988] IRLR 512 (EAT).
[43] Brown Wilkinson, J., *Sillifant* v. *Powell Duffryn Timber Ltd.* [1983] IRLR 91 (EAT); approved in *Polkey* v. *A. E. Dayton Services Ltd.* [1988] ICR 142 (HL) by Lord Bridge.

are relevant to the question of whether the employer acted reasonably, but a failure to comply with those principles does not necessarily render the dismissal unfair, and a tribunal's failure to apply those principles does not amount to an error of law. Thus a failure by an employer to give an employee an opportunity to cross-examine witnesses before a disciplinary hearing is not unfair,[44] though of course such a failure in the context of a criminal trial would be impermissable.

Nor have the courts insisted that any hearing should be conducted by an impartial tribunal or arbitrator before a fair dismissal can be carried out. Although the EAT has occasionally revealed a disposition towards applying the principles of natural justice to disciplinary hearings,[45] the predominant view, recently expressed by the Court of Appeal in *Slater* v. *Leicestershire Health Authority*,[46] is that a dismissal can still be reasonable where the person dismissing had effectively been also principal investigator, prosecutor, and judge, even though this violated ideals of impartiality. Here the manager investigated an allegation by another employee that a nurse had slapped an old person twice on the buttocks and had seen marks consistent with this, though it was also compatible with the appellant's account that he had had to use reasonable force to restrain a difficult patient. The same manager then held a hearing which led to dismissal. The Court of Appeal held that the procedure was fair despite a violation of the requirement of natural justice that the hearing should be conducted by an impartial body. This principle of natural justice was not an independent ground for attacking a dismissal decision, but only part of the general reasonableness requirement.

This unwillingness to implement the principles of natural justice for disciplinary dismissals seems to be grounded in efficiency considerations. It is sometimes justified on the ground that, for small employers, it may not be practicable to find management who are not implicated in the decision to dismiss, though the problem could be overcome by the use of private arbitration. The real reason for the denial of the requirement of an impartial hearing in employment seems to be the likely cost to the employer.

It is very important that internal appeals procedures run by commercial companies (which usually involve a consideration of the decision to dismiss by one person in line management by his superior) should not be cramped by legal requirements imposing impossible burdens on companies in the conduct of their personnel affairs.[47]

---

[44] *Ulsterbus Ltd.* v. *Henderson* [1989] IRLR 251 (CA N. Ireland).

[45] *Moyes* v. *Hylton Castle Working Men's Social Club and Institute Ltd.* [1986] IRLR 482 (EAT): (2 members of disciplinary committee were also the main witnesses of charges of sexual harassment; EAT allows employee's appeal on ground that apparently biased committee rendered dismissal procedurally unfair); *Whitbread & Co. PLC* v. *Mills* [1988] ICR 776 (EAT): (applies doctrine in *Calvin* v. *Carr* [1980] AC 574 (PC) that breaches of natural justice at original hearing can only be cured by a complete rehearing).

[46] [1989] IRLR 16 (CA).

[47] *Rowe* v. *Radio Rentals* [1982] IRLR 177 (EAT).

These considerations of cost run directly counter to the justification for strict procedural standards based upon the individual's right to dignity. The courts' refusal to be bound by the principles of natural justice, even in cases of disciplinary dismissals where they are most apt, indicates that this model cannot provide a useful interpretative principle of their practice.

Nor does the second model of democratic participation throw much light on the practice of the tribunals. The courts have placed little importance on the participation of workers or their representatives in disciplinary matters. A dismissal may be fair even though it is made in breach of a collectively agreed procedure which provides a role for union officials.[48] It is only in cases of economic dismissals that one discovers signs of the model of democratic participation playing a part in determining the standards of procedural fairness.

Statutes guide the courts towards the application of the democratic participation model to economic dismissals in two instances. EPCA 1978, s. 59(b), renders dismissals for redundancy unfair if the employer fails to comply with a customary arrangement or a collectively agreed procedure in the absence of special reasons justifying a departure from those arrangements.[49] This section has been interpreted in a manner inconsistent with the democratic model, however, for it does not include procedural agreements but solely substantive criteria for choosing between employees for dismissal.[50] The courts view the intention of the section as one of protecting the individual's seniority rights in the event of redundancy rather than one of promoting consultation and collective bargaining with respect to redundancies.

Secondly, the provisions on consultation with recognized trade unions contained in Employment Protection Act 1975, Part IV, though not directly connected to the law of unfair dismissal, set a standard for good industrial practice which appears to be reflected in the courts' views on the nature of fair procedures in the context of collective redundancies. In *Williams* v. *Compair Maxam Ltd.*,[51] having recited the statute in full as evidence of good industrial practice, Browne-Wilkinson, J., suggested, as guidelines for procedural standards in dismissals for redundancy, two principles reflecting the democratic model:

1. The employer will seek to give as much warning as possible of impending redundancies so as to enable the union and employees who may be affected to take early steps to inform themselves of the relevant facts, consider possible alternative

---

[48] *Bailey* v. *BP Oil Kent Refinery Ltd.* [1980] ICR 642 (CA) (failure to notify union official in breach of grievance procedure not unfair). This was a decision during the second period described above, but its attitude towards collective agreements persists to this day: see Ch. 3.

[49] See Cyril Grunfeld, *The Law of Redundancy* (3rd edn., London, 1989), at pp. 303–10.

[50] *McDowell* v. *Eastern British Road Services Ltd.* [1981] IRLR 482 (EAT).

[51] [1982] ICR 156 (EAT), approved in *Polkey* v. *A. E. Dayton Services Ltd.* [1987] ICR 301 (CA).

solutions and, if necessary, find alternative employment in the undertaking or elsewhere.

2. The employer will consult the union as to the best means by which the desired management result can be achieved fairly and with as little hardship to the employees as possible. In particular, the employer will seek to agree with the union the criteria to be applied in selecting the employees to be made redundant. When a selection has been made, the employer will consider with the union whether the selection has been made in accordance with those criteria.[52]

These principles reflect the spirit of the legislation on collective redundancies, though their emphasis upon agreement with the union approximates even more closely to the democratic participation model of procedural fairness. But it has to be said that few tribunals and courts have been prepared to adopt the democratic model to the extent envisaged by Browne-Wilkinson, J. His principles of procedural fairness have been demoted to the status of guidelines for tribunals which may occasionally be relevant and helpful in indicating the standards of good industrial practice.

At bottom the democratic participation model runs counter to the courts' perception of the legislation as a matter of corrective justice between employer and individual employee. Although the employer's failure to respect collectively agreed procedures may exemplify poor industrial relations practices, the job of the tribunals is to ensure that justice is done to employees, not to control the manner in which management handles its relations with organizations of workers. Outside the narrow field of collective redundancies, where statute provides a modest lead towards democratic participation, the emphasis of the interpretation of the standards of procedural fairness consistently reflects a concern for the treatment of the individual employee, not the elements of some ideal of industrial democracy.

The third model of procedural justice based upon efficient managerial decisions accords much more closely with the practice of the tribunals.[53] Under this model the aim is to require procedures which will produce efficient decisions for management. The required procedures will often involve investigations and hearings. The degree of investigation must be such that it amounts to reasonable inquiries appropriate to the circumstances.[54] Employers may also have to conduct hearings in disciplinary matters to ensure that they reach a conclusion based upon a correct impression of the circumstances, including mitigating factors. This normally requires that 'someone accused should know the case to be met; should hear or be told the important parts of the evidence in support of that case; should have an opportunity to criticise or dispute that evidence and to adduce his

---

[52] [1982] ICR 156, at p. 162.

[53] For a similar interpretation, see S. Fredman and S. Lee, 'Natural Justice for Employees: The Unacceptable Faith of Proceduralism' (1986), 15, *ILJ* 15, at p. 29.

[54] *Weddel (W.) & Co. Ltd.* v. *Tepper* [1980] ICR 286 (CA); *British Home Stores Ltd.* v. *Burchell* [1980] ICR 303 (EAT) (Note).

own evidence and argue his case'.[55] Where the facts are clear, however, or the offence so serious that mitigating factors could not change the decision, then it would be a waste of expenditure to conduct an investigation or a hearing: so the law does not require one. In addition, the nature of the required procedure must reflect the cost considerations pertaining to person-nel management, so that cumbersome and expensive procedures which comply with principles of natural justice need not be adopted.

In economic dismissals, the point of the procedure of consultation is to ensure that the employer is making a wise selection of employees to be made redundant and jobs to be eliminated. The process may also reveal an opportunity for the employer to redeploy the worker elsewhere in the business, thereby retaining the benefits of a trained employee and fostering loyalty in the workforce. In short, the reasonable employer is the efficient employer, the one who adopts procedures conducive to cost effective manpower management. It is this subtle combination of the costs and benefits of dismissal procedures which best accounts for the diversity and flexibility of the courts' and tribunals' standards of procedural fairness.

The match between the efficiency model and the practice of the tribunals is not exact. As well as the decisions referred to above which give intimations of support for the other two models, the interpretation of procedural fairness adopted by the courts and tribunals probably undervalues the element of carefulness in reaching decisions which is as important in the context of efficiency as the attention to reliable fact-finding mechanisms. The inherent flexibility of the approach endorsed in *Polkey* v. *A. E. Dayton Services Ltd.* springs largely from its emphasis upon investigation of the facts at the expense of demanding as well that in every case the employer should demonstrate that he has followed a procedure which ensures that all relevant considerations have been taken into account and irrelevant ones have been excluded.

This missing element of the efficiency model may be illustrated by *Mathewson* v. *R. B. Wilson Dental Laboratory*.[56] The tribunal recognized that, by the employee's admission that his arrest for possession of cannabis had caused him to return to work from lunch an hour late, the principal facts of the matter were put beyond dispute. But by concluding that the procedure was not unfair, the Industrial Tribunal omitted to realize the importance under the efficiency model of procedural fairness of requiring the employer nevertheless to conduct a hearing to check that all relevant considerations were being considered and that irrelevant ones were not influencing the decision. In this case the mitigating factors that the employee had never taken drugs to work and that there was no evidence that his work had been affected in any way should have been considered as strong reasons

---

[55] *Spink* v. *Express Foods Group Ltd.* [1990] IRLR 320 (EAT) per Wood, J., at p. 323.
[56] [1988] IRLR 512 (EAT).

for doubting whether the drugs offence in itself sufficed to justify dismissal. Although the Industrial Tribunal in permitting the absence of such a hearing was probably following the lead of the House of Lords accurately, the decision shows how the practice of the courts does not fit precisely the efficiency model of procedural fairness.

But we can turn this dissonance into an opportunity for constructing the best interpretation of the concept of procedural fairness. Because the efficiency model fits so closely the practice of the courts and tribunals, it can be adopted as the underlying moral principle to guide an interpretation which seeks to present the practice in its best light. We should stress those decisions which embody both dimensions of the efficiency model, both its attention to rectitude in fact-finding and its requirement of carefulness or rationality in reaching conclusions on the facts. Support for this interpretation can be found from another reading of *Polkey* v. *A. E. Dayton Services Ltd.*, one which stresses the positive statements of principle quoted at the beginning of this chapter, such as Lord Bridge's view that, 'in the case of misconduct, the employer will normally not act reasonably unless he investigates the complaint of misconduct fully and fairly and hears whatever the employee wishes to say in his defence or in explanation or mitigation'[57] This interpretation then presents the standards of procedural fairness in their best light by treating any derogation from such a principle, for the reasons of diversity and flexibility, as being unsound unless it can be justified both by reference to the completeness of the factual inquiry and the fullness and rationality of the assessment of the facts by the employer.

If this is indeed the best interpretation which can be placed upon the practice of the courts and tribunals with respect to the standards of procedural fairness, then I think that we have reason to doubt whether this approach fully accords with the aims of the legislation. In Chapter 1 we concluded that one of the principal reasons for the enactment of the unfair dismissal legislation was to improve respect for the dignity of the individual in the workplace. This justification for the legislation obviously fits much more closely the first model of procedural fairness which insists upon strict standards of natural justice. It is possible, of course, as we noted in the context of the interpretation of the standards of substantive fairness in the previous chapter, that the standards of fairness in their application to particular cases will be influenced by additional moral principles and pragmatic considerations. But what seems to have happened in the context of procedural fairness is that initially the tribunals permitted the moral principle of dignity to provide the underlying moral vision for their interpretation of the legislation, even though the concern for procedure had pragmatic origins in the concern for the strike problem and the desire to avoid a major threat to the autonomy of managerial disciplinary decisions.

[57] [1988] ICR 142 (HL) at pp. 162–3.

Later on, however, considerations of efficiency were permitted to eviscerate this aim of the legislation until they amounted to a rival moral vision which took its place as the foundation.

4. COMMON LAW IN TRANSITION

The law of unfair dismissal was enacted to reform the common law of dismissal. The common law imposed no independent requirement of fair disciplinary procedures. The claim for wrongful dismissal insisted upon damages for breach of the terms of the contract of employment, and it was assumed that neither the express nor the implied terms of the agreement contained a contractual right to a fair procedure. From this perspective the law of unfair dismissal achieved a considerable advance in promoting fair disciplinary procedures in the workplace. But since the inception of the legislation the common law has evolved in two directions which could significantly improve an employee's legal rights to procedural justice.

A crucial development in the remedies afforded by private law must be set against a new industrial relations background and altered contracting practices. The advent of the law of unfair dismissal with its threat of compensation for procedurally unfair dismissals compelled employers to reconsider whether dismissal procedures devised in accordance with the ACAS Code of Practice on Disciplinary Procedures might prove to their economic advantage for they would reduce the risk of awards of compensation. There is considerable evidence, to be examined in greater detail in Chapter 8, which supports the view that the vast majority of employers quickly instituted dismissal procedures in each workplace, either unilaterally or through collective agreement. Many of these disciplinary procedures appeared to be incorporated into the individual contracts of employment, either by express reference in the particulars of employment issued under the statutory duty to provide a statement,[58] or by implication from the custom of the workplace. These alterations in the terms of the contract of employment to include dismissal procedures then raised the question whether or not the new procedural terms might be enforceable under the ordinary law of contract.

The obstacle to such claims lay primarily in the weak remedy for breaches of the contract of employment. If the employee could merely claim a small level of damages for breach of this term of the contract, then there would be little financial incentive for employers to abide by them aside from the need to conform in order to avoid paying compensation for unfair dismissal. But if the employee could win an injunction from a court, which in effect would require the employer to carry out the procedure on pain of fines, sequestration, and imprisonment for contempt of court, then the common law would

---

[58] EPCA 1978, s. 1.

offer a new and substantial opportunity for employees to insist upon fair procedures. In short, although the statutory remedies for the procedural standards required by the law of unfair dismissal turned out to be largely illusory, especially during the second period described above, the award of an injunction at common law would in effect enforce those standards strictly in a different forum and the employee could gain the benefit of procedural justice by other means. When, shortly before the implementation of the law of unfair dismissal in 1971, the Court of Appeal in *Hill* v. *C. A. Parsons & Co. Ltd.*[59] accepted that in some cases at least an employee might win an injunction to enforce the contract of employment, the stage was set for a rapid expansion of a new direction for the establishment of procedural justice in the workplace. The Court of Appeal declared that the established rules for the award of injunctions had to be reconsidered in the light of new social values.

Over the last two decades there has been a marked trend towards shielding the employee, where practicable, from undue hardships he may suffer at the hands of those who may have power over his livelihood—employers and trade unions. So far has this now progressed and such is the security granted to an employee under the Industrial Relations Act 1971 that some have suggested that he may now be said to acquire something akin to a property in his employment. It surely is then for the courts to review and where appropriate to modify, if that becomes necessary, their rules of practice in relation to the exercise of a discretion such as we today have to consider—so that its practice conforms to the realities of the day.[60]

At about the same time, the assumption that the common law did not require employers to follow fair procedures for dismissal of employees also took a knock. From the decision of the House of Lords in *Ridge* v. *Baldwin*,[61] it was clear that certain workers, in that case a Chief Constable of Police, though not all employees, could succeed in having a dismissal declared null and void for breach of the principles of natural justice under public law. Although the House of Lords insisted that ordinary employees were not entitled to the protection of the principles of natural justice, they left the scope of public law and its application to employees rather obscure. This encouraged some employees to seek the public law prerogative remedies in the hope of extending the application of the principles of natural justice to a broader range of employment. A public law claim therefore offered the 'glittering prize'[62] of reinstatement pending the adoption of procedures complying with the principles of natural justice, not only a stricter standard

---

[59] [1972] 1 Ch 305 (CA).

[60] [1972] 1 Ch 305, per Sachs, LJ., at p. 321.

[61] [1964] AC 40 (HL).

[62] J. Beatson and M. Freedland, 'The Contract of Employment: The Role of Public Law' (1983), 12, *ILJ* 43.

of procedural fairness than that offered by the law of unfair dismissal, but also a stronger remedy.[63]

The fundamental reason for the attraction of these new remedies for employees derives from their basis in a moral vision which accords with the model of procedural justice grounded in the right to dignity. The public law jurisdiction endorses the principles of natural justice because of its concern to protect the dignity of the individual against encroachment by the State. The private law jurisdiction also finds its vision in respect for the dignity of the individual though in a more attenuated way. By insisting upon perform-ance of contractual agreements, the courts respect the right of the contracting parties to determine the content of their relationship and to make it binding upon them. Although the main emphasis in the enforcement of contracts lies in promoting and respecting the autonomy of the parties to the contract, this freedom of contract also respects the dignity of individuals to settle their own economic affairs for themselves.

Both public law and private law jurisdictions share important implications for procedural justice in the workplace. They affect the employer's decision with respect to the implementation and scope of a dismissals procedure. To the extent that these remedies are available, they offer many employees a better chance to enjoy the benefit of procedural standards which more closely approximate to those found in the model derived from the right to dignity. But the availability of these remedies turns on complex points of law of civil procedure as well as subtle principles for the exercise of judicial discretion, so we should now turn to the details of these two avenues of redress to discover what hope they may realistically offer to employees of securing procedural justice.

PUBLIC LAW

The principal advantage of a remedy in public law springs from its stricter adherence to the rules of natural justice. Although judicial review of public authorities does not require strict compliance to the ideal model described at the beginning of this chapter, derogations from the rules requires ample justification. Instead of the rules of natural justice being regarded as merely a point of reference which may be ignored and must not be slavishly followed as in the case of the unfair dismissal jurisdiction, once public law principles

---

[63] For other advantages of public law procedures, see M. Stokes, 'Public Law Remedies for Dismissal' (1985), 14, *ILJ* 117, at pp. 120–1; H. Carty, 'Dismissed Employees: The Search for a More Effective Range of Remedies' (1989), 52, *Modern Law Review*, 449. The prerogative remedies are ultimately discretionary, which creates the possibility that the court will avoid an order which in effect compels reinstatement when this appears impracticable, e.g. *Chief Constable of the North Wales Police* v. *Evans* [1982] 3 All ER 141 (HL) (declaration issued, but no order of *mandamus*). There is a clear risk that in the exercise of discretion the courts will be unwilling to challenge managerial disciplinary authority too directly, thereby substantially weakening the attraction of the public law remedy, a risk considered in greater detail in Ch. 7.

apply to a case then the rules must be followed unless a departure creates no risk of unfairness and no possible perception of unfairness.[64]

It is sometimes suggested that in judicial review of public authorities the courts subject natural justice to a test of futility, so that if a fair procedure would have made no difference, then there is no breach of natural justice.[65] If this view of public law were correct, it would undermine substantially the difference between the standards of procedural fairness in the law of unfair dismissal and those employed in judicial review of public authorities. Although such a doctrine has occasionally been approved by the courts,[66] it seems out of line with the 'weight of authority',[67] and even in the context of dismissal from employment it has been consistently rejected by the House of Lords.[68] It seems better to conclude, therefore, that the public law jurisdiction offers an employee a much better chance to be able to insist upon strict observance of the rules of natural justice.

To gain this advantage, however, the employee must demonstrate not only that he or she is entitled to the application of the principles of natural justice, but also that his or her claim falls under the procedure for judicial review contained in Order 53 of the Rules of the Supreme Court. To fall within this jurisdiction, it is neither necessary nor sufficient that the employee be employed by the State. How then do the courts decide when to apply the principles of natural justice through administrative law to the termination of employment?

The history of the case-law reveals considerable confusion over the appropriate test.[69] The courts have not always separated clearly the distinct issues of jurisdiction and entitlement to natural justice. Instead they have proffered three inconsistent tests for the application of natural justice to dismissals which elide these two issues. In *Ridge* v. *Baldwin*,[70] the House of Lords excluded ordinary employees from bringing claims for natural justice, but permitted such claims from 'office holders' who benefit from statutory protection of the tenure of their jobs. A completely different approach emerged in *Stevenson* v. *United Road Transport Union*,[71] where the Court of Appeal linked the application of natural justice to any exercise of a discretionary power which was conditional on the establishment of certain

---

[64] R. v. *Chief Constable of Thames Valley Police, ex parte Cotton* [1990] IRLR 344 (CA).

[65] S. Fredman and S. Lee, 'Natural Justice for Employees: The Unacceptable Faith of Proceduralism' (1986), 15, *ILJ* 15.

[66] *Cinnamond* v. *British Airports Authority* [1980] 1 WLR 582 (CA); *Glynn* v. *Keele University* [1971] 1 WLR 487 (CA); *Malloch* v. *Aberdeen Corporation* [1971] 1 WLR 1578 (HL), at pp. 1595, 1600.

[67] P. P. Craig, *Administrative Law* (2nd edn., London, 1989), at p. 213.

[68] *Chief Constable of North Wales Police* v. *Evans* [1982] 1 WLR 1155, 1160–1, 1174–5; and the majority of the House of Lords in *Malloch* v. *Aberdeen Corporation* [1971] 1 WLR 1578.

[69] B. A. Walsh, 'Judicial Review of Dismissal from Employment: Coherence or Confusion?' (1989), *Public Law*, 131.

[70] [1964] AC 40 (HL).

[71] [1977] ICR 893 (CA).

facts. The Court of Appeal subsequently revised its approach in *R*. v. *East Berkshire Area Health Authority, ex parte Walsh*,[72] by making the public law action contingent on the nature of the right being claimed: if the employee's claim is essentially one for breach of contract then private law applies, but if the claim concerns the exercise of a statutory power, then public law can be used.

None of these approaches establishes clear limits to the public law jurisdiction, because they fail to disentangle the question of jurisdiction from the issue of entitlement to the principles of natural justice. Under the first approach, the distinction between 'office holders' and employees is opaque, and the idea of statutory protection of tenure is sufficiently vague that it may extend to any case where statute establishes dismissal procedures, which is of course true for any workers covered by the unfair dismissal legislation. The term 'office holder' is trying to resolve both the jurisdictional question and the issue of entitlement to natural justice in one fell swoop, but such an uncertain concept cannot perform that dual task satisfactorily. The second approach overlooks the jurisdictional issue entirely, so unless the public law jurisdiction applies to all workers, it would have to be restricted in some way.

The third test attempts to resolve both issues by drawing an untenable and arbitrary distinction relating to the essential nature of the cause of action. In *R*. v. *East Berkshire Area Health Authority, ex parte Walsh*, the employee, a senior nurse in the National Health Service, claimed that he had been dismissed without an opportunity of being heard under the disciplinary procedure laid down in regulations by the Secretary of State. The Court of Appeal interpreted this claim not as one for breach of natural justice, but rather as one alleging breach of the terms of the contract of employment which incorporated the disciplinary procedure, a matter for the private law of contract. Reliance upon such a distinction will produce arbitrary results, for whether or not such procedures are incorporated into a contract of employment depends upon historical accident,[73] and the puzzling issue of whether some employees of the State have contracts at all.[74] But, more importantly, this approach surely conceals instrumental reasoning, for in truth Mr Walsh's claim had no essential nature except that he believed he had been unfairly treated. The conceptual classification of his claim by the court did not depend upon its essential nature, but on the important potential consequences of classification for the extension of principles of natural justice to state employees.

---

[72] [1984] ICR 743 (CA).

[73] S. Fredman and G. S. Morris, *The State as Employer* (London, 1989), at pp. 268–9, pointing out that equivalent procedures for prison officers, fire service, and police are not incorporated into contracts.

[74] See *R*. v. *Civil Service Appeal Board, ex parte Bruce* [1988] 3 All ER 686 (DC); *McLaren* v. *Home Office* [1990] IRLR 338 (CA).

This instrumental reasoning brings out one common theme in all these approaches to determining the limits of the public law jurisdiction. The courts seek to limit the application of the principles of natural justice to a small category of dismissals. They have resisted strongly any attempt to use the public law jurisdiction to introduce the principles of natural justice across the board in employment relations. Underlying this resistance is surely the assumption that the right to dignity which the State must respect in its dealings with citizens should have no application to the economic relations of the labour market. In the absence of the possibility of adjusting the principles of natural justice to accord with the favoured efficiency conception of procedural fairness in employment relations, the courts are compelled by this ideology to reject the public law jurisdiction entirely. For this reason, few employees can expect to succeed in public law claims for breach of natural justice in dismissals.

Recent decisions of the Court of Appeal, however, have separated more clearly the two issues of public law jurisdiction and the substantive entitlement to natural justice. According to Woolf, LJ, in *McLaren* v. *Home Office*,[75] jurisdiction under Order 53 over dismissals in breach of natural justice should be limited to two types of case. The first concerns dismissals of individuals under machinery established by statute (or royal prerogative) which not only provides a tribunal with the power to dismiss but also specifies the conditions under which this power of dismissal may be exercised. Judicial review of such tribunals' decisions will be available in principle to ensure that they remain within the law governing their powers and the conditions for its exercise. A right to natural justice before such tribunals will normally be implied as a matter of course. The second type of case concerns broad policy decisions of public authorities which may be reviewed for their fairness and rationality. Where the policy decision affects individual employees, as, for example, a change in the terms and conditions of employment,[76] or dismissals for redundancy,[77] then those employees may bring a claim under the public law jurisdiction for judicial review of the fairness and rationality of the policy decision. A breach of natural justice may render such a decision unfair, as in *R.* v. *Secretary of State for Foreign and Commonwealth Affairs, ex parte The Council of Civil Service Unions*.[78] Here the House of Lords decided that the Minister for the Civil Service would have been in breach of the rules of natural justice, when she varied the terms and conditions of staff so that they would no longer be permitted

---

[75] [1990] IRLR 338 (CA), at p. 342; see M. R. Freedland, 'The Emerging Law of Public Employment' (1990), 19, *ILJ* 199.

[76] *R.* v. *Hertfordshire County Council, ex parte NUPE* [1985] IRLR 258 (CA).

[77] *R.* v. *Liverpool City Council, ex parte Ferguson* (*The Times*, 20 Nov. 1985) (declaration that notices of termination were *ultra vires* and void for illegality), noted G. S. Morris, 'Employment Rights and Public Law Remedies' (1986), 15, *ILJ* 194; *R.* v. *Hillingdon Authority, ex parte Goodwin* [1982] ICR 800 (QB).

[78] [1985] IRLR 28 (HL).

to be members of trade unions, but for the fact that their legitimate expectation of prior consultation was overriden in this particular instance because of evidence that consultation might have posed a threat to national security.

Even if an employee's claim for judicial review fits into either of these two categories, however, the public law jurisdiction may still be denied if the employee enjoys adequate remedies for his or her complaint through private law or under the statutory law of unfair dismissal. At this stage the court examines the precise nature of the applicant's claim, and if he or she could proceed to have his or her precise claim heard by way of an action for breach of contract in private law, as in *R.* v. *East Berkshire Health Authority, ex parte Walsh*, then the court will deny public law jurisdiction.[79] Similarly, if the employee's claim for dismissal could be handled by an Industrial Tribunal, the court will deny public law jurisdiction.[80] At this second stage of the jurisdictional question, therefore, most claims will fail because of the availability of adequate alternative remedies. It will only be where the precise substance of the employee's claim cannot be properly investigated by the alternative judicial forum that the court will permit proceedings under Order 53 with the consequence that the superior remedies of public law will be available.[81]

This dual test for public law jurisdiction, first the question of principle, and then, secondly, the more pragmatic discretionary exclusion of jurisdiction on the ground of adequate alternative remedies, seems likely to block almost every claim for a dismissal to be avoided for breach of natural justice. Once again, therefore, the courts have striven to avoid the imposition upon employers of standards of procedural fairness which reflect the ideal of respect for the dignity of individuals. The basic stance of the common law, which denies that ordinary employees should be entitled to procedural justice out of respect for individual dignity, not only triumphed in connection with the statutory claim for unfair dismissal but also served to confine the expansion of public law remedies.

PRIVATE CONTRACT

Under the ordinary contract of employment an employee may have a contractual right to a disciplinary procedure. The right may derive from an

---

[79] See also *McLaren* v. *Home Office* [1990] IRLR 338 (CA).

[80] *R.* v. *Civil Service Appeal Board, ex parte Bruce* [1988] 3 All ER 686 (Div. Ct.).

[81] *R.* v. *Secretary of State for the Home Department, ex parte Benwell* [1985] IRLR 6, [1984] 3 All ER 854 (QB) (prison officer's complaint that there had been a departure from the statutory code of procedure, which was appropriate for public law since he sought an order for the carrying out of that procedure); *R.* v. *Civil Service Appeal Board, ex parte Cunningham* [1990] IRLR 503 (QB) (prison officer could not have recourse to Industrial Tribunal, so review of the measure of compensation awarded by Civil Service Appeal Board permitted); noted in M. R. Freedland, 'The Emerging Law of Public Employment' (1990), 19, *ILJ* 199.

express term, often one which incorporates some other document such as a collective agreement or the employer's personnel handbook, or an implied term based upon custom or reasonable necessity. These days the vast majority of workers are likely to be able to point to their employer's formal disciplinary procedure and ask the court to enforce it.

It is not always clear whether such disciplinary procedures constitute terms of the contract of employment. In the absence of a term which expressly incorporates the procedure, a court may conclude that an employer's personnel handbook is an exercise in administrative discretion by management which does not give rise to contractual rights.[82] If the procedure is contained in a collective agreement, a court may similarly reason that the procedure is intended to regulate collective industrial relations between union and management rather than to accord individual workers contractual rights.[83] But on the assumption that it is accepted that the procedure has been incorporated into the individual contract of employment, the crucial question becomes whether a court will issue an injunction to enforce compliance with the procedure or alternatively award additional damages for breach of procedure over and above the normal damages for wrongful dismissal?

The award of an injunction to enforce an agreed disciplinary procedure apparently runs counter to the traditional rule against specific performance of contracts of employment.[84] This equitable principle has been justified on the ground that specific performance would become tantamount to slavery and also that it would be impracticable because of the loss of the necessary mutual trust and confidence between employer and employee. These arguments have always been overstated and will be critized in greater detail in Chapter 7. The fear of slavery only applies to actions against the employee, which are in any case prohibited by the Trade Union and Labour Relations Act 1974, s. 16. The requirement of continuing trust and confidence between employer and employee has been regarded as having dubious validity in the context of large organizations, and has been avoided recently by examining not the relation between the employee and his or her immediate supervisor but that between the employee and the organization as employer.[85] It may be suggested, indeed, that in large organizations the employer cannot reasonably claim a loss of confidence and trust in the employee until the case against the employee has been demonstrated in accordance with its normal disciplinary procedures.

In any case, it makes little sense to apply the requirement of continuing

---

[82] See above, p. 85.

[83] See Lord Wedderburn, *Worker and the Law* (3rd edn., Harmondsworth, 1986), at pp. 339–43.

[84] The same principles apparently apply to declarations: *Gunton* v. *Richmond-upon-Thames London Borough Council* [1980] ICR 755 (CA).

[85] *Irani* v. *Southampton Health Authority* [1985] IRLR 203.

trust and confidence to the enforcement of a disciplinary procedure. One of
the major purposes of the introduction of such procedures is to provide a
forum when there is a risk of a breakdown of trust and confidence which
needs to be resolved one way or the other if the employment relation is to
continue satisfactorily. Consistent with this view, the Court of Appeal in
Jones v. *Lee*[86] granted an injunction which entitled a headteacher to a
contractually agreed hearing before dismissal without taking any notice of
any breakdown of trust or confidence. If such a breakdown in relations has
occurred, then any difficulties may be avoided by allowing in the court's
order for an employee to be suspended pending the final outcome of the
disciplinary proceedings.[87]

It has even been suggested by Woolf, LJ, that the existence of a formal
disciplinary procedure provides a reason for issuing an injunction:

The existence of the disciplinary proceedings may be highly material to indicate that
the category of employee concerned, unlike an ordinary employee, is not limited to a
claim for damages but can in the appropriate circumstances in an ordinary action seek
a declaration or an injunction to ensure that the proceedings are conducted fairly.[88]

If, as I have argued, these traditional objections to the issuance of an
injunction to prevent a breach of a disciplinary procedure are unfounded and
irrelevant, then clearly the common law now offers potentially stronger
support for disciplinary procedures than either the law of unfair dismissal or
public law. Because an employer will be held strictly liable for breach of a
contractual procedure, subject to any waiver of breach by the employee,[89]
there is no room for most of the arguments by which courts and tribunals
diminish procedural standards. Unlike in the law of unfair dismissal, it
cannot be alleged that the breach of contract is a mere technicality.[90] Nor
can the futility of the exercise defeat the claim, as it might for the law of
unfair dismissal as determined in *West Midlands Co-operative Society Ltd.* v.
Tipton.[91] Nor could compensation be reduced for contributory fault or on
the ground that it would be just and equitable as in *Devis & Sons Ltd.* v.
Atkins.[92] Nor would the plaintiff have to risk a denial of the remedy in public
law as an exercise of residual discretion.[93] Instead the court should simply
order the employer to fulfil his or her contractual obligation to carry out the
disciplinary procedure in full.

Any right to an injunction to enforce the disciplinary procedure is lost,

---

[86] [1980] ICR 310 (CA).

[87] *Robb* v. *London Borough of Hammersmith and Fulham* [1991] IRLR 72 (QB).

[88] *McLaren* v. *Home Office* [1990] IRLR 338 (CA), at p. 342.

[89] *R.* v. *BBC, ex parte Lavelle* [1983] ICR 99 (QB); and Shaw, LJ, in *Gunton* v. *Richmond-
upon-Thames London Borough Council* [1980] ICR 755 (CA), at p. 761.

[90] *Post Office* v. *Marney* [1990] IRLR 170 (EAT).

[91] [1986] ICR 192; [1986] AC 536 (HL).

[92] [1977] ICR 662; [1977] AC 931 (HL).

[93] *Chief Constable of the North Wales Police* v. *Evans* [1982] 3 All ER 141 (HL).

however, if the court infers from the employee's conduct that he or she has accepted that the employment relation is over.[94] This conduct is usually in the form of an acceptance of another job. But according to the important decision in *Gunton* v. *Richmond-upon-Thames London Borough Council*,[95] the employee may then pursue an action for damages, not only for wrongful dismissal to the sum of the net wages due under the contractually required period of notice, but also a sum representing the period of time of continued employment which would have occurred had the employer faithfully fulfilled his or her obligations under the contractual disciplinary procedure. Because this additional compensation may amount to more than double the normal level of damages awarded for wrongful dismissal, the decision provides employers with a strong financial incentive to carry out the agreed procedure.[96]

This branch of the common law would become even more important if there was an implied term granting entitlement to natural justice. Although such an idea was rejected for ordinary employees in *Ridge* v. *Baldwin*,[97] in *R.* v. *East Berkshire Area Health Authority, ex parte Walsh*, where there was a contractual disciplinary procedure, Purchas, LJ, said that: 'The rules of natural justice may well be imported into a private contractual relationship.' In *R.* v. *BBC, ex parte Lavelle*,[98] Woolf, J., argued that the existence of an elaborate disciplinary procedure took the employment relationship out of the category of a pure contract of employment and that it was appropriate to imply the principles of natural justice into the disciplinary procedures. The employer was therefore in breach of its contractual obligations by failing to give adequate notice to an employee of a disciplinary hearing, though this breach was waived by the employee when after independent advice she chose to exercise the next appeal stage of the procedure which was conducted fairly.

Such an implied term in a contract can be easily justified on traditional common law grounds as representing the unexpressed intentions of the parties. Moreover, it is common for courts to introduce similar implied terms in the analogous cases concerning trade union disciplinary action against members, where the term serves to flesh out the bare bones of the union's disciplinary procedure.[99] Similarly, it should not be difficult for the

---

[94] *Dietman* v. *London Borough of Brent* [1988] IRLR 299 (CA).

[95] [1980] ICR 755 (CA); followed in *Dietman* v. *London Borough of Brent* [1988] IRLR 299 (CA).

[96] Paradoxically the award of substantial damages may have an adverse effect on the award of injunctions, for the court might no longer regard damages as inadequate to meet the justice of the case. *Gunton* v. *Richmond-upon-Thames London Borough Council* [1980] ICR 755 (CA) confirms, however, that the award of damages will be reduced by the normal principles of mitigation of loss, so this risk may not materialize. In addition, the courts seem sympathetic to the view that deprivation of a contractually agreed procedure cannot easily be compensated by an award of money damages: *Robb* v. *London Borough of Hammersmith and Fulham* [1991] IRLR 72 (QB).   [97] [1964] AC 40 (HL).   [98] [1983] ICR 99 (QB).

[99] *Lawlor* v. *Union of Post Office Workers* [1965] Ch 712 (Ch.); *Radford* v. *National Society of Operative Printers, Graphical and Media Personnel* [1972] ICR 484 (Ch.).

courts to add to a contractually agreed disciplinary procedure any appropriate principles of natural justice.

It would be a bolder step to imply a term of natural justice into a contract of employment which made no mention of any disciplinary procedure, for this would run headlong into the doctrine that ordinary employees have no entitlement to natural justice established in *Ridge* v. *Baldwin*.[100] Nevertheless, this may be on the verge of happening as a result of the closing down of the remedies available under public law. In their determination to exclude most employees from the public law action, the courts have translated employees' claims for natural justice into actions for breach of contract. This has led to the suggestion that contracts of employment do include normally an implied term of natural justice prior to dismissal.[101] If so, then any employee, even in the absence of an express disciplinary procedure contained in his or her contract may seek an injunction or damages against breach of the principles of natural justice in private law. The decision in *Ridge* v. *Baldwin* may be distinguished on the ground that it concerned solely the question of natural justice under the public law jurisdiction, whereas here we are considering the question of the terms of private contracts of employment. There is a considerable irony here of course. In their determination to prevent claims for natural justice through public law procedures the courts may have paved the way for the use of the ordinary private law of contract to create unprecedented rights to procedural fairness.

The advent of routine awards to enforce contractually agreed dismissal procedures should have considerable significance for the personnel practices of employers. It renders the employer's decision to institute such procedures more complex, for on the one hand they are necessary to avoid claims for unfair dismissal, yet on the other hand, once incorporated into the contract of employment, they tie the employer's hands to the inflexible course envisaged by the dismissal procedure. This legal positon provides employers with a strong incentive to attempt to avoid any contractual obligation by an express disclaimer of intention to enter a binding contractual agreement with respect to all or part of the disciplinary procedure contained in a collective agreement or personnel handbook. Such disclaimers in front of personnel handbooks have become commonplace in the USA, though they will not necessarily prevent a court from concluding that at least some aspects of the personnel handbook including the dismissal procedure have nevertheless been incorporated into the contract of employment by custom.[102]

---

[100] [1964] AC 40 (HL).

[101] K. D. Ewing and A. Grubb, 'The Emergence of a New Labour Injunction?' (1987), 16, *ILJ* 145, at p. 156 (natural justice for any employee protected by contractual or statutory rights from dismissal at will).

[102] M. R. Witt and S. R. Goldman, 'Avoiding Liability in Employee Handbooks' (1988), 14, *Employee Relations Law Journal*, 5; M. W. Finkin, 'The Bureaucratization of Work: Employer Policies and Contract Law' (1986), *Wisconsin Law Review*, 733.

5. SUBVERSION BY CONCILIATION

All these legal developments may have little effect in practice in the vast majority of dismissals. The first step in the legal procedures governing claims for unfair dismissal after a claim has been filed is that an ACAS conciliation officer tries to persuade the parties to settle their dispute. Many employers also consult ACAS after a dismissal even before a claim has been filed by the employee.[103] They do so in order to seek advice but also in the hope that a settlement of a dispute will include a legally binding provision against any further proceedings in the matter.[104] Only about a third of applications filed proceed to a tribunal hearing, leaving about 43 per cent settled between the parties and 24 per cent withdrawn without any settlement having been agreed. Almost all of those cases where ACAS has been approached informally by the employer will be settled out of court as well.[105] Taking together all dismissals where ACAS is consulted, only one-fifth are likely to proceed to a tribunal hearing.[106] For 80 per cent of dismissed employees, therefore, the conciliation system bears heavily on the outcome of their case, either by encouraging a settlement or by inducing a withdrawal of the claim. The importance of the conciliation procedure for the impact of the law governing the requirement of fair procedures has not been considered, but I believe that a comprehensive study of procedural fairness in the law of unfair dismissal would be seriously incomplete without consideration of two conjectures about its likely deleterious effects.

My first suggestion is that the incentive for the employer to comply with a fair procedure to reach the right result under the legislation will be reduced to the extent that the case is unlikely to be adjudicated by a tribunal, for an agreed settlement is likely to reflect the general substantive merits of the case far more than formal compliance with appropriate disciplinary procedures. Since the level of compensation paid on pre-trial settlements is usually substantially lower than that awarded by tribunals, the median level being less than one-half of tribunal awards,[107] we can see the pattern emerging of employers offering a relatively modest sum which reflects the merits of the case and the costs to the employer of proceeding to trial without any routine award of compensation for breach of the standards of fair procedure. As so few cases proceed to a hearing, we can surmise that in practice conformity

---

[103] This role for ACAS derives from EPCA 1978, s. 133(3).

[104] The binding effect of such settlements is protected by EPCA 1978, s. 140(2)(g).

[105] P. Lowry, *Employment Disputes and the Third Party* (London, 1990), at p. 147.

[106] ACAS, *Annual Report 1988*, at p. 30.

[107] K. Williams, 'Unfair Dismissal: Myths and Statistics' (1983), 12, *ILJ* 157, at p. 159; Dickens *et al.*, *Dismissed*, at p. 162. Some doubt must be cast on these findings as an accurate description of current practice in the light of a more recent study, which claims that in agreed settlements the amount of compensation was about the same as the median awarded by tribunals: N. Banerji, D. Smart, and M. Stevens, 'Unfair Dismissal Cases in 1985–86: Impact on Parties' (1990), 98, *Employment Gazette*, 547, at p. 551.

to procedural standards plays a very small part indeed in influencing the majority of outcomes of disputed dismissals. The public good of affirming the importance of procedural fairness is subverted by the ease of and pressures for private settlements.[108]

The conciliation process is also likely to undermine procedural standards in a second way. In an important sense the discussions with the conciliation officer represent for many employees a kind of preliminary appeal against the employer's decision to terminate the employment relation. The conciliation officer hears what the employee has to say and then seeks to achieve a settlement of the case. Under EPCA 1978, s. 134(1) the duty of the conciliation officer is 'to endeavour to promote a settlement of the complaint without its being determined by an industrial tribunal'. Thus the principal function of the officer is to prevent the case from going to a hearing, so there is no duty to ensure that the settlement is fair to the employee.[109] The official view of ACAS is that the officer acts purely as a neutral and impartial conciliator who facilitates agreements to settle the case.[110] In practice it seems from empirical surveys that conciliation officers point out the strengths and weaknesses of the case to the parties.[111] But they do not adopt a paternalist role towards the employee, helping him or her to put forward a case in its best light. In most cases the officer assists a bargaining process and advises the employee to accept the employer's first offer.[112]

Judging by the high proportion of cases settled out of court, this conciliation process indubitably functions well to reduce the costs to the State of the administration of the system of Industrial Tribunals. But it should be clear that the duty of conciliation officers to achieve settlements prevents them from adopting a truly impartial stance, one which gives the parties the opportunity to hear a relatively expert opinion on their likely chances of success before a tribunal. The employee, who normally lacks the assistance of lawyers, is likely to mistake the advice to settle for a small sum of compensation as an impartial assessment of the merits of his or her case. But the advice is far from impartial by the standards of the principles of natural justice: it is tainted by the State's bias to reduce the amount of litigation. One survey revealed dramatically the inherent bias of this conciliation procedure. It found that in 13 per cent of cases where the claimant had

---

[108] Cf. Jules L. Coleman, *Markets, Morals and the Law* (Cambridge, 1988), at pp. 202–15. For other pressures to settle out of court springing from the Employment Protection (Recoupment of Unemployment Benefit and Supplementary Benefit) Regulations 1977, SI 1977, No. 674, see R. W. Rideout, 'Unfair Dismissal—Tribunal or Arbitration: A Discussion Paper' (1986), 15, *ILJ* 84, at p. 85.

[109] *Moore* v. *Duport Furniture Products* [1982] ICR 84 (HL).

[110] P. Lowry, *Employment Disputes and the Third Party* (London, 1990), at p. 121.

[111] P. Lewis, 'The Role of ACAS Conciliators in Unfair Dismissal Cases' (1982), 13(3), *Industrial Relations Journal*, 50; cf. P. J. White, 'ACAS and the Lawyers: Some Survey Evidence' (1989), 20, *Industrial Relations Journal*, 280.

[112] Dickens *et al.*, *Dismissed*, at pp. 174–7.

subsequently been successful before the Industrial Tribunal in his or her claim for unfair dismissal, the ACAS conciliation officer had encouraged the claimant to withdraw his or her case on the grounds that there was little or no chance of winning.[113] This finding also suggests that as well as violating the strict standards of natural justice, the conciliation system also fails the efficiency approach to the standard of procedural fairness to ensure the correct outcomes at the least cost. The conciliation process is clearly not designed to ensure correct outcomes, but to minimize the cost to the State of bad ones.

These conjectures on the impact of the conciliation process on the conduct of discipline reveal that British law has missed a major opportunity to establish fair disciplinary procedures. The conciliation officers could have been used to buttress the efficiency approach to procedural fairness by pushing the employer to go through all the reasonable steps necessary to reach a careful decision on the correct information. They could have been empowered to advise the employee against settling his or her case until such procedures had been properly conducted.[114] This would have led employers to adopt those procedures in order to gain the benefit of the cheaper settlements out of court. Yet instead of performing a role which would at once have been conducive to fairness towards the dismissed employee and at the same time beneficial to harmonious industrial relations, the conciliation officers routinely and subtly undermine the force of procedural requirements by encouraging employees to take quick settlements which reflect a mixture of the substantive merits of their cases and their employers' estimates of the likely costs of litigation.

6. CONCLUSION

Considerations of cost dominate the principles governing the fairness of the procedures which employers are required to adopt prior to a dismissal. The cost to the State of the administration of the tribunal system leads to the heavy reliance upon conciliated cash settlements which seem likely to reflect almost entirely the merits of the substantive grounds for dismissal. In the hearing before the tribunal itself, the general principles requiring employers to comply with reasonable procedures reflect, both in their detailed provisions on investigations and hearings, and also in the exceptions when no procedure is required at all, the consideration that the employer should reach an efficient decision. This model of procedural fairness is not required by the legislation, but has been imposed by the courts and tribunals as an interpretation of the standard of fairness in the law of unfair dismissal.

At variance with this dominant interpretation of the law of unfair

---

[113] Lewis, 'The Role of ACAS Conciliators in Unfair Dismissal Cases', at p. 54.
[114] See the analogous proposal in Justice, *Industrial Tribunals* (London, 1987).

dismissal, we have glimpsed some recent decisions of the common law courts which uphold a contractual basis for rights to a fair procedure. An injunction may be awarded against an employer who fails to comply with the provisions of his own disciplinary code, notwithstanding the possibility that such procedures may prove an expensive and futile gesture. This common law jurisdiction rests upon a rights-based conception of justice as opposed to the goal-based efficiency criterion governing procedural fairness in the law of unfair dismissal.

It should be apparent, however, that neither jurisdiction acknowledges the force of the strict principles of natural justice grounded in the individual's right to respect. The context of business management in which the principles of fair procedure in dismissals have been forged appears to have steered the courts away from acknowledging that individuals should be entitled to a fair procedure as of right. When the public law jurisdiction seemed to promise just such a possibility, the courts developed an elaborate and flimsy set of rules to exclude applicants for judicial review precisely to stop this from happening.

Yet this rejection of the ideals of natural justice in the workplace runs directly contrary to one of the aims of the legislation as we interpreted them in Chapter 1. Fair procedures for administering the bureaucratic framework of the workplace are an essential step in fostering opportunities for autonomy and ensuring respect for the dignity of the individual. Arguments based upon conflicting considerations of cost should not be permitted to undermine this important aspect of the legislation.

What seems to be required is more detailed legislative guidance on the necessary steps for an employer to adopt prior to a valid dismissal. A comparison with the French Code du Travail is instructive. There the Code requires a registered letter warning the employee of dismissal and inviting him or her with a fellow worker of his or her choice to a hearing by the employer; at the hearing the employer must explain the grounds for the proposed dismissal; then, after the hearing, the employer must send another registered letter informing the employee of the decision to dismiss.[115] If some similar procedure were to be mandated by British legislation, then many of the uncertainties and complexities concerning standards of procedural fairness revealed in this chapter would be overcome.

---

[115] Code du Travail, L. 122–14 *et seq.*; see M. Despax and J. Rojot, *Labour Law and Industrial Relations in France* (Deventer, 1987), at pp. 114–16.

[5]

Economic Dismissals and Social Cost

WHEN a factory pollutes a river we all suffer. Leaving aside the important interest of animal and plant life in a supportive environment, human beings enjoy reduced amenities and incur considerable costs in cleaning up the river to make it safe again for consumption and irrigation. These costs may be shouldered by the community itself out of general taxation or they may be imposed on the owners of the factory. Many techniques may be employed to force the owners of the factory to internalize the costs of pollution within the business. The community may impose a charge to compensate it for the cost of cleaning, or it may increase the burden of taxation on businesses liable to pollute the environment, or it may impose mandatory legal restrictions on factories against pollution backed up by fines which are likely to render it inefficient for the factory to continue to pollute the river. Whatever technique is used, its purpose is to compel the business to internalize some or all of the costs of pollution rather than externalizing them on to the community as a whole.

In many respects economic dismissals impose analogous costs on the community to those provoked by pollution. When an employer dismisses all or part of the workforce for business reasons, the community immediately begins to bear such costs as financial support for the unemployed workers and their dependants and assistance for their search for fresh jobs. In the absence of any regulation designed to compel employers to internalize the costs of economic dismissals, these costs either will be borne by the community through its social security system and its active manpower programmes for relocating workers in new jobs, or left to lie where they fall on the individual workers. Again the State may utilize many techinques for shifting all or part of the burden of social cost back on to the employer. The employer may be forced to pay a charge in the form of a severance payment to the individual worker, or, through taxation of business, there may be a form of compulsory pooling of the social costs on owners of capital, or the community may even seek to prevent economic dismissals altogether through penalties.

One policy which often guides the law's regulation of pollution consists in the minimization of social costs. It directs that regulation should impose the costs of pollution upon owners of factories when their costs in avoiding pollution are less than the cost to the community in cleaning it up. The law transfers the expense of reduction of pollution only to the extent that it remains cheaper for the factory to take precautions rather than for the State to take measures to purify the water. The general aim is to minimize the social costs of pollution by placing liability upon the most efficient cost avoider. Such a policy does not prohibit pollution altogether, but rather permits it where the costs of clean up are less than the expense of fail-safe precautions. Should a similar policy operate in connection with economic dismissals?

The policy of minimizing social costs would compel employers to internalize some but not all of the costs of economic dismissals.[1] The law would transfer the burden to employers if either of two criteria were satisfied. First, where an employer could meet a social cost such as income maintenance for the dismissed worker more efficiently than the State, then liability should be imposed upon the employer. This criterion will rarely be satisfied with respect to most social costs. It seems unlikely, for example, that the payment of a variable sum of money to dismissed workers to maintain their income during an uncertain period of unemployment could be more cheaply administered by the employer than the State. It seems more probable, however, that an employer's co-operation in attempts by state agencies to find new jobs for workers, to train them for available work, and all the other dimensions of an active manpower programme will reduce its costs, so in that instance the first criterion may be satisfied.

The second criterion for transfer of social cost demands that measures be taken to keep employees in their jobs where the cost of continuing employment is less than the social costs of unemployment. This might occur, for example, during a temporary downturn in the business, where the social security costs of income maintenance for dismissed workers during unemployment exceed the costs of preserving their jobs by a combination of reduced wages and a temporary employment subsidy from the State.

But these examples should not obscure the complexity of the calculus of social cost. We should recognize that any transfer of cost on to the employer is likely to have an impact upon the labour and capital markets. In so far as legal regulation increases the cost of labour to the employer, then this may reduce the employer's demand for labour or lead to a loss of competitiveness in the international markets unless the employer compensates for such costs by reducing wages. Compulsory severance payments may thus increase overall levels of unemployment in the long term. Increased regulation may also divert capital investment towards those sites with lower labour costs. In

---

[1] Cf. D. R. Kuhn and C. E. Zech, 'Plant Closings and Public Policy: Achieving an Optimal Level of Plant Closings' (1988), 10, *Law and Policy*, 63; F. Raday, 'Costs of Dismissal: An Analysis in Community Justice and Efficiency' (1989), 9, *International Review of Law and Economics*, 181.

either case, the general welfare of the community may be reduced. A full analysis of the social costs should incorporate this element into its calculus.

The precise effect of legal regulation of economic dismissals depends upon the freedom of owners of capital to respond to it. On the most pessimistic view for job security, the law is necessarily impotent against the structural constraints of the market-place. This view holds that the product-market dictates a limited role for labour law, for in the absence of purchasers of the firm's product, even the most generous government will decline to keep pouring subsidies into a redundant business. In addition, the capital market accentuates this limited role for labour law, since capital moves quickly towards the most profitable centres of business, stepping lightly over national boundaries and divisions between market sectors. Any supplemental labour costs, such as protection of workers against lay-offs, will induce capital investors to seek more profitable terrain elsewhere, typically in the third world. In the absence of further capital investment, the prognosis for any business must be short, so any protection of jobs which imposes costs on the employer may in the long run increase levels of unemployment. To a limited extent, indubitably, the State may supply the missing capital and so preserve the firm and jobs, but the constraints of the product-market severely curtail the number of worthwhile opportunities for such intervention in the capital market. In the light of these structural considerations stemming from the market system itself, this pessimistic view asserts that expectations of job security beyond protection from disciplinary dismissals without cause must remain pipe-dreams, and society should dispel these illusions rather than seek to reinforce them.[2]

But this pessimistic view assumes both considerable freedom of capital to change its location of investment and that any legal regulation of economic dismissals necessarily increases the labour costs of the business. The second assumption will be challenged in the third section of this chapter, and shown to be partly false. The first assumption plainly ignores the legal and practical difficulties of capital investment in different parts of the globe, which deter for the most part the gravitation of all capital investment towards the least regulated labour markets. The effect of regulation of economic dismissals upon levels of capital investment must therefore depend upon a complex equation which balances the advantages of relocation against its additional risks. It cannot be assumed therefore that any legal regulation will have a commensurate impact upon levels of capital investment and employment.

This chapter argues that the policy of minimizing social cost should comprise one of the principal guides to legal regulation of economic dismissals. This approach leads to a series of criticisms of the current British

---

[2] Richard B. McKenzie, *Restrictions on Business Mobility: A Study in Political Rhetoric and Economic Reality* (Washington, DC, 1979).

law, especially the award of severance payments under the redundancy payments legislation in the Employment Protection Consolidation Act 1978, Part VI. The first section of this chapter addresses the task of justifying this social cost approach to economic dismissals, for it may be thought to run contrary to the argument in Chapter 1 that regulation of dismissals is justified by its improvement for job security. A second section intervenes in the argument to inspect more closely the nature and causes of economic dismissals. We highlight the source of economic dismissals in changing demands for labour, the fluidity of capital markets, the growing practice of vertical disintegration, and anti-union industrial relations strategies. The third section addresses the problem of the potential deleterious effects of any regulation of economic dismissals upon levels of employment and wages. Contrary to the pessimistic view described above, I argue that many regulatory measures will not significantly increase labour costs, and that the costs of many others will prove minimal. It follows that the fear of capital disinvestment should not deter legislatures from regulating economic dismissals. The fourth section examines what types of regulation of economic dismissals may be justified by the policy of minimizing social cost. This attempts to measure in a broad-brush way the likely costs and benefits of particular types of regulation, in order to support concrete proposals for reform of the current regulatory framework. A brief conclusion summarizes these proposals.

1. THE CLAIM OF JOB SECURITY

To pose the policy question about the legal regulation of economic dismissals in terms of minimizing social cost runs against the grain of many justifications for the redundancy payments legislation and similar schemes for severance benefits. Just as one may find it instinctively abhorrent that the law should tolerate any pollution of rivers notwithstanding its efficiency, so too some view the paramount reason for regulation of economic dismissals as one to prevent them occurring at all. Job security, it is said, is a vital interest of workers, so that the law should ensure that economic dismissals never occur, or at least make it economically inadvisable for employers as long as the business remains solvent. Such a policy seems to me unworkable, inefficient, and above all without substantial justification.

This section considers and rejects three possible justifications for granting an employee a right to protection of job security against economic dismissals in the form of a severance payment designed to deter them. These may be identified as: (a) the protection of a property right in the job; (b) a concern for the dignity and autonomy of individuals; and (c) a redistributive criterion based on fairness. Having considered and rejected these three potential forms of justification for defending job security against economic dismissals, the section concludes in (d) by exploring the rival attractions of an alternative approach based upon minimizing social cost, an approach which necessarily rejects the protection of job security as a central goal for legal regulation.

(a) Property Right

An initial difficulty in assessing the concept of a property right in a job as a justification for protecting job security against economic dismissals springs from the vagueness of the alleged right.[3] Consider, for example, the following judicial commentary upon the British system of redundancy payments:

A redundancy payment is compensation for loss of a right which a long-term employee has in his job. Just as a property owner has a right in his property and when he is deprived he is entitled to compensation, so a long-term employee is considered to have a right analogous to a right of property in his job, he has a right to security, and his rights gain in value with the years . . .[4]

On examining this quotation closely, we can detect considerable ambiguity in its concept of job property. Indeed, three conceptions of job property figure in the judgment.

Three Conceptions of Job Property

Despite the appeal to the idea of ownership of property, with the implication that the employee's possession of his or her job should be protected, in fact the judgment places much greater emphasis upon a weaker conception of a right to security which can be infringed at will by the employer on payment of financial compensation. In the judge's mind, the right to security is like a bottle of fine claret, increasing in value with age, though available for anyone to consume on payment of compensation. The primary ambiguity in the rhetoric of property rights in a job thus concerns the fundamental issue whether the right mandates protection of the employee in his possession of a job or whether it merely posits an interest to be compensated by those who damage it. A property right in a job could be conceived either as (1) a right to possession of a job (that is an immunity from dismissal),[5] or (2) a right to compensation for compulsory alienation, or (3) merely a right to an extended period of notice prior to dimissal.

With respect to (1), we have already noted the complexity and artificiality of devising a conception of a property right which both finds a useful analogy with existing property rights recognized by the law and yet approximates to

---

[3] For earlier discussions of this idea, see Chs. 1 and 3. For a perceptive overall analysis of the notion of job property and its application to the law of dismissal, see Paul Davies and Mark Freedland, *Labour Law: Text and Materials* (2nd edn., London 1974), at pp. 428–32.

[4] *Wynes* v. *Southrepps Hall Broiler Farm Ltd.* [1968] ITR 407 (IT) per Sir Dairmid Conroy, QC, at p. 407.

[5] J. Singer, 'The Reliance Interest in Property' (1988), 40, *Stanford Law Review*, 611, at p. 688.

the goal of respecting job security.[6] But assuming that this difficulty could be overcome, perhaps by the analogy of equitable proprietary estoppel, then economic dismissals present one further difficulty and ambiguity in the relevant conception of ownership.

A distinction must be drawn between a right to *a* job and a right to *the* job. Is it a claim for a right to a particular job, that is, either a specified grade in the organization or an identifiable set of tasks such as typing or welding, or is the right merely one of employment by a particular employer (or associated employers), whatever tasks are assigned? The latter meaning probably corresponds to the expectation of white-collar workers and Japanese employees governed by the regime of lifetime employment, for they intend to rise through the bureaucratic hierarchy or to move sideways into new kinds of tasks for which they must be trained. In contrast, manual workers in most industrial countries, whether skilled or not, probably expect a more confined conception of job property, limited to the tasks for which they were initially hired.

This difference between a right to the particular job and a right to employment becomes critical when the employee is required to take on new tasks but refuses or is incapable of so doing. As the pace of changes in technology increases, this issue becomes integral to many claims involving economic dismissals. On one view, an employer's insistence upon adjustment counts as an infringement of a property right in the job, whereas, on the other, the employer is merely living up to his obligation to provide employment. Advocates of a job property right must either resolve this ambiguity or accept that the right changes according to the expectations of the parties.

The weaker conception of job property in (2) seeks merely to compensate the employee for the loss of his or her expectation of future employment. If we take seriously an employee's expectations under an implicit contract of career development, promotion, incremental pay increases,[7] and job security during good behaviour—expectations normally fostered by management in order to induce co-operation, effort, and investment in human capital and firm-specific skills[8]—then this provides a basis for a measure of compensation in economic dismissals. Indeed, it is perhaps for these reasons that many British employers augment severance or redundancy pay well above statutory minimum payments.[9]

[6] See Ch. 1.

[7] E. P. Lazear, 'Agency, Earnings Profits, Productivity and Hours Restrictions' (1981), 71, *American Economic Review*, 606–20.

[8] S. J. Grossman and O. D. Hart, 'Implicit Contracts, Moral Hazard and Unemployment' (1981), 71, *American Economic Review*, 301; S. Rosen, 'Implicit Contracts: A Survey' (1985), 23, *Journal of Economic Literature*, 1144.

[9] A. Booth and M. Chatterji, 'Redundancy Payments and Firm-specific Training' (1989), 56, *Economica*, 505; A. L. Booth, 'Extra-statutory Redundancy Payments in Britain' (1987), 25, *British Journal of Industrial Relations*, 401.

This justification for a severance payment would lead to a quantification based on the difference between the likely income produced by continued employment and the actual income of the employee subsequent to dismissal. The difference comprises not only the gap between social security levels and wages, but also the probable inferior remuneration arising from a new job on account of the employee's lack of seniority and firm-specific skills. In practice, no legal system attempts to quantify severance payments in this way. The British Redundancy Payments legislation, like most European legal systems, quantifies payments by reference to the three factors of length of service, rate of pay, and age of employee.[10] One possible rationale for this practice is that these factors very roughly correspond to the forces which create the differential in income resulting from dismissal: the greater the seniority, the greater the likely diminution of income from new employment; the greater the age of the employee, the longer the likely period of unemployment; the higher the pay, the further you have to fall.

It is also possible to attribute some meaning to the idea of job property by the idea in (3) which suggests that ownership of a job involves an extension of the time clause in the contract of employment. Much like the practice of tenured jobs for teachers in universities, the right would involve a promise by the employer of a job until retirement age or at least of a substantial period of notice prior to dismissal. Any precipitate dismissal would be a breach of this clause, giving rise either to specific relief by way of reinstatement or substantial damages. Here the measure of compensation would comprise the regular net wages for the required period of notice, with perhaps a deduction for any likely income representing future earnings from employment, in order to provide dismissed workers with an incentive to look for work for the same reasons of efficiency which support the normal principles of mitigation of loss in contractual damages.

Justifications of Job Property

Whichever conception of job property is envisaged, however, it does raise the question of why the law should recognize such a novel individualized right? Moreover, if such an argument of principle can be sustained, which conception of job property does it support? Here we consider two arguments of principle which, I believe, represent the main strands of the current debate: (1) a return upon capital investment; and (2) the obligation from necessity.

Return on Capital Investment   In support of (1), Barron argues that employees recognize that in establishing wage levels a company must retain sufficient

---

[10] EPCA 1978, Sched. 4.

profits to permit further capital investment.[11] By holding back on wage demands in order to establish long-term job security, the workers gain a right to part of the eventual capital proceeds of the business. At present, of course, that capital is solely represented in the value of the share, so the shareholder acquires it all. But the employees' decision to refrain from bargaining so fiercely that retained profits are completely swallowed up by wages entitles them, on this view, to a share in the profits in the form of capital retained by the firm. This argument applies not only when a business is closed and sold, but also where there are reductions in the workforce through lay-offs, because those employees who lose their jobs have made a similar investment which they should now be able to realize. Indeed, in theory, the argument extends to any kind of dismissal, even that for good cause, for during the period of employment every employee has presumably contributed to the sum of retained profits.

This argument can also be put in a similar though not identical Marxist vein. The source of the firm's profits lies in the difference between the exchange value of labour (the wages paid) and the use value of labour (the value added to the product by the labour, judged by the product's sale price). Marx calls the difference between exchange and use value, the surplus value, and argues that surplus value is the source of the firm's profits.[12] The surplus value created by the expropriation of labour can be returned in part to the employees on the termination of their connection with the business. Hence a severance payment would represent all or part of the surplus value appropriated by the firm.

Whichever way the argument is put, it would justify a conception of job property which was limited to the payment of a severance benefit. It differs slightly from the second conception of job property identified above, for instead of compensating expectations, it provides restitution of a hypothetical investment or forgone income. In practice, however, similar factors would guide the assessment of the severance benefit, for the length of service and the actual wage paid would be the best indicators of the amount of income forgone, on the assumption that workers forgo wages or surplus value in proportion to their pay. Logically, no doubt, the amount of the severance benefit should depend also upon the level of profits of the firm during the period of service, for in the absence of retained earnings or profits, the employees would have sacrificed nothing and should receive no severance benefit.

Of course, this justification for the recognition of a property right in the

---

[11] P. Barron, 'Causes and Impact of Plant Shutdowns and Relocations and Potential Non-NLRA Responses' (1984), 58, *Tulane Law Review*, 1389–1408, at p. 1408. This might also be described as a form of compulsory saving for employees to provide for economic loss in the event of dismissal: Santosh Mukherjee, *Through No Fault of Their Own* (London, 1972), at pp. 44–5.

[12] Karl Marx, *Capital*, i (1867; Harmondsworth, 1976), ch. 1.

job presupposes that the workforce have forgone the exercise of power to demand and receive higher wage levels. In most cases it seems unlikely that such power exists, so this argument could founder on the objection that the entitlement to severance pay rests upon forgoing a right or power which never existed or which in fact was not forgone.

A further puzzling feature of this justification of severance benefits concerns their distribution. Because economic dismissals, or dismissals generally, trigger the payment, only employees who lose their jobs before resignation or retirement appear entitled to their share of reserved profits or surplus value. Workers who have kept their jobs, perhaps because their skills are especially valuable to the firm or because of their willingness to adapt to new technologies, will discover that ironically they will not see their cut of the profits even though they may have done more than most to contribute to them. This proposed distribution therefore seems inequitable.[13] The only remedy would be to expand the range of persons entitled to payment to encompass all employees regardless of the fact that they have not been dismissed.

This brings us to perhaps the most stubborn difficulty with this capital investment argument for severance pay, though strangely this difficulty may help to resolve the foregoing distributive paradox. Severance benefits awarded on the ground of capital investment may involve double compensation for the workforce. Given that the reason why employees refrain from demanding wages at levels which soak up all the profits is that they wish to preserve the viability of the firm in order to ensure the continuation of their stream of income, to give them severance pay in addition to their anticipated benefit of job security may be compensating them twice for the same act of forgoing higher wages. Of course, it is true that job security has not materialized in cases of economic dismissals, so perhaps in these cases the double compensation problem does not arise, though this is true only if the wages forgone represent an attempt to eliminate the risk of job loss altogether, not simply to reduce it. The Marxist version of this justification for recognition of job property may be less susceptible to this problem of double compensation, since it regards the extraction of any surplus value from the workforce as an expropriation by the employer. But the avoidance of double compensation may provide the solution to the earlier distributive paradox, for this reason may explain why employees who retain their jobs never see a return on their capital investment.

At bottom, however, this justification for recognition of a right to job property in the form of severance benefits falls down because of the flimsiness of any reasoning concerning hypothetical contracts. As soon as one steps down the road of supposing people to have made contracts which they did

---

[13] S. Rottenburg, 'Property in Work' (1961–2), 15, *Industrial and Labor Relations Review*, 402, at p. 404.

not, or to have included terms which never occurred to them, the exercise becomes not only speculative but also vulnerable to large numbers of equally plausible alternative versions of the hypothetical contract. Variables such as the degree to which employees prefer to avoid the risk of unemployment and the extent to which they refrain from exercising their full bargaining power can be manipulated to produce any result ranging from substantial severance payments to none at all. Surely, if the claim for ownership of jobs with a right to compensation for deprivation of this form of property can be substantiated, it should rest upon firmer foundations than these eminently contestable hypothetical contracts?

The Obligation from Necessity   The second justification for a property right in a job starts from the premiss that both the employee and the local community suffer from being heavily dependent upon the local business. Especially in a single company town, we find a relation of dependence or subordination between the fortunes of the company and the local economy. This economic interdependence reflects the intensive division of labour in advanced industrialized societies and may warrant the invocation of diffuse contractual duties based upon reliance between the company and its employees.[14] Moreover, the relation of domination in single company towns may justify the imposition of moral and legal duties to refrain from misrepresentation. But to found a moral right to job property, that is, a right which supersedes contractual arrangements and which founds a correlative duty to compensate, a stronger justification for overriding the freedom of the employer in the market-place must be found.

Such an argument must invoke the moral principle of *necessité oblige*.[15] This principle holds that where one individual is heavily dependent upon another for his or her welfare, that other owes a duty to care for the vulnerable individual. The paradigm case comprises the relation between parent and child. One reason why a parent owes a duty to care for a child is the child's need and dependence upon the parent. Where a parent fails in this duty, the community will undertake the obligation, but it remains in principle morally entitled to charge the cost of this care to the parent.

This moral principle of *necessité oblige* extends by analogy to the relation between employer and individual employee. Because the employee's income, social status, and way of fulfilling his or her life through work is so heavily dependent upon his or her employer, that employer owes a duty of care. Breach of this duty of care by economic dismissals entitles the individual employee to compensation equivalent to fulfilment of the duty. Since the community will have to provide support for the worker through social security payments, to that extent the local community should also be compensated by the employer.

[14] J. Singer, 'The Reliance Interest in Property' (1988), 40, *Stanford Law Review*, 611.
[15] 'Necessité Oblige', in Tony Honoré, *Making Laws Bind* (Oxford, 1987).

The kind of legal provision which this argument warrants is a duty upon the employer to provide income maintenance for a period of time in which it is reasonable for the employee to find another job. To the extent that the community acts as surrogate for this duty through payment of social security benefits, it could be recompensed by the employer. Perhaps the most straightforward way of organizing this provision would be to place a duty upon the employer to continue to pay wages for a period of time, for example six months or until the employee finds another job, whichever is the shorter. The employer might object to this latter proposal on the ground that through taxation which funds social security benefits he or she has already contributed once to fund this moral obligation to care for the employee, so that the additional payments of wages would amount to a duplication of this duty. If this argument is accepted, the original proposal could be qualified so that the employer could recoup the amount of social security benefits to which the unemployed worker is entitled from the State. This latter system operates already in Britain for sickness benefits and maternity pay.[16]

Framed in this way, the moral argument based upon *necessité oblige* justifies the third conception of a job property right outlined above. It extends the time clause in employment by requiring the employer to be responsible for the continuation of the employee's stream of income for a period of time after his or her services are no longer required. This is the weakest conception of job property, but it would involve a substantial obligation upon the employer. We should consider, however, whether the moral argument can withstand closer scrutiny.

An initial weakness of the argument stems from the factual premiss of dependence. In single company towns, where no alternative employment is available, the employee's dependence must be considerable. But this is an unusual situation; in most cases of economic dismissals other employers exist in the vicinity. Of course, these employers may not have jobs to offer the dismissed workforce, but once the facts are altered in this way, the moral argument must be viewed in a different light. Instead of the dependence upon an employer arising from the fact that he or she is the sole employer in the district, it now arises from the absence of other job opportunities which is profoundly affected by the general level of unemployment. In this general form, the argument is plainly untenable, for in some regions or economies there may in fact be a shortage of labour. Thus, because this justification for job property depends in part upon the buoyancy of the local labour market, it falls short of providing a general justification for recognition of the right.

Even if this difficulty could be overcome, perhaps by asserting that generally speaking the labour market is sufficiently close to equilibrium to ignore the few aberrations which occur, we must question whether the

---

[16] Social Security and Housing Benefits Act 1982, Part 1; Statutory Maternity Pay (General) Regulations 1986, SI 1986, No. 1960.

employee's degree of dependence really warrants the imposition of a duty of care. The parent and child example of a relation of dependence which merits the imposition of a duty of care differs because we accept in all kinds of moral issues that children's lack of maturity makes them a special case. Their inability to fend for themselves truly creates a necessity for someone to care for them. But can the same be said for the average adult worker without diminishing the degree of necessity required so far as to weaken the justification for the imposition of a duty of care? The moral principle of *necessité oblige* creates a narrow exception to the general principle of respect for the autonomy of individuals. Normally we do not owe our neighbours a duty to care for them, even if they have fallen on hard times. Charity may be a virtue, but not a duty with a correlative right.[17] The question then is whether the relation of dependence between employer and employee is sufficiently intense to warrant a departure from the normal principle of autonomy.

Leaving this question aside, for opinions will differ on how to draw the line in this borderline case, one final criticism should be ventured. The content of the duty of care, even when plainly acknowledged as in the relation of parent and child, must be limited both to what is reasonable and to what the parent can afford. The State cannot take a child into care because her parents fail to give her *filet mignon* once a week. Even supposing that the duty of care applies to the employer, the duty must be limited to what the employer can afford. In cases of economic dismissals, inevitably the available sums for compensation may be small. Compelling the employer to pay out wages long after the employee has been made redundant may simply force further dismissals to keep the employer solvent. A duty cannot reasonably be stated in advance, such as a duty to give six months' wages on termination, without ignoring the essential qualification to the duty which respects the shortage of the employers' resources.

None of these objections to the justificiation for a conception of job property based upon the moral argument of *necessité oblige* completely succeeds in discrediting it. Apart from the special case of single company towns, however, where the employer's duty may be raised in the light of the relation of dependence, the end result must be a weak conception of job property which amounts to little more than a duty upon the employer to contribute to income maintenance after the dismissal to the extent that this is financially possible. As has been indicated, this idea of job property is perhaps better analysed as a duty upon the employer to make a contribution to the social security system of background support for unemployed workers. Employers may fairly argue that they already perform this duty by paying

---

[17] Contra: Thomas Reid, in Sir W. Hamilton (ed.), *The Works of Thomas Reid* (6th edn., Edinburgh, 1863).

their contributions to National Insurance, so there is no case for requiring them to pay in addition a severance benefit.

Conclusion   These criticisms of standard justifications for a property right in a job largely dispose of this possible rationale for regulation of economic dismissals. The capital investment argument suffers from its contingency upon an unrealistic hypothetical contract. The argument from necessity seems inapplicable to the generality of economic dismissals, though it works satisfactorily in connection with problems engendered by single company towns. At the most these justifications support weak conceptions of job property, which imply some duty upon the employer to contribute to the social cost of dismissal. They certainly cannot provide a justification for legal regulation which seeks to prevent or deter employers from making economic dismissals in the ordinary run of cases. But once one inspects closely the premisses behind these justifications for severance payments, they provide little ground for the imposition of redundancy payments upon the generality of employers.

(b) Contribution to Autonomy

In Chapter 1 it was argued that the general aim of unfair dismissal legislation is best understood in terms of a response to a right to dignity and a contribution to autonomy. The question now is whether that general aim of the statutory law of unfair dismissal warrants any regulation of economic dismissals, and, if so, does it justify the requirement of severance payments by the employer?

Justifications for Regulation

In general, the right to dignity, as it was interpreted in Chapter 1, has no application to economic dismissals. The employee's grievance is not grounded in a complaint that the management's reasons for dismissal display a lack of respect for the individual employee. In the absence of any work to be done, or a pressing need to improve labour productivity to meet competitive pressures, the employer no more displays disrespect to the dismissed workers than any person who chooses not to buy a service because he or she cannot afford it. Disrespect to the dismissed workers only arises where the employer fails to follow a fair procedure or adopts suspect criteria for selection of those employees to be made redundant. In those circumstances the law of unfair dismissal renders the dismissals unfair.[18] But the employer who carries out economic dismissals is not normally derogating from the employee's right to dignity in the way in which we defined it

---

[18] See Ch. 2.

earlier. This right therefore cannot provide a justification for the protection of job property and the award of redundancy payments.

The other aim of the law of unfair dismissal, to establish conditions conducive to the enjoyment of autonomy, does justify in principle one form of regulation of economic dismissals. An employer who makes workers redundant without substantial economic justification has failed to adopt a rational manpower planning policy which is an essential feature of a workplace environment which fosters the capacity for autonomy. In the absence of sound economic reasons for dismissal, management's attitude towards its labour force veers towards treating it as merely another commodity, one of the factors of production to be purchased in the precise quantity and quality needed without any regard being had to the human needs and aspirations of the workers. This possible derogation from autonomy raises the question whether employers should be required to demonstrate to a neutral forum that market conditions do compel or make advisable some shedding of labour. The problem here, as we shall see below, is to devise a workable mechanism for challenging economic dismissals by means of an independent assessment of the employer's labour requirements. Though sound in principle, such a mechanism seems to be unworkable in practice.

Assessment of Manpower Decisions

Under the British law of dismissal, no direct method exists for challenging the advisability of dismissals. Employees have, however, sought to persuade courts to review management's decision to make redundancies by bringing a claim for unfair dismissal and then seeking to rebut the employer's defence that the workers were redundant. Such arguments have usually failed. In a typical example, *Moon* v. *Homeworthy Furniture Ltd.*,[19] the employees claimed that a factory was economically viable so there was no need to close it and make them redundant. The tribunals declined to go behind the fact that there had been a cessation of business, the statutory test for redundancy, regarding evidence as to the reasons for the factory closure as not only irrelevant but also potentially dangerous, because this would embroil the court in venturing an opinion on the merits of an industrial dispute. Such judgments firmly place the decision to make redundancies within the scope of unreviewable managerial discretion.

The sole possibility for employees who believe their dismissals to be unnecessary is to question the employer's decision on the ground of unfair selection for redundancy. In these cases the employees tackle the employer's manpower planning strategy by seeking to demonstrate its unfairness in allocating unemployment in response to market conditions. For example, in *Watling & Co. Ltd.* v. *Richardson*,[20] the employers were engaged in electrical

[19] [1977] ICR 117 (EAT).
[20] [1978] ICR 1049 (EAT).

contracting, moving their workers from one site to the next as the jobs became available. The employers dismissed the claimant when work at one site had finished, but kept on two other employees hired only ten days before to work on another site (though because of an emergency they had in fact temporarily worked alongside the claimant). The claim for unfair dismissal succeeded on the ground of unfair selection for redundancy, the employer's decisions falling outside the range of reasonable responses. This judgment reveals the possibility of an indirect attack on management's manpower decisions which exists in cases of selection for redundancy between different workers. The employer's manpower policy, which paid scant respect to the length of service of particular individuals, but simply dismissed all workers on a particular site when the job was finished unless they could be transferred to a new site, fell foul of the reasonableness requirement of the law of unfair dismissal. Similarly, a selection for redundancy from a beauty salon in *Orr* v. *Vaughan*,[21] was unfair because the employer had not properly investigated the reasons for the business losing money and had not properly considered in the light of such an investigation (and the length of service of the three employees) which one, if any, should be dismissed. What is not possible is any direct challenge to the employer's decision to reduce the workforce at all.

At the end of the day, it is largely for the employer to decide, on the material which is available to the employer, what is to be done by way of re-organisation of the business; and it is for the employer to decide whether the requirement of the business for employees to carry out the particular work have ceased or diminished. If the employer acts on reasonable information reasonably acquired, then that is the test and no more.[22]

Is it possible to devise a form of legal regulation of economic dismissals which permits a neutral third party such as a tribunal or government official to evaluate the grounds of management's decision to make economic dismissals? Apart from the considerable social cost of administering such a system, many doubt whether any agency or court has the expertise and confidence to second-guess business decisions concerning the product and capital markets. Although the difficulties surrounding such an exercise should not be exaggerated, since so much of the decision will depend upon unverifiable business judgement, it is hard to insist that government agencies would make better decisions in even the majority of cases. The French and Dutch experience with such second-guessing of management's decision does not provide one with much encouragement.

Looking, for example, at the Dutch system of permitting challenges to management's decision before a court on the ground that the decision

---

[21] [1981] IRLR 63 (EAT).
[22] Per Slynn, J [1981] IRLR 65. For a different interpretation of this decision, see Fraser Davidson, *The Judiciary and the Development of Employment Law* (Aldershot, 1984), ch. 3.

exhibits 'mismanagement',[23] what we discover is that management's judgements about the product market are hard to impugn. Some success in preventing plant closures has been won, however, by challenging the redistribution of capital between divisions in a conglomerate. In these circumstances, management's plan envisages closure of one plant and an expansion at another location. The court or official may be able to reason that the savings derived from an amalgamation of production at one site will not exceed the costs of plant closure to the firm. Even so, these calculations will be complex, and one suspects that the court's decision is biased in favour of retaining the industry within its jurisdiction.

In addition to those practical considerations, the potential costs of maintaining such a government agency to review managerial decisions about the necessity for economic dismissals must deter regulation. These costs of administrative regulation, whether borne by the State or the employer, must push up the social costs of dismissals unless, in a substantial number of cases, dismissals are reduced or avoided altogether.

Administrative review may, however, present one potential saving to employers which should be weighed against these objections to regulation based upon its cost. Before the French regulatory system was largely dismantled at the end of 1986,[24] prior to making economic dismissals, an employer had to receive an authorization from a public official, the labour inspector. This authorization was contingent upon the inspector finding that the employer had consulted his workforce, had drawn up a social plan to help employees find new work, and that the economic dismissals were justified. Although few economic dismissals were actually prevented under this regulatory system—perhaps 10 per cent at most[25]—many were delayed for a few months. Despite the apparent cost and inconvenience to the employer which led the new conservative government to abolish these regulations, Loubéjac argues that it conferred considerable benefits upon employers.[26] An administrative authorization of the economic dismissals provides employers with a public recognition of the necessity of the workforce reduction. This legitimization of the decision tends to reduce criticism and undermine potential resistance from the workforce itself. In short, in so far as industrial conflict may arise from the announcement of economic dismissals (and this depends heavily upon the traditions of

[23] A. Jacobs, 'Voluntary Plant Closings and Workforce Reductions in the Netherlands' (1986), 16, *Georgia Journal of International & Comparative Law*, 235.

[24] Code du Travail, L. 321–9, abolished in part by Loi 30/12/86; P.-L. Frier, 'Le Contentieux administratif des "grands" licenciements économiques: une fausse sortie?' (1987), 9/10, *Droit Social*, 678; J.-E. Ray, 'Le Nouveau Droit de licenciement (1985–1987)' (1987), 9/10, *Droit Social*, 664.

[25] F. Loubéjac, 'Sur la suppression de l'autorisation de licenciement' (1986), 3, *Droit Social*, 213, at p. 214.

[26] Ibid. 213.

solidarity within the workforce) then administrative approval may deflect industrial action and avoid its potential costs to the employer.

Thus there may be benefits accruing to an employer from independent manpower assessments to offset the social costs of administrative regulation. But this argument lacks the strength to undermine the previous conclusion that in general public control of economic dismissals is likely to prove costly both to the community and the employer.

Conclusion

The arguments for control over economic dismissals on the ground of respect for individual dignity and augmenting autonomy thus mandate at most a limited field for intervention. The right to dignity leads to the application of standards of procedural standards of fairness in the form of consultation with the individual worker. It also supports an examination of the employer's grounds for selection of particular workers to be made redundant, which can in some instances involve an examination of the fairness of the employer's whole manpower strategy. A concern for autonomy also supports administrative measures designed to test the soundness of the employer's economic calculations for making dismissals, but for reasons of cost and practicability this appears an unwise course to pursue. But none of these considerations supports the recognition of any right to a redundancy payment as a matter of course for economic dismissals.

(c) Distributive Justice

A third possible justification for severance payments demands a fair distribution of the benefits of economic dismissals. When an employer improves productivity by reducing labour costs through economic dismissals, then it may be argued that those workers who have sacrificed their jobs should partake of some of the benefits to general welfare derived from superior productivity. The case for severance payments thus rests upon a fair distribution of the benefits of business reorganization by compelling the employer to relinquish some of those profits to those who stand to lose the most.

The questionable assumption behind this argument is whether economic dismissals improve the profits of the business. Although this may prove to be the case in some business reorganizations, in other instances of economic dismissals, such as plant closures and lay-offs due to declining demand for the product, the dismissals merely serve to reduce the employer's losses. A severance payment in these circumstances does not redistribute profits so much as undermine the employer's trading position even further. Instead of tackling an issue of a fair distribution of benefits springing from a business reorganization, in most economic dismissals the law must address the problem of distributing the economic losses between employer and employees, so the argument based upon a fair distribution of profits has no application.

Even where the argument from distributive fairness does apply to economic dismissals in cases of business reorganization, we should be concerned that by increasing the cost to the employer of effecting such a reorganization by requiring severance payments, this will deter other welfare maximizing manpower planning. This objection leads on to the question of how to minimize the social cost of economic dismissals, bearing in mind that any regulation may have an adverse effect on the levels of employment. We should conclude, therefore, that the argument from distributive fairness has only limited application to economic dismissals, and that even where it does apply it necessarily raises broader questions concerning the welfare maximizing potential of severance payments which must be considered in the general context of the task of minimizing social cost.

(d) Conclusion

This examination of arguments put forward in support of the compulsory imposition of redundancy payments reveals that none of them can survive close scrutiny. The argument based upon protection of a property right dissolves into the question whether employers can provide income support more efficiently than state agencies, which is the central question in the analysis of social cost. Arguments based upon the right to dignity of the worker seem irrelevant and any strengthening of autonomy in the workplace seems impracticable and potentially deleterious to social costs. Considerations of distributive fairness seem inapplicable to most economic dismissals, and, where they do seem pertinent in the case of business reorganizations, they merely pose in a different form the problems concerning the calculus of social cost. For these reasons, it makes better sense to abandon the attempt to find a principle on which to justify the award of severance payments and to examine instead what responses from the law to economic dismissals may be warranted by the criterion of minimizing social costs.

2. NATURE AND CAUSES OF ECONOMIC DISMISSALS

Before engaging in a detailed examination of how to minimize social costs, it is useful to consider the variety of causes behind economic dismissals.[27] We shall discover that the appropriate response from the law depends upon the exact nature of the economic dismissal under inspection.

[27] P. J. White, 'The Management of Redundancy' (1983), 14(1), *Industrial Relations Journal*, 32.

DEMAND FOR LABOUR

In many instances the causes of economic dismissals will be plain. A downturn in the demand for a product will force cut-backs in production, thereby reducing the employer's demand for labour. If, because of obsolescence of the product or the unlikelihood of product demand returning, the plant permanently closes, temporary lay-offs will become dismissals. In these cases, the hope to preserve job security appears forlorn, for in effect the employer is being compelled by market forces to go out of business and no amount of regulation can prevent this.

In less drastic cases, changing technologies of production may force the employer to seek new employees with different skills, whether it be the secretary who must now be able to operate a word processor or a production line manager who must now oversee robots rather than people. Here, new technologies change the nature of the demand for labour, leading in many instances to economic dismissals. Greater opportunities for job security arise in this context, for the employer could be required to pay the costs of retraining the existing workforce so that they can handle the new technology. Such a requirement is, however, likely to prove more costly to the employer and may prove inefficient in the context of social costs if unemployed workers with suitable skills are available to replace the existing workforce.

Measures designed to improve the efficient use of labour are also likely to provoke economic dismissals. An employer may respond to increasingly competitive markets by altering job specifications, such as new hours of work or reduced rates of pay, for the purpose of reducing labour costs or keeping them constant whilst improving productive output. Such fundamental changes in the contract of employment amount to a repudiatory breach by the employer, entitling the employee to regard himself or herself as having been dismissed. Of course, the employee will be more likely to opt for 'constructive dismissal' in these circumstances if the law provides substantial remedies for economic dismissal. The preservation of job security is again possible here, but it can only be achieved by either insisting that employees should be flexible in relation to their terms and conditions of employment or by prohibiting the employer from responding to competitive pressures, the latter option being unconducive to job security in the long run as the business loses its position in the market. The calculus of social costs points strongly against any remedy for employees in such cases, since the costs of unemployment will actually be increased if the employee is permitted to regard himself or herself as having been dismissed and claim a severance benefit. Perhaps to reduce the incentive to enter unemployment, the British courts have rejected claims for redundancy payments in similar circumstances.[28]

---

[28] *Chapman* v. *Goonvean and Rostowrack China Clay Co. Ltd.* [1973] ICR 310 (CA); *Johnson* v. *Nottinghamshire Combined Police Authority* [1974] ICR 170 (CA); *Lesney Products & Co. Ltd.* v. *Nolan* [1977] ICR 235 (CA); *Hollister* v. *National Farmers Union* [1979] ICR 542 (CA); *Richmond Precision Engineering* v. *Pearce* [1985] IRLR 179 (EAT).

FLUIDITY OF CAPITAL MARKETS

In recent years another cause of economic dismissals has come to the fore. Capital may be easily shifted from one investment to another and capital markets naturally tend to push capital towards the point of most profitable return. This fluidity of capital is accentuated in conglomerate corporations, or multi-divisional firms, for there an internal capital market operates, steered by head office, directing the available capital to its most profitable uses within the conglomerate. We can illustrate the drastic effects of the fluidity of capital upon the number of economic dismissals with a simple example.

Imagine that a corporation which produces coal operates three types of mines. Type (a) can only produce coal profitably if the price is set above the current spot price on world markets. Type (b) produces coal profitably at a price below the price set by world markets. Type (c) is the same as (b) except that coal is produced so cheaply that these mines reap much greater profits than type (b). Economic dismissals will occur as a result of the unprofitability of the mine in type (a) unless there is some reason to suppose that world markets will drastically alter in the near future. Similarly, however, type (b) mines will close if the capital can be reinvested in further type (c) mines, for the internal capital market will dictate that the capital be invested in the most profitable place. Moreover, with the fluidity of capital across national boundaries, the gravitation of investment towards type (c) mines can occur in a world arena. Thus one of the ironies of the threat of third-world competition to the industrial base of western societies has been that often the competition emanates from subsidiaries of western conglomerates.[29] The key point to notice, however, is that economic dismissals can be generated in type (b) mines, regardless of the fact that there is demand for the product and that it can be produced profitably. In these type (b) mines it would be possible to preserve job security, of course, though at the expense of restricting investment in type (c) mines.

In this example, the nature of the product has been kept constant, but of course, in a conglomerate which has a finger in many pies, the profitability of type (b) mines will be judged against all the other avenues of investment such as oil, publishing, automobiles, etc. In these circumstances, even type (c) mines may be closed by the conglomerate, or at least sold off, in order to put the capital to more productive use in other sectors of the economy. Although these mine closures might occur in the absence of a conglomerate in line with the normal operation of the external capital market, the existence of an internal capital market permits constant scrutiny of comparable profitability of market sectors, reduces the costs of transferring capital from

---

[29] B. Rhine, 'Business Closings and their Effects on Employees: Adaptation of the Tort of Wrongful Discharge' (1986), 8, *Industrial Relations Law Journal*, 362, at pp.363–4.

one sector to another, permits the use of depreciation write-offs in one business to provide tax savings and retained profits for investment elsewhere,[30] and reduces the corporate need to remain in one particular sector of the market where it has established its reputation and expertise. Given the profitability of type (c) mines, it should be possible to protect job security. Since the business is likely to be sold as a going concern rather than have its assets realized and the plant closed, the protection of job security here takes the form of guaranteeing to workers their existing legal rights despite a transfer of the enterprise, as under the Transfer of Undertakings Regulations 1981.[31]

VERTICAL DISINTEGRATION

Another aspect of modern business organization makes economic dismissals more frequent, though in this instance the event is obscured. One strategy for improving productivity is to offer guarantees of job security to the workforce.[32] Often this guarantee can only be realistically made to a core group of workers. Firms thus engage in vertical disintegration, that is, subcontracting tasks to independent employers with their own workforces. Alternatively the firm divides its labour force formally into permanent staff and temporary and casual workers. Outside the workers in the core firm with job security there then exists a periphery consisting of temporary workers for the firm and subcontractors and their employees. In the event of economic dismissals being required, the core employer can quickly reduce labour costs and production by eliminating temporary workers and declining to place further orders with subcontractors. This organizational framework passes under the name of the 'flexible firm'.[33]

This pattern of core and periphery employees, which corresponds in part to the distinction between primary and secondary labour markets, has been widely used by major businesses. Unfortunately, from the perspective of this chapter, this device for managing labour requirements serves to disguise the source of the decision to make economic dismissals. It permits large firms to lay off workers by remote control through the termination of requirements contracts with subcontractors. The full implications of this capital structure can be appreciated by considering a typical automobile manufacturer. 'British Leyland maintains subcontracting relations with about 4,000 firms

[30] Barry Bluestone and Bennett Harrison, *The Deindustrialization of America: Plant Closings, Community Abandonment, and the Dismantling of Basic Industry* (New York, 1982), at pp. 7, 149–60; L. Kay and K. Griffin, 'Plant Closures: Assessing the Victims' Remedies' (1983), 19, *Willamette Law Review*, 199.

[31] SI 1981, No. 1794, based on EC Directive 77/187.

[32] J. F. Bolt, 'Job Security: Its Time has Come' (1983), 61, *Harvard Business Review*, pt. 6, pp. 115–23.

[33] J. Atkinson, 'Flexibility or Fragmentation? The United Kingdom Labour Market in the Eighties' (1987), 12, *Labour and Society*, 87.

and about 65 per cent of the value of an average Leyland car represents "bought out" parts and components.'[34] By declining to place further orders with subcontractors, the automobile manufacturer compels those employers to make the economic dismissals. In legal systems such as Britain which provide severance benefits in the event of economic dismissals, examples of the effects of this pattern of core and periphery abound. In *Delanair Ltd*. v. *Mead*[35] the employer, Delanair, manufactured heating systems primarily for Ford cars. After a long strike at Fords, the demand for heating systems substantially declined. Delanair, having cut production nearly in half as a result, reduced its labour force by 10 per cent including the individual claimant, Mead. In reality Fords were responsible for this economic dismissal, though of course formally Delanair had terminated the contract of employment. Perhaps because the EAT appreciated Delanair's complete lack of control over the events, it instructed the Industrial Tribunal not to award a redundancy payment to the claimant, if the dismissal occurred from financial exigency rather than a careful reappraisal by Delanair of its need for labour. Although this decision amounts to a dubious interpretation of the relevant legislation,[36] it illustrates the sympathy of the courts for the predicament of peripheral employers, though this concern had the unfortunate effect in this case of depriving the employee of his right to a severance payment.

The core and periphery phenomenon of capital structures alerts us to a serious obstacle to the preservation of job security. Since employers can determine the size of the firm and contract out any part of its operations to independent businesses, major employers could comply with regulations requiring respect for job security for their own employees, whilst at the same time preserving almost complete flexibility in manpower numbers, by using the expedient of external contracting to smaller businesses for fluctuating aspects of production.

A shift in the direction of the flexible firm is likely to result eventually in the increasing redundancy of redundancies, in the sense of lay-offs, since firms will be concerned with expanding small core labour forces rather than reducing large workforces by shedding peripheral members.[37]

For example, the computer firm IBM usually avoids laying off any of its permanent staff by using overtime working, temporary workers, and subcontracting to small manufacturers and suppliers.[38] Since these small employers are often unable to provide stable employment, job security for the core workers may therefore imply reduced security for the periphery, the social cost thus being redistributed simply from one group of workers to another.

---

[34] Andrew L. Friedman, *Industry and Labour* (London, 1977), at p. 118.

[35] [1976] IRLR 340; [1976] ICR 522 (EAT).

[36] Cyril Grunfeld, *The Law of Redundancy* (2nd edn., London, 1980), at p. 195.

[37] C. L. Harris, 'Redundancy and Class Analysis', in Raymond M. Lee, *Redundancy, Layoffs and Plant Closures* (London, 1987), 24, at p. 25.

[38] Bolt, 'Job Security', at p. 118.

When we realize that workers in the periphery will often be drawn from minorities and women, the desirability of such a redistribution becomes even more deeply suspect. In addition, when we discuss below the possible requirements of notice and bargaining over economic dismissals, we will see how this core and periphery arrangement also effectively frustrates potentially worthwhile measures from the perspective of social cost.[39]

ANTI-UNION STRATEGIES

One final cause of economic dismissals should be noted at this point, though these cases will not be considered below. In the USA anti-union sentiment plainly motivates plant closures or, more frequently, relocation of plants. One study suggests that in decisions to relocate plants, although factors like the availability of raw materials, labour costs, and proximity to markets play a part, more important in practice are vague concerns such as business climate and the popularity of unions. In these cases of economic dismissals, it is difficult to disentangle the anti-union sentiment from the concern to reduce labour costs, and the US courts scarcely try to pin down infringements of the right to free association.[40] It is far from clear that anti-union sentiment plays such an important role in generating economic dismissals in Britain, however, and so this topic is more conveniently considered in the context of the general question of the extent to which freedom of association should be protected by the law of dismissal, which will be assessed in Chapter 6.

3. THE EFFICIENCY OF REGULATION

Before examining the details of legal regulation charged with the task of reducing the social costs of economic dismissals, we should consider one crucial preliminary issue. It is normally assumed that any regulation which imposes some burden on the employer in connection with economic dismissals, whether it be a simple notification requirement or a general scheme of severance payments, will inevitably impose additional costs upon employers. These extra labour costs would then have to be included in the calculus designed to discover those measures which lead to a minimization of social costs. Yet, on deeper reflection, it seems likely that not all regulations will impose a significant burden upon employers and that some may indeed prove conducive to more efficient manpower use. To appreciate when this may prove to be the case, we need to examine more carefully the circumstances in which economic dismissals take place.

Against legal intervention in economic dismissals stand the normal eco-

[39] See further, H. Collins, 'Independent Contractors and the Challenge of Vertical Disintegration to Employment Protection Laws' (1990), 10, *Oxford Journal of Legal Studies*, 353.
[40] *Textile Workers Union* v. *Darlington Manufacturing Co.*, 380 US 263 (1965); *NLRB* v. *Transportation Management Corp.*, 103 S. Ct. 2469 (1983).

nomic arguments against any control over dismissals. These arguments, it will be recalled, suggest that regulation of dismissals will increase the cost of labour, resulting either in additional costs to the business with the possible consequences of a reduction of labour demand or loss of competitiveness in the international product market, or some adjustment of wage levels downwards. Against these important considerations, we noted that although improvements to job security impose costs upon employers, these should not be without benefits such as better morale, deeper loyalty to the enterprise, a lower turnover of labour, and a diminution of industrial conflict, all of which tend to improve productivity. The example of lifetime employment in some Japanese companies has been frequently held up as a model for European and American companies to follow, not because of the justice of the arrangement, but because of its efficiency from an employer's cost–benefit calculation. The question whether regulation of economic dismissals invariably imposes a net cost upon employers may be examined in connection with a number of typical measures.

SEVERANCE PAYMENTS

The liability to pay dismissed workers a fixed cash sum clearly increases the cost of labour to employers. It may also have long-term adverse effects upon levels of capital investment and employment, since one of the causes of economic dismissals is the transfer of capital to locations where labour costs are low. Regulation of economic dismissals by requiring severance payments has several possible effects on this phenomenon. The required payment will initially place a brake upon capital flight, for it increases the costs to the employer of relocation. On the other hand, it will also provide a disincentive to further investment in a location which insists upon severance payments, because it ties down capital in one particular place and therefore imposes opportunity costs. In the absence of worldwide standards, therefore, the economic analysis suggests that capital will gradually shift towards investment in countries without such regulation or where the sums payable remain relatively small. For this reason, of course, the European Community has tried to establish uniform standards across member states to prevent any one from being at a competitive disadvantage against the rest,[41] and the US Federal Government imposed a uniform notice requirement upon larger employers.[42]

Yet this economic analysis of the likely impact of severance payments on labour costs and capital investment is gravely flawed and incomplete. One

[41] EEC Directives: 75/129 (notification and consultation for collective redundancies); 77/187 (acquired rights on transfer of undertakings); 80/987 (employees' right in insolvency).

[42] The Worker Adjustment Retraining Notification Act or the Plant Closing Notification Act 1988; see W. B. Gould, 'Job Security in the United States: Some Reflections on Unfair Dismissal and Plant Closure Legislation from a Comparative Perspective' (1988), 67, *Nebraska Law Review*, 28.

effect of the provision of severance benefits is to weaken resistance to change on the part of the workforce. If they are required to adapt to new technology, operate new systems of work, adopt flexible working practices, and so forth, they may prove more accommodating if those workers who are adversely affected by the changes receive compensation for loss of their jobs. It was probably with this objective in mind that the Redundancy Payments Act 1965 was first introduced in Britain. Compensation for economic dismissal was designed not to improve job security, but rather to reduce resistance to change. The underlying aim of government was to increase the international competitiveness of domestic industry by providing guidance on suitable inducements to remove restrictive working practices, and to promote the use of new technologies. The legislation built upon the technique of cash payments already devised by many employers, and which they continue to use more generously than the statutory minimum sums,[43] for the sake of these general welfare considerations.

In a sense, therefore, redundancy payments were designed to make economic dismissals an acceptable practice to the workforce, not to strengthen their job security.[44] If the Government is successful in altering workers' perceptions of the justice of economic dismissals, then there may be strong economic arguments in favour of severance benefits as a technique for increasing labour mobility and flexibility and so improving the international competitiveness of business in the long term. The alleged adverse effects on capital investment and levels of employment will not materialize, and the costs to the employer of severance benefits will be more than offset by the legitimating channel provided by the redundancy payments scheme which can be counterposed to potentially costly industrial action. Evidence from a study of the operation of the redundancy payments legislation reports some success in achieving these goals.[45] From the point of view of the efficiency of the firm, therefore, severance payments may make sense, though this does not mandate compulsory redundancy payments, since their efficiency must depend upon the likelihood of organized worker opposition to dismissals which varies from one workplace to the next.

NOTIFICATION

A duty to give notice to employees liable to be dismissed would in itself place a minute administrative burden upon employers. Objectors to a notice

---

[43] For a summary of the available evidence of employer's use of severance payments in Britain both before 1965 and afterwards, Booth and Chatterji, 'Redundancy Payments and Firm-specific Training', 505; Booth, 'Extra-statutory Redundancy Payments in Britain', 401.

[44] Paul Davies and Mark Freedland, *Labour Law: Text and Materials* (2nd edn., London, 1984), at p. 529.

[45] S. R. Parker, C. G. Thomas, N. D. Ellis, and W. E. J. McCarthy, *Effects of the Redundancy Payments Act* (London, 1971), at pp. 9–16.

requirement, however, insist that the consequential loss to the employer could be considerable.

They suggest, first, that advance warning of dismissal will reduce productivity, both because employees will lose their motivation to work hard and because many will leave early, thereby disrupting the production process. Although common sense indicates the possibility of shirking and even strikes, the limited empirical evidence often points to the contrary result.[46] In some cases this can be explained by the hope of the workforce that an increase in productivity will cause management to alter its decision to make economic dismissals. The problem of early leavers does have more substance, though it should not be exaggerated.[47] It is true that good employees with marketable skills may quit early in order to secure their future position and avoid uncertainty. On the other hand, employees with firm-specific skills are unlikely to be able to find alternative employment at similar rates of pay quickly. Moreover, in a business climate of uncertainty, labour turnover is likely to be high in any case, so the marginal increase in early leaving when precise news is given may not prove significant. Much depends upon how management presents the problems facing the company. Often it is better that precise, reliable information is given out rather than rumours be allowed to foster insecurity and militancy in the workforce. At little extra cost, management may ease the sense of insecurity caused by rumours of economic dismissals by offering counselling services or time off work to apply for other jobs, and in this way avoid the adverse effects upon productivity.

The second kind of consequential loss to the firm concerns customers of the employer, who may be reluctant to continue to deal with that enterprise for fear of being stranded with unfulfilled orders or inadequate post-sales service. Nevertheless any loss of customers will depend heavily upon the type of product. In any case, surely these customers deserve adequate protection for their contractual entitlements to post-sales service? The publicity surrounding the closure will ensure that adequate provision is made.

Finally, and perhaps this is the most serious objection from the point of view of management, disclosure of impending economic dismissals may reduce the value of the stock, which in turn may prejudice or jeopardize the economic rationale behind the reduction in the workforce. Yet the impact upon stock prices cuts both ways, for if the capital market is convinced that a relocation of investment makes sense, then the stock price will rise.

None of the objections to a notice provision on the ground of the costs to the employer therefore appears to carry much weight. Although some firms

[46] A. R. Weber and D. P. Taylor, 'Procedure for Employee Displacement: Advance Notification of Plant Shutdown' (1963), 36(3), *Journal of Business*, 302, at pp. 312–15; Office of Technology Assessment, *Plant Closings: Advance Notification and Rapid Response—Special Report* (Washington, DC, 1986), 22.

[47] Weber and Taylor, 'Procedure for Employee Displacement', 312–15.

might incur substantial costs in complying with a notice requirement, the picture is less clear with respect to the average company. Against these costs must be set the kinds of benefits arising from improvements in productivity described above. Secure in the knowledge that there will be no economic dismissals without notice, employees are more likely to feel inclined to identify with the interests of the company, and to stay with the business even when they might earn more elsewhere. There exists, therefore, a strong possibility that a mandatory notice requirement would not increase the labour costs of businesses, so that a mandatory notice requirement would be warranted even on a narrow cost–benefit analysis.[48]

DUTY TO BARGAIN WITH EMPLOYEES

Before we can apply a cost–benefit analysis to the regulation of the practices of collective industrial relations, some further distinctions need to be drawn. A duty to bargain with representatives of the workforce may occur in a strong and a weak form. In the weak form, it comprises a duty to listen to and respond to proposals from representatives of the workforce, personified either by the union or works council. In the strong form, a good faith requirement is added, which, though uncertain in its precise implications, demands from the employer reasonable efforts to reach an agreement with representatives of the workforce. Under European Community law, the weaker form prevails,[49] usually expressed by the separate national laws as a duty to consult either the recognized union as in Britain,[50] or the Works Councils. Under the US labour law system, unions have claimed with only limited success the stronger duty to bargain in good faith over economic dismissals.

This brings us to a second distinction. Many aspects of economic dismissals might be discussed with the workforce, ranging from management's assessments of the capital and product markets, through decisions concerning the selection of particular workers to be laid off, to severance payments and opportunities for retraining. In the USA the courts have fashioned a distinction between the reasons for the economic dismissals and their effects or consequences on the workforce.[51] Only the latter has been regarded as a mandatory subject for collective bargaining in good faith,

---

[48] For a summary of the US studies and a similar conclusion, see R. G. Ehrenberg and G. H. Jakubson, 'Advance Notification of Plant Closing: Does it Matter?' (1989), 28, *Industrial Relations*, 60.

[49] EEC Directive 75/129 (1975).

[50] Employment Protection Act 1975, s. 99. On the meaning of 'consultation', see *TGWU* v. *Ledbury Preserves (1928) Ltd.* [1985] IRLR 412 (EAT); *Spillers-French (Holdings) Ltd.* v. *USDAW* [1979] IRLR 339 (EAT).

[51] *First National Maintenance Corp.* v. *NLRB*, 452 US 666 (1981); *Otis Elevator Co.*, 269 NLRB No. 162 (1984); R. A. Gorman, 'The Negligible Impact of the National Labor Relations Act on Managerial Decisions to Close or Relocate' (1984), 58, *Tulane Law Review*, 1354.

which permits an employer to refuse to discuss the reasons for the economic dismissals. In Europe, the duty to consult representatives of the workforce is not so confined, for the Directive includes both ways and means of avoiding collective redundancies or reducing the number of workers affected as well as mitigating the consequences.[52] Nevertheless, both kinds of legal provision have given rise to a sense of frustration on the part of the workforce, because of the absence of any duty placed upon the employer to justify the decision to make the dismissals in the first place.

Yet the arguments against a duty to bargain in good faith over the reasons for economic dismissals (as opposed to their incidence and effects) are strong. In most instances, management's decision to make economic dismissals will be grounded in a reasonable assessment of both the product and capital markets. Of course, management may make mistakes about the future, but they have a strong incentive to make the best decision on the available evidence in order to satisfy shareholders and protect their personal positions. Although there is a possibility that representatives of the workforce could point to mistakes in management's calculations, the chance must be small. Against this chance must be set the costs of collective bargaining or consultation, as well as the costs of delays which might be incurred in order to fulfil the duty to bargain in good faith. Because bargaining is time consuming and realistically will have little chance of significant alteration on management's plans, a duty to bargain over the whole economic misfortune of the company is unlikely to produce gains to outweigh the costs.

Nevertheless, with respect to grounds for economic dismissals other than the product and capital markets, there may be scope for an insistence upon the stronger duty to bargain in good faith, which could be supported by the cost–benefit analysis. Two kinds of argument which might be put forward by the representatives of the workforce could be treated as mandatory topics of bargaining in good faith, because the potential savings which they might produce for the employer could exceed the costs of negotiation. These two arguments focus upon possible mistakes which management may have made in assessing the labour market. In certain circumstances the workforce may be in a better position to provide information about the true costs of reductions in the labour force, and they may also be able to alter the total sum of labour costs in a way which profoundly alters the accounting calculations which lie behind the decision to make reductions in the workforce. We can envisage the possibility that the workforce or their representatives could perceive two kinds of mistakes in management's calculations.

The first kind of mistake is an underestimation of the extent to which the workforce are prepared to make concessions on wages or other aspects of

[52] EEC Directive 75/129 (1975), art. 2(2).

labour costs in order to avoid or reduce job losses.[53] During the recession in the early 1980s in America, a number of strong unions have been prepared to enter into concession bargaining rather than face lay-offs.[54] In effect they have traded wage levels for job security, and management have appreciated that this is the most efficient way of handling a downturn in production because labour costs are reduced without losing the services of skilled employees. The movement toward concession bargaining was less pronounced in Britain, perhaps because of the absence of a legally enforceable collective agreement. An individual worker may attempt to frustrate concession bargaining by refusing to accept new terms and conditions of employment,[55] though such a refusal runs the risk of providing the employer with a substantial reason for dismissal sufficient to justify dismissal without compensation.[56] In so far as closures depend upon the movement of capital to more profitable sites, then items such as a reduction in labour costs may make the original plant or industry appear less unattractive as an investment. In short, only the labour force itself can know the extent to which labour costs can be reduced without serious industrial conflict other than by economic dismissals, and they must be in a better position than management to consider the possible savings in that regard. A duty to bargain in good faith over such proposals of concessions in wages could easily satisfy the cost–benefit analysis.

The second kind of mistake which might be made by management and which representatives of the workforce might identify more accurately is a failure to appreciate the impact of dismissals upon aspects of production which are hard to quantify in monetary terms in advance.[57] Two examples are the quality of the product and the health and safety of the workforce. If all that is contemplated by management is a reduction in the workforce, they may be contemplating what turns out, on proper reflection informed by collective bargaining, to be false economies in staff. Although such information would have been available to management, the costs of inquiry may have inhibited a search hitherto. With the co-operation of representatives of the workforce, however, the cost of acquiring this information will be reduced and a duty to consider and discuss the implications of this information may well satisfy a cost–benefit analysis. At the very least, it may influence management's decision about the incidence of dismissals, even if it does not alter the total sum.

These two potential errors in management's calculations indicate that

---

[53] C. J. Arup, 'Redundancy and the Operation of an Employment Termination Law' (1983), 9, *Monash Law Review*, 167, at p. 174.

[54] J. T. Addison, 'Job Security in the United States: Law, Collective Bargaining, Policy, and Practice' (1986), 24, *British Journal of Industrial Relations*, 381.

[55] *Robertson* v. *British Gas Corporation* [1983] ICR 351, [1983] IRLR 302 (CA); *Gibbons* v. *Associated British Ports* [1985] IRLR 376 (QB).

[56] *Hollister* v. *National Farmers' Union* [1979] ICR 542 (CA).

[57] Arup, 'Redundancy and the Operation of an Employment Termination Law', p. 174.

some bargaining in good faith with the workforce prior to the decision to make economic dismissals would be efficient solely from the point of view of the firm. Although the range of bargaining would be confined to the two kinds of costly errors which management could be making, as described above, again this analysis demonstrates that a wholesale rejection of a duty to bargain in good faith over economic dismissals on the ground of the cost to the employer is misconceived.

CONCLUSION

Enough has been said with respect to the cost–benefit analysis from the perspective of the firm to cast doubt on the assumption that all regulation of economic dismissals would impose net costs upon employers. Severance payments do risk the normal costs associated with any attempt to improve job security, and in addition might discourage capital investment in the long run despite providing an initial brake upon capital flight. On the other hand, the provision of severance benefits can be designed to facilitate adaptation on the part of the workforce to new technologies and working practices, and in these circumstances it may establish more attractive industrial practices and competitive labour market conditions for investors. Exactly how these costs and benefits balance out must turn on such variables as the size of payments and the willingness of workers to forgo the exercise of industrial action and pursue the regulatory pathway towards resignation and acceptance of compensation.

With respect to other types of regulation of economic dismissals, again the economic arguments against regulation are only partially convincing. A case can be made that a provision for advance notice would be neutral to employers in relation to its costs and benefits, and that a limited duty to bargain in good faith could in fact benefit firms on average. If so, then these forms of regulation can be supported without harming the profitability of a business or indirectly harming the job security and job opportunities of other workers.

In the light of these conclusions, we turn next to possible justifications for the regulation of economic dismissals which take into account considerations other than the efficiency of the particular firm. The purpose of reflecting first upon the efficiency of regulation has been to point out that, unlike disciplinary dismissals, the efficiency arguments against legal control of economic dismissals are less persuasive.

4. MINIMIZING SOCIAL COST

We are now in a position to consider what types of regulation of economic dismissals satisfy the principle of reduction of social cost. The application of this principle determines when employers should be required to internalize some of these costs.

We concluded above that under this principle the law should transfer the burden to employers if either of two criteria are satisfied: first, when an employer can handle a social cost at less cost than the State; and secondly, when the cost of continuing employment is less than the social costs of unemployment. We should now examine in the light of the relevant social costs what types of regulation could satisfy either of these two criteria.

Three kinds of social costs arising from economic dismissals stand out for attention. First, there are the immediate economic costs of providing income maintenance for the worker and dependants during the ensuing period of unemployment. Plainly this cost depends heavily upon the general level of unemployment which profoundly affects an employee's chances of regaining a steady source of income. In addition, workers differ considerably in their likelihood of regaining equivalent jobs, with older, poorly qualified, women, and minority groups usually suffering relative disadvantage in this respect.[58] Any new job found may be at a lower rate of pay, which may reflect a social cost in wasted investment by the worker in firm-specific skills or more general investments in skills and knowledge (that is, human capital).[59] Secondly, in the longer term, we must reckon on the additional costs of breakdowns in both mental and physical health which appear to be connected with the anomie resulting from termination of employment.[60] Substantial, though not entirely incontrovertible, evidence links the economic dislocation to a family caused by dismissal to physical and mental illness, as well as an increased incidence of certain kinds of criminal behaviour such as spouse and child abuse. Thirdly, many studies demonstrate the cost-effectiveness of active manpower policies. Retraining or redeployment of the worker reduces the likely period of unemployment, that is, the amount of the first kind of social cost described above, but of course these active manpower policies themselves impose additional burdens of administrative and educational expenses. Although worthwhile manpower policies do not increase social costs, they do present the distributive question whether society or the employer making the economic dismissals should bear the expense.

Many of these social costs cannot be redistributed because of their nature. For example, injury to physical and mental health necessarily falls upon the

[58] Bluestone and Harrison, *The Deindustrialization of America: Plant Closings, Community Abandonment, and the Dismantling of Basic Industry*, at pp. 54–5; S. S. Mick, 'Social and Personal Costs of Plant Shutdowns' (1975), 14, *Industrial Relations*, 203, at p. 205.

[59] D. S. Hamermesh, 'The Costs of Worker Displacement' (1987), 102, *Quarterly Journal of Economics*, 51.

[60] Bluestone and Harrison, *The Deindustrialization of America: Plant Closings, Community Abandonment, and the Dismantling of Basic Industry*, at pp. 63–6; Mick, 'Social and Personal Costs of Plant Shutdowns', at p. 205; Carolyn C. Perrucci, Roberts Perrucci, Dena B. Targ, and Harry R. Targ, *Plant Closings: International Context and Social Costs* (New York, 1988), ch. 5.

worker, though the costs of medical care could be redistributed on to either the community or the employer. Similarly, an active manpower policy can only be run effectively by an organization rather than an individual worker, although the individual could be required to contribute to the cost by paying for the retraining. In so far as the social costs can be redistributed, however, in practice the choice will boil down to a bipartite selection between the employer and the community, since the individual employee with only limited resources at his or her disposal will have to depend upon one of the others to pay for most of the costs outlined above. In a nutshell, therefore, the distributive question to be addressed is whether particular social costs arising from economic dismissals should be borne by society or the employer making the dismissal? The discussion proceeds by considering each of the three types of social cost in turn.

INCOME MAINTENANCE

The first social cost is economic hardship caused to the worker through loss of regular income. In considering measures to provide income support, we face the relatively simple distributive question whether the employer should bear some of the cost or whether the State's social security system should pick up the whole tab. The law could redistribute the cost of income maintenance back on to the employer by a number of techniques: (1) it could require the employer to keep the employee in work, or at least continue wages, for a period of time; (2) the employer could be required to make a lump sum severance payment; (3) the employer could be required to increase his or her contribution to the social security system, or to supplement the benefits by direct payments.

The most common legally required contribution by an employer takes the form of a severance payment, either in accordance with a statutory scheme such as the British redundancy payments legislation or as a private contractual inducement to the workforce to avoid industrial conflict. Although these payments indubitably serve the function of income maintenance and have been represented as such, they are rarely calculated by reference to the needs or regular income of the dismissed worker. Instead they reflect principally the length of the employee's service, with the largest sums going to the employees who have worked for the employer for the longest period of time. Often this has the perverse effect of inducing older workers who will find it much harder to gain new employment to accept redundancy first, thus both increasing the social cost of unemployment and the cost to the employer.[61] When, however, as in Australia, attempts are made to reconcile the aim of

---

[61] W. W. Daniel, 'The United Kingdom', in M. Cross (ed.), *Managing Workforce Reduction: An International Survey* (London, 1985), at p. 71; L. S. Root, 'Britain's Redundancy Payments for Displaced Workers' (1987), 110, *Monthly Labor Review*, 18, at p. 22. The system of rebates for employers was intended in part to reduce this perverse effect.

income maintenance with the practice of calculating severance payments on the basis of length of service, this leads to a muddled basis for assessments.[62] This dissonance between the traditional basis of quantification and the goal of income maintenance renders severance payments a clumsy medium for the goal of income maintenance. In addition, the inevitable risk of over- or under-compensation involved in aggregating an uncertain future stream of income loss into a lump sum makes severance payments an inaccurate method for achieving the aim of income maintenance. It is possible, for example, for the recipient of a severance payment to walk immediately into a higher paying job. Thus the inappropriateness of severance payments as a technique of income maintenance places them out of the reckoning in this discussion, despite the widespread practice of using them, for the other techniques of maintaining income are much better tailored to their task.

But can any of the other techniques satisfy the criteria of a reduction of social cost? A reduction in social cost must be ruled out in general, since the object of income maintenance is to provide the employee with a sum of money, which imposes a similar cost whether it is paid by the State or the employer. That only leaves open the possibility that the administrative costs to the employer of providing income maintenance will be less than the costs to the State of providing social security benefits. Even supposing this to be the case, the argument would still only warrant the imposition upon the employer of a duty to administer the benefits, but not necessarily to pay for them. In other words, although the employer would continue to pay some fraction of wages, this sum would be recouped from the State, which amounts to a version of the third technique described above.

The only real chance of a reduction of social costs by diverting the expense of income support on to the employer depends upon the possible reaction from the employer of avoiding economic dismissals altogether. If this happens, then all the social costs of economic dismissals will be avoided though at the expense to the employer of keeping redundant workers on the payroll. This result poses the difficult speculative question whether the savings achieved outweigh the costs of the inefficient use of capital by deterring economic dismissals.

This key issue cannot be answered in the abstract. Neither side of the equation is susceptible to precise quantification. On the one hand, the costs of health care, the criminal justice system, and active manpower policies, cannot be predicted with precision. On the other hand, limitations upon the free movement of capital place a burden which depends upon the opportunity cost, which varies according to the improvement of profitability by moving capital. For example, the rate of return upon the investment may only be

---

[62] See the Australian version which tries unsuccessfully to reconcile the goal of income maintenance with the concept of severance payments by reducing the weight attached to length of service in V. Taylor and D. Yerbury, 'Australia', in Cross (ed.), *Managing Workforce Reduction*, at p. 142.

improved marginally by relocating a plant or it may be doubled overnight. In the former case, a general welfare calculation may suggest that the employer be required to continue to pay the workers in order to reduce social costs, but in the latter case the losses to general welfare from forgoing a profitable investment would exceed the savings in social costs. Moreover, as we have seen, economic dismissals occur for a variety of reasons which complicates the calculations considerably. If the reason for the economic dismissals is not capital flight but rather technological change or a decline in product demand, deterrence of the dismissals by transferring all or part of the social cost of income maintenance on to the employer may endanger the long-term viability of the whole business in internationally competitive markets. Severance payments or continuation of wages might even tend to reduce the aggregate demand for labour over the business cycle and inhibit the formation of new capital, thereby increasing the level of unemployment generally.[63]

These complexities in the calculus of social cost discourage any firm conclusions about the advisability of transferring any of the burder of income support on to the employer. Such measures are unlikely to be neutral in their impact upon the total social cost and there is a considerable risk in many cases that there will be a long-term increase in social cost with no appreciable improvement in job security. So the case for severance payments, or other measures designed to provide income support, probably cannot be made under the criteria of reduction of social cost.

HEALTH AND CRIMINAL JUSTICE COSTS

No one can make a reliable estimate of these social costs. Although the anomie resulting from economic dislocation can be documented in particular instances, it would be foolish to try to generalize from particular studies. For every story of poverty, sickness, and family breakdown resulting from economic dismissals, we can find anecdotes of people finding exciting new careers once jolted out of their routines by economic dismissals. On the whole, of course, we can guess with some limited statistical support that dismissals cause more harm to health than good and that the incidence of certain kinds of criminal behaviour increases (though some may diminish). One American study[64] allows $2,000 per person saved from unemployment to represent the benefit to society from the avoidance of crime, which is not an improbable figure in certain contexts of urban youth unemployment.

The question here is whether this evidence provides sufficient grounds for

---

[63] J. T. Addison and P. Portugal, 'The Effect of Advance Notification of Plant Closings on Unemployment' (1987), 41(1), *Industrial & Labor Relations Review*, 3–16, at p. 13 (discussing the potential similar effect of a notice provision).

[64] D. A. Long, C. D. Mallar, C. V. D. Thornton, 'Evaluating the Benefits and Costs of the Job Corps' (1981), 1, *Journal of Policy Analysis and Management*, 55–76.

switching some of the social cost on to the employer. This could mean either steps to avoid economic dismissals altogether, or to require the employer to contribute to the costs of maintaining the health and criminal justice services. Since we have ruled out the former option, that is, granting permanent possession of jobs, we are left with a possible redistribution of costs. In effect this means a tax upon the employer, in addition to the general level of taxes, for the additional burden which the economic dismissals are likely to impose upon the community in these respects. Against the imposition of such a tax stands the benefits to the general welfare likely to be gained in the long run from permitting economic dismissals and the possibility that some of those benefits will be lost by providing tax disincentives.

Again we are confronted with a complex equation of social cost. The level of the tax would indubitably affect the incidence of economic dismissals. It might be kept to such a low marginal rate that it could be collected without reducing the incidence of economic dismissals (the presumed benefit side of the equation) but at the same time reduce the cost to the community by the taxation contribution. At a much higher level of taxation, economic dismissals would be reduced losing the benefit of economic efficiency but gaining the benefit of avoidance of unemployment and indirect social costs.

ACTIVE MANPOWER POLICY

An active labour market policy involves government intervention in order to preserve the demand for labour, increase the quality of the labour supply, improve geographical mobility, and to remove other impediments to successful job searches. Most states have experimented with a variety of policies such as the provision of employment agencies which notify workers of vacancies, retraining schemes to give dismissed workers marketable skills, temporary employment subsidies, and financial support for geographical mobility (either by means of tax relief or direct payment).

The case for an active manpower policy run by government rests on the reduction of the total social cost attributable to economic dismissals. The question is, can governments devise measures, to help workers find new jobs or keep them in their present employment, which cost less than the social costs of unemployment? It will always be much harder to evaluate the benefits of such programmes compared to the certain costs of administration of the scheme and any mandated financial assistance to employees or employers.[65] Although one clear benefit is the reduction in the amount of unemployment assistance furnished, the precise measure of the reduction must remain open to dispute, since an uncertain percentage of workers

[65] H. L. Wilensky, 'Nothing Fails Like Success: The Evaluation-Research Industry and Labor Market Policy' (1985), 24, *Industrial Relations*, 1.

would have found alternative employment or set themselves up in business[66] without the assistance of such programmes. Fortunately these difficulties of quantifying the advantages of an active manpower policy need not detain us, for the central issue of this inquiry is not whether the State should pursue active manpower policies but rather whether some of the burden of the costs of such programmes, assuming that they have been shown to be cost effective, should be placed upon the employer. This narrow focus eliminates many dimensions of an active manpower policy, because the State can take advantage of economies of scale and better sources of information. It would be a mistake, for example, to require the employer to run an employment agency. Only a few aspects of active manpower policies appear to satisfy the criteria for a reduction of social cost.

Retraining

Improvements in the quality of the labour supply prove particularly important in helping an economy adjust to a rapidly changing technological environment. Training provides a vital role here. It is often most successful in both providing new skills and matching workers to new kinds of jobs if it combines formal education and work experience.[67] But training only succeeds as a method of helping workers to adjust to changing economic conditions if the cost of education is heavily subsidized. When money is short as a result of unemployment and the benefits of retraining uncertain, most workers will be reluctant to commit themselves to expensive retraining.[68] Here the State can play a valuable role by improving the skills of the workforce as a whole, the costs of which may be repaid by preserving the economy's competitive position in the world market. Given, therefore, that states are likely to provide financial assistance for retraining of the dismissed workforce, the question arises whether employers should contribute to these measures.

An employer's contribution to retraining could take the form of taxation to support the State's measures or an independent programme. Could an employer's independent programme successfully retrain workers at lower cost or more effectively than the State's measures? The evidence suggests that general educational systems do not pick up dismissed workers as effectively as localized programmes tailored to individual needs, but this result merely indicates that the State should set up special units close to the plant which can place workers in programmes suitable to their needs and

---

[66] Self-employment cannot be expected to be a solution for most workers unless they have personal non-firm-specific skills even where the law requires or the employer provides generous severance payments as a source of start-up capital; see Raymond M. Lee, 'The Entry to Self-employment of Redundant Steelworkers' (1985), 16(2), *Industrial Relations Journal*, 42.

[67] Wilensky, 'Nothing Fails Like Success', 1.

[68] Jeanne P. Gordus, Paul Jarley, and Louis A. Ferman, *Plant Closings and Economic Dislocation* (Kalamazoo, 1981), at p. 117.

aptitudes. The Massachusetts Industrial Services program provides a useful model in this respect, for it establishes a Worker Assistance Center near the plant closing down, staffed by dismissed workers, which channels all the available assistance with retraining and job search through a single local agency.[69] Yet a case can be made for requiring the employers' co-operation, because they may be in the best position in view of the employee's record to judge the suitability of retraining schemes for the individual. For example, after Ford announced the closure of its San José assembly plant, a collective bargaining agreement established a committee which provided for all employees vocational assessment and advice on suitable training opportunities. The take-up rate of retraining opportunities compared very favourably to the normal rates without such a special scheme.[70] This hypothesis about the value of employers' co-operation suggests that employers could reduce the costs of retraining by loaning the services of their personnel departments to the state agency in order to assist in accurate placement of workers on retraining programmes. If such a step renders the retraining measures more cost effective, then the State should be willing to pay the salaries of the personnel staff. So this suggests that the employer should be required by law to co-operate with retraining schemes, but not necessarily pay for the wages of employees whose services are lent to the State.

Another possible way of encouraging employers to participate in the retraining of their workforce is to provide public funds to assist the employer's programme. In Italy, for example, firms can submit a plan for reorganization and retraining to a public authority, which can provide financial assistance to the employer if it approves the plan.[71] Unfortunately this cumbersome system is necessary to avoid the squandering of public resources, but it may prove attractive to employers faced with the challenge of new technology.

Temporary Employment Subsidy

A government may be prepared to finance continuing levels of employment in those businesses subjected to severe product market pressures during a temporary set-back through such measures as temporary employment subsidies. Under these schemes a government contributes to the wage costs of the employer at a rate lower than or commensurate with unemployment benefits for a limited period of time. The contribution can take many forms, including direct weekly payments to employees or their employer, or short-term loans to the business on advantageous terms. The benefits of such measures from the perspective of general welfare is that the long-term social

[69] R. McGahey, 'State Economic Development Policy: Strategic Approaches for the Future' (1986–7), 15, *New York University Review of Law and Social Change*, 43.

[70] Gary B. Hansen, 'Preventing Layoffs: Developing an Effective Job Security and Economic Adjustment Program' (1985), 11, *Employee Relations Law Journal*, 240, at pp. 262–4.

[71] Edward Yemin, *Workforce Reductions in Undertakings* (Geneva, 1982), at p. 23.

costs of lay-offs are avoided at the relatively minor expense of short-term employment subsidies and temporary refinancing.

Should the employer be required to shoulder a greater burden in these cases of temporary employment subsidies? In one sense the employer receives a windfall, for in effect the State pays for part of the payroll. Moreover, the employer saves the costs of rehiring workers and possibly training new ones when the business picks up again. Further indirect savings may include the avoidance of operational disadvantages from 'bumping' (that is, the practice of moving skilled workers to unskilled jobs and dismissing unskilled workers), lower labour turnover, and a reduction of worker militancy. Do these savings justify the imposition upon the employer of making a further contribution to the cost of keeping employees in work? I think it would be a mistake to require such a contribution, because the employer already incurs the costs of keeping employees on the payroll to the extent of the gap between subsidy and actual wage. Any additional burden upon employers might deter them from co-operating with the scheme, especially as the employer may be undergoing cash-flow problems with the uncertainty surrounding the viability of the business, thereby reducing employees' chances of job security.

Refinancing the Business

Earlier we distinguished economic dismissals predicated upon declines in the product market from those motivated by movements in the internal and external capital markets. Although intervention in dismissals responding to product market decline may be pointless, unless there is a substantial chance that the market will pick up in the near future, the same conclusion does not apply to economic dismissals originating in capital market changes. Given that the pressure from the capital market is leading the owners of the company to wish to reinvest their capital elsewhere, we should recognize that the plant to be closed or slimmed down may still be profitable much in the way that the type (*b*) mines described above could be profitable. In these circumstances, the cost to the community of refinancing the plant out of its own funds may be less than picking up the social costs of mass dismissals. The purpose of an active manpower policy would then become an investigation into the possible refinancing of the business in order to avoid the potentially greater social costs of dismissals.

Indeed the net cost to the community of refinancing the plant may turn out to be small. The community may be able to attract private capital from banks to support the venture. This may happen in the case of the closure of a division of a conglomerate where the return on capital investment throughout the conglomerate is greater than the average return in the external capital market. In this case, although the conglomerate will wish to reinvest its capital in other more profitable divisions of the business, the external capital market may still find the plant an attractive business proposition. Of course, if the capital market worked efficiently, these private investors might come forward in any case. The advantage of introducing the State would be to establish business confidence in the plant by guaranteeing adequate capital investment, so that smaller investors could be encouraged to risk their capital. This step was taken in Britain in the early 1980s under the Loan Guarantee Scheme, through which the Government offered guarantees on 80 per cent of loans up to £75,000 from banks and financial institutions for two to seven years.[72] So in effect the community would sell stocks and shares in the plant to as many private investors as possible, thereby refinancing the business entirely out of private capital with a considerable reduction in the social costs. These considerations in favour of state backing for reopening a business apply with particular force to employee or management buy-outs,[73] for these small investors require a major capital resource. By providing or guaranteeing the initial capital outlay, the community will enable the workforce to keep the business alive, and then over a number of years the employees can acquire the equity in the plant.

Should the law require an employer to co-operate in the refinancing of the business? An employer might not be willing to disclose its books to the public for fear of adverse publicity. Moreover, if the employer plans to set up an identical business in some other location, it may fear competition from the existing plant if it were to reopen. These potential obstacles to co-operation and the reduction of the social costs of dismissals suggest a role for legal intervention. To require full disclosure of the financial position of the firm imposes a small cost on the employer but the savings in social costs are great. The employer's fear of competition from a reopening of a plant should be discounted, however, because if the plant really presented serious competition, the employer would have no reason to close it in the first place.

But co-operation beyond a compulsory disclosure of the firm's accounts may impose substantial costs upon the employer and it would be hard to formulate the duty in concrete legal terms. How, for example, could we express in law a duty to keep the plant in operational condition for as long as possible in order to prevent machinery from deteriorating? Similarly, how could we monitor a duty to bargain in good faith with employees who seek to buy the business without in fact determining what is a fair price?[74] There is a way through taxation, however, which could provide the employer with incentives to co-operate with a refinancing of the business. The reduction in

[72] *Report of the Select Committee of the House of Lords on Unemployment* (London, 1982), i. 63 ff.

[73] D. G. Olson, 'Employee Ownership: An Economic Development Tool for Anchoring Capital in Local Communities' (1986–7), 15, *New York University Review of Law & Social Change*, 239; M. Wright, J. Coyne, and H. Lockley, 'Management Buyouts and Trade Unions: Dispelling the Myths' (1984), 15(3), *Industrial Relations Journal*, 45.

[74] G. Schatzki, 'Some Comments on the Labor–Management Law applied to Plant Closures and Relocations' (1984), 58, *Tulane Law Review*, 1373, at p. 1387.

social costs could be sufficiently large where plant closures are avoided altogether, that the community could afford to grant tax concessions to the original owners of the business if they co-operated with a scheme of refinancing through the State. This approach would also relieve the problem of discouraging further capital investment in new businesses for fear of having capital trapped in a particular location.

Notification Requirement

Once again we must pinpoint the importance of notification of impending economic dismissals, though in this instance the notice should be given to the community in order that it may prepare an adequate response through its manpower machinery. Advance notification can significantly reduce the costs of the community's programme for helping the dismissed workforce to find new employment and at the same time is likely to improve the programme's rate of success because of the availability of a greater time span in which to plan.[75] As a consequence, all three types of social cost described above may be reduced. This burden of giving notice should be placed on the employer, if the cost to the employer is less than the additional cost to the community of preparing for an unexpected dislocation caused by lay-offs, and the advance notification improves the job security of employees. In the majority of cases this appears to be the likely result, since the costs to the employer of any notification requirement should be small, following the arguments considered above.

We should note at this point, however, one difficulty to be overcome by any legal requirement of notice. Earlier we considered the typical business pattern of core and periphery. We observed how the core employer's decision to reduce production effectively caused the economic dismissals of the peripheral employer. There exists a danger that the core employer would provide little by way of notice to the peripheral employer of its intention to cut back production, leaving the peripheral employer scant chance to give adequate notice to the community and its workforce. This difficulty could only be overcome by requiring the core employer to give advance notice where it knows, or ought reasonably to foresee, that the effect of its decision will be to cause economic dismissals in the peripheral employer's business. Such a proposal would be hard to formulate and enforce, though without it much of the benefit of a notice requirement would be lost.

The possible sanctions for breach of a duty to give notice offer further dimensions to an active manpower policy. Although some countries view the right to notice as an individual right of the employee, entitling the individual to compensation in the event of the employer breaking the duty, in the

---

[75] See, for evidence to support this claim, N. R. Folbre, J. L. Leighton, and M. R. Roderick, 'Plant Closings and Their Regulation in Maine, 1971–1982' (1984), 37(2), *Industrial and Labor Relations Review*, 185; Ehrenberg and Jakubson, 'Advance Notification of Plant Closing: Does it Matter?'.

context of an active labour market policy, it makes better sense to follow West Germany and to impose a tax upon the employer for failure to give adequate notice for state authorities to be in a position to respond to the economic dislocation.[76] British law in ss. 100 and 105 of the Employment Protection Act 1975 provides for a small fine for failure to notify the Secretary of State of impending redundancies.[77] Perhaps a more subtle version would be to give exemption from a tax to the extent that the employer creates new employment opportunities in the region.[78] Essentially this last proposal looks to stimulate the demand side for labour through tax incentives for employers to create their own manpower programmes.

Job Creation

Should the employer be required to create a demand for labour, rather than be simply given certain tax incentives to do so? In other words, should the law impose a duty upon the employer to create a social plan, as in many European countries, which encompasses proposals to create job opportunities for the dismissed workforce? In support of such an idea, some empirical evidence suggests that large companies can be in a good position to create job opportunities and to attract investment in a way in which local government agencies cannot. For example, the employer may be in a position to steer substantial subcontract work in the direction of a new venture which employs some of its former workforce, as in the case where Massey Ferguson financed a new company to employ part of the workforce following plant closure and agreed to give it substantial subcontract work.[79] Yet, however successful some of these ventures turn out, plainly few companies facing closure or lay-offs will enjoy the market position and surplus capital to go far down this road of job creation. Nor will the companies necessarily have the expertise at their disposal to assess the viability of such job creation schemes. It would prove hard to distinguish cases where such ambitious social plans were feasible from the ordinary case of plant closure by a small company, and the necessary administrative oversight would be expensive and possibly prone to error. The better course appears to be to offer employers certain tax incentives to adopt job creation schemes, without compelling them to do so.[80] The cost to the employer of running such a

[76] Gerhard Bosch, 'West Germany', in Cross (ed.), *Managing Workforce Reductions*, at p. 178.

[77] The possible financial incentive to notify in order to gain a redundancy rebate disappeared with the rebates; D. Bird, 'Redundancies in Great Britain' (1990), 98, *Employment Gazette*, 450, at p. 453.

[78] *Report of the Select Committee of the House of Lords on Unemployment*, i. 83, discussing the examples of British Steel and Pilkingtons.

[79] C. Baldry, S. Henderson, N. Haworth, and H. Ramsey, 'Multinational Closure and the case of Massey Ferguson, Kilmarnock' (1984), 15(4), *Industrial Relations Journal*, 17, at p. 23.

[80] *Report of the Select Committee of the House of Lords on Unemployment*, i. 83, discussing the examples of British Steel and Pilkingtons.

scheme, less the tax rebate, could well be less than the cost to the community of mounting a similar job creation scheme attaining equivalent results.

Job Search

If job creation seems unrealistic in most instances, how about requiring the employer to contribute to the task of assisting employees to find alternative employment? To set up a full-scale employment agency would be unrealistic and duplicate, probably less efficiently, both specialist private enterprise and government services. Yet the employers' contacts in the business world may afford them special leads on jobs for their former employees. Moreover, a large conglomerate may be in a position to offer employment in its other divisions. A Canadian Commission of Inquiry into Redundancies and Layoffs found that employees' job searches have been most successful when their existing employer participates actively in the search for new employment possibilities.[81] Do these latter considerations warrant the imposition of a duty upon the employer to assist with job searches in some way?

A minimum legal requirement, recognized already in Germany and Britain, is to permit employees time off work prior to dismissal to search for alternative employment. The cost to the employer of planned absenteeism is small compared to the advantage to society of reducing the amount of unemployment by hastening an employee's job search. A more difficult issue concerns the employer's liability to pay wages when the employee absents himself or herself to look for work. The British statute forges a compromise on this point. It permits the employee a general right to a reasonable time off to look for new employment, or to make arrangements for training for future employment,[82] but only provides for pay during absence up to a maximum of two-fifths of a week's pay.[83] This keeps the cost to the employer down below any level which could raise a concern that this form of assistance with job searches fails to satisfy the wealth maximization criterion.

A bolder legal requirement would impose a procedural duty upon an employer to consider the possibility of hiring dismissed employees in other plants owned or controlled by the firm or associated companies. The duty could be satisfied by advertising suitable vacancies and offering priority in hiring to dismissed employees. The additional costs to the employer of such a measure would be minimal since he or she will have the expense of filling these vacancies in any case. The benefits to the community would also be small, however, since the procedure does not increase employment levels, but merely avoids some of the harmful effects of sudden dislocation resulting from dismissal. The main benefit might be a reduction in the time of unemployment between jobs. The benefit could be increased if the duty

---

[81] Yemin, *Workforce Reductions in Undertakings*, at p. 29.
[82] EPCA 1978, s. 31(1).
[83] Ibid., s. 31(9).

were to be strengthened in line with the German provision which provides for compensation to a dismissed employee where alternative employment was available even though the job would only be suitable after retraining.[84] But this duty would impose considerable costs upon the employer, and if other unemployed workers have the necessary skills, then the greater duty would not satisfy the criteria of reduction of social cost.

The main practical difficulty with the weaker proposal lies in devising a suitable mechanism to ensure performance of the procedural duty. If the duty comprises giving priority consideration to dismissed employees, the employer may be able to argue in every case that such consideration was given, but that other applicants appeared more suitable for the job. Hence the failure of dismissed employees to secure employment could not prove breach of the duty. In effect the procedural duty could turn out to be devoid of serious content, allowing the employer to go through the motions without ever holding a serious intention of rehiring existing employees. The closest approximation to this duty achieved by most legal systems with provisions regulating economic dismissals is to give employers exemption from payment of a severance benefit if they offer an employee suitable alternative employment.[85] But this does not amount to a duty to contribute to an active manpower policy, merely an incentive to do so at the discretion of the employer. The British law approaches the imposition of such a duty through the law of unfair dismissal, for in some cases it has been held that the employer acted unfairly in failing to consider the possibility of redeployment where such possibility existed to the knowledge of the employer.[86] Despite the slim advantages offered by a mandatory procedural duty, it should be supported because it recognizes, if only symbolically, the importance to be attached to job security as part of the general legislative aim of fostering conditions conducive to autonomy in the workplace.

5. CONCLUSION

This chapter has examined the strengths and weaknesses of justifications for the legal regulation of economic dismissals. We discovered in section 1 that the arguments for protecting job security against economic dismissal by administrative measures, or deterring dismissals through compulsory severance payments such as redundancy payments, foundered because they were either incoherent, irrelevant, or wholly impractical. We suggested instead that the appropriate principle for guiding a regulatory scheme for economic dismissals should be one which aims to reduce their social cost by compelling

---

[84] Bosch, 'West Germany', at p. 170; Manfred Weiss 'West Germany', in *International Encyclopaedia for Labour Law and Industrial Relations* (Deventer, 1987), v. 91.

[85] Maine Code Annotated 26, s. 625-B 3.C; EPCA 1978, s. 82(3)–(7).

[86] *Vokes Ltd.* v. *Bear* [1973] IRLR 363 (NIRC); *Oakley* v. *The Labour Party* [1988] IRLR 34 (CA); *Thomas & Betts Manufacturing Ltd.* v. *Harding* [1980] IRLR 255 (CA).

the employer to internalize those costs in particular cases. In the pursuance of this policy, we established in section 3 that not all regulation invariably imposes net costs upon employers, so that selective regulatory measures need not cause adverse effects on levels of employment and remuneration which would have to be included in the calculus of social cost.

Judged by the criteria of minimizing social cost, we concluded in section 4 that a few measures of legal regulation of economic dismissals appear warranted. The criteria are satisfied by a notification requirement which insists that the employer should give both the community and the workforce advance warning of the dismissals. Breach of this duty should be sanctioned by a tax upon the employer payable to the community to offset the social costs of dismissals. The employer could earn an abatement or exemption of this tax by an active manpower policy of his or her own, often known as a social plan.

In addition, the employer should be required to bargain in good faith with employees' representatives over all aspects of labour costs and the incidence of dismissals amongst the workforce. Breach of this duty must be sanctioned by specific relief and, if necessary, punitive damages.

Furthermore, the policy of minimizing social costs gives strong support to a requirement upon the employer to contribute to the cost and administration of various active manpower policies. These measures include co-operation between employer and the State with respect to retraining and refinancing the business, and the right for employees to have opportunities to take time off work to look for a new job.

These conclusions do not excite the imagination. All of them, in one form or another, are in place in many countries throughout the world.[87] Their novelty lies rather in the reasoning behind them. The analysis strives to avoid misplaced rhetorical claims for job security and the equally superficial rejection of legal intervention based upon abstract economic models of the market. In addition, these proposals may prove striking because they contain some notable omissions, for example, the kind of severance benefits which lie at the heart of the British redundancy payments legislation. But it should be stressed that this discussion has focused upon legal requirements which set minimum standards for an entire community. No law should prevent gifts from owners of capital to the workforce in the form of severance benefits, but equally none should require them.

[87] See B. Hepple, 'Security of Employment', in R. Blanpain (ed.), *Comparative Labour Law and Industrial Relations* (3rd edn., Deventer, 1987), ch. 22; Erika M. Szyszczak, *Partial Unemployment: The Regulation of Short-Time Working in Britain* (London, 1990)..

[6]

Civil Liberties in the Shadow of Managerial Prerogative

A FAILURE to respect civil liberties constitutes one of the principal sources of injustice in the law of unfair dismissal. Although most liberal states protect basic rights against abuse of power by agencies of the State, their laws generally fall short of adequate protection of civil liberties against the economic power exercised by employers.[1] In the absence of a Bill of Rights in Britain, one must doubt whether civil liberties receive adequate weight in the legal system as a whole. But even if a Bill of Rights were enacted to curb the actions of the State, it should not be forgotten as well that the enjoyment of civil liberties often remains vulnerable to the chilling effect of explicit or implicit threats of disciplinary action. The British law of unfair dismissal reveals its derisory protection for civil liberties against the employer's power of dismissal in two complementary ways.

In the first place, it lacks the general category of public rights dismissals outlined in Chapter 2, with the consequence that only one right, freedom of association, achieves anything commensurate to special protection for a fundamental right. A dismissal on grounds of membership or non-membership of a trade union is not only automatically unfair but also gives rise to a penal award of damages to reflect the affront to public values. The right to equality of opportunity achieves a lesser degree of protection through the sex and race discrimination legislation, but this does not fulfil the requirements for a proper vindication of civil liberties outlined in Chapter 2. Other rights such as freedom of speech, however, receive no such special treatment at all.

In the absence of a distinct category of public rights dismissals for other basic rights, most cases involving civil liberties fall to be decided under the general test of fairness for disciplinary dismissals. Under the 'range of reasonable responses' test, which the tribunals use to determine questions of fairness, considerations of respect for the civil liberties of employees rarely surface in the reasoning of the courts and tribunals. Even when they do, they seem to be easily swamped by considerations reflecting respect for the breadth of managerial prerogative. When the privacy of the employee's

---

[1] L. E. Blades, 'Employment at Will vs. Individual Freedom: On Limiting the Abusive Exercise of Employer Power' (1967), 67, *Columbia Law Review*, 1404.

domestic life comes into question, for instance, the employer's assertions of potential harm to his or her business from a loss of trust and confidence quickly obliterates any residual worries of the tribunal about respect for the liberty of the individual. So the second weakness of the law of unfair dismissal in connection with civil liberties is the interpretation of the fairness standard which places insufficient weight upon respect for individual rights.

To illustrate this double failure, consider a case where an employee exercised his right to freedom of speech. From a newspaper report,[2] we gather that Dr Ross Hesketh was dismissed in 1983 from his job with the Central Electricity Generating Board after questioning his employer's role and the Government's statements on the export of civil plutonium to the USA, and after revealing in public that international safeguards applied in Britain and the USA were inadequate to prevent diversion of civil material into weapons' use. Could Dr Hesketh claim that his dismissal was unfair on the ground that he was merely exercising his right to freedom of speech in the public interest? Since the unfair dismissal legislation contains no special provisions in connection with the right to freedom of speech, the claim would fall under the general test of whether the employer's action lay within the range of reasonable responses of employers to such circumstances. The tribunal would almost certainly have focused on the point that Dr Hesketh had deliberately broken any rules promulgated by the employer about confidentiality of information and that his actions could have an adverse effect upon the employer by diminishing public confidence in the use of nuclear power. Add to this the employer's claim that he had lost confidence in the employee, and the tribunal would have quickly concluded that the dismissal was fair. In so reasoning, the tribunal would almost certainly have given little or no weight to the consideration that Dr Hesketh was purporting to exercise his right to free speech. This important right would be dissolved into the host of competing considerations making up the determination whether the employer acted within the range of reasonable responses. The right to freedom of speech becomes merely one factor which a reasonable employer ought to bear in mind, but one with relatively little weight in the balance against the assertions of potential harm to the business.

Similar results are likely to greet other employees dismissed in circumstances where arguably they were exercising other civil liberties. In *Saunders v. Scottish National Camps Association*,[3] a case considered earlier because it was one of those who initiated the 'range of reasonable responses' test of fairness, the employer's dismissal of a caretaker of a children's summer camp because he was a homosexual was held to be fair, with no mention of the employee's freedom to exercise his sexual preference and respect for his privacy. The tribunals were satisfied by the evidence suggesting that other

[2] *Guardian* (8 Sept. 1983).
[3] [1981] IRLR 277 (CS).

employers would be unwilling to employ a homosexual in proximity to children, without giving any weight to the employee's personal freedom.

The tribunals' approach to questions of fairness in this context appears to mirror quite closely the decisions of the Supreme Court of the United States. Although the jurisdiction of that court consists in the application of constitutional provisions including the Bill of Rights, the court does not grant the same measure of protection to employees of their rights against their state employers as it does for citizens against the government. Although generally a strong upholder of freedom of speech, the Court allows state employers to impose severe constraints on the exercises of this right.[4] The Bill of Rights cannot be invoked against ordinary private employers, and here the common law provides no protection at all for employees exercising their right to freedom of speech,[5] unless the speech consists in informing public authorities of criminal activity.[6] We have already considered in Chapter 4 a similar pattern in connection with the right to procedural fairness or due process, a right of state employees which disappears in the workplace, where, in the absence of explicit statutory provisions or perhaps contractural procedures issued by a public authority, the US courts are unwilling to discover a right to natural justice or procedural due process.[7] As we saw in Chapter 4, the British tribunals similarly do not require employers to adopt the high standards of natural justice applied in the realm of public law.

Underlying this similarity of approach, I suggest, lies a common conception of a division between the public and private realm. When a citizen has rights infringed by the State, this is a matter of public concern deserving legal sanction. But when those same rights are effectively infringed by dismissal or threats of dismissal, then it is a private matter between employer and employee which should be determined by the contractual relations between them. In the first section of this chapter we examine critically this public–private distinction, because it appears to provide the ideological foundation-stone which accounts for the two weaknesses of the law of unfair dismissal described above.

1. THE PUBLIC–PRIVATE DISTINCTION

DEFINITION

We should commence by asking what is the public–private distinction, and why does it matter? My suggestion is that to comprehend why civil liberties

---

[4] *Connick* v. *Myers* 461 US 138 (1983).
[5] *Schultz* v. *Industrial Coils, Inc.*, 125 Wis. 2d 520, 373 NW 2d 74 (1985); *Geary* v. *United States Steel Corp.*, 456 Pa. 171, 319 A. 2d 174 (1974).
[6] *Palmateer* v. *International Harvester Co*, 85 Ill. 2d 124, 421 NE 2d 876 (1981).
[7] *Board of Regents* v. *Roth*, 408 US 564 (1972); *Perry* v. *Sindermann*, 408 US 593 (1972).

are so undervalued in the law of unfair dismissal, we need to appreciate how this abstract distinction colours the interpretation of the law. The assertion that an economic or social relation falls into one category or the other at once both presupposes and determines that a particular set of values should be brought to bear in assessing the conduct of the parties. But the dissonance of values betrayed by the public–private distinction is difficult to expose with precision, because the distinction itself possesses three interrelated connotations.

Privacy

Sometimes the concept of private equates with privacy, so that lawyers employ the contrast to justify the absence of legal regulation. We have already noted that one of the crucial themes of the background ideology of the common law pertaining to dismissal was the view that the hiring and firing of employees was a private matter for employers, a domestic household matter, and so none of the law's business, except in so far as debts such as unpaid wages were left outstanding. The result was the legal doctrine of termination at will or on brief notice, without a judicial power of review of the justice of dismissal. The implicit contrast here lies between private matters best left to the discretion of the individual and public matters of concern to the State where power must be regulated and controlled. As long as dismissal from employment is categorized as a private matter, then the State need not be concerned for the liberty and equality of its citizens.

Jurisdiction and Status

When referring to the public–private distinction on other occasions, lawyers adopt the traditional Roman law contrast between public law and private law.[8] In modern legal systems this denotes either a division of jurisdiction between courts[9] or a difference between the legal status and privileges of state institutions and ordinary individuals.[10] In British labour law the latter point emerges in the controversy over whether civil servants can and do have an ordinary contract of employment, or whether the State as employer is exempt from this traditional category of private law on the ground that a contract would fetter its discretion with potential harm to the public interest.[11] In Chapter 7 we will examine how employees of the State have sought better job security than that provided by the law of unfair dismissal

---

[8] Digest of Justinian (Ulpian), 1.1.2.

[9] M. Waline, Droit administratif (9th edn., Paris, 1963), ch. 2, para. 29.

[10] John Austin, Lectures on Jurisprudence, ed. R. Campbell (3rd edn., London 1869), lecture XLIV, who follows in this respect Sir Matthew Hale and Sir William Blackstone.

[11] See B. Napier, 'The Contract of Employment', in Roy Lewis (ed.), Labour Law in Britain (Oxford, 1986), ch. 12 at p. 333; and now McLaren v. Home Office [1990] IRLR 338 (CA). The public interest being at stake is often regarded as a sign of public law jurisdiction: J. W. Jones, Historical Introduction to the Theory of Law (Oxford, 1940), pp. 159–63.

by attempting to use the public law jurisdiction of the courts, with its differing procedures, principles, and remedies.

More importantly here, the contrasting principles between public and private law play some role in colouring the law's approach to civil liberties at work. As long as the employment relation is viewed as a species of private law contract, and issues of civil liberties are regarded as falling within the province of public law, then the distinction between public and private law presents a conceptual obstacle to the introduction of civil liberties into the workplace. The obstacle is not a complete barrier, for occasionally the courts countenance the introduction of public law principles into employment, as in the example of natural justice considered in Chapter 4. But the obstacle remains, even if its location is moved from time to time, for it remains difficult to introduce public law concepts into legal argument concerning private contractual matters such as employment.

Social Spheres

A third, deeper, but more diffuse use of the public–private distinction finds its roots in a theory of liberal society which postulates the separateness of social spheres. The values which should govern private economic relations such as employment should differ, if not in name, then in meaning, from those applicable to relations of public political power such as that between the citizen and the State. Although freedom and equality are regarded as cardinal principles in both spheres, they receive radically different interpretations. In the private sphere of contract, liberty and equality are regarded as satisfied by the freedom of all persons to enter and choose the terms of a contract.[12] But in the public sphere, liberty demands protection against the abuse of power, and equality requires protection against discrimination. Thus under the values of a private sphere a man should be free to decline to make a contract with a woman for reason of her sex, for this represents an exercise of freedom of contract which the woman enjoys equally. In contrast, in the public sphere such discriminatory treatment of women violates the fundamental principle of equality and reduces their freedom in society.

The separation of these spheres of social life, where different value systems operate, is often explicitly recognized and justified in liberal political philosophy, as in the work of Michael Walzer, *Spheres of Justice*.[13] His principal aim is to define and justify the boundaries between many social spheres. In the case of democracy, for example, Walzer argues that ownership of property should not be permitted to influence political power, but that, in an ordinary factory, he suggests that the subject-matter of political power, sovereignty, a sustained control over men and women, is rarely at stake, so that democratic principles need not be strictly observed within the

---

[12] Hugh Collins, *The Law of Contract* (London, 1986), ch. 2.
[13] (Oxford, 1983).

workplace.[14] It is more common, however, for liberal political theory to suppress the significance of separate spheres of justice. John Rawls's conclusion in his celebrated *A Theory of Justice*,[15] that principles of justice must be divided into two parts, the former protecting individual rights and the latter securing welfare aims, does not on its face subscribe to a separation of spheres of social life. Yet, when one examines closely the content of the individual rights proposed, it is apparent that they apply primarily to the field of civil liberties against government coercion. It seems to be assumed that simple contractual relations will suffice to organize production, subject to redistributive mechanisms like taxation to satisfy the welfare criterion,[16] with scarcely any entry of those individual rights into the private sphere. For example, Rawls regards forms of worker democratic control as compatible with his theory of justice, but does not pause to consider whether they are required by it.[17]

On closer examination, this separation of value systems denoted by the public–private distinction articulates and legitimizes a vital contrast between principles of distributive justice. Private rights protect historical entitlements to property and other forms of wealth, whereas public law offers the possibility of redistributive measures.[18] Justice in the private sphere consists of restoration and compensation for wrongs, whereas broader considerations of general welfare and secure enjoyment of rights provide the touchstone for justice in the public sphere. Classifications of relationships into either public or private imply what kind of justice should be the appropriate concern of the law. Inevitably, therefore, the public–private distinction can function in rhetoric as a means of legitimizing patterns of distributive justice. By labelling a relationship as a private one, it becomes much harder to suggest the law should seek to redistribute wealth rather than to compensate for any wrongs done. Not only does legal regulation of the private realm of the contract of employment perceive its goal in terms of corrective justice, but also it makes it hard to present the augmentation of welfare or increased security for rights as a legitimate purpose of the law.

With regard to the distribution of power in the social spheres, the public–private distinction marks a contrast between the kind of substantive rights enjoyed by a citizen.[19] Public law concerns itself with redressing imbalances of power, whereas private law denies the existence of a problem by asserting a strong presumption of equality. In a liberal state, a citizen's

---

[14] Ibid. 298–303.
[15] (Oxford, 1972).
[16] Ibid. 274–84. Rawls accepts a limited invasion of the private sphere in that the State should enforce equality of opportunity in economic activities and free choice of occupation (at p. 275).
[17] Ibid. 280.
[18] N. E. Simmonds, *The Decline of Juridicial Reason* (Manchester, 1984), p. 128.
[19] Sir Thomas Erskine Holland, *The Elements of Jurisprudence* (13th edn., Oxford, 1924), p. 128.

rights under public law aim to protect the dignity and liberty of an individual. Normally public law also provides a democratic procedure for government in which each citizen participates in the selection of policies. Moreover, public law ensures that those wishes are respected by upholding the principles of the Rule of Law which prevent the agencies of government from overstepping their delegated powers.[20] The rights of a citizen in private law, however, are primarily designed to protect interests in property and to provide the necessary framework for orderly market transactions between equal citizens. Contractual rights do not embrace conceptions of dignity and self-determination except in so far as the equal right to enter binding contracts reflects those values. Hence, by classifying a relationship as falling within the private sphere, no question can arise of rights to dignity, liberty, and self-determination.

In the context of the employment relationship, therefore, by regarding it as an ordinary market transaction within private law, claims for industrial democracy and self-determination appear irrelevant. More importantly, the routine creation of power relations of subordination through the contract of employment lies beyond the perspective of private law principles. Provided that the employer performs his side of the bargain in the form of payment of wages, oppressive terms placed upon the employee must be enforceable and unreviewable by courts. The problem of legitimizing the employer's power over his workforce is neatly avoided by escaping from the category of public. Hence the absence of a distinct category of public rights dismissals reflects the view that in the private sphere of employment no questions about harm to rights can arise.

The public–private distinction and its application to employment issues proves exceedingly hard to assess and challenge because of these three intertwining strands of thought: the appeal to privacy from state intervention, the jurisdictional and procedural emphasis on private law, and separation of spheres of justice in contemporary political theory which is reflected in the law. As a rhetorical device, moreover, the public–private contrast may be constantly manipulated to justify particular policies,[21] so that, for example, trade unions are held to be public institutions at one moment in order to justify legal controls over their internal government, but at the next instant they become private bodies in order to justify their subjection to ordinary private law principles of liability in tort. There can be little doubt, however, that it is the third contrast between public and private in terms of spheres of justice which proves the most fundamental and decisive obstacle to the recognition of civil liberties in the workplace.

---

[20] Sir Harry Woolf, 'Public Law—Private Law: Why the Divide? A Personal View' (1986), *Public Law*, 220, at p. 221.

[21] K. Klare, 'The Public/Private Distinction in Labor Law' (1982), 130, *University of Pennsylvania Law Review*, 1358.

POWER

The most important implication of the separateness of spheres of social life for the protection of civil liberties in the workplace is the view that no such problem arises. The employer's power to dismiss the worker for his or her opinions or way of life raises no risk to civil liberties, for it is merely an exercise of contractual rights, the proper remedy for which is corrective compensation for any unavoidable losses caused.

This denial that a problem exists can perhaps be explained by reference to a narrow conception of power. Liberal theory generally assumes that problems of illegitimate power arise primarily from the use of force. This danger of coercive power which threatens liberty and equality is met, first, by granting to the State an exclusive monopoly on the exercise of force, and secondly, by controlling the State through laws demanding respect for the rights of individuals and the proper exercise of powers under the law.

This view of the source of illegitimate power has often been questioned, with radical political theory pointing out that both economic power derived from ownership of the means of production and ideological power gained from control of the media and professions are in practice far more important in the stable western countries. In addition, one can suggest that the hierarchical structures of workplace organization are in themselves a denial of equality and a dangerous source of power against civil liberties.[22]

It must be admitted, of course, that different forms of power pose different problems of control and legitimization. There is no reason to suppose that the remedies for potential abuse of economic power need be the same as those appropriate to control the use of physical coercion. But it does not follow that economic control does not pose a real threat to liberty and equality in the workplace, nor that the protection of individual rights may prove the most appropriate way of countering any potential abuse of economic and bureaucratic power.

2. LEGITIMIZATION TECHNIQUES OF BOUNDARY MAINTENANCE

This separation of public and private spheres receives three kinds of explicit legitimization in contemporary liberal philosophy. Here I shall describe in outline these three arguments and consider some major objections which can be levelled against them. My argument is that none of them sufficiently justifies that division between public and private spheres which effectively excludes the values of liberty and equality from the workplace.

[22] H. Collins, 'Liberty and Equality in the Workplace' (1990), 42, *Archives for Philosophy of Law and Social Philosophy*, 148.

FREEDOM OF CONTRACT

The traditional justification for denying civil liberties in the workplace springs from ideas of freedom of contract. It is argued that the consensual terms of a contract of employment cannot derogate from liberty and equality any more than any other contractual arrangement. On the contrary, the freedom of the parties to choose whether or not to enter a contract and to select its terms is the hallmark of liberty, and the equality of contracting parties in the market-place is the emblem of formal equality. Only this kind of freedom of association, it is asserted, is truly compatible with political institutions which respect liberty.[23]

To this argument it is often objected that the worker lacks any real freedom or equality when entering into an employment relationship. The employer's ownership of the means of production puts him or her in a strong bargaining position and the worker's need for employment in order to earn a subsistence income really prevents him or her from having any choice but to enter the contract on the employer's terms. In its weak form, this argument points to the inequality of bargaining power of the employee to undermine the legitimacy of the contract of employment.[24] In its strong form, the economic system is said to coerce the worker to sell his or her labour power in a way analogous to physical coercion, which removes any freedom or equality from the transaction.[25]

The problem with these criticisms of the free contract model is that they both seem overstated. It is surely not the case that every employee has inferior bargaining power to the employer, for certain workers may possess skills in high demand, and furthermore labour shortages generally in the economy must considerably strengthen the worker's hand. The strong version of the argument depends ultimately for its persuasive power on the analogy between economic necessity and physical coercion. Although it is true to say that both sources of pressure may effectively reduce a person's options, it is surely wrong to insist that they are exactly the same, so that the employment relation differs not at all from slavery imposed by coercion.

A better way to challenge the legitimization of freedom of contract seems to be to question the premiss that ordinary contracts do not derogate from equality and liberty. We can show, for example, that an ordinary sale of goods to a consumer often deprives the consumer of any choice in the terms and establishes great inequalities of power, since the manufacturer drafts the

---

[23] Rawls, *A Theory of Justice*, at p. 310.

[24] M. Rheinstein (ed.), *Max Weber on Law in Economy and Society* (Cambridge, Mass., 1954), at p. 188; Claus Offe, 'The Political Economy of the Labour Market' and 'Two Logics of Collective Action' in id., *Disorganized Capitalism* (Cambridge, 1985).

[25] Karl Marx, *Capital* (1867; Harmondsworth, 1976), i. 283–92, 798–9, 1063–4; Herbert Marcuse, *Reason and Revolution* (2nd edn., New York, 1963), at pp. 273–312; G. Cohen, 'The Structure of Proletarian Unfreedom' (1983), 12, *Philosophy of Public Affairs*, 3.

terms in order to absolve itself from any responsibility for damage or default. Ordinary contracts are therefore suspect by comparison with the standards of liberty and equality, and the contract of employment partakes of this derogation from liberal values in at least equal measure. Indeed, it is possible that the contract of employment presents a particularly grave problem, not because of inequality of bargaining power, but because the courts endorse the view that management must have strong powers to govern the organization of production with corresponding duties on the part of employees to comply with its instructions. In other words, the paradigm employment relation guarantees considerable control to the employer through the implied terms of the contract or the general rules of construction of the relation, whereas in contrast the paradigm sale of goods to a consumer attempts to even up the disparity in power because it is infused with implied terms which guarantee the quality of the product and therefore gives the consumer some power to demand satisfactory performance.[26] It is this legal endorsement of the social stereotype of subordination in employment which undermines the attempt to legitimize the denial of liberty and equality in the workplace by reference to the ideology of freedom of contract.

INDUSTRIAL PLURALISM

Advocates of industrial pluralism suggest that the denial of the values of equality and liberty in the workplace has been, or should be, remedied by the advent of collective bargaining.[27] In its ideal form the collective organization of workers bargains with the employer on all matters at the workplace, using their improved bargaining power through collective action and control over the labour supply to institute rules which bind managerial prerogative and to gain a fair share of the income of the business. The institutions of collective bargaining themselves are said to represent the embodiment of democratic government.

This account of collective bargaining suffers from two major weaknesses. In the first place, collective bargaining rarely achieves more than an improvement of the basic terms and conditions of employment. In order to support demands for improvements, workers must be prepared to withdraw their labour with a corresponding loss of income. Such potential hardship militates against the scope of collective bargaining stretching beyond the immediate concerns of wages and hours. Far from challenging the hierarchies and inequalities of the workplace, collective bargaining seems at most to set

---

[26] Sale of Goods Act 1979; Unfair Contract Terms Act 1977.
[27] See H. Collins, 'Against Abstentionism in Labour Law', in John Eekelaar and John Bell (eds.), *Oxford Essays in Jurisprudence Third Series* (Oxford, 1987), 79, at pp. 80–4.

the principle terms on which the organization of domination should operate.[28]

Secondly, and this is my major objection to the philosophy of industrial pluralism, it seems wrong in principle to make important civil liberties depend upon market forces and collective strength. For example, if we consider a right to procedural fairness prior to a dismissal from employment, why should this right depend upon the solidarity of the union and the general condition of the labour market? Despite broad aspirations towards industrial democracy, collective bargaining approaches the issue of liberty and equality in the workplace from a private perspective, thereby bolstering the public–private distinction and effectively denying a proper realization of the values of liberty and equality in the workplace.

THE NECESSITY OF AUTHORITY RELATIONS

A third way of legitimizing the public–private distinction is to insist upon the necessity for differentiation because of the exigencies of productive activities. In its strongest form, known as the theory of the firm, this view asserts that the general welfare requires efficient business arrangements, and that efficiency in many forms of productive activity requires managerial hierarchies much in the same way as armies need generals.[29] In a weaker and more subtle version of this argument, it is suggested that workers must choose to divide their activities between leisure, remunerated work, and participation in management of production, and that workers freely choose the current balance between these three interests; this balance normally results in participation being traded off for greater wages and more leisure.[30] In effect workers choose to sacrifice certain aspects of liberty and equality for the sake of greater material wealth and leisure. The stronger version therefore justifies workplace hierarchies on the ground of economic necessity; the weaker version views the hierarchies as the result of complex choices in a world in which an increasing division of labour is feasible and where inequality and subordination are chosen by the workers themselves as a means to greater prosperity and leisure.

The question whether hierarchies at work are necessitated by the nature of productive activities does not admit of a simple answer. Theories of the firm demonstrate rather that different productive activities benefit from different kinds of arrangements, and that even in conveyor-belt production

---

[28] D. E. Feller, 'A General Theory of the Collective Bargaining Agreement' (1973), 61, *California Law Review*, 663; Collins, 'Against Abstentionism in Labour Law', at p. 93.

[29] A. A. Alchian and H. Demsetz, 'Production, Information Costs, and Economic Organization', (1972), 62, *American Economic Review*, 777; O. E. Williamson, *Markets and Hierarchies* (New York, 1975), ch. 4.

[30] Charles Taylor, *Philosophy and the Human Sciences: Philosophical Papers* (Cambridge, 1985), ii. 278–80.

it is far from clear that simple hierarchies of authority function more efficiently than forms of small group production such as quality circles.[31] But even if it could be shown that hierarchies are economically determined or mandated by general welfare considerations, that surely does not warrant the conclusion that liberty and equality need be denied in the workplace. Legal regulation designed to protect civil liberties and equality by treating them as side constraints upon the pursuit of efficient production, as in the example of sex and race discrimination law, is surely possible without subverting the efficient organization of production. Such legal regulation would also protect these interests of workers without requiring them to sacrifice leisure time.

The legitimization of authority relations in the workplace by reference to the imperatives of efficient production therefore does not warrant the total occlusion of the values of liberty and equality in the private sphere. It rather suggests that these rights should be recognized as legal side-constraints upon private bureaucratic power. Although hierarchy may sometimes prove necessary, just as in the case of the exercise of state power, that provides no reason why it cannot be tempered by respect for individual rights.

The weaker version of the argument which regards the hierarchy and subordination of the workplace as the result of a hypothetical contract between workers and employers cannot be so easily discounted. As Charles Taylor argues, the argument only becomes vulnerable if one treats the preferences of workers for greater material prosperity over the realization of the ideals of liberty and equality in the workplace as distorted preferences.[32] Workers choose the maximization of consumer goods because this is what capitalism does best, and this choice is reinforced by all the ideologies of consumerism circulating in a capitalist society in the forms of politics and advertising. In short, the choice is merely to play in the system rather than to reject it in its entirety, and this should not be regarded as an unfettered exercise of autonomy. To question the workers' choice in these circumstances does not pose a challenge to their liberty and dignity, but rather seeks to remove the conditions which effectively subvert any fair opportunity for a meaningful choice.

3. RIGHTS AND GOODS

The above argument suggests that the absence in the law of unfair dismissal of a distinct category of public rights dismissals and the inadequate support for civil liberties afforded by the general 'range of reasonable responses' test of fairness reflect a public–private distinction in which employment is

---

[31] H. Collins, 'Independent Contractors and the Challenge of Vertical Disintegration to Employment Protection Laws' (1990), 10, *Oxford Journal of Legal Studies*, 354, at pp. 356–62.
[32] Taylor, *Philosophy and the Human Sciences*.

characterized as a purely contractual relation based upon free exchange between equal parties. This image of employment and its location in the private sphere is supported by three legitimating ideologies. The fundamental weakness of this perspective engrained in the law lies in its failure to appreciate how managerial authority, organized and deployed through a bureaucracy, constitutes an independent source of domination in the workplace. The rules, procedures, and sanctions of the workplace disciplinary code reveal the independence of this source of power from the bargaining of the market-place. A dismissal is not simply the termination of an economic relation, but an exercise of institutional power.

This bureaucratic power is liable to misuse in much the same way as state power by government agencies. The experience of liberal politics during the last couple of centuries reveals that one highly successful technique for safeguarding individual liberties against the misuse of state power consists in the establishment of constitutional guarantees for individual rights. It is tempting, therefore, to suggest that in defence of individual rights in the workplace, the legislation on unfair dismissal should include a public-rights category which serves the similar function of guaranteeing individual rights against the abuse of managerial authority.

Yet I think that such a simple transplant of ideas and institutions should be resisted. Following the arguments of Joseph Raz, we should recognize that the individual rights protected by such constitutional documents as Bills of Rights are not justifiable simply because they protect certain individual interests. The protection of rights is not an end in itself, but should be seen from the perspective of its protection and promotion of certain collective goods in society. The rights identified in Bills of Rights are those which from historical experience are necessary to ensure the flourishing of a particular public culture. For example, the right to freedom of speech should not be regarded purely as serving some individual interest in liberty.

[S]ome aspects of freedom of speech cannot be explained at all except as protecting collective goods, i.e. preserving the character of the community as an open society. The freedom of the press illustrates the point. In most liberal democracies the press enjoys privileges not extended to ordinary individuals. These include protection against action for libel or breach of privacy, access to information, priority in access to the courts or to Parliamentary sessions, special government briefings, and so on. They are sometimes enshrined in law, sometimes left to conventions. The justification of the special rights and privileges of the press are in its service to the community at large. The interest of individuals in living in an open society is not confined to those who desire to benefit from it as producers or consumers of information or opinion. It extends to all who live in that society, for they benefit from the participation of others in the free exchange of information and opinion.

What is true of freedom of the press is also true of many other aspects of freedom of speech. The precise boundaries of freedom of speech are notoriously controversial, but its core is and always was the protection of political speech and of the free exchange of information which is of public interest. It benefits all those who are subject to that political system. Thus while political theorists often highlight the protection for the individual dissident which it provides, in practice its primary role has been to provide a collective good, to protect the democratic character of society.[33]

These arguments suggest that it would be wrong to devise a category of public rights dismissals which simply imitates the list of rights established in liberal democracies. Books which propose such a simple transplant invariably fail to develop a convincing argument, because they must acknowledge both that these rights must be restricted in special ways, and furthermore that certain rights should be recognized in the workplace even though they have no corresponding right in the public sphere.[34]

A more instructive guide to the range and scope of rights appropriate for the workplace may be gleaned from the Termination of Employment Convention 1982 of the International Labour Organization.[35] Articles 5 and 6 of this Convention enumerate reasons which do not constitute valid reasons for dismissal. These are union membership or participation in union affairs; seeking office as, or acting or having acted as, a workers' representative; the making of a bona fide complaint against an employer for violation of law; race, colour, sex, marital status, family responsibilities, pregnancy, religion, political opinion, national extraction or social origin; absence from work during maternity leave; temporary absence from work because of illness or injury. The ILO has also promulgated a guideline Termination of Employment Recommendation which suggests that age should not constitute a valid reason for dismissal, subject to national law and practice regarding retirement.

Using these ILO standards as a working list of possible examples of public rights dismissals rather than the normal liberal constitutional standards, before adopting them we should subject them to the two criteria for recognition of public rights in the workplace implicit in Raz's argument. First, we should look for instances of the special vulnerability of particular individual interests from the abuse of an employer's bureaucratic power. This criterion reflects the historical origins of the development of legal protection of rights: the complex institutional process necessary to guarantee those rights should only be invoked where individual interests can be demonstrated to be especially vulnerable to attack. Secondly, protection of an individual right should only be afforded when that serves an important collective good, either in its contribution to the nature of the employment

---

[33] Joseph Raz, *The Morality of Freedom* (Oxford, 1986), at pp. 253–4.

[34] e.g. Alan F. Westin and Stephan Salisbury (eds.), *Individual Rights in the Corporation* (New York, 1980); Robert E. Smith, *Workrights* (New York, 1983); David W. Ewing, *Freedom Inside the Organisation* (New York, 1977).

[35] Brian Napier, 'Dismissals; the new ILO Standards' (1983), 12, *ILJ* 17; R. Blanpain, 'Equality and Prohibition of Discrimination in Employment', in id. (ed.), *Comparative Labour Law and Industrial Relations* (3rd edn., Deventer, 1987), ch. 21.

relation, or in its regulation of how the workplace affects other aspects of social life. In assessments of the collective good, we should bear in mind that the general welfare considerations against restricting managerial disciplinary powers also should be balanced in the establishment of a list of protected rights, for those welfare considerations also represent important collective goods.

4. WHAT RIGHTS?

The implications of these two criteria for the establishment and content of a distinct category of public rights dismissals may be illustrated through a number of examples.

THE CLOSED SHOP AND FREEDOM OF ASSOCIATION

In the context of the workplace, the right to freedom of association has been used to defend the formation of trade unions against aggressive anti-union tactics by employers. The history of employers' attempts to suppress the formation of trade unions provides ample support for the view that the individual's interest in joining a trade union is especially vulnerable.[36] At the same time, the dominant labour law policy of industrial pluralism has supported the claim that because the formation of trade unions is a necessary precondition to the growth of collective bargaining, the right to freedom of association satisfies the requirement of contributing to a collective good. In addition, the formation of trade unions may contribute to other collective goods, such as the provision of adequate grievance procedures for individual employees. Although, therefore, the right to freedom of association clearly deserves inclusion in a list of public rights, so that a dismissal motivated by anti-union sentiment should be automatically unfair, the precise meaning and extent of this right in the context of the workplace has proved controversial, especially in connection with the closed shop.

A closed shop comprises an agreement between an employer and a trade union that all employees, or all employees of a particular class, should be members of the union. Unions seek such agreements both to consolidate their collective bargaining power and as a symbolic affirmation of their position as joint regulators of the workplace and the solidarity of the workforce behind their representatives.[37] Employers can benefit from the avoidance of multiple unions and the assurance that the workforce will abide by collective agreements.[38] But from the point of view of a simple theory of individual rights, the closed shop interferes with the right of freedom of

[36] S. Evans and R. Lewis, 'Anti-union Discrimination: Practice, Law and Policy' (1987), 16, *ILJ* 88.
[37] Stephen Dunn and John Gennard, *The Closed Shop in British Industry* (London, 1984).
[38] M. Hart, 'Why Bosses Love the Closed Shop', *New Society* (15 Feb. 1979), 352.

association. Because employees are likely to lose their employment if they refuse to join the appropriate trade union, their freedom not to associate with a particular group is impaired.

The law of unfair dismissal, as it stands in 1991, accepts this analysis of the infringement of the right to freedom of association. It determines that a dismissal is automatically unfair if the reason for the dismissal is either that an employee is a member of a trade union or is not a member of one.[39] In effect, an employer may only dismiss an employee for refusing to join a trade union on pain of paying the punitive damages of the special award.[40] This legislation simply transplants the right to freedom of association forged in connection with the development of political parties in a liberal democracy to the workplace and applies it without qualification to membership of trade unions.

Under my proposed criteria, however, the result would not necessarily be the same. The first question to be asked is whether employees' individual interest in this aspect of their freedom can be demonstrated to be especially vulnerable to the abuse of managerial prerogative. Whether or not the individual interest in not being compelled to join a trade union has been oppressed is controversial.[41] In a few scattered cases we can find evidence that unions and employers have used the closed shop to exclude workers who have genuine objections to membership of particular trade unions or any trade union whatsoever.[42] But most union membership agreements have not been strictly enforced. Often they have not been applied to existing employees prior to the inauguration of closed shops,[43] and they normally recognize certain exceptions to protect employees with deeply held personal convictions against union membership.[44] On the dubious assumption, however, that sufficient abuse of power has taken place in the past to satisfy the first test, we should next consider the second criterion which asks whether the defence of the right would serve some important collective good?

Again, however, it is far from clear that the negative aspect of freedom of association, the freedom not to belong to a trade union, serves a worthwhile collective good. Where is the collective good in permitting subversion of the solidarity of trade union membership by permitting free riders, weakening the collective-bargaining power of trade unions, and sowing the seeds of disruption through unofficial industrial action?[45] The good, if it exists, must

---

[39] EPCA 1978, s. 58, as amended by Employment Act 1988, s. 11. The same principle also applies to access to employment: Employment Act 1990, s. 1.

[40] EPCA 1978, s. 75A.

[41] O. Kahn-Freund, 'Trade Unions, The Law and Society' (1970), 33, *Modern Law Review*, 241.

[42] Dunn and Gennard, *The Closed Shop in British Industry*, pp. 124–37.

[43] Ibid. 122 ff.; B. Weekes, 'Law and the Practice of the Closed Shop' (1976), 5, *ILJ* 211; R. Benedictus, 'Closed Shop Exemptions and Their Wording' (1979), 8, *ILJ* 160.

[44] Dunn and Gennard, *The Closed Shop in British Industry*, pp. 23–4.

[45] See Royal Commission on Trade Unions and Employers' Associations, Cmnd. 3623 (1965–8) (Donovan Commission), para. 599.

lie either in reducing the wage increases of workers for the sake of improving the profitability of capital investment, or in a revised attitude towards collective bargaining which now sees individual bargaining as the prefered market mechanism for settling terms and conditions of employment.[46]

This discussion of the closed shop reveals that my criteria for inclusion of rights within a distinct category of public rights dismissals do not provide cut and dried answers to important questions. Since rights deserve protection when the individual interests at stake are especially vulnerable and serve an important public good, empirical questions relating to their vulnerability and political questions about the scope of public goods must be answered before it can be said whether a particular right should be included on the list. My conclusions with respect to the closed shop probably indicate that some limited scope for the enforcement of union membership agreements should be permitted, perhaps along the lines of the Employment Act 1982, which built in guarantees for deeply held personal convictions and insisted that prior to the inception of a closed shop an affirmative ballot of the workforce should be held. The individual guarantees would reflect the first criterion of the special vulnerability of particular individuals such as those whose religious faith mandated non-membership of a trade union, and the secret ballot would test the validity of the claim of solidarity of support behind a particular trade union. But these conclusions might have to be modified if conceptions of the public worth of collective bargaining alter so dramatically that it is no longer perceived as serving a worthwhile goal in shaping the nature of employment relations. What I reject is the simplistic transplant of the right of freedom of association from its political context to the workplace without further examination of the justifications and goals secured by the protection of individual rights against the abuse of private bureaucratic power.

PRIVACY

The ILO standards give at least two examples where the nature of the invalid reason for dismissal embraces the value of protecting the private life of individuals. These are dismissals based upon religion and political opinion. But should the protection against managerial disciplinary power which infringes the private life of the individual outside work be confined to these two instances?

Many of the cases of disciplinary dismissals considered in this book concern instances where the reason for dismissal relates to other kinds of activities outside the workplace. Dismissals for shoplifting during a lunch-

---

[46] Lord Wedderburn, 'Freedom of Association and Philosophies of Labour Law' (1989), 18, *ILJ* 1; Ferdinand von Prondzynski, *Freedom of Association and Industrial Relations* (London, 1987), ch. 11.

break,[47] for being arrested for possession of prohibited drugs in the park,[48] or for being a homosexual,[49] all fall into this category. Other examples might include dismissal for sexual relations regarded by the employer as immoral such as adulterous relations,[50] or for remarriage after divorce by a teacher in a Catholic school.[51] All these examples will be handled under the current law of unfair dismissal by the ordinary test of fairness.

We have noted that the 'range of reasonable responses' test of fairness tends to endorse management's decision to dismiss in these circumstances. The tribunal decided that Mr Mathewson's dismissal for being arrested for possession of cannabis during his lunch-break in the park was 'harsh but fair'. But these cases pose the question whether some civil liberty of the employee is being invaded by the exercise of managerial disciplinary powers in such circumstances. This civil liberty may be described as a right to privacy, the freedom from supervision and control by an employer of one's life outside working hours.

Of course, this turns the idea of privacy in employment on its head. The dominant perspective of the nineteenth century viewed the fulfilment of privacy in the protection of the master in governing his own domestics as he saw fit, and this could certainly include control over every aspect of their lives.

May I not refuse to trade with any one? May I not forbid my family to trade with any one? May I not dismiss my domestic servant for dealing, or even visiting, where I forbid? And if my domestic, why not my farm-hand, or my mechanic, or my teamster?[52]

In the modern context of employment, the idea of respect for privacy becomes one of protecting employees from attempts by their employers to control what they do outside working hours.

Here again a simple transplant of rights from the constitutional sphere to the workplace would be undesirable. Since these constitutional rights do not generally protect those who have infringed the criminal law, no right would exist to protect many of these individuals dismissed for activities outside work. Thus the potential force of the employee's objection to discipline for these reasons would be lost altogether.

Applying my proposed criteria, however, we can begin to develop a case for special protection against dismissal for activities outside work, whether they be lawful or unlawful. We would first have to identify the special

---

[47] *Moore* v. *C. & A. Modes* [1981] IRLR 71 (EAT).

[48] *Mathewson* v. *R. B. Wilson Dental Laboratories* [1988] IRLR 512 (EAT).

[49] *Saunders* v. *Scottish National Camps Association* [1980] IRLR 174 (EAT); affirmed [1981] IRLR 277 (Ct. Sess.).

[50] *Spiller* v. *F. J. Wallis Ltd.* [1975] IRLR 362 (IT).

[51] *Jones* v. *Lee* [1980] ICR 310 (CA); see, generally, G. Giugni, 'Political, Religious and Private Life Discrimination', in Folke Schmidt (ed.), *Discrimination in Employment* (Stockholm, 1978), ch. 4; J. M. Thompson, 'Crime, Morality, and Unfair Dismissal' (1982), 98, 423; B. Teyssié, 'Personnes, entreprises et relations de travail' (1988), *Droit Social*, 374.

[52] *Payne* v. *Western & Atlantic R. R. Co.*, 81 Tenn. (13 Lea) 507, (1884) at p. 518.

vulnerability of certain types of individual interest in liberty and privacy to disciplinary action. This might be established by many examples of discrimination against homosexuals and strict codes against drugs promulgated by employers.

The second stage would be to ask whether the protection of a right to privacy in such circumstances would serve an important collective good, either in its contribution to the nature of the employment relation, or in its regulation of how the workplace affects other aspects of social life. Tolerance of criminal offences committed outside work does not in itself qualify as a collective good, of course, but the collective good in these instances concerns the relation between the workplace and other dimensions of social life. One of the key ingredients of respect for autonomy consists in the establishment of conditions which permit individuals to be the authors of their own lives. The danger which invasions of privacy by employers pose is that, in making one choice, the choice to take a particular job, the individual indirectly and unwillingly commits himself or herself to the adoption of certain other standards in the remainder of his or her life. By virtue of the employer's expansive disciplinary code, the employee commits himself or herself not only to hard work but also the duty to live the remainder of his or her life in a manner which the employer sees fit. Mr Mathewson must not only prove himself a skilled craftsman but also must refrain from smoking cannabis at weekends; and Mr Saunders must not only care for the school premises but also refrain from exercising his sexual preference on a Saturday night in town. The underlying aim of the law of unfair dismissal, it has been argued, is to foster autonomy by establishing opportunities to enter into worthwhile employment opportunities. Here the value of autonomy indicates that we should also ensure that managerial disciplinary power should not overreach itself, so that this individual's choice to enter employment should not determine his or her choices with respect to other aspects of his or her life. If this were to be permitted, then it would be the employer, not the employee, who would be author of the employee's life.

Applying these principles to our various examples, they require different treatment. In the case of discrimination against homosexuals, there seems sufficient empirical evidence of victimization to support a claim for protection of an interest. The collective good which clinches support for categorization as a public rights dismissal lies not in the uncertain public support for homosexual relations but in the protection of autonomy. This reasoning may be strengthened by recognizing that to attempt to deprive someone of his or her identity as a member of a particular group such as gays also impinges upon an important aspect of autonomy, for being autonomous does not require isolation but the ability to participate in groups which give individuals their sense of identity and worth.[53]

---

[53] Raz, *The Morality of Freedom*, at p. 254.

In our other examples of drugs and shoplifting, however, the historical pattern of victimization is less clear at present, and the worth of these choices must be doubted. Therefore, the two criteria suggest merely that in applying the test of fairness the tribunals should recognize the danger to autonomy presented by expansive disciplinary codes, and should find such dismissals unfair unless the employer presents substantial evidence of the risk of harm to the business. A good example of this approach to criminal offences committed away from work was set in *Norfolk County Council* v. *Barnard*.[54] Here the employee worked as a trainer of drama teachers. He was driving home late one evening when he was stopped by the police for a breath test. The police searched his car and discovered a small quantity of cannabis. He pleaded guilty to a charge of possession. The local authority then dismissed him for misconduct. The Industrial Tribunal found the dismissal was unfair, expressing the relevant principles in these terms:

If a conviction for an offence outside employment seriously and genuinely affects the employee's relationship with his fellow employees then the dismissal might be justified. The same proposition is put forward if the nature of the offence upon which the conviction rests made the employee a danger to others particularly children. Certainly in that case dismissal would be justified. In certain circumstances dismissal for a criminal conviction might justify dismissal if the reputation or the business of an employer could be genuinely and seriously affected adversely. We cannot find in this case any of these conditions present.

The EAT approved the decision and the reasoning of the tribunal. In its emphasis upon the need to demonstrate a serious adverse effect on the business, this decision more fully accords with the aim of respecting autonomy which lies behind the legislation than other reported cases such as *Mathewson* v. *R. B. Wilson Dental Laboratories*.[55]

FREE SPEECH

We have already noted the striking contrast between the protection of freedom of speech afforded by constitutions in a public context compared to the complete absence of safeguards for whistle-blowers in the private realm of ordinary employment.[56] When the potential whistle-blower on corruption or defective products is faced by the dilemma of either being disloyal to his or her employer or deceiving the public and betraying his or her conscience,

---

[54] [1979] IRLR 220 (EAT).

[55] [1988] IRLR 512 (EAT).

[56] I confine my comments here to speech and writing, but of course freedom of speech might be construed more broadly to include expression of personal taste through clothes (*Tardif* v. *Quinn* 545 F 2d 761 (1976) (CA First Circ.)); badges (e.g. *Boychuck* v. *H. J. Symons Holdings Ltd*. [1977] IRLR 395 (EAT)); and grooming (*Kelley* v. *Johnson* 425 US 238 (1975) (Supreme Court)), where the considerations raised will be rather different including sex stereotyping (*Earwood* v. *Continental Southeastern Lines Inc*. 539 F 2d 1349 (1976) (CA Fourth Circ.)).

the law generally counsels the employees to keep quiet. Although a court may decline to issue an injunction which would prohibit employees revealing to the public or at least the police confidential information of the employer which betrays possible illegality,[57] neither the common law nor the law of unfair dismissal offers the employee significant protection against dismissal. But should we extend the protection of freedom of speech to the workplace without modification? Again such an immediate transplant of constitutional rights would be a mistake.

Although freedom of speech is clearly an individual interest which is especially vulnerable to threats of disciplinary action, the collective good necessary to support the establishment of a category of public rights dismissals in this context must be examined closely. The collective good may spring from two sources.

First, there may be a public interest in the continuation of aspects of the open society into the workplace. This might apply to employees who disclosed to the public the criminal activity of their employers,[58] or the concealed dangers of the products of the firm.[59] In the public sector, revelations of corruption and mismanagement might also satisfy this public interest.[60] Such whistle-blowers exercise freedom of speech precisely for those kinds of reasons which an open society values, such as legality and respect for legal duties, and they should receive protection against disciplinary action.

A second source of potential collective good arising from the protection of freedom of speech concerns the operation of the workplace itself. Freedom of speech may support efficient decisions, for management will be kept properly informed of all the relevant information when they make their decisions.[61] The danger of controls over freedom of speech in these instances derives from junior employees fearing disciplinary action from exposing the incompetence or mistakes of their immediate superiors. Another related reason for supporting freedom of speech depends upon whether there is a public value in promoting versions of participatory democracy at work. To the extent that this is collectively regarded as a desirable goal, then, for the same reasons as democracy in government flourishes best under conditions of freedom of information and expression, so too workplace democracy would function best if freedom of speech were protected.

---

[57] *Initial Services* v. *Putterill* [1968] 1 QB 405 (CA); *Lion Laboratories* v. *Evans* [1984] 3 WLR 539 (CA); *Schering Chemicals* v. *Falkman* [1982] QB 1 (CA); *Re a company's application* [1989] 2 All E.R. 248 (Ch.D) see Eric Barendt, *Freedom of Speech* (Oxford, 1987), at pp. 132–3.

[58] *Palmateer* v. *International Harvester*, 85 Ill. 2d 124, 421 NE 2d 876 (1981).

[59] *Geary* v. *United States Steel Corp.*, 456 Pa. 171, 319 A. 2d 174 (1974).

[60] US federal law gives express protection for whistle-blowers in the public sector, but the level of protection for employees seems unsatisfactory in practice: T. M. Devine and D. G. Aplin, 'Whistleblower Portection: The Gap between the Law and Reality' (1988), 31, *Howard Law Journal*, 223.

[61] For similar lines of reasoning using transactions costs economics, see O. E. Williamson, 'The Organization of Work' (1980), 1, *Journal of Economic Behavior and Organization*, 1.

In my estimation, these considerations probably only support at present the creation of a public right in connection with speech which serves the collective good described as the public interest. This would protect whistle-blowers against dismissal where they have disclosed corporate misfeasance which involves criminal or dangerous practices. But this protection for freedom of speech would not extend to the revelation of trade secrets or confidential, market-sensitive, information. Nor would it extend to remarks which seriously undermined useful authority structures in the workplace, though this should not prevent constructive criticism. As Kenneth Walters has observed,

It is one thing to expect employees to commit themselves to pursuing broad organizational objectives; it is quite another to see the contract of employment as a faustian bargain in which employees suspend all critical judgment to serve their superiors.[62]

Disentangling these different aspects of freedom of speech would no doubt prove difficult in some instances, but the principles governing the distinction should be clear. In *Connick* v. *Myers*,[63] a case before the US Supreme Court concerning speech in a district attorney's office, the court characterized the issue, as it had in previous cases,[64] as one of balancing the interest of the employee as a citizen in commenting upon matters of public concern and the employer's interest in the efficiency of its operations. After examining the questions circulated by the appellant in an internal office memorandum, the Court determined that one raised an issue of public concern, namely whether or not employees were forced to work in political campaigns, but that the remaining questions raised issues of internal management, such as confidence in supervisors, office morale, and the need for grievance procedures, which did not deserve constitutional protection. The majority of the Court upheld the dismissal as lawful, but the dissenting minority argued both that, even if only one question was on a constitution-ally protected issue, the dismissal should be unlawful, and that in any case questions of trust and morale in the office of the district attorney fell within the province of matters of public interest. The disagreement here largely concerns the exact scope of speech in the public interest, an issue confused by the public nature of the employer, but the general principles seem worthy of general application through a public rights category of unfair dismissal.

All the members of the Supreme Court seem to have assumed that the second possible justification for a collective good in freedom of speech should

---

[62] Kenneth D. Walters, 'Your Employees' Right to Blow the Whistle', in A. F. Westin and S. Salisbury (eds.), *Individual Rights in the Corporation* (New York, 1980).

[63] 461 US 138; 103 S. Ct. 1684 (1983).

[64] See *Pickering* v. *Board of Education* 391 US 563, 88 S. Ct. 1731 (1968); *Givhan* v. *Western Line Consolidated School District*, 439 US 410, 99 S. Ct. 693 (1979).

not be credited. They believe apparently that a tension exists between, on the one hand, efficient and good management, and on the other, the freedom to speak one's mind in the workplace. Robert Ladenson presents this argument in terms of individuality or autonomy.

Specifically in regard to the workplace, one can argue that individuality on a wide scale can flourish only under background conditions of general economic well-being. Certain modes of discipline in a work setting, however, are indispensable for the maintenance of efficient production or delivery of services. Accordingly, freedom of expression in the workplace must not extend so far as to undermine seriously the conditions of material prosperity upon which individuality also depends.[65]

This inevitably rules out a broader protection of freedom of speech as a useful ingredient of efficient decisions or a necessary adjunct of democratic participation in management. Hence US courts assume that dismissal is justified if the published speech might cause loss of respect for management and problems of morale in the workforce.[66]

The complexity of the issue of the exact limits of freedom of speech in the workplace can be illustrated further by a case involving a clash between the value of participatory democracy at work and the need for orderly industrial relations. In *British Airways Engine Overhaul Ltd.* v. *Francis*,[67] following a meeting of women workers employed by the company, their shop steward spoke to the press to complain that her union was not actively pursuing its policy of seeking equal pay for women at the company. The company reprimanded the shop steward on the ground that her statements to the press violated company regulations. The EAT upheld her complaint that the reprimand amounted to action deterring her from taking part in the activities of an independent trade union, or penalizing her for so doing, contrary to s. 23(1) of EPCA 1978. This avenue for protection of free speech through the guarantees for trade union activities has been confined usually to communications connected to bargaining with a recognized trade union.[68] For example, in a claim for unfair dismissal under s. 58 of EPCA 1978 when a union member organized a petition to complain that the machinery which the employees used was not safe, the EAT decided that the fact that few employees were members of the union and the employer had not recognized the union prevented the dismissal from being unfair for penalizing a trade union activity.[69] In the *Francis* case, the shop steward fell just within the scope of the protection of trade union activities, because she could be regarded as a spokesperson for the recognized union and her remarks were made in the context of a dispute about equal pay. But it seems clear that

[65] Robert F. Ladenson, *A Philosophy of Free Expression* (Totowa, NJ, 1983), at p. 117.
[66] *Schultz* v. *Industrial Coils Inc.* 125 Wis. 2d 520, 373 NW 2d 74 (Ct. App. 1985).
[67] [1981] ICR 278 (EAT).
[68] For a slightly broader interpretation of the protection, see *Dixon*, v. *West Ella Developments Ltd.* [1978] ICR 856 (EAT).
[69] *Chant* v. *Aquaboats Ltd.* [1978] ICR 643 (EAT).

without her qualification as shop steward her remarks to the press which were of course critical of the union and the established bargaining process would have been outside the statutory protection for trade union activities. The tribunals seem to want to confine this indirect protection for freedom of speech to statements which they regard as an inevitable part and parcel of collective bargaining. Outside this field, the concern for participatory democracy becomes overwhelmed by the dual factors of protection of managerial disciplinary power and support for orderly collective bargaining through recognized channels and procedures.

In the future, however, the strength of public support for democratic participation in management might increase, and, if so, then this aspect of freedom of speech might deserve protection as a public right, thus encompassing even speech which undermined managerial authority in some instances. European countries have moved further in this direction by protecting speech connected to the activities of Workers Councils. But even the recent French legislation which purports to enact a new right of freedom of expression is limited by the countervailing concerns of protection of the interests of the business. It permits employees freedom of expression with respect to the content, organization, and terms of work.[70] This falls short of recognition of a general right to freedom of speech in the workplace, for the liberty is confined to those matters which can be described as the terms and conditions of employment and does not encompass broader issues such as the policy of the firm on ethical matters or the environment.

SAFETY

Health and safety legislation imposes a general regulatory framework on the workplace of criminal penalties for breach of regulatory standards. But the system of enforcement through workplace committees and government inspectors cannot always respond adequately to individual cases of danger. Hence the case arises of a worker being dismissed for refusing to follow instructions, giving as his reason for disobedience the dangerous condition of the workplace. Should such a dismisal be regarded as automatically unfair,[71] and, if so, should it be categorized as a public rights dismissal thus earning special protection?

The case for regarding safety at work as a suitable public right is strong. The personal safety of the individual is plainly a vital individual interest. To place him or her in the position of either having to risk his or her health or give up employment seems an invidious choice which individuals should not

---

[70] Code du Travail, Art. L. 461–1. See P. Jestaz and P. Godé, 'Libertés des salariés dans l'entreprise' (1982), 81, *RTDC* 814.
[71] Cf. France, Code du Travail, Art. 231–8–1.

be required to make. The number of industrial accidents reported each year indicates how often such a choice must be made.[72]

We can also argue under the second criterion for recognition of a right that there now reigns a public culture of improving safety at work. Not only does an elaborate regulatory system attempt to enforce a 'duty of every employer to ensure, so far as is reasonably practicable, the health, safety and welfare at work of all his employees',[73] but also the common law recognizes that an employer is under a duty to provide 'a proper working environment' and to 'take reasonable steps to prevent exposure to unnecessary risk'.[74] These well-accepted legal standards reflect a general belief in the collective good of ensuring so far as is practicable a safe working environment. The right to a reasonably safe place of work therefore satisfies the criteria for recognition of a public right in the context of the law of dismissal, even though such a right does not usually figure in constitutional Bills of Rights.

STRIKES

In contrast, many constitutions recognize a right to strike, and labour legislation also endorses a similar right. British law, however, has no such constitutional or legislative safeguard; it merely provides certain limited immunities against criminal and civil sanctions. Section 62 of the EPCA 1978 removes the jurisdiction of Industrial Tribunals to hear claims for unfair dismissal where the complaint was taking part in a strike or other industrial action, unless the employer was victimizing the complainant by dismissing him or her but not others who were also on strike at the date of the dismissal. Blanket dismissals of all strikers therefore avoid any sanction from the law of unfair dismissal, but victimization falls to be determined under the ordinary principles of fairness for disciplinary dismissals. A recent amendment also removes the jurisdiction of the tribunal if the employee is taking part in unofficial industrial action, that is, action not authorized or endorsed by his or her trade union.[75] The effect of removing jurisdiction is to leave the employee without a remedy for dismissal, unless collective pressure can achieved re-employment or some financial settlement. This leaves the worker's right to strike unprotected by any claim which might deter the employer's sanction of dismissal except in some cases of victimization of workers taking part in an official strike.

A strong case can be mounted here for incorporating the right to strike in

---

[72] T. Nichols, 'Industrial Injuries in British Manufacturing in the 1980s' (1986), 34(2), *The Sociological Review*, 290; B. Barrett and P. James, 'Safe Systems: Past, Present—and Future?' (1988), 17, *ILJ* 26.

[73] Health and Safety at Work Act 1974, s. 2(1).

[74] *Graham Oxley Tool Steels Ltd.* v. *Firth* [1980] IRLR 135 (EAT); *Dutton & Clark Ltd.* v. *Daly* [1985] IRLR 363 (EAT).

[75] EPCA 1978, s. 62A, as amended by Employment Act 1990, s. 9.

a category of public rights dismissals in so far as the dismissal involves victimization. The individual interest in job security is especially vulnerable to such selective dismissals, unless the individual can rely upon an unusual degree of solidarity within the remaining workforce. This satisfies the first criteria, and, for the second, it is merely necessary to find a public culture which support's the individual's right to strike, a right which may be qualified by the necessity of following certain democratic procedures prior to industrial action. Although these considerations support the view that victimization should be regarded as a public rights dismissal, the arguments are less persuasive for incorporating blanket dismissals of all strikers as well.[76]

Dismissals of all workers engaging in industrial action do not so directly challenge the individual interest in job security. An employer plays this card in order to strengthen his or her position in any negotiations towards a settlement of the dispute. The dismissals are directed towards improving a bargaining position in the labour market rather than attacking the individual interest in job security. Because of this focus, these collective dismissals do not satisfy the first criterion for the recognition of a public rights dismissal, namely the special vulnerability of an individual interest to the power of management. Rather it makes sense to view collective dismissals during industrial action as a form of economic dismissal, that is, one connected to the interplay of market forces. This would lead either to the system of remedies envisaged in Chapter 5 or to the award of redundancy payments under current legislation. At present, however, redundancy payments may only be awarded in cases of collective dismissals where the industrial action is provoked by the employer's prior notice of dismissal for reasons of redundancy or lay-off.[77] Another approach would simply regard any collective dismissals during industrial action as ineffective, thereby putting the contract of employment into suspension,[78] though some additional remedy would be required for the few cases where the dispute is not settled before the business closes down.

EQUALITY

The ILO standards support a strong idea of equality by prohibiting dismissals on the grounds of race, colour, sex, and marital status. The British sex and race discrimination legislation condemns dismissals on these

---

[76] For the contrary view, see K. D. Ewing, 'The Right to Strike' (1986), 15, *ILJ* 143, at pp. 149–53; B. Napier, 'Strikes and Lock-outs' (1988), 17, *ILJ 50*.

[77] EPCA 1978, s. 92.

[78] This is the French approach, subject to the exception of *faute lourde*: Code du Travail, L. 521–1. J. Pélissier, 'Fautes des grévistes et sanctions patronales' (1988), *Droit Social*, 650. It has been proposed in the Labour Party: Policy Review, *Meet the Challenge, Make the Change* (London, 1989).

grounds. But a full protection of the public right to treatment as an equal through the scheme of public rights dismissals could extend to any instance where the employer's motive for dismissal could be impugned on the ground that it involves treating the individual with disrespect on the ground of his or her unalterable characteristics, such as age or disability. Provided that the characteristic was one where it was recognized that individuals were unusually vulnerable to adverse discrimination, then the public culture of supporting the right to be treated as an equal would support incorporation into the proposed scheme of public rights dismissals.

We have already noted that the current law of unfair dismissal makes no special provision for discrimination, with the partial exception of pregnancy related dismissals. The tribunals can be expected to find such dismissals unfair even under the loose 'range of reasonable responses' test, but any additional compensation to reflect society's condemnation of such derogation from equality must be derived from the relevant sex and race discrimination legislation. Under this legislation, unlike the law of unfair dismissal, a court may award damages for injury to feelings from the insult,[79] and it has been observed that such compensation 'should not be minimal, because this would tend to trivialise or diminish respect for the public policy to which the Act gives effect'.[80] These damages may be increased beyond mere compensation in the form described as aggravated damages,[81] where the defendant has behaved in a high-handed, malicious, insulting, or oppressive manner.[82] In addition, the damages may escape the limitations of mere compensation if the court makes an exemplary award against a public authority found guilty of deliberate discrimination.[83] These principles go some way to make up for the absence of any special treatment of discriminatory dismissals under the law of unfair dismissal itself, though in practice their subjection to the same upper limits of compensation as that applicable to unfair dismissal reduces their deterrent effect.[84]

No such additional compensation will be available in cases of discrimination against the elderly or the disabled. The existence of the Disabled Persons (Employment) Act 1944 suggests the existence of a public culture which disapproves of discrimination against disabled persons. Section 9 of that Act provides a criminal penalty for dismissals of registered handicapped persons, if the employer does not employ his or her appropriate quota of handicapped workers, unless the employer has reasonable cause for the dismissal. Further support for the existence of a public culture of providing special protection for disabled persons comes from evidence that tribunals

[79] *Skyrail Oceanic Ltd.* v. *Coleman* [1981] ICR 864 (CA).
[80] *Alexander* v. *Home Office* [1988] ICR 685 (CA) per May, LJ, at p. 692.
[81] *Rookes* v. *Barnard* [1964] AC 1129 (HL) per Lord Devlin at p. 1221.
[82] *Alexander* v. *Home Office* [1988] ICR 685 (CA).
[83] *City of Bradford* v. *Arora* [1991] IRLR 165 (CA).
[84] EPCA 1978, s. 76.

support greater use of reinstatement as a remedy for unfair dismissal in cases of disability.[85] These indicators might be relied upon to justify including such discrimination in a scheme of public rights dismissals. Under the present legislation, of course, dismissal of disabled persons must be judged under the range of reasonable responses test. This often provides scant protection. In *Seymour* v. *British Airways Board*,[86] the employers sought to reduce labour costs by redeploying or dismissing 'non-effective' staff. Following a back injury at work, the employee could no longer perform the heavy lifting aspects of his job as a baggage handler at an airport. The tribunal decided that the employer had acted reasonably in selecting this employee for dismissal. The EAT agreed that, although an employer should give special consideration to dismissals of registered disabled workers, the applicable standard, even when the 1944 Act was involved as in this case, was no more than one of reasonableness. This standard falls below that which might be obtained by an acknowledgement of a public right designed to foster equality of opportunity for disabled workers.

No legislation has been enacted so far in Britain to combat age discrimination. But this may occur in the foreseeable future in imitation of the law in the USA which prohibits, with certain exceptions such as top executives and firemen, dismissal on the sole ground of age, unless the employer can demonstrate that age is a genuine occupational qualification.[87] Most British employers operate a compulsory retirement age. This is legal, provided that this age limit upon employment does not discriminate between men and women.[88] Section 64(1) of EPCA 1978 withdraws the right to claim unfair dismissal from employees after they reach the normal retiring age laid down by the employer, or in the absence of such provision the age of 65. Far from prohibiting age discrimination, therefore, the current legislation facilitates it by removing the need for the employer to justify the dismissal on a ground such as lack of capacity to perform the work.

To alter these provisions would entail a major transformation in the social composition of the workforce and create the need to rewrite most occupational pension plans. These obstacles are not insuperable, however, as the experience of the United States has demonstrated, and a growing concern for equality of opportunity for ageing workers may provide the impetus to change the legal position from one of condoning dismissal on ground of age to that of deterring it.

---

[85] K. Williams and C. Lewis, *The Aftermath of Tribunal Reinstatement and Re-engagement*, Department of Employment Research Paper No. 23 (London, 1981), at p. 31.

[86] [1983] ICR 148 (EAT).

[87] Age Discrimination Act Pub. L. 90–202, 15 Dec. 1967, 81 Stat. 602; 29 USCA 621.

[88] Sex Discrimination Act 1975, ss. 6(4) and 82(1A), as amended by Sex Discrimination Act 1986, s. 2.

FAMILY LIFE

The ILO Convention also lists as an invalid reason for dismissal the idea of family responsibilities. An employee may seek permission for time off work to deal with a family emergency, such as a child's illness or the funeral arrangements for a close relative, but if this permission is refused and the employee is dismissed for taking time off work without permission, should this count as an unfair dismissal? More significantly, should this dismissal count as an invasion of a public right leading to a finding of automatic unfairness?

The nature of the right envisaged in the ILO Convention differs from the previous examples because it links the right to an acknowledged social duty. The right concerns an aspect of autonomy. In these cases managerial disciplinary power threatens to interfere with another sphere of an employee's life, his or her family life. At the same time managerial disciplinary power is coercing employees to fail to live up to their social responsibilities to their families. Employees are presented with the invidious choice of either keeping their jobs and abandoning their families or sacrificing their jobs for the sake of family responsibilities.

The case for recognizing a public right in such circumstances depends in the first instance on whether there is evidence to suggest that employers do not present employees with such an invidious choice. Industrial practice may depend here upon the size of the employer, with larger employers being more disposed to make provision for 'personal leave' or 'emergency leave'. But no such practice was acknowledged for small employers in *Warner* v. *Barbers Stores*.[89] Mrs Warner worked as a sales assistant in a small shop. She asked her employer if she could have a day off work, because her young son, who suffered from diabetes, was leaving hospital and she wanted to supervise his diet and insulin injections on his first day at home. The employer refused permission because of the difficulties which her absence would create, and so Mrs Warner resigned and claimed unfair dismissal. The claim failed at the first hurdle; the tribunal decided that she had not been constructively dismissed. The EAT agreed that there was no implied term in the contract of employment which gives employees a reasonable amount of time off during an emergency, so the employer was not in breach of contract, so there could be no constructive dismissal. Although an isolated decision, one which is less sympathetic to the employee's predicament than other reported cases,[90] it does reveal that in some instances at least the employee is faced with the invidious choice between keeping a job or fulfilling family responsibilities.

---

[89]   [1978] IRLR 109 (EAT).
[90]   *Thornton* v. *Champion Associated Weavers Ltd*. [1977] IRLR 385 (IT) (dismissal unfair, but compensation reduced by 45% for contributory fault).

Under the second criterion for acknowledging a public right, we should surely acknowledge the collective good derived from observance of family responsibilities. Although the collective good in efficient production may qualify the extent to which personal leave should be granted and require advance notice if at all possible, our scale of values surely places care for the family above the profitability of business. If so, then the case for acknowledging a public right becomes established.

5. WHAT REMEDIES?

To complete this picture of how a scheme of public rights dismissals might be developed, we should turn to the question of what remedy should be afforded to vindicate the right? Should the tribunals insist upon reinstatement of the worker as a symbolic affirmation of society's disapprobation of such abuse of managerial power, or would financial penalties serve this purpose better?

Reinstatement may appear the toughest remedy. By compelling the employer to re-employ the worker, the law makes it clear that this sort of abuse of power will not be tolerated. Under the Polish law of dismissal, for instance, a labour court may order re-engagement of a worker who has been dismissed for political activities, membership of a trade union, or activity on the Workers Council, and the employer is deprived of any defence such as a claim that re-engagement is not practicable because the vacancy has been filled.[91] But, on closer inspection, it is less clear that reinstatement will achieve the goal of deterring violations of public rights as effectively as punitive damages, that is, compensation which exceeds the actual losses incurred by the dismissed worker.

Reinstatement is normally a cheap remedy from the point of view of the employer, unless he or she values dearly the loss of face. The employer merely has to re-employ the person and pay any remuneration due during the intervening period between dismissal and reinstatement. In contrast, an award of punitive damages, if set at a prohibitive level, renders such dismissals exceedingly expensive for employers. If we examine the question of remedy from the perspective of what sanction is likely to deter such dismissals most effectively in the future, then the punitive financial sanction seems likely to count for more in the employer's mind than simply the additional loss of face involved in not only losing the case but having to reinstate the worker as well. Punitive damages strike at management at the point where they are most sensitive, the balance sheet of the firm, for it is by this criterion alone that the owners of capital who hire them tend to evaluate their performance.

In addition, one must question whether reinstatement could prove a

---

[91] I am grateful to Professors Andrzej Swiatkowski and Barbara Wagner for this illustration.

practicable remedy in many instances of public rights dismissals. Reinstatement without subsequent official monitoring to ensure that the employer does not victimize the employee through the almost invisible operation of the internal labour market for promotion and betterment seems to me to be an almost useless remedy. One US study of reinstatement after anti-union discrimination reveals that most employees refused the offer, and, among those who returned to work, 87 per cent left within a year complaining of unfair company treatment.[92] The necessary supervision of the employer's conduct in order to detect instances of such unfavourable treatment motivated by reasons which infringe public rights seems almost beyond the competence of any state agency and extremely costly to run. At the least, reinstatement orders would have to be policed through a novel institutional framework established in the workplace such as the German Works Councils.[93]

For these reasons, if the law of dismissal is to take the invasion of public rights seriously, the case for a general remedy of punitive damages seems overwhelming. Punitive damages may also appeal because in their quantification tribunals may reflect the degree of fault of the employer and any contributory fault on the part of the employee. But whatever the exact rules adopted, their aim, which is to deter the abuse of managerial power with respect to individual rights, should be kept in mind as the paramount consideration.

[92] W. H. Chaney, 'The Reinstatement Remedy Revisted' (1981), 32, *Labor Law Journal*, 357; for a broader study, see A. A. Malinowski, 'An Empirical Analysis of Discharge Cases and the Work History of Employees Reinstated by Labor Arbitrators' (1981), 36, *The Arbitration Journal*, 31.

[93] S. Estreicher, 'Unjust Dismissal Laws: Some Cautionary Notes' (1985), 33, *American Journal of Comparative Law*, 310, at p. 319.

[7]
The Search for Legal Guarantees of Job Security

THE idea of reinstatement is to place the employee back in his or her former job, with full back pay, as if no dismissal had ever taken place. Many believe that reinstatement should be the normal remedy for unfair dismissal. This view seems to rest on the supposition that, since the aim of the legislation is to promote job security, then this is best achieved by giving the dismissed worker his or her job back. The legislation implies an acceptance of this supposition by awarding some degree of priority to the remedy of reinstatement over compensation. It imposes a preliminary duty upon the Industrial Tribunal at the remedial stage of the proceedings to explain to successful claimants what orders for reinstatement may be made and ask them whether they wish the tribunal to make such an order.[1] Yet the tribunals rarely order reinstatement. The statistics reveal that orders for reinstatement are made at most in 5 per cent of successful claims, and in some years this drops to as little as 2 per cent.[2]

This dissonance between the widespread expectation that reinstatement should be the normal remedy and its rarity in practice provokes the two central questions of this chapter. In the first place, for reasons of justice should reinstatement be the normal remedy for unfair dismissal? Here we examine the foundations of the intuition which supports reinstatement as the primary remedy, in order to test them against the justifiable goals which the remedial system should pursue. Secondly, we must ask why the apparent legislative intention to make reinstatement the normal remedy has failed so spectacularly? Should we attribute some blame to the Industrial Tribunals or are other forces in fact at work here?

Before addressing these questions directly, however, it is worth considering the likely shape of any practical remedial system for unfair dismissals.

---

[1] EPCA 1978, s. 68(1); see *Pirelli General Cable Works Ltd.* v. *Murray* [1979] IRLR 190 (EAT).

[2] The official statistics are unreliable because of misrecording, the absence of records where the parties agree a settlement, and the failure to take into account the outcome of appeals. Nor do these figures record actual outcomes as opposed to tribunal orders. See Linda Dickens, Michael Jones, Brian Weekes, and Moira Hart, *Dismissed: A Study of Unfair Dismissal and the Industrial Tribunal System* (Oxford, 1985), at pp. 108–11.

Remedial strategies in law are rarely so uncomplicated as to be explicable by reference to one overriding aim such as the protection of job security or full compensation for loss. At the remedial stage of legal proceedings, numerous additional policy considerations affect the type and measure of the remedy.[3] In the criminal law, where the general aim may be to deter deviant behaviour, the punishment reflects not only considerations of general deterrence but also efforts to reform the criminal, to take into account his or her degree of moral culpability in the light of social background and motives, and to reduce the public cost of sanctions by, for example, avoiding imprisonment. Similarly, we should not expect that remedies for unfair dismissal will pursue a univocal end. This point is already implicit in my tripartite typology of dismissals, which separates out economic and public rights dismissals as meriting distinctive remedial treatment. But even in the central case of disciplinary dismissals, important policy considerations other than the protection of job security or compensation for loss are likely to affect the remedies available in the tribunals.

1. THE INTEREST IN JOB SECURITY

Let us suppose for a moment, however, that the dominant goal of the remedial strategy should be to further the general aim of the law of unfair dismissal to improve job security. Before jumping to the conclusion that the reinstatement remedy is bound to achieve that goal more successfully and completely than any other remedy, we should recall in detail exactly why the interest in job security deserves protection. We shall discover, I suggest, that it is far from clear that reinstatement best serves the aim of promoting job security.

In Chapter 1 we rejected the idea that the law of unfair dismissal should be understood to protect job tenure come what may. General welfare considerations argue strongly against the aim of ownership of jobs, and, in any case, by recognizing the possibility of fair dismissals grounded in the fault of the employee, the legislation clearly did not intend to grant such a degree of protection to job security. Instead, I suggested that the legislation should be interpreted as extending protection to job security for two reasons. First, it aims to protect the dignity of individuals against abusive treatment during the exercise of managerial disciplinary powers. Secondly, the legislation promotes the collective good of establishing worthwhile opportunities for employment for the sake of establishing important conditions for the fostering of autonomy or freedom. These aims combine to establish the purpose of the legislation primarily in improving the justice of disciplinary practices and job structures, but not necessarily in keeping people in their jobs.

---

[3] For a fuller discussion of the complexity of remedial strategies, see H. Collins, *The Law of Contract* (London, 1986), at pp. 178–81.

In a successful claim for unfair dismissal, if we accept that a dominant goal of the remedy awarded should be to promote the ends of the legislation, then what remedy will best serve these dual ends of protection of dignity and autonomy? It is far from clear that reinstatement will succeed better than financial compensation in securing the aim of the transformation of the working environment. Reinstatement, if quickly ordered, will be a cheap, almost costless sanction against the employer, providing little incentive to alter any abusive disciplinary practices.[4] In contrast, a substantial financial penalty strikes at the employer where it hurts most, the balance sheet, and may force a review of those practices. For example, an employer who fails to adopt a fair disciplinary procedure and is therefore judged to have dismissed a particular worker unfairly, can reinstate the employee and continue as before, realizing that at most there will be the occasional loss of face when a tribunal insists upon reinstatement. A financial penalty, on the other hand, cannot be so easily ignored, for it will be incurred every time the abusive disciplinary procedure is followed; at some level of compensation, it must become uneconomic for the employer to persist in such practices. It was for this reason, among others, that I suggested that the most effective remedy for the vindication of public rights against dismissals lay in punitive damages. Similarly, in the context of ordinary disciplinary dismissals, it seems clear that the ends of the law in improving the working environment are likely to be promoted more effectively by substantial compensation than a remedy of reinstatement.

This argument dramatically weakens the strength of the supposition that the remedy of reinstatement best serves the goal of the law in promoting an employee's interest in job security. Financial compensation would prove more effective, provided that it was calculated with this end in view. The fact that compensation is not calculated with this end in mind reveals a missed opportunity for the law to pursue its ends, but does not undermine the general point that, if the dominant goal of the remedial strategy is the same as that of the legislation as a whole, then financial compensation rather than reinstatement should be the primary remedy.

Although the supposition that reinstatement is the most appropriate remedy for unfair dismissal therefore proves false, this does not eliminate the possibility that for the sake of some other remedial purpose reinstatement should be awarded as the normal remedy. In describing the aim of compensation, the courts and tribunals usually speak in terms of corrective justice, that is, providing a sum of money which restores the claimant's position to the extent of making him or her no worse off financially than if he or she had not been unfairly dismissed. If, as seems likely, corrective justice in this sense constitutes an important ingredient in the remedial

---

[4] M. S. West, 'The Case Against Reinstatement in Wrongful Discharge' (1988), *University of Illinois Law Review*, 1, at p. 64.

policy of the legislation, then we may ask whether reinstatement could better achieve this goal than awards of compensation.

2. CORRECTIVE JUSTICE

The tribunals have always made it clear that in the calculation of monetary compensation their goal is one of corrective justice rather than a transformation of the workplace environment:

[T]he purpose of assessing compensation is not to express disapproval of industrial relations policy. It is to compensate for financial loss.[5]

The aim of compensation is backward-looking, to provide a monetary award which covers all the employee's financial losses caused by the unfair dismissal.

This aim of corrective justice could also be achieved by the remedy of reinstatement. By returning the employee to his former job with back pay to cover the period between dismissal and reinstatement, all the financial losses engendered by the dismissal would either be compensated or avoided. Indeed, it seems likely that reinstatement achieves a fuller and more accurate measure of corrective justice than an award of compensation. The legislation imposes artificial limits on the total sum of compensation, and in addition the interpretation of the legislation by the courts and tribunals places limits on the types of loss which may be recovered by a successful claimant through a monetary award. Here we shall consider the types of loss which monetary awards usually fail to address and consider whether the reinstatement remedy could better serve the aim of corrective justice with respect to these limitations.

In the absence of an order for reinstatement or re-engagement, a successful claimant for unfair dismissal must receive a basic award and a compensatory award.[6]

BASIC AWARD

The basic award, which is the same as a redundancy payment, is calculated by reference to the three variables of length of service, age, and weekly wage.[7] Typically the employee receives a sum representing one week's wages for each year of service for the employer. The basic award makes no attempt to connect the measure of compensation to the actual loss suffered. Its purpose here is obscure, for the compensatory award should perform the task of corrective justice. The basic award may serve the purpose of ensuring

---

[5] *Clarkson International Tools Ltd.* v. *Short* [1973] ICR 191 (NIRC), per Sir John Donaldson, at p. 196.
[6] EPCA 1978, s. 72.
[7] Ibid., s. 73.

that all unfairly dismissed employees receive some compensation, even though a few may not have suffered any loss, as a way of signifying and disapproving the wrongfulness of the employer's behaviour, a purpose which can be undermined by the provisions on contributory fault.[8] The basic award may also avoid complexity in calculation of compensation where the tribunal finds that the employee was dismissed unfairly for reasons of redundancy. More pertinent to our enquiry here, it may be suggested that the basic award supplies a crude tool for compensating some of those losses which are hard to quantify and which the tribunals in assessing the compensatory award exclude altogether.

The exact purpose of the basic award may be shortly the subject of judicial scrutiny. Because the basic award is tied to length of service with a particular employer, it seems likely that it has an indirect discriminatory effect upon women, because they, unlike men, often take a break from careers for the purpose of child-rearing and thus break their continuity of employment with a particular employer. The legislation may thus have the indirect discriminatory impact of compensating men more generously than women on average in claims for unfair dismissal. If the basic award is regarded as a form of pay, women will be able to allege that the statute contravenes the principle of equal pay for equal work contained in Article 119 of the Treaty of Rome. For this purpose pay is defined as all benefits in cash or in kind, present or future, provided that they are paid, albeit indirectly, by the employer to the worker in connection with her employment.[9] Under European law, which permits challenges to British statutes,[10] the basic award will then have to be justified by satisfying the test laid down in *Bilka-Kaufhaus GmbH* v. *Weber von Hartz*,[11] that it serves a genuine non-discriminatory purpose and is reasonably necessary to achieve that aim. Before the ECJ the Government will be compelled to try to justify the basic award (or the redundancy payments legislation, since it is calculated in the same way) according to this strict standard and this will reveal whether or not the basic award serves any worthwhile goal. It may be found that since the basic award does not satisfy the principle of corrective justice then it lacks an objective justification. Its most promising defence may lie in the observation in Chapter 5 that the factors which vary the amount of compensation correspond roughly to the social and market forces which cause reduced wages in subsequent employment after dismissal. It might then be possible to present the basic award as

---

[8] Ibid., s. 73(7B).

[9] *Barber* v. *Guardian Royal Exchange Assurance Group* [1990] IRLR 240 (ECJ); *Kowalska* v. *Freie und Hansestadt Hamburg* [1990] IRLR 447 (ECJ); *Hammersmith and Queen Charlotte's Special Health Authority* v. *Cato* [1988] ICR 132 (EAT) (redundancy pay is pay within Art. 119); see E. Szyszczak, 'The Effect of EEC Law on Sex Discrimination and Redundancy Payments' (1988), 17, *ILJ* 115.

[10] *Rinner-Kühn* v. *FWW Spezial-Gebaudereinigung GmbH* [1989] IRLR 114 (ECJ); noted, E. Szyszczak (1990), 19, *ILJ* 114.

[11] [1986] IRLR 317 (ECJ).

consistent with the goal of corrective justice. Alternatively, the objective justification for the basic award might lie in regarding seniority as a fair proxy for greater productivity, as suggested in *Handels-og Kontorfunktiona-ererness Forbund i Danmark* v. *Dansk Arbejdsqiverforening (acting for Danfoss)*,[12] though economic analysis tends to cast doubt on this link.[13]

COMPENSATORY AWARD

A compensatory award should succeed in fully compensating dismissed employees for any type of loss easily reducible to a cash sum. Under s. 74(1) of EPCA 1978:

the amount of the compensatory award shall be such amount as the tribunal considers just and equitable in all the circumstances having regard to the loss sustained by the complainant in consequence of the dismissal in so far as that loss is attributable to action taken by the employer.

The main item of recovery is normally the loss of net wages during the period of unemployment following the dismissal. The tribunals also routinely compensate the employee for loss of fringe benefits such as deprivation of a company car, private medical insurance, subsidized housing, pension or superannuation rights,[14] loss of privileges under a company share-option scheme, and any other contractual benefits.[15]

The actual figures set by Industrial Tribunals under these headings cast doubt on whether they use their full powers to achieve corrective justice with respect to these cash sums. In particular, the tribunals seem reluctant to award compensation under the heading of future loss of income through unemployment on the basis of a realistic prediction of the likely period of unemployment. The tribunals enjoy a broad discretion to estimate future employment prospects, drawing upon their knowledge of the local labour market and the characteristics of the complainant,[16] but they seem to underestimate the length of time involved. Although the average level of compensation awarded by tribunals does appear to increase in periods of high unemployment, the difference appears to be no more than two or three extra weeks of pay.[17] The tribunals may legitimately discount this type of loss in recognition of the accelerated receipt of earnings, but against this the tribunals do not indicate an awareness that claimants may experience greater difficulty in regaining employment because they have contested the dismissal

---

[12] [1989] IRLR 532 (ECJ).

[13] J. L. Medoff and K. G. Abraham, 'Experience, Performance, and Earnings' (1980), 95, *Quarterly Journal of Economics*, 703.

[14] *Scottish Co-operative Wholesale Society.* v. *Lloyd* [1973] ICR 137 (NIRC).

[15] See Steven D. Anderman, *The Law of Unfair Dismissal* (2nd edn., London, 1985), at pp. 302–3.

[16] *Fougere* v. *Phoenix Motor Co.* [1976] ICR 495 (EAT).

[17] Linda Dickens *et al.*, *Dismissed*, at p. 124.

before a tribunal.[18] These observations suggest that an order of reinstatement is likely to achieve better corrective justice than an award of compensation when the claimant is likely to remain unemployed for a substantial period of time.

The tribunals experience considerable difficulty in fixing a cash sum for loss of expectations arising from the implicit contract of the firm's internal labour market.[19] The employee may reasonably expect that promotion prospects will open up through seniority and training in firm-specific skills, so that his or her lost income from continued employment in the same firm will increase and persist long after the dismissal. Since these losses are speculative and contingent upon numerous uncertain factors such as the employee's diligence and the firm's growth, the tribunals may seriously undercompensate the claimant. They will only augment compensation for loss of wages if a salary increase was a high probability, and even then the sum will be reduced to reflect a discount for the risk that the raise would not have been forthcoming.[20] A claimant seems unlikely to receive any compensation for the possibility of promotion and appropriate salary increases during subsequent years. Seniority rights to better job security comprise another feature of the implicit contract which is unlikely to receive adequate compensation. The tribunals award modest sums to reflect a claimant's loss of statutory rights by lacking the requisite qualifying period of employment in a new job,[21] such as two years for the right to bring a claim for unfair dismissal, but the claimant has to prove that any future employment will be less secure than his or her former job in order to win compensation for the loss of implicit contractual expectations of job security.[22] Since financial compensation seems unlikely to reflect the full losses arising from deprivation of a position in an internal labour market, a remedy of reinstatement seems to promise more satisfactory relief from the perspective of corrective justice. The hitch is, of course, that having been dismissed, the employee may reasonably doubt whether his or her former expectations of betterment through the internal labour market will be realized if he or she is compulsorily reinstated contrary to the wishes of management.

Another way in which compensation is likely to fall short of perfect corrective justice arises from the nature of the work itself which may possess a form of 'consumer surplus value' for employees.[23] Their former jobs may

---

[18]   Ibid., 128.

[19]   R. J. Flanagan, 'Implicit Contracts, Explicit Contracts, and Wages' (1984), 74, *American Economic Review Papers*, 345.

[20]   *York Trailer Ltd.* v. *Sparkes* [1973] ICR 518 (NIRC).

[21]   Set at £100 in *Muffett (S. H.) Ltd.* v. *Head* [1986] IRLR 488 (EAT). The loss of the statutory right to a redundancy payment became less significant after the introduction of the basic award: EPCA 1978, s. 74(3).

[22]   *Norton Tool Co. Ltd.* v. *Tewson* [1972] ICR 501 (NIRC).

[23]   D. Harris, A. Ogus, and J. Phillips, 'Contract Remedies and the Consumer Surplus' (1977), 95, *LQR* 581.

possess the twin features of satisfying a sense of vocation and maximizing their return on investments in human capital (that is, earning high wages as a result of spending time and effort in acquiring particular skills and knowledge).[24] They may reasonably believe that any alternative employment will only afford diminished returns in these two respects. Suppose, for example, a person has set her sights on becoming a heart-transplant surgeon. After years of training she is unfairly dismissed and its seems unlikely that she will be able to regain employment in this specialized field but will have to settle for some other branch of surgery. A remedy of reinstatement here will provide better corrective justice for the element of vocational fulfilment, for a tribunal will only compensate the financial loss linked to investments in human capital which can be proven from the surgeon having to take a job at lower pay in another branch of surgery.[25] A similar loss in consumer surplus value may result from the employee being compelled in his or her search for another job to move home, thereby perhaps losing touch with friends and relatives and disrupting family life. But the rules on mitigation of loss, which we shall consider shortly, may require the employee to look for work in other regions, and failure to do so will result in a reduction of compensation.

One important type of loss suffered by a dismissed employee concerns the harm to his or her reputation. This may persist even after a successful claim for unfair dismissal, for the stigma of dismissal seems to make it more difficult to gain fresh employment.[26] It may also compel claimants to accept worse jobs in the future, for about half of applicants to tribunals report that their new job is worse in terms of status and pay than the original one.[27] This lower rate of pay may be reflected in the award of compensation, but damage to reputation itself has not been regarded as a compensable head of recovery, and it does not seem to affect the tribunals' estimates of the likely period of unemployment, unless perhaps evidence of this damage is buttressed by a false unsatisfactory letter of reference from the employer,[28] or some other strong evidence that the manner of dismissal has damaged employment prospects.[29] Reinstatement may avoid this loss more successfully than compensation.

The tribunals have also opposed awards for injured feelings, the unpleasant manner of dismissal, and the emotional suffering resulting from unfair dismissal. In *Vaughn* v. *Weighpack Ltd.*,[30] the employee was summoned from

---

[24] G. S. Becker, 'Investment in Human Capital: A Theoretical Analysis' (1962), 70, *Journal of Political Economy*, suppl., 9.

[25] *Scottish Co-operative Wholesale Society Ltd.* v. *Lloyd* [1973] ICR 137 (NIRC); *Winterhalter Gastronom Ltd.* v. *Webb* [1973] ICR 245 (NIRC).

[26] Linda Dickens *et al.*, *Dismissed* at pp. 121 and 128.

[27] N. Banerji, D. Smart, and M. Stevens, 'Unfair Dismissal Cases in 1985–86: Impact on Parties' (1990), 98, *Employment Gazette*, 547, at p. 552.

[28] *Canter* v. *Bowater* [1975] IRLR 323 (IT).

[29] *Norton Tool Co. Ltd.* v. *Tewson* [1972] ICR 501 (NIRC).

[30] [1974] ICR 261 (NIRC).

his home to the office on a Sunday morning and then summarily dismissed by the managing director. The court recognized that this was a 'most distressing experience' and the employee suggested that, in the small community in which he lived, news of this abrupt manner of dismissal travelled fast and he felt disgraced. The court declined to award any compensation for these items of loss in the absence of firm evidence that the manner of dismissal made it more difficult to find employment, and expressed the pious hope that the tribunal's finding of unfair dismissal would rectify any temporary mischief. It is not clear whether reinstatement could provide a superior remedy for injured feelings: it would provide a more dramatic vindication of the employee, but it occurs too late to wipe out the immediate emotional distress.

The most important limitation upon the quantification of compensation originates from the test of causation. The tribunals deny full compensation for losses sustained, if they discover a break in the chain of causation between the dismissal and the loss. If after dismissal, for example, the employer offers the worker his or her job back and he or she unreasonably refuses this offer, then the tribunal will deny compensation on the ground that it was not the dismissal which caused the employee's losses but his or her own unreasonable refusal of reinstatement. Similarly, where the dismissal is shown to be unfair on the ground of an unfair procedure, the compensation should be reduced to nil if the tribunal is satisfied that the unfair procedure could have made no difference to the outcome because of the strength of the employer's case.[31] If a fair procedure had been adopted, the employee would have been dismissed fairly, so he has suffered no loss from the unfairness of the dismissal,[32] except perhaps that it was a little sooner than it might otherwise have been.[33] Similarly, if the employer can demonstrate that the employee would have been dismissed for redundancy in any event, then the compensatory award must be reduced to reflect the point that the unfair dismissal had not caused a loss of income beyond the probable date of redundancy.[34] These strict tests of causation run a serious risk of undercompensation because the causation inquiry is necessarily speculative. There appears to be an unevenness of treatment here, for speculative claims of losses on the part of the employee are quickly discounted, but equally contingent assertions of probable breaks in causation as in the case of impending redundancies seem to be accepted quite readily by the tribunals. These speculative grounds for diminution of compensation could be avoided

[31] *British United Shoe Machinery Co. Ltd.* v. *Clarke* [1978] ICR 70 (EAT).

[32] *Earl* v. *Slater Wheel (Airlyne) Ltd.* [1972] ICR 508 (NIRC); *Clarkson International Tools Ltd.* v. *Short* [1973] ICR 191 (NIRC).

[33] *Abbotts* v. *Wesson-Glymved Steels Ltd.* [1982] IRLR 51 (EAT).

[34] *Young's of Gosport Ltd.* v. *Kendell* [1977] ICR 907 (EAT); *Daley* v. *A. E. Dorsett (Almar Dolls Ltd.)* [1985] IRLR 385 (EAT) (company subsequently goes into liquidation). The tribunals will not question whether the redundancies were necessary or premature: *James W. Cook & Co. (Wivenhoe) Ltd.* v. *Tipper* [1990] IRLR 386 (CA).

by an award of reinstatement, though of course this might prove futile in many instances such as impending redundancy.

As well as these limitations on the heads of compensable loss devised by the courts and tribunals, s. 75 of the EPCA 1978 also imposes an absolute upper limit on the measure of the compensatory award. Although few employees receive awards approaching this sum, currently set at £10,000, older senior management employees dismissed from their jobs are likely to receive substantially less than full compensation. As an illustration of the undermining of the principle of corrective justice, in *O'Laoire* v. *Jackel International Ltd.*,[35] the deputy managing director was unfairly dismissed at a time when he earned a gross annual salary approaching £40,000, plus stock options, private medical insurance, pension provision, and a company car. The Industrial Tribunal reckoned that his actual losses exceeded £100,000, but due to s. 75 only awarded him £12,185 (comprising a basic award of £155, a compensatory award of the maximum at that time of £8,000, and a maximum additional award of £4,030 for the failure of the employers to comply with a reinstatement order). Upholding this decision in the Court of Appeal, Lord Donaldson, MR called for a fundamental review of the limits imposed by s. 75 in view of this injustice to higher-paid employees.[36] It is clear that a reinstatement order would better fulfil the aim of corrective justice in any case where the statutory maxima are likely to be exceeded.

What this study of the compensation remedy reveals is that it often falls short of full corrective justice for the losses sustained by the dismissed worker. In most instances a remedy of reinstatement would probably achieve a more accurate and complete recovery for the claimant's losses. It appears therefore that the primacy of the reinstatement remedy could be justified on the ground that it best fulfils the remedial aim of corrective justice. There is some evidence to support the view that tribunals tend to award reinstatement in those cases where special circumstances such as the loss of investment in human capital and position in an internal labour market, as, for example, in the case of apprentices, highlights the inadequacy of the compensatory remedy by the standards of corrective justice. Similarly, there is an association between awards of reinstatement and districts of high unemployment to deal with the risk of undercompensation from estimates of likely periods of unemployment.[37] But before we conclude that, for reasons of corrective justice, reinstatement should be the normal remedy for unfair dismissal, it is vital to consider the significance of other possible policy objectives within the remedial strategy.

---

[35] [1990] IRLR 70 (CA).
[36] Ibid., at p. 74.
[37] K. Williams and D. Lewis, *The Aftermath of Tribunal Reinstatement and Re-engagement*, Department of Employment, Research Paper No. 23 (London, 1981), at p. 31.

3. QUALIFYING CONSIDERATIONS

Whether or not improvements in job security or corrective justice should be regarded as the dominant policy of the remedial strategy, it is clear that three other policies substantially impinge on the pursuit of those goals. Each of these policies firmly points to compensation rather than reinstatement as the most justifiable primary remedy for unfair dismissal. The three policies may be described as: proportionality in the light of the employee's degree of fault; the minimization of social cost; and the defence of managerial authority structures.

PROPORTIONALITY

Section 74(6) supplies the tool for introducing proportionality into assessments of the compensatory award:

Where the tribunal finds that the dismissal was to any extent caused or contributed to by any action of the complainant it shall reduce the amount of the compensatory award by such proportion as it considers just and equitable having regard to that finding.

A similar provision permits reduction of the basic award,[38] and the special award.[39] By virtue of these provisions an employer can rely upon those reasons for dismissal which failed to justify the dismissal as fair in order to persuade a tribunal to reduce the measure of compensation. The more that the employee was the author of his or her own misfortune, the greater will be the reduction of the level of compensation.

The uneven application of the principle of proportionality by the law of unfair dismissal is startling. It is extremely difficult for employees to challenge dismissals on the ground that this sanction was too severe and that some lesser penalty should have been imposed. As we saw in connection with *British Leyland (UK) Ltd.* v. *Swift* in Chapter 3,[40] provided that dismissal was within the employer's range of reasonable responses to the employee's conduct, even though the tribunal regards the penalty as harsh, it will find it to be fair. Yet when the employer's interest in proportionality comes to the fore in assessments of compensation, the tribunals engage in a minute inspection of the fault of the employee in order to give the employer the benefit of any shred of justification he or she can put forward.

Unless an employer lacks any reason for dismissal at all, in every case he or she can allege that the employee's actions caused or contributed to the dismissal. The tribunal must then decide whether it would be just and equitable to reduce the award of compensation for this reason, and if so, to

---

[38] EPCA 1978, s. 73(7B).
[39] Ibid., s. 75A(4).
[40] [1981] IRLR 91 (CA); above, p. 98.

what extent. This decision necessarily embarks the tribunal on its own objective delineation of what kind of fault on the part of the employee merits disciplinary action and the relative gravity of different sorts of misconduct. The reluctance to set objective standards produced by the problem of juridification described in Chapter 1 is dramatically abandoned at this point in the proceedings when it serves the interests of employers.

How then have the courts and tribunals described the type of fault which merits disciplinary action? In *Nelson* v. *British Broadcasting Corporation (No. 2)*,[41] the corporation abolished the employee's post and offered him alternative employment subject to a condition providing for a three months' report on his performance. Mr Nelson refused the offer because he objected to the condition. The Industrial Tribunal reduced his compensation for unfair dismissal by 60 per cent. On appeal to the Court of Appeal, the claimant argued that he was not at fault in the required sense or to such a degree as to warrant such a large reduction. In dismissing this point of the appeal, Brandon, LJ, provided significant guidance to the tribunals on what kinds of conduct constitute fault in the relevant sense:

It is necessary, however, to consider what is included in the concept of culpability or blameworthiness in this connection. The concept does not, in my view, necessarily involve any conduct of the complainant amounting to a breach of contract or a tort. It includes, no doubt, conduct of that kind. But it also includes conduct which, while not amounting to a breach of contract or a tort, is nevertheless perverse or foolish, or, if I may use the colloquialism, bloody-minded. It may also include action which, though not meriting any of those more pejorative epithets, is nevertheless unreasonable in all the circumstances. I should not, however, go so far as to say that all unreasonable conduct is necessarily culpable or blameworthy; it must depend on the degree of unreasonableness involved.[42]

When applying these principles to the facts of the case, Brandon, LJ accepted the tribunal's finding that the condition attached to the offer of alternative employment was a reasonable one for the employers to make, but argued that it did not necessarily follow that Mr Nelson's conduct in objecting to it was so unreasonable as to be culpable or blameworthy in the required sense. On the other hand, the tribunal had found that Mr Nelson had been so upset by the condition attached to the offer that he had made the worst possible decision which he could have made in the circumstances. Brandon, LJ, accepted this as a finding of fault sufficient to justify a reduction in the award. It appears then that foolish behaviour counts as fault, even when the employee is led to this foolishness by emotional distress, but that an objection to a reasonable management instruction may not suffice.

These principles may be interpreted to state the view that the fault of the

---

[41] [1980] ICR 110 (CA).
[42] Ibid., at p. 121.

employee meriting disciplinary action should concern acts of insubordination, foolishness, or carelessness. It is insufficient to justify a reduction, that
the employee lacks the talent to measure up to expected high standards,[43]
though if this failure results from a lack of diligence or an unwillingness to
heed advice, a reduction will be warranted.[44] This amounts to a broad
interpretation of the fault criterion, one which bears only a weak connection
to the criterion of harm to the interests of the firm, which, as we noted in
Chapter 3, is the test used to determine the initial question of the fairness of
the dismissal.

The just and equitable standard contained in s. 74(6) of the EPCA 1978
also leaves the tribunals with a broad discretion to set the proportion of
reduction of compensation. The reduction may be anything from nil to 100
per cent.[45] Normally the appeal courts decline to review this aspect of a
tribunal's decision, regarding it as a pure question of fact.[46] Thus in *Nelson*
v. *British Broadcasting Corporation (No. 2)*,[47] the Court of Appeal left
untouched the stiff reduction of 60 per cent, arguing that the tribunal had
not acted perversely on the facts. This refusal to review the extent of
proportionality bears witness to a resurgence of the problem of juridification,
the appeal courts being aware that to meddle with percentages will necessarily embroil them in defining with precision the exact nature and degree of
fault which should suffice to render a dismissal fair.

On the other hand, the appeal courts cannot resist the temptation to
reduce compensation if facts emerge subsequent to the tribunal hearing
which confirm the employer's substantive ground for dismissal. In *Ladup
Ltd.* v. *Barnes*,[48] the employee of a casino was arrested and charged with
growing and possession of cannabis. On hearing of the arrest the employers
summarily dismissed the employee. A claim for unfair dismissal was
successful on the ground that the employers had failed to follow a fair
procedure, but the Industrial Tribunal declined to reduce the award of
compensation on the ground of contributory fault. After the employee had
been convicted of the criminal offence by a Crown Court, the employers
sought review of the tribunal's decision not to reduce compensation. The
EAT intervened and ordered a contribution of 100 per cent, thereby
depriving the employee of any compensation. It is hard to see how the
employee's subsequent conviction of the criminal offence could have contributed in any way to his dismissal. The willingness of the EAT to reduce
compensation can only be explained by a desire to insist upon proportionality
in favour of the employer.

[43] *Kraft Foods Ltd.* v. *Fox* [1978] ICR 311 (EAT).
[44] *Finnie* v. *Top Hat Frozen Foods* [1985] ICR 433 (EAT).
[45] *Devis & Sons Ltd.* v. *Atkins* [1977] ICR 662 (HL).
[46] *Hollier* v. *Plysu Ltd.* [1983] IRLR 260 (CA); but see *Nairne* v. *Highlands & Islands Fire
Brigade* [1989] IRLR 366 (Ct. Sess.) and *Coalter* v. *Walter Craven Ltd.* [1980] IRLR 263 (EAT).
[47] [1980] ICR 110 (CA).
[48] [1982] ICR 107 (EAT).

The same desire repeats itself in assessments of the compensatory award under EPCA 1978, s. 74(1). Because this general provision governing the compensatory award requires a tribunal to assess what measure is just and equitable in the circumstances, Davies and Freedland suggest that this discretion, which also applies to the basic award,[49] permits a tribunal to reduce awards to ensure that the employee only receives his or her 'just deserts'.[50] In this vein, Viscount Dilhorne in *Devis (W.) & Sons Ltd.* v. *Atkins* insisted that:

No compensation should be awarded when in fact the employee has suffered no injustice by being dismissed.[51]

Following this decision, the courts have adopted a broad discretion under EPCA 1978, s. 74(1) to reduce compensation in the light of all the circumstances known to the tribunal according to the principle of whether or not the employee suffered an injustice.[52]

The meaning of injustice here apparently goes beyond both the idea of blameworthy conduct, which satisfies the test of contributory fault, and the strict test of causation governing attribution of losses. Compensation may be reduced where the misconduct was unknown to the employer at the time of the dismissal and so this fault could not have caused or contributed to the decision to dismiss. In most of these cases, however, the employee's claim for substantial compensation would be defeated under the principle of causation, for he or she could only recover compensation for loss of wages until such time as the fault was discovered. In *Devis (W.) & Sons Ltd.* v. *Atkins*, however, on these facts the House of Lords seemed unwilling to give any compensation at all, thereby suggesting that the concept of injustice to the employee runs free of any causal link with the dismissal at all.[53] Their Lordships' view of the justice of the case was decisively influenced by the preceding common law which permitted an employer a complete defence to a claim for damages for wrongful dismissal in such circumstances. Here the

---

[49] EPCA 1978, s. 73(7B).

[50] Paul Davies and Mark Freedland, *Labour Law: Text and Materials* (2nd edn., London, 1984), at p. 501.

[51] [1977] ICR 662 (HL), at p. 679. See also *Townson* v. *The Northgate Group Ltd.* [1981] IRLR 382 (EAT).

[52] *Polkey* v. *A. E. Dayton Services Ltd.* [1988] ICR 142 (HL); *Sillifant* v. *Powell Duffryn Timber Ltd.* [1983] IRLR 91 (EAT); *Tele-Trading Ltd.* v. *Jenkins* [1990] IRLR 430 (CA).

[53] It is possible that the principles of causation, as developed in the common law, could account for the denial of any compensation in such cases. An employee guilty of fraudulent behaviour should not be able to recover any arrears of wages in an action for wrongful dismissal, if the fault was sufficiently serious for the employer to have avoided the contract or to claim that the performance of work fell so far short of the expectation as to deprive the employer of any substantial benefit. If such a claim for wages would have failed, then the employee has suffered no loss from the premature dismissal, so on a strict application of the principle of causation the award of compensation for loss of wages should be nil. This reasoning suggests that the principles of causation may account after all for any reductions applied by the tribunals apart from those provided for under the auspices of the contributory fault doctrine.

justice of the case was measured by the standards of the common law, despite the reforming aim of the legislation. But, more generally, this interpretation of the discretion implicit in assessing the compensatory award permits the courts' desire to ensure proportionality in compensation for the benefit of the employer to inflate the discretionary power so that it floats freely over all awards of compensation without any conceptual limit.

The remedy of compensation thus offers the tribunals a much better opportunity for introducing a principle of proportionality than is afforded by the remedy of reinstatement. Davies and Freedland are correct to detect, in the courts and tribunals, 'a preference for giving effect to value-judgments by providing monetary compensation rather than by granting or withholding reinstatement or re-engagement'.[54] An order of reinstatement would place the employee back in the same position as before without any account being taken of his or her contributory fault. The legislation envisages a way around this problem by the alternative order of re-engagement, but this lacks the requisite flexibility for a full application of the principle of proportionality. An order for re-engagement is really designed to deal with the case where the tribunal considers that putting the employee back in exactly the same job is not practicable or sensible, but that the employer should be required to offer him or her alternative employment elsewhere in the enterprise. But the order for re-engagement could be used to introduce an element of proportionality, for it permits a tribunal to insist upon re-engagement at a lower rate of pay with the loss of any rights of privileges formerly earned and without back pay if the complainant caused or contributed to some extent to the dismissal.[55] Such orders have rarely been made for clearly this is a complex and finicky procedure for introducing the principle of proportionality. This suggests that for the sake of this principle, compensation should be the normal remedy within the remedial strategy.

MINIMIZING SOCIAL COST

In devising a remedial strategy, the legislature and the courts usually have an eye to the total social cost involved. The total social cost includes the financial losses to the claimant and the legal costs in bringing a claim.

Complicated procedures are likely to push up the legal costs for the parties and the costs of the administration of justice by the courts. For this reason, as we have seen, the legislation promotes the use of conciliation through ACAS in order to reduce the burden of litigation. The function of conciliation officers is 'to endeavour to promote a settlement of the complaint without its being determined by an industrial tribunal'.[56] These officers

---

[54] Davies and Freedland, *Labour Law: Text and Materials*, p. 494.

[55] EPCA 1978, s. 69(6)(*c*). But there can be no deduction for failure to mitigate loss: *City and Hackney Health Authority v. Crisp* [1990] ICR 95 (EAT).

[56] EPCA 1978, s. 134(1).

achieve settlements in about half of the cases where a formal complaint has been issued.[57] The Industrial Tribunals also follow a pre-hearing procedure in order to weed out weak cases before they come to trial. The courts have constantly emphasized the importance of avoidance of technicality in the practices of the tribunals, refusing to insist upon mandatory procedures and legal principles enforceable by law, in order to expedite hearings and to reduce the number of appeals. All these measures reduce the social cost of dismissals.

Considerations of social cost also mandate the application of the principle of mitigation of loss to the compensatory award.[58] Dismissed workers must seek alternative employment, even if they have asked for the remedy of reinstatement, in order to reduce their loss. If they succeed in finding another job, then their compensation must be diminished since they have suffered a reduced loss;[59] and if they fail through a lack of reasonable endeavours, then a tribunal will reduce compensation by a similar amount. The application of the mitigation rule involves the tribunal in making a speculative hypothetical inquiry into what would have happened with respect to the claimant's loss if he or she had acted reasonably in seeking to reduce his or her loss,[60] and, once the supposed course of events has been estimated, the tribunal should reduce the compensation according to the ordinary principles of causation.[61] The policy behind mitigation here, as elsewhere in the law of contract, is to reduce the social cost of termination of contracts, though of course the principal beneficiary is the employer.

The practice we have already mentioned of the tribunals underestimating the likely period of future unemployment of unfairly dismissed employees is functionally equivalent to the rules concerning mitigation. Because a successful claimaint is unlikely to receive compensation for the full length of his or her period of unemployment during a recession, this gives him or her a strong incentive to accept whatever employment may be found as soon as possible rather than rely upon an award of compensation. This shortfall in the compensatory award, together perhaps with the other respects in which it fails to meet the strict requirements of corrective justice, may therefore be explicable by reference to the qualifying consideration of minimizing social cost.

It makes sense from the point of view of both corrective justice and minimizing social cost to avoid double compensation for the employee in respect of lost wages by not permitting him or her to claim both social security payments and compensation from the employer. From the perspec-

---

[57] Pat Lowry, *Employment Disputes and the Third Party* (London, 1990), at p. 116.

[58] EPCA 1978, s. 74(4).

[59] For a minor exception to that rule, see *Fentiman* v. *Fluid Engineering Products Ltd.* [1991] IRLR 150 (EAT).

[60] *Fyfe* v. *Scientific Furnishings Ltd.* [1989] IRLR 331 (EAT).

[61] *Gardiner-Hill* v. *Roland Berger Technics Ltd.* [1982] IRLR 498 (EAT).

tive of corrective justice the employer should take the benefit of any avoidance of double compensation, as in the law of wrongful dismissal, since the dismissal has not caused any loss which is covered by social security payments. The policy of minimizing social cost, however, points in the opposite direction. If the State is relieved of this expenditure, this reduces the general taxation burden and places the burden on the employer who is in the best position to avoid the loss. Regulations therefore permit the Secretary of State to recoup the 'prescribed element' in an award of compensation, that is, the sum payable for lost wages which has in fact been provided by the State up to the time of the completion of the proceedings before the Industrial Tribunal.[62]

These aspects of remedial strategy designed to minimize the social cost of dismissals clearly qualify the pursuit of corrective justice through awards of compensation. A remedy of reinstatement might not serve such a policy equally well. If reinstatement were the normal remedy, then this would give an employee an incentive not to search for alternative employment until the tribunal hearing, since reinstatement would not be affected by such concerns as mitigation. In addition, the remedy of reinstatement requires additional hearings to determine whether it is practicable and the reasons for an employer's failure to comply with an order, both of which add to the social costs of the administration of justice. For these reasons, the award of a remedy of compensation rests more easily with the qualifying consideration of minimizing social cost.

MANAGERIAL AUTHORITY

The foregoing qualifying considerations are patent on the face of the statute, but the final consideration worthy of mention hides from sight. In the context of the law of unfair dismissal, it seems perhaps improbable that one of the remedial strategies consists in the protection of managerial disciplinary authority. One of the chief aims of the statute must be to control that prerogative for the sake of the employee's interest in job security. Yet there are several aspects of the legislation and the practice of the tribunals which appear inexplicable except by reference to a policy of protecting the disciplinary authority of management.

We have already encountered one example of this phenomenon. The upper limits on an award of compensation provided by EPCA 1978, s. 75, run counter to the principle of corrective justice. What purpose then do these limits serve? It seems to me most likely that the underlying policy is to meet the concern that no dismissal should be prohibitively expensive for employers, so that in the last resort any employee can be dismissed without

---

[62] Employment Protection (Recoupment of Unemployment Benefit and Supplementary Benefit) Regulations 1977, SI 1977, No. 674.

wrecking the business.[63] The alternative explanation that the legislature deliberately sought to discriminate against higher paid employees seems improbable, though perhaps it was assumed that these employees would be able to take care of themselves through 'golden parachutes' in the terms of their contracts. But I suggest that the main aim of the statutory limits on compensation consists in the protection of the ultimate power of dismissal, no matter how unjustifiable, for the sake of ensuring that management has the final authority to make any dismissals which it chooses.

For the same reason we must suspect that the legislature was unwilling to give tribunals effective power to enforce orders for reinstatement and re-engagement. If an employer fails to comply with such an order, the sanction against the employer is not fines, sequestration, and imprisonment for contempt of court, but the employee must bring a further action to seek an additional award under s. 71(2) (b) for a cash sum representing between thirteen and twenty-six weeks pay.[64] As Lord Donaldson, MR, has observed, this means that an order for reinstatement is 'wholly unenforceable'.[65] Not only do employees lack any legal mechanism for compelling reinstatement in practice, but also they cannot sue for their back pay from the date of the dismissal until the reinstatement order was made, or when it became clear that the employer proposed to ignore the order, so the reinstatement order has no financial consequences for an employer apart from the risk of an additional award.[66] Even this additional award remains in doubt, for an employer may attempt to satisfy the tribunal, at a further hearing for determining whether the employee should be granted an additional award, that reinstatement was not practicable, and if the employer succeeds with this argument, then no award can be made.[67] The effect of this absence of effective sanction for non-compliance with orders of reinstatement is once again to support management's ultimate authority to determine who shall remain on the payroll of the business. This contrasts vividly with Italian law where the device of punitive damages which cumulate by the day secures a

---

[63] H. Collins, 'Reinstatement and Upper limits of Compensation' (1990), 19, *ILJ* 193. The Donovan Commission recommended an upper limit so that employers could insure against the risk of awards of compensation, but since the limit of awards has been kept so low it seems that employers have in recent years internalized the risk: Royal Commission on Trade Unions and Employers' Associations, Cmnd. 3623 (1965–68), para. 554. The current limits are set by: The Employment Protection (Variation of Limits) Order, SI 1991, No. 464; The Unfair Dismissal (Increase of Compensation Limit) Order, SI 1991, No. 466; The Unfair Dismissal (Increase of Limits of Basic and Special Awards) Order, SI 1991, No. 467.

[64] For the exercise of this discretion taking into account the fault of the employer and the loss to the employee, see *Morganite Electrical Carbon Ltd.* v. *Donne* [1988] ICR 18 (EAT). It should depend on 'all the merits of the case': *Mabirizi* v. *National Hospital for Nervous Diseases* [1990] ICR 281 (EAT) per Knox, J., at p. 289.

[65] *O'Laoire* v. *Jackel International Ltd.* [1990] IRLR 70 (CA), at p. 73.

[66] Ibid.

[67] EPCA 1978, s. 71(2)(b).

high degree of compliance with reinstatement orders since compliance will normally be much cheaper for the employer.[68]

By removing any potential sting to managerial authority from orders of reinstatement, the legislation therefore ensures that reinstatment does not comprise an entirely distinct remedial option for a tribunal. An order for reinstatement is a gesture, no more, for ultimately a recalcitrant employer will merely have to pay slightly larger compensation. This qualifying consideration of deference to managerial authority in the last resort ensures that reinstatement must play a peripheral role in the remedial strategy pursued by the legislation. Whether or not such a policy is justifiable is a question now being urgently examined under the province of the common law equitable jurisdiction to issue injunctions, a matter we shall consider after having first examined the reasons for the rarity of the award of the reinstatement remedy by the tribunals.

4. DISTORTION BY PRIVATE INTEREST

Much debate has centred on the question of why the Industrial Tribunals so seldom order reinstatement. It is tempting to argue that the tribunals themselves are mostly to blame for their failure to exercise this power. They may be thought to be too orientated towards management's interest in avoiding loss of face and maintaining disciplinary authority.[69] Without discounting this possibility entirely, I suggest that the major reason for the absence of reinstatement orders is the predictable result of the distortion of this apparent policy of the legislation by the private interests of both employers and employees.

We have already noted that the legislation initially gives reinstatement priority as a remedy. Before making such an order, however, the tribunal must check that the complainant wishes to be reinstated and decide whether it is 'practicable' and 'just' for the employer to comply with an order.[70] These terms delegate a broad discretion to tribunals,[71] which certainly could be used to thwart the apparent legislative intention of making reinstatement the normal remedy.

The term 'just' introduces the idea of contributory fault, which grants the

[68] Lord Wedderburn, 'The Italian Workers' Statute: Some British Reflections' (1990), 19, *ILJ* 154, at pp. 158–9, and 185–9; M. Rocella, 'Reinstatement of Dismissed Employees in Italy' (1989), 10, *Comparative Labor Law Journal*, 166. As Wedderburn points out, at p. 189, Law 108 of 11 May 1990 alters the law so that as an alternative to reinstatement plus the minimum of 5 months' wages in compensation, the employee may choose 15 months' wages.

[69] Dickens *et al.*, *Dismissed*, at p. 111: see also L. Dickens, M. Hart, M. Jones, and B. Weekes, 'Re-employment of Unfairly Dismissed Workers: The Lost Remedy' (1981), 10, *ILJ* 160, at p. 169.

[70] EPCA 1978, s. 69(5).

[71] Ibid., s. 70(1), only provides guidance on the meaning of 'practicable' in the case of the employment of a permanent replacement. But see *Freemans PLC* v. *Flynn* [1984] IRLR 486 (EAT).

tribunal a broad discretion to deny the remedy if the employee's conduct was blameworthy or culpable. The tribunals have interpreted the term 'practicable' to be a narrower concept than 'possible', so that the order must be capable of being carried into effect with success. They have declined to order reinstatement where it would provoke industrial action.[72] They have also proved reluctant to make reinstatement orders against small employers on the ground that it is not practicable to compel reinstatement in the context of the personal relationships necessary to the successful functioning of small businesses.[73] These decisions reveal that the term practicable is not confined to the question whether the employer has a suitable vacancy for the claimant, but also takes into account the whole potential working environment including the sentiments of the employer and the workforce. But the tribunals have not required certainty that the order will be successful, for if it proves not practicable the employer has a complete defence to the sanction of the additional award.[74]

Although this discretion does afford the tribunals the power to deny reinstatement in a broad range of cases, their interpretation of what is practicable and just does not appear to rule out orders in most cases. In larger firms the possible adverse reaction of immediate supervisors should not make reinstatement impracticable even on the current interpretation of the term, and Williams and Lewis find accordingly an association between greater numbers of orders of reinstatement and larger organizations. Moreover, it is surely an unusual case where the workforce as a whole does not support the individual's quest for reinstatement, and again there is an association between union support for a claim and increased use of the remedy of reinstatement. One must conclude that the small numbers of orders for reinstatement depends much more heavily on pressures on the tribunal coming from both employer and employee.

Employers apparently routinely resist orders for reinstatement despite having lost the case and the issue of principle. This attitude presumably reflects an unwillingness to permit tribunals to determine in the last resort who should be employed by them. Even if an order is made, employers seem to ignore it, hoping either that the claimant will not pursue his or her remedy for an additional award, a hope usually justified in fact, or being prepared to pay the additional sum in order to ensure a break of contact with the employee. Williams and Lewis report one instance 'where a Tribunal told an employer in advance that the cost of not complying with the order would be £138 it was promptly accepted as a bargain'.[75] This resistance to interference bears witness to the attitude that discipline at work is essentially a private

---

[72] *Coleman* v. *Magnet Joinery Ltd.* [1974] IRLR 343 (CA).

[73] *Enessy Co. SA t/a The Tulchan Estate* v. *Tulchan* [1978] IRLR 490 (EAT).

[74] *Timex Corporation* v. *Thomson* [1981] IRLR 522 (EAT).

[75] K. Williams and D. Lewis, *The Aftermath of Tribunal Reinstatement and Re-engagement*, Department of Employment Research Paper No. 23 (London, 1981), at p. 37.

matter, one which should not be subject to interference by the State. Faced with such resistance, the employee's desire for reinstatement seems likely to diminish substantially. As Dickens argues, 'What applicants "want" is often determined by the employer's known or assumed position'.[76] When the tribunal adjourns proceedings, after having declared its determination that the dismissal was unfair in order to see if the parties can agree a settlement of the case, these attitudes expressed by the employer are likely to discourage the claimant from pursuing the question of reinstatement further.

At the same time, employees have independent reasons for tending not to press for reinstatement. They focus naturally on their own personal interests rather than the more general concerns of the legislation to improve the working environment through the control of managerial prerogative. These personal concerns will normally be mainly related to financial loss and vindication of reputation through a successful claim. This focus on personal interest explains why, according to Lewis's survey, although, at the commencement of proceedings, 75 per cent of claimants want reinstatement, only 20 per cent want it when they have won their case.[77] Lewis reports that the reasons which applicants give for this change of heart are generally in the categories of breakdown of relationship, fear of victimization, and belief that the employer's behaviour was so bad that the worker would not want to be employed by that employer again. He suggests that it is administrative delay which defeats the reinstatement remedy, which leads to the suggestion that private arbitration may be much more effective. But what his analysis misses is the point that the employee's personal interests govern his or her application for an order of reinstatement, and in this calculation of personal interest it will rarely be the case that the interest extends to reinstatement, though this may occur in instances of potential undercompensation as outlined above. This analysis explains better why in cases settled through conciliation by ACAS, presumably more speedily than tribunal hearings, an even smaller percentage of claimants are re-employed.[78] Against this economistic interpretation of the claimant's motivation, Dickens suggests that the choice of applicants for the remedy of compensation arises precisely because they think that the tribunal lacks sufficient clout to restore them properly to their position as before. Whilst this may be true in part, it seems to me improbable that at the conclusion of proceedings most employees have more in mind than an interest in extracting the maximum compensation available.

[76] Dickens et al., Dismissed, at p. 118.

[77] P. Lewis, 'An Analysis of why Legislation has Failed to provide Employment Protection for Unfairly Dismissed Workers' (1981), 19, BJIR 316. These statistics have been doubted as a result of a different survey which found that only a quarter of applicants put re-employment down on the original claim form as the preferred remedy: Dickens at al., Dismissed, at p. 116. See also the rejoinder by P. Lewis (1983), 21, BJIR 232.

[78] ACAS, Annual Report 1987 (London) reports re-employment in only 1.6% of settlements.

What these arguments tend to suggest is that, even if the legislation intends reinstatement to be the primary remedy for unfair dismissal, the private interests of employers and employees are likely to combine to ensure that compensation remains the standard remedy. This will remain true even if the tribunals adopt a more relaxed test as to when reinstatement is practicable and just.

5. INJUNCTIONS

Since claimants can rarely expect to win reinstatement through a claim for unfair dismissal, in recent years they have increasingly turned to the common law for assistance. They can seek injunctions against dismissals or some lesser form of disciplinary action, the effect of which is to prevent the employer from acting without becoming in contempt of court. Injunctions may be pursued either through the public law procedures of Order 53 or through the ordinary private law of contract. Either route, however, is fraught with technical complexities and dim prospects of success.

PUBLIC LAW

The public law remedies include injunctions and also prerogative orders such as *mandamus* and *certiorari* which, if applied, would have the equivalent effect of invalidating a dismissal and restoring the employee to his or her former position. The public law cause of action is subject to the procedural restraints described in Chapter 4 in connection with claims for natural justice. But even assuming that a state employee can successfully invoke public law procedures against dismissal, it seems unlikely that he or she will receive a remedy equivalent to reinstatement. The historical origins of such a claim lie in the notion of public office being akin to a property right,[79] but in the modern context of ordinary employment by the State, the courts stress the contractual and discretionary nature of the relation. Although in theory an unlawful action should be declared void, which in the case of dismissal would have the effect of reinstatement, the courts seem disinclined to follow the logic of this conceptual reasoning, and instead insist upon retaining a discretion with respect to remedies.[80]

In *Chief Constable of North Wales* v. *Evans*,[81] the House of Lords declined to grant *mandamus*, a positive injunction to reinstate a probationary police officer who had been forced to resign following procedures which were in breach of natural justice. The court was unwilling to order reinstatement because this would in effect assume the power of the Chief Constable to

---

[79] P. P. Craig, *Adminstrative Law* (2nd edn., London, 1989), at p. 418.
[80] See Sandra Fredman and Gillian S. Morris, *The State as Employer* (London, 1989), at pp. 266–8.
[81] [1982] 1 WLR 1155 (HL).

determine the membership of the police force. In addition, the court was unwilling to order reinstatement because of 'practical problems' arising from the officer's exclusion from the police force during the four years of litigation and the undercurrent of ill-feeling which would undermine relations with superiors in the force. Instead the court issued a declaration that he had been unlawfully dismissed and left the officer to seek a remedy in damages.

This decision may be distinguished because it concerned solely a claim for an order of mandamus, and so it is possible that the courts would be more willing to make other prerogative orders available. For example, in *R. v. Secretary of State for the Home Department, ex parte Benwell*,[82] the court granted *certiorari* to quash the decision to implement a dismissal. But since all the prerogative orders are discretionary, it seems likely that the policy considerations adumbrated by the House of Lords will influence the award of all public law remedies. The concern not to remove management's ultimate authority to determine who should remain on the payroll, a concern already noted in connection with the remedies for unfair dismissal, seems bound to defeat claims for reinstatement through public law remedies in most instances.

PRIVATE LAW

Under the common law, the action for wrongful dismissal could only afford a remedy in damages. But the courts of equity offered the additional possibility of securing remedies of specific performance and injunctions. By winning such an action, an employee would in effect secure reinstatement backed up by all the penalties for contempt of court. The courts of equity, however, operated a discretion which routinely prevented employees from gaining such remedies for their employer's breach of contract. In recent years the precise principles under which this discretion should be exercised have come under closer scrutiny. A slim chance now exists that employees may succeed in gaining reinstatement by means of an injunction against termination of the contract of employment issued under the equitable jurisdiction of the ordinary courts.

The procedure for gaining an injunction has an important bearing on the outcome of these cases. In most instances the plaintiff employee seeks an interlocutory injunction, which is an injunction issued pending full trial of the contentious issues between the parties when a permanent injunction may be issued. The normal aim of interlocutory injunctions is to preserve the relative positions of the parties until the court decides in favour of one side or the other. In practice, of course, the interlocutory injunction may well terminate the litigation, for the employer will be compelled to reconsider the decision to dismiss and to seek a settlement with the employee. Under the

---

[82] [1985] IRLR 6 (QB).

general principles of civil procedure, an interlocutory injunction will be issued if, first, the plaintiff can convince the court that there is a serious question to be tried, and secondly, the balance of convenience lies in favour of issuing an injunction.[83]

The first part of the test tends to lead the court to ask whether the plaintiff has any hope of succeeding in obtaining an injunction, a question which raises in outline the principles on which a court will issue permanent injunctions, but does not require the court to make a final determination on how these points will ultimately be resolved. In recent years, the courts have rejected the simple view that no employee can have any hope of succeeding in obtaining an injunction at full trial of the issues, for it has been plain that some employees will succeed since *Hill* v. *C. A. Parsons & Co. Ltd.*[84] Instead, the court examines the principles on which injunctions will be issued in order to determine whether the employee appears to enjoy some chance of success. This test greatly improves the chances for employees of gaining an interlocutory injunction.

The second part of the test concerning the balance of convenience or the balance of the risk of doing an injustice looks at the practical difficulties which might be created for the parties if an interlocutory injunction were to be issued by the court. For example, if the effect of the injunction were to prevent the employer from running his business efficiently, then the interloctory injunction would be refused.[85] In most instances, however, the terms on which an interlocutory injunction is issued may avoid serious inconvenience to the employer. The employee can give the court undertakings which will satisfy the employer's legitimate concerns, as in *Wadcock* v. *London Borough of Brent*,[86] where the employee undertook to work in accordance with the orders, instructions, and wishes expressed by management. This test of the balance of convenience should thus present only a small obstacle to the employee's claim.

It is the first part of the test for issuing interlocutory injunctions which is therefore likely to prove the only significant hurdle to be overcome. The courts have traditionally put forward a number of reasons for declining to exercise their discretion to award specific performance and injunctions in favour of employees. First, it was urged that such orders might be tantamount to the imposition of slavery and therefore contrary to public policy. Of course, this argument should be irrelevant if the employee is seeking the remedy, and statute now prohibits the employer from winning the remedy.[87]

---

[83] *American Cyananmid Co.* v. *Ethicon* [1975] AC 396 (HL).

[84] [1972] Ch. 305 (CA).

[85] *R.* v. *National Heart and Chest Hospitals, ex parte Pardhanani* (unreported), 21 Sept. 1984 (CA).   [86] [1990] IRLR 223 (Ch. D.).

[87] Trade Union and Labour Relations Act 1974, s. 16; employers may nevertheless enforce post-employment restrictive covenants: P. Goulding, 'Injunctions and Contracts of Employment: The *Evening Standard* Doctrine' (1990), 19, *ILJ* 98; M. R. Freedland, 'Paradigms and Gardens in the Law of Restraint of Trade' (1989), 18, *ILJ* 112.

In the nineteenth century, this argument was even more disingenuous, since the employer could in effect compel specific performance through the threat of criminal penalties for leaving work under the Master and Servants Acts.[88] The argument relied upon Fry's false doctrine of mutuality, which prevented one party to a contract gaining a remedy unavailable to the other, a doctrine which has since been substantially modified.[89] Now the requirement of mutuality will normally be satisfied as long as the employer does not lose the right to terminate the contract for fresh reasons or after a proper inquiry.

The second reason given by the courts for declining to award equitable relief was the argument that the employment relation depends for its success upon continuing trust and confidence between the parties and that, following a dismissal, such qualities in the relationship are likely to be absent or severely impaired. This argument cannot provide a complete bar to an injunction, since in some unusual circumstances the employer may retain complete trust and confidence in the worker, as in *Hill* v. *C. A. Parsons & Co. Ltd.*,[90] where the employer was compelled to dismiss the employee as a result of union pressure to support a closed shop. An employer's conduct in keeping on the employee in some other job after an incident may also defeat this argument.[91] The assumption behind this principle for the exercise of discretion may also be challenged. In a large bureaucratic organization, good working relations with fellow employees appear less significant than in the case of a small workshop. Following this line of thinking in *Irani* v. *Southampton and South-West Hampshire Health Authority*,[92] the court argued that although the employee's immediate supervisor may have lost trust and confidence in him, this was not true for his employer, the entity of the Health Authority running the hospital. It should only be possible for employers to rely on this ground where they can demonstrate that plausible evidence of imcompetence or misconduct had been brought to their attention. In addition, I have also suggested in Chapter 4 that the requirement of trust and confidence should be regarded as irrelevant to claims directed at the enforcement of internal grievance procedures for the reason that the whole purpose of such procedures is to resolve doubts of this nature. In any case, an injunction should be able to take this factor of trust and confidence into account in the terms on which it is ordered. The court may command the employer to keep the employee on the payroll but suspend performance

---

[88] Mark Freedland, *The Contract of Employment* (Oxford, 1976), at p. 272; A. Merritt, 'The Historical Role of Law in the Regulation of Employment: Abstentionist or Interventionist?' (1982), 1, *Australian Journal of Law and Society*, 56, at p. 73.

[89] *Price* v. *Strange* [1978] Ch. 337 (CA).

[90] [1972] Ch. 305 (CA).

[91] *Powell* v. *London Borough of Brent* [1987] IRLR 466 (CA); *Hughes* v. *London Borough of Southwark* [1988] IRLR 55 (QB).

[92] [1985] ICR 590 (Ch. D.).

of work pending some further inquiry.[93] The presence or absence of trust and confidence is not really the issue: 'although the courts will only rarely grant the plaintiff injunctive relief against his employer, the all important criterion is whether the Order sought is workable.'[94]

Before granting equitable relief the courts also apply a standard test of assessing whether alternative remedies available to the plaintiff are adequate or whether an injunction or specific performance is necessary to achieve justice in the case. As we have seen, damages for wrongful dismissal are far from generous and some courts have regarded this as a good reason to justify the award of equitable remedies in employment cases.[95] But it would not be difficult to point to many kinds of losses which are not compensated by an award of damages for breach of the contract of employment which could be met by an injunction. The express terms of the contract may offer the employee a better chance to fight the fairness of the dismissal, if, for example, the contract provides that dismissal should only take place for grossly immoral or negligent conduct.[96] Similarly, the value of the opportunity to contest the dismissal by following the employer's internal grievance procedure is not adequately compensated by the award of damages which merely secures the net pay during the time in which the grievance procedure would have taken place,[97] for this does not include the loss of the opportunity to reverse the dismissal decision entirely.[98] Damages will also not compensate the plaintiff for the unpleasant manner of the dismissal.[99] Damages may under-compensate for breach of aspects of the implicit contract of the internal labour market, such as the opportunity to develop skills or to realize promotion prospects, an issue at stake when an injunction was granted in *Powell* v. *London Borough of Brent*.[100] The employee may foresee loss of investment in human capital because of the absence of alternative opportunities to use skills as in the case of a doctor dismissed from the National Health Service, a virtual monopoly employer.[101] Similarly, the employee may place a particular value on the job because of its vocational satisfaction or his or her investment in human capital. In *Hughes* v. *London Borough of Southwark*,[102] the plaintiff social worker was employed at the Maudsley Hospital in a multi-disciplinary team working with doctors, nurses, and

---

[93] e.g. *Irani* v. *Southampton and South-West Hampshire Health Authority* [1985] ICR 590 (Ch. D.); *Robb* v. *London Borough of Hammersmith and Fulham* [1991] IRLR 72 (QB).

[94] *Robb* v. *London Borough of Hammersmith and Fulham* [1991] IRLR 72 (QB) per Morland, J., at p. 75.

[95] *Irani* v. *Southampton and South-West Hampshire Health Authority* [1985] ICR 590 (Ch. D.), at pp. 604–5.

[96] See K. D. Ewing, 'Job Security and the Contract of Employment' (1989), 18, *ILJ* 217.

[97] *Gunton* v. *Richmond-upon-Thames London Borough Council* [1980] ICR 755 (CA).

[98] *Robb* v. *London Borough of Hammersmith and Fulham* [1991] IRLR 72 (QB).

[99] Ibid.

[100] [1987] IRLR 466 (CA).

[101] *Irani* v. *Southampton and South-West Hampshire Health Authority* [1985] ICR 590 (Ch. D.).

[102] [1988] IRLR 55 (QB).

other staff in the field of child abuse. For financial reasons the local authority decided to transfer her part-time to a community area of the borough to help with a growing problem of child abuse. The plaintiff complained that such a transfer was a breach of her contract and that it would disrupt the vital service offered by the hospital. In granting an interlocutory injunction which had the effect of compelling the local authority to withdraw the instruction pending trial, the court recognized that an award of damages would not compensate the plaintiff for the loss of her job satisfaction, distress, and the whole point of her grievance which was the unwillingness to be taken away from work for which she had been specially trained and which she believed to be more important than the alternative.[103] For all these different sorts of reasons a remedy in damages for breach of contract may prove inadequate to meet the justice of the case, so in many instances this test should present no obstacle to the award of an injunction.

None of these bars to the award of an injunction therefore seems to carry sufficient weight to rule out the remedy in cases where the plaintiff desires reinstatement strongly. The crucial test remains the one requiring the continuation of trust and confidence, but if this is inapplicable to cases involving breach of grievance procedures as the Court of Appeal seemed to indicate in *Jones* v. *Lee*,[104] and if it is circumspectly applied to large organizations, then it should no longer present a serious obstacle to claimants. But these difficulties do not exhaust the legal problems surrounding a successful claim for an injunction at common law. We must consider two further problems, one a conceptual difficulty for the plaintiff seeking an injunction, and the other a bar to an equitable remedy arising from subsequent conduct.

The conceptual argument has not yet been tested properly in the courts, but it is potentially fatal to any claim for an injunction or specific performance. In substance an equitable order commands the parties to respect their existing contractual duties. If the contract between them has been terminated, however, then no duties remain for the court to enforce. The normal principle in the law of contract insists that a contract will not be terminated except by the injured party's acceptance of the repudiatory breach by the other party. The contract therefore subsists despite serious breach and the court may order its continued observance. But it has often been suggested that a summary dismissal by an employer, even though in breach of contract, terminates the contract forthwith.[105] If so, then no contractual obligations remain for the court to enforce by way of injunction, except the secondary duty to pay damages for wrongful dismissal.

---

[103] Ibid. at p. 58.
[104] [1980] ICR 310 (CA).
[105] e.g. Shaw, LJ, in *Gunton* v. *Richmond-upon-Thames London Borough Council* [1980] ICR 755 (CA); Lord Donaldson, MR, in *R.* v. *East Berkshire Health Authority, ex parte Walsh* [1984] ICR 743 (CA).

This conceptual argument may appear casuistic, but it lies at the bottom of the second obstacle to equitable relief arising from subsequent conduct. In *Dietman* v. *London Borough of Brent*,[106] the plaintiff was summarily dismissed and successfully claimed wrongful dismissal. She was denied an injunction against dismissal prior to the completion of formal disciplinary proceedings, however, the court finding that, because the employee had obtained employment elsewhere pending trial, she had impliedly accepted the employer's repudiation of the contract so that it had been terminated. This decision presents a considerable bar to injunctive relief, since the plaintiff is under a duty to seek alternative employment as part of his or her duty to mitigate loss. But it also confirms the force of the conceptual reasoning that once the contract has been terminated then no injunction can be awarded.

The crucial question therefore becomes whether summary dismissal in breach of contract has the effect of terminating the contract of employment without the need for the employee to accept the repudiation either by words or conduct. The House of Lords has avoided the issue,[107] and the Court of Appeal has expressed conflicting views. By a majority the court held in *Gunton* v. *Richmond-upon-Thames London Borough Council*[108] that summary dismissal could not terminate all the obligations under the contract unilaterally, but subsequently a differently constituted court has doubted that reasoning.[109] The Full Court of the Federal Court of Australia has applied the ordinary rule of contract law that a repudiation has to be accepted in order to terminate the contract of employment.[110] My own interpretation of the law is that a contract of employment persists after wrongful summary dismissal by an employer. The policy behind the general law of contract here is to permit the injured party to protect his or her interests in the way he or she perceives to be best. There seems no good reason for departing from that policy simply because the injured party happens to be an employee. The contrary view has arisen because in practice no doubt a summary dismissal is quickly accepted by the employee, who will be compelled both by economic necessity and the legal duty to mitigate loss to seek alternative employment.

In order to avoid these problems derived from conceptual difficulties concerning the termination of the contract of employment, dismissed employees will be best advised to seek an interlocutory injunction forthwith. The interlocutory injunction can be quickly obtained and will resolve any

---

[106] [1987] IRLR 259 (QB); an appeal against the finding of wrongful dismissal was refused: [1988] IRLR 299 (CA).

[107] *Rigby* v. *Ferodo Ltd.* [1987] IRLR 516 (HL).

[108] [1980] ICR 755 (CA).

[109] *R.* v. *East Berkshire Health Authority, ex parte Walsh* [1984] ICR 743 (CA).

[110] *Turner* v. *Australian Coal and Shale Employees Federation* (1984) 55 ALR 635; see G. Smith, 'Specific Performance of Contracts of Employment' (1985), 14, *ILJ* 248.

doubt that the employee seeks to preserve the existing contractual relation if possible. Any purported dismissal would then amount to contempt of court for breach of the injunction, so that the employer is unlikely to raise the conceptual argument. Furthermore, it is worth noting that the conceptual argument may backfire on the employer. In *Irani* v. *Southampton and South West Hampshire Health Authority*,[111] the court used the risk that the employer would be able to terminate the contract of employment prior to trial as a reason for issuing an interlocutory injunction, since without the interlocutory injunction the employee's claim for a full injunction appeared bound to fail.

These developments in the common law have occurred quite independently from the statutory law of unfair dismissal. Except for EPCA 1978, s.77, which provides for interim relief in the form of continuation of employment where an Industrial Tribunal believes that it is likely that the reason for dismissal was motivated by membership or non-membership of a trade union, the tribunals have no power to intervene at such an early stage of the dispute and order reinstatement pending the outcome of the hearings. This gap in the legislation is gradually being filled by the common law, but the complexities and anomalies of the common law seem destined to prevent the development of a coherent scheme of interim relief pending a full hearing.

Perhaps the best way forward might be to amend the provisions which provide for a pre-hearing assessment of the case by an Industrial Tribunal or an appointed official.[112] The current aim of this pre-hearing assessment consists in discouraging claims which have no reasonable prospect of success by making an order for costs against the claimaint and by requiring a deposit of £150 before the claimant may proceed. The role of the pre-hearing assessment could be augmented so that, if the employee appears to have a reasonable prospect of success, then the tribunal could order the continuation of employment or suspension on full pay pending the outcome of the full tribunal hearing. Similarly tribunals could make orders for continuation of employment pending the outcome of appeals before the EAT.[113] Such orders would be equivalent to the injunctions issued by the common law courts, but would have several advantages over that procedure.

This new procedure could be informal with quick and easy access to employees. The real substantive issues at stake could be considered, rather than the arcane considerations which so dominate the reasoning of the common law courts. It would also introduce a degree of equity into pre-hearing assessments, which at present serve entirely the employer's interest

---

[111] [1985] ICR 590 (Ch. D.).

[112] EPCA 1978, Sched. 9, as amended by Employment Act 1989, s. 20; Industrial Tribunals (Rules of Procedure) Regulation 1985, SI 1985, No. 16, Sched. 6.

[113] For similar developments in Germany, see A. Döse-Digenopoulos and A. Höland, 'Dismissal of Employees in the Federal Republic of Germany' (1985), 48, *Modern Law Review*, 538, at p. 548.

under the guise of minimizing the social cost of litigation. But, above all, the availability of such a procedure would greatly increase the chances that reinstatement might remain a viable and attractive option to the parties.

6. INTIMACY AND ESTRANGEMENT IN EMPLOYMENT

Drawing together the strands of the above argument, I have suggested that justice does not necessarily require reinstatement to be the primary remedy for unfair dismissal. The principal aim of the legislation of improving job security is likely to be better served by generous awards of compensation. Furthermore, a remedial strategy should not be dominated by a univocal end such as the protection of the employee's interest in job security or the application of the principle of corrective justice, and a compensatory remedy often better serves other worthwhile policies such as proportionality and minimizing social cost. Nevertheless, as the law governing compensation for unfair dismissal stands, it seems inadequate to compensate claimants fully for their losses. It takes too narrow a view of the aims of the legislation, ignores various heads of loss which should be included in a full scheme of corrective justice, and is too ready to reduce compensation on grounds of speculative hypothetical causal inquiries and overly broad assessments of contributory fault. In these circumstances there may be an important role for the remedy of reinstatement, either by statute or the common law, to achieve better corrective justice and to satisfy the employee's interest in job security.

The reluctance of the courts and tribunals to order reinstatement either under the statute or at common law seems ultimately to derive from a perspective which views the contract of employment as a personal relation between the parties. It is believed that the intimacy required between employer and employee for their successful co-operation at work cannot be imposed by the court. This argument appears under the statute when the tribunal decides that it would be impracticable to order reinstatement because of the hostility of the employer or other employees. It resurfaces in the exercise of discretion in awarding public law remedies and injunctions at common law in the common requirement that trust and confidence should subsist between the parties. This reasoning both repeats the idea underlying the common law that the employment relation is too intimate or private a matter to be imposed by an external body, thus justifying complete absten-tion by the courts, and simultaneously turns the idea on its head to say that, because the relations between the parties have become estranged, then it would be inappropriate to compel them to work together once more.

Against this perspective of the privacy of the contract of employment lies the brute fact of the modern bureaucratic relations of production through which large organizations use impersonal rule systems to manage and steer the workforce. I have argued that one of the principal justifications for the law of unfair dismissal must be its attempt to subject this bureaucratic power to some external control in order to avoid abuse. To accept this perspective of the privacy of employment again at the remedial stage, as in the examples where the legislation and the courts ensure that management has the ultimate power to determine who will remain on the payroll, is to accept an ideology which the law of unfair dismissal was intended to challenge and undermine. The old common law, which respected the privacy of the employment relation by abnegating any power of control, effectively granted management an unbridled prerogative to determine tenure of jobs. Although the effects of the resurgence of this perspective as part of the remedial strategy are less detrimental to employees' interest in job security than before, they can nevertheless defeat claims for reinstatement in cases where that remedy could best serve the interests in job security and corrective justice.

The strong preference for monetary compensation evidenced by the courts and tribunals also springs from another perspective on the contract of employment, one which reflects the economism of the law of contract as a whole. The pre-eminence of damages as the remedy for breach of contract reflects the commodification of all economic relations. The point of entering such contractual relations is perceived by the courts to be one of wealth maximization through the exchange of commodities in the market. An adequate remedy must be to give the injured party the money which he or she expected to make from the broken contract. This perspective of the law of contract applies to the contract of employment, surfacing in the narrow identification of compensable losses in the law of unfair dismissal and wrongful dismissal.

The error in the economism of the law of contract is that it ignores the power relations established through market transactions. Nowhere is this more apparent than in the employment relation where the paradigm contract contains an exchange of wages for the power to direct and control. A just remedial strategy should attempt to combat invidious power relations established in economic transactions for the sake of fostering autonomy. This strategy may usually be served best by generous awards of compensation, as in the case of public rights dismissals, but in other instances an award of reinstatement may control the abuse of power more immediately and effectively. The reinstatement remedy may also foster the idea that the employment relation should comprise more than an economic exchange; it should entitle a person to membership of an organization in which the right to participate and to be consulted in the decision-making process is part of the democratic principles on which the organization should be run.

[8]

The Social and Economic Effects
of Dismissal Law

PREVIOUS chapters in this book have focused primarily on a critical examination of the law of termination of employment from the perspective of the coherence and justice of its rules. But this study would be incomplete without an examination of the available evidence about the social and economic effects of dismissal law.

An immediate difficulty confronts us in assessing the evidence about the effects of the legislation. What the law requires of employers in theory may be a long way from what they do in practice in response to the law of unfair dismissal. The owner of the market stall where I shop for vegetables recently vouchsafed the popular wisdom that an employer has to give an employee three warnings before dismissal, but readers of this book will have noticed that neither the legislation, nor the tribunals, nor any Code of Practice has ever promulgated such a rule, and indeed the courts have insisted that in egregious cases instant dismissal is permissable. Mr Matthewson could correct her on the law from bitter experience, but if this popular wisdom is widespread, as I believe it is from similar anecdotal evidence,[1] and a survey of small firms which demonstrated considerable ignorance of the legislation,[2] then this misperception of the law may have a considerable impact on employers' disciplinary practices, rendering them far more respectful of the principles of procedural fairness than the law in fact requires. Employers seem also to believe that the level of compensation awarded by Industrial Tribunals is far higher than it is in fact, leading them to share the view expressed by Norman Lamont in 1978, as Opposition spokesman on industry, that the legislation 'has made it prohibitively expensive for firms to dismiss even workers for whom they have no jobs'.[3] If such absurd claims by public figures are given credence by employers, the effects of the

---

[1] See P. Lewis, 'Employment Protection: a Preliminary Assessment of the Law of Unfair Dismissal' (1981), 12(2), *Industrial Relations Journal*, 19.

[2] Richard Clifton and Charlotte Tatton-Brown, *Impact of Employment Legislation on Small Firms*, Department of Employment Research Paper No. 6 (London, 1979), at p. 33.

[3] Quoted in K. Williams, 'Unfair Dismissal: Myths and Statistics' (1983), 12, *ILJ* 157, at p. 162.

legislation may be quite different from the standards which the law actually imposes.

The empirical evidence to support any firm conclusions about the social and economic effects of the unfair dismissal legislation itself is unfortunately slender and sometimes contradictory. With the notable exception of the major study co-ordinated by Linda Dickens,[4] researchers often rely heavily upon surveys sent by post to employers or upon telephone interviews so that replies may prove unreliable. For example, one survey conducted in 1968 produced the statistic that only 58 per cent of works managers ever imposed disciplinary penalties upon their workforce, a result which defies belief.[5] What we lack most of all is a systematic study of disciplinary practices prior to the enactment of the legislation followed up by a survey of the same subjects ten years later to discover the probable impact of the legislation. The opportunity for such a study has now been lost, so we must rely upon patchy evidence concerning both periods, together with some simple economic models which suggest likely effects of the legislation. We can examine this evidence under a number of headings in order to determine whether in fact, if not in law, the legislation on unfair dismissal has achieved any or all of its aims.

1. DISCIPLINARY PRACTICES

Since the principal aim of the legislation was to improve the working environment for employees by controlling abuse of managerial discretion over discipline, we should commence by asking whether there is evidence to support the view that employers have indeed altered their rules and practices with respect to discipline at work?

FORMAL PROCEDURES

Firm evidence supports the finding that employers have responded to the legislation by instituting formal internal grievance procedures. Millward and Stevens, in their survey of a sample of over 2,000 firms with more than twenty-five employees in 1984 drawing on both the manufacturing and service industries in the public and private sectors, discovered the existence of such grievance procedures for dismissals in 90 per cent of firms.[6] There was little difference in the incidence of such procedures between the various

---

[4] Linda Dickens, Michael Jones, Brian Weekes, and Moira Hart, *Dismissed: A Study of Unfair Dismissal and the Industrial Tribunal System* (Oxford, 1985).

[5] Government Social Survey, *Workplace Industrial Relations* (London, 1968), SS 402, at p. 84.

[6] Neil Millward and Mark Stevens, *British Workplace Industrial Relations 1980–1984* (Aldershot, 1986), at pp. 169–85. Almost identical percentages are reported from a 1977–8 survey of private manufacturing establishments employing 50 or more employees: William Brown (ed.), *The Changing Contours of British Industrial Relations* (Oxford, 1981), at pp. 42–7.

industrial sectors. Nor was there a great deal of difference between small and large firms, though all establishments with more than 500 employees had a disciplinary procedure. Comparing their evidence with a similar survey conducted four years earlier, we can discern a steady increase in the incidence of such procedures.[7]

But comparing these findings with studies prior to the introduction of the legislation, we discover a significant proliferation of disciplinary procedures. Exact comparisons prove difficult because of the different scope of surveys. In addition, many surveys counted disputes procedures recognized by employer's federations at national level even though such procedures were seldom activated in practice for instances of individual dismissals.[8] Even allowing for these differences between the samples, the surveys reveal strikingly different pictures.[9] In the worst picture presented, a 1969 Government Social Survey of 1,100 private sector establishments employing over twenty-five workers reported that works managers acknowledged a formal plant-level disciplinary procedure in only 8 per cent of cases, though in larger firms the figure was nearer 50 per cent.[10] Other estimates from the same period suggest less than 20 per cent of firms overall had internal grievance procedures,[11] but that 65 per cent of firms employing more than 150 employees had a formal grievance procedure at plant level.[12] Although the true picture of disciplinary practices prior to 1971 therefore remains uncertain, even the most optimistic assessments from that period reveal a significant change occurring after the advent of the legislation.

Can this marked development in disciplinary procedures be attributed to the advent of the law of unfair dismissal? The timing of these developments certainly suggests a causal connection. Furthermore, in a survey of managers in manufacturing industry about the effect of employment protection laws in general, they asserted that the law of unfair dismissal had had an important effect on the introduction of disciplinary and dismissal procedures.[13] Another survey of medium-sized manufacturing firms conducted in 1972–3 reported that about a third of firms said that they had initiated or modified their disciplinary procedures because of the law of unfair dismissal.[14] In 1978

[7] W. W. Daniel and Neil Millward, *Workplace Industrial Relations in Britain* (London, 1983), at p. 163.

[8] Government Social Survey, *Workplace Industrial Relations*, SS 402, at p. 82.

[9] The crude results of these various surveys are conveniently tabled in Dickens *et al.*, *Dismissed*, at p. 235.

[10] Sandra J. N. Dawson, *Disciplinary and Dismissal Practices and Procedures*, Government Social Survey (London, 1969), reported in W. W. Daniel and E. Stilgoe, *The Impact of Employment Protection Laws*, Policy Studies Institute Report 44/577 (London, 1978), at pp. 58–60.

[11] K. W. Wedderburn and P. L. Davies, *Employment Grievances and Disputes Procedures in Britain* (Berkeley, Calif., 1969), at p. 138.

[12] Government Social Survey, *Workplace Industrial Relations*, SS 402, at p. 82.

[13] W. W. Daniel, 'The Effects of Employment Protection Laws in Manufacturing Industry' (1978), 86, *Department of Employment Gazette*, 660.

[14] Brian Weekes *et al.*, *Industrial Relations and the Limits of the Law* (Oxford, 1975), at p. 22.

another survey of employers who had recently defended unfair dismissal claims revealed that 12 per cent of establishments had introduced a procedure subsequent to the unfair dismissal claim being brought.[15] Indubitably other factors contributed to the growth of formal disciplinary procedures, such as union bargaining strength, the devolution of collective bargaining to plant level, and the greater professionalization of personnel management, but, notwithstanding these factors, the cumulative evidence points almost conclusively to the success of the legislation in compelling employers to adopt more formal disciplinary procedures.

How important is this success in the light of the goals of the legislation? A formal disciplinary procedure in itself does not guarantee fair outcomes. Nor does the existence of a procedure without its application have any virtue, though the survey evidence suggests that employers normally stick to promulgated procedures.[16] Yet the procedure itself has value, as I have argued, both in its contribution to respect for the dignity of individuals and in its likely improvement of the efficiency of disciplinary measures. Furthermore, these formal procedures constitute a key element in the establishment of a working environment conducive to conditions for the exercise of autonomy. The procedures largely remove the threat of irrational discipline, for the subjection of the employer's reasons for dismissal to further scrutiny seems likely to eliminate ill-founded and irrelevant considerations. In short, the institution of formal procedures was a necessary goal of the legislation for it to achieve its ultimate ends, and all the evidence points directly to its considerable degree of success.

BUREAUCRATIZATION

Other effects of the legislation on disciplinary practices of employers seem also to be welcome in the light of the aims of the legislation. The surveys all report the extension of managerial hierarchies with responsibility for dismissal. Firms have responded to the risk of litigation by removing the power of dismissal from the immediate supervisor and vesting it in senior management. One survey from 1972–3 found that 30 per cent of firms had changed the responsibility for dismissal by moving the decision up the managerial hierarchy in response to the advent of the legislation.[17] In the period 1985–6 it is reported that three-quarters of all cases arising in multi-establishment organizations were handled at head-office level.[18] We see at the same time

---

[15] Dickens et al., Dismissed, at p. 234; for similar evidence from a more recent period, see N. Banerji, D. Smart, and M. Stevens, 'Unfair Dismissal Cases in 1985–86: Impact on Parties' (1990), 98, Employment Gazette, 547, at p. 552.

[16] Millward and Stevens, British Workplace Industrial Relations, at p. 185, report that worker representatives believe that procedures are followed in 90% of cases.

[17] Weekes et al., Industrial Relations, at pp. 21–2. This finding was constant between large and medium-sized firms.

[18] Banerji, Smart, and Stevens, 'Unfair Dismissal Cases in 1985–86', at p. 549.

greater importance being attached to personnel management.[19] In the 1980s one survey also reports a much greater use of ultimate appeals under disciplinary procedures to higher-level management external to the plant,[20] suggesting that disciplinary matters have increasingly become issues of corporate concern and not simply the business of plant managers.

These developments should be welcomed. Although higher-level management may have a tendency to back the disciplinary decisions of line managers in order to buttress authority relations in the workplace, they enjoy greater liberty to question the general policy behind the dismissal and should be relatively immune from the personality conflicts which may be at the root of the trouble. This depersonalization of the dispute should permit a cooler assessment both of the merits of the case against the employee and of the employer's needs for particular standards of conduct on the part of employees. This should in turn reduce the incidence of abuse of managerial power and promote efficient disciplinary decisions. Although the reinforcement of hierarchies at work is not always welcome, this effect of the legislation in formalizing hierarchies within management itself seems to promote significant goals of the legislation.

Small firms have the greatest difficulty in adapting to this bureaucratic style of management. From that source comes the most vociferous protests about the degree to which the legislation impinges on their disciplinary practices.[21] During the 1980s, Parliament has responded sympathetically to these criticisms.[22] It adjusted the fairness standard in the law of unfair dismissal so that the tribunal is expressly alerted to the problems encountered by small firms in satisfying strict and formal legal standards.[23] The legislation also increased the qualifying periods for claims for unfair dismissal, so that fewer employees of small employers were entitled to protection.[24] Recent legislation has eliminated the requirement for small employers to issue particulars of disciplinary procedures.[25]

Although one has sympathy for small employers who do not wish their businesses to become bogged down by tiresome administration, we should question whether these reforms of the law are justified. In the first place, it is one thing to reduce the formal requirements upon small employers, but surely quite another to remove the protection for a whole class of employees altogether. Secondly, we should note that the most burdensome administra-

---

[19] Brown, *Changing Contours of British Industrial Relations*, at pp. 32–3; Daniel and Stilgoe, *The Impact of Employment Protection Laws*, p. 41.

[20] Millward and Stevens, *British Workplace Industrial Relations*, at p. 180.

[21] Dickens *et al.*, *Dismissed*, at p. 268.

[22] See I. T. Smith, 'Employment Laws and the Small Firm' (1985), 14, *ILJ* 18.

[23] EPCA 1978, s. 57(3) as amended by Employment Act 1980, s. 6.

[24] Ibid., s. 64A, inserted by Employment Act 1980, s. 8(1); but the Unfair Dismissal (Variation of Qualifying Period) Order 1985 subsequently extended the 2-year qualifying period to all full-time employees.

[25] EPCA 1978, s. 2A, inserted by Employment Act 1989, s. 13.

tive requirements upon small employers consist of forms and accounting for the purpose of taxation and national insurance, and these have remained, so we must suspect that it is dislike for the law of unfair dismissal itself, rather than any absolute concern about imposing bureaucracy, which has motivated this legislation. In any case, this concern for small firms is largely misplaced, for we have noted that Industrial Tribunals adopted flexible standards at all stages of the fairness inquiry which can respond adequately to the practical difficulties of compliance for small employers. What is striking about the operation of the law of unfair dismissal, however, despite the adoption of flexible standards of fairness, is that employees of small businesses enjoy a well above average success rate in their claims for unfair dismissal before Industrial Tribunals.[26] This suggests that it is precisely in these small businesses that employees have most to fear from arbitrary disciplinary power. Indeed, a survey of small employers reported that 65 per cent said that the law of unfair dismissal had made no difference to their disciplinary practices,[27] thereby revealing both perhaps the cause of the high success rate of applicants and at the same time their need for legislative protection.

In so far as the legislation has added to the bureaucratization of work, this seems to be a small price to pay for establishing fair and reasonable working conditions. Simitis makes a profound mistake in perceiving an antithesis between individual freedom and the bureaucratization of work,[28] for it is only by the subjection of managerial disciplinary power to rules that workers can begin to enjoy the necessary conditions for autonomy.

JOB SECURITY

Many will not be satisfied by these credits to the legislation, however, for they will want to know the bottom line: are employees more secure in their jobs? I have argued that the protection of job tenure in itself was not, and should not be, an aim of the legislation. But if the better aim of improving the working environment for employees has been achieved, we would certainly expect a reduced incidence in the number of dismissals since the introduction of the legislation. Here again the evidence, though not conclusive, points to a dramatic reduction in disciplinary dismissals. A government survey of 1969[29] found that 6 per cent of establishments employing more than 500 workers had dismissed 6 per cent of the workforce or more each year, but by 1977 none had dismissed more than 3.5 per cent of the

---

[26] M. Stevens, 'Unfair Dismissal Cases in 1985–6: Characteristics of Parties' (1988), 96, *Employment Gazette*, 651.

[27] Clifton and Tatton-Brown, *Impact of Employment Legislation on Small Firms*, at p. 23.

[28] S. Simitis, 'The Juridification of Labor Relations' (1985), 7, *Comparative Labor Law*, 93; id., 'Juridification of Labor Relations', in Gunther Teubner (ed.), *Juridification of Social Spheres: A Comparative Analysis in the Areas of Labor, Corporate, Antitrust and Social Welfare Law* (Berlin, 1987), 113.

[29] Dawson, *Disciplinary and Dismissal Practices and Procedures*.

workforce.[30] The number of disciplinary dismissals continued to decline into the 1980s, so that across all firms employing more than twenty-five workers the average fell to between 1 and 2 per cent of the workforce.[31] As one would expect, the bulk of the dismissals fell on new employees with less than one year's service.[32]

These figures point to a marked improvement in the job security of employees since the legislation was introduced. Again the causal connection cannot be proven conclusively, but the link seems highly likely. At the same time the legislation clearly does not deter employers from dismissing employees, especially during the probationary period, when they believe that they have sufficient disciplinary grounds. These results fit closely the aim of the legislation to improve job security without harming the efficiency of business by making it impossible to dismiss unsatisfactory workers. Once again the legislation should be credited with considerable success, even if some of this success is due to popular misconceptions of its requirements.

What none of these statistics reveal, however, is the extent to which the legislation has forced employers to reconsider the grounds on which they are prepared to dismiss workers. We have seen that the range of reasonable responses test of fairness in fact gives management considerable latitude in formulating the substantive standards of good conduct at work. But even this test sets a boundary on the kinds of reasons regarded as sufficient to justify a dismissal. Given the widespread ignorance of the details of the law amongst employers, however, one wonders whether the legislation has redefined these substantive rules of conduct at all. We have no available study of this aspect of disciplinary practices, but can only infer from the reduced incidence of disciplinary dismissals that some alteration in employers' definitions of conduct meriting dismissal may have taken place.

This absence of evidence about the substantive grounds for dismissal adopted by employers leaves a gaping hole in any assessment of the success of the legislation. We cannot yet be sure whether the routine practices of employers now qualify as rational manpower policies, free from abuse of discretion, which enhance opportunities for individuals to be authors of their own lives.

It seems to me unlikely, however, that the law of unfair dismissal on its own could achieve such a major reform of disciplinary practices. Because the law fixes solely on the point of termination of employment and emphasizes compensation for loss of a job, it does not offer the possibility of reviewing directly the disciplinary rules of the workplace for the purpose of proposing reforms. Management retains the discretion to insist upon its works rules at the price of the compensatory award. French legislation, in contrast,

---

[30] Daniel and Stilgoe, *The Impact of Employment Protection Laws*, at pp. 62, 75.
[31] Millward and Stevens, *British Workplace Industrial Relations*, at pp. 186–7.
[32] Ibid. 187–8.

empowers a government labour inspector to examine works rules to check that they do not contain provisions which infringe the law, or the civil liberties of individual employees, or the *principes généraux* of the legal system.[33] Unless such infringements can be demonstrated to be justifiable and proportionate to the business objectives of the employer, the labour inspector may require modifications of the works rules with the ultimate sanction of criminal penalties.

The clear advantage of this approach to disciplinary practices over that restricted to litigation over dismissals must be its prophylactic effect, that is, the way it forces employers to consider the justice of works rules before they are promulgated rather than only after they have been breached. European law seems to be moving in this direction, so this approach may eventually be imposed on national law. For example, the Equal Treatment Directive requires national legislation to eliminate any sex discrimination in the 'internal rules of undertakings'.[34] I suggest that the law of dismissal needs to operate in tandem with prior scrutiny of disciplinary rules if it is to be completely successful in its goal of transforming the workplace environment.

2. COLLECTIVE INDUSTRIAL RELATIONS

In Chapter 1, I argued that the law of unfair dismissal represents a radical departure from the traditional labour policy of industrial pluralism. Instead of promoting collective bargaining as the mechanism for resolving questions of justice at work, the unfair dismissal legislation diverts grievances into a legal forum which assesses individual rights. Instead of bargaining power determining outcomes, legal argument and interpretations of legal principles dictate results. At the same time, however, we noted that the Donovan Commission hoped that the provision of a legal avenue of redress for unfair dismissal would have an impact on collective industrial relations by reducing the incidence of industrial conflict connected with dismissals. When considering the social effects of the legislation, therefore, we should ask what impact the legislation has had on collective industrial relations and in particular upon the incidence of strikes.

UNION RECOGNITION

In one respect, unions and management could embrace a concerted response to the advent of the legislation. As we have noted, management introduced formal disciplinary procedures in order to comply with the legislation.

---

[33] Code du Travail, L. 122-33–L. 122-39; A. Jeammand, 'Les Contrôles de la légalité du règlement intérieur' (1983), 9–10, *Droit Social*, 520; J. Savatier, 'Le Contrôle administratif du règlement intérieur' (1987), 9–10, *Droit Social*, 645.

[34] EC Directive 76/207; the corresponding national legislation is Sex Discrimination Act 1986, s. 6(1)(*b*).

Unions normally supported this development and almost invariably where the union had already achieved recognition the disciplinary procedure was shaped by a collective agreement.[35]

A more challenging issue is whether the development of disciplinary procedures actually caused employers to grant recognition to unions for the first time, so that the legislation had the effect of actually promoting the values of industrial pluralism. Although the Donovan Commission hoped that this would occur,[36] the Industrial Tribunals did not require joint agreement with the union for a disciplinary procedure to be fair,[37] so the statute provided little inducement for employers to recognize unions.[38]

From its commencement the legislation has offered the possibility of a grant of exemption from the province of the statute by the Secretary of State, if he is satisifed that a collective agreement provides procedures and remedies as beneficial to employees as the statute.[39] Although intended to stimulate collective bargaining over disciplinary matters, this provision has only been used once following a tribunal decision which was unsatisfactory to both employer and union.[40] There seems to be little incentive for employers to seek formal exemption, since the employee's right to job security cannot be diminished; and, for trade unions, the prospect of being seen to deprive their members of a possible legal avenue of redress must seem equally unattractive. Instead of stimulating joint disciplinary procedures, this provision has simply been ignored.

The legislation also protected the right of workers to join trade unions,[41] which may have improved the chances of collective bargaining relations developing. Until the advent of the special award in 1982, however, the slim chances of success (probably due to problems of proof of anti-union discrimination), combined with the low levels of compensation, could hardly have deterred employers from adopting an anti-union stance.[42] The courts and tribunals tend also to adopt a narrow interpretation of trade union membership and activities which diminishes the support for collective bargaining. In *Carrington* v. *Therm-A-Stor Ltd.*,[43] almost all of the employees

---

[35] Daniel and Millward, *Workplace Industrial Relations in Britain*, at pp. 165–7; Millward and Stevens, *British Workplace Industrial Relations*, at p. 179; one survey reports a much less active involvement by unions: S. Evans, J. Goodman, and L. Hargreaves, 'Unfair Dismissal Law and Changes in the Role of Trade Unions and Employers' Associations' (1985), 14, *ILJ* 91, at p. 96.

[36] Royal Commission on Trade Unions and Employers' Associations, Cmnd. 3623 (1965–8), para. 540.

[37] *Neefjes* v. *Crystal Products* [1972] IRLR 118 (NIRC).

[38] Weekes *et al.*, *Industrial Relations*, at p. 31.

[39] EPCA 1978, s. 65.

[40] Dickens *et al.*, *Dismissed*, at pp. 238–40; C. Bourn, 'Statutory Exemptions for Collective Agreements' (1979), 8, *ILJ* 85. For a discussion of the operation of this exceptional case, see L. Rico, 'Legislating against Unfair Dismissal: Implications from British Experience' (1986), 8, *Industrial Relations Law Journal*, 547, at p. 573.

[41] EPCA 1978, ss. 58, 59(a).

[42] Dickens *et al.*, *Dismissed*, at pp. 245–7.

[43] [1983] ICR 208 (CA).

in a new factory joined a trade union and the union's district secretary applied to the employer for recognition. The employer reacted by dismissing more than a quarter of the workforce for redundancy, though without selecting for dismissal on the basis of union membership. The Court of Appeal held that the employer had reacted to trade union activities in general rather than any particular individual employee's membership or activities in a trade union, so the dismissals were not automatically unfair. The legislation thus fails to support union recognition claims at the critical moment. After the introduction of the special award, ironically enough, levels of union membership began to fall. It therefore seems unlikely that the protection of the right to become a member of a union by the law of unfair dismissal played any significant part in encouraging plant-level bargaining.

It is true, of course, that union recognition at plant level increased rapidly in the 1970s, but this development could be explained entirely by employers' need to establish orderly pay negotiations. There is no direct evidence to support the view that the law of unfair dismissal contributed to any significant extent in the growth of collective bargaining at any level.

UNION MEMBERSHIP

But if the legislation did not promote collective bargaining, did it deter it? Did the alternative avenue of redress for grievances provided by the Industrial Tribunals, together with the introduction by employers of grievance procedures, reduce employees' support for union representation? Did the law succeed in expropriating conflict over dismissals,[44] as the Donovan Commission intended?

Before the advent of the legislation most unions said that they preferred dismissals to be handled through collectively agreed procedures.[45] Unions in the United States have also voiced the fear of a possible adverse impact on levels of membership, for one of their main attractions offered to workers as an inducement to join the union is the introduction of labour arbitration using the standard of just cause to regulate discipline at work. In recent years, however, this resistance to legislation from American unions has been dropped.[46] Were these fears about potential adverse effects upon union membership and hence bargaining strength well grounded?

In Britain it seems unlikely that the legislation had any negative impact on levels of union membership and the extent of collective bargaining. Trade union officials were clearly prepared to continue their past practices of

---

[44] G. Teubner, 'Juridification: Concepts, Aspects, Limits, Solutions', in Teubner (ed.), *Juridification of Social Spheres*, 3, at pp. 7–8.

[45] Dickens *et al.*, *Dismissed*, at p. 251, quoting report in *The Times* (15 Mar. 1965).

[46] T. J. St Antoine, 'A Seed Germinates: Unjust Discharge Reform Heads Towards Full Flower' (1988), 67, *Nebraska Law Review*, 56.

negotiating disciplinary procedures with employers and of participating in those procedures to the extent of representing their members at disciplinary hearings.[47] They continued to press grievances through agreed procedures without resorting to law, but at the same time were also prepared to undertake the novel and valuable task of assisting members in representing their claims before Industrial Tribunals. About one-third of applicants for unfair dismissal receive advice from trade union officials, and about one-half of applicants who are members of trade unions have an official or shop steward represent them before the Industrial Tribunal.[48] In addition, unions could argue persuasively that the degree of protection of job security afforded by collective action was likely to be superior to that offered by Industrial Tribunals.[49] Reinstatement is a more likely outcome of collective bargaining than in the tribunals, and through bargaining unions can compel employers to adopt disciplinary standards more favourable to employees. Thus union membership was probably not affected by the legislation because the unions could still offer real benefits in terms of job security through collective bargaining and at the same time present themselves as a body to turn to for advice and representation in the event of litigation.

INDUSTRIAL ACTION

Indeed there is every sign that unions continued to press grievances against disciplinary action in exactly the same way as before the advent of the legislation. It is clear, for example, that stoppages of work concerned with disciplinary dismissals of workers constitutes approximately the same percentage of strikes as before.[50] Evidence before the Donovan Commission suggested that about 10 per cent of stoppages of work in the period 1964–6 concerned dismissals other than redundancies;[51] for 1982 the corresponding figure was 9 per cent of stoppages;[52] and for 1988 and 1989 the corresponding figures were 11 per cent and 8 per cent respectively.[53] No doubt as long as the workforce perceives a collective interest to be at stake in individual disciplinary action, they will continue to use collective strength to protect their interests.[54] For this reason it seems unlikely that the legislation could

---

[47] Dickens et al., Dismissed, at p. 237.
[48] Banerji, Smart, and Stevens, 'Unfair Dismissal Cases in 1985–86', at p. 550.
[49] H. Collins, 'Capitalist Discipline and Corporatist Law' (1982), 11, *ILJ* 78.
[50] Dickens et al., Dismissed, at pp. 224–7.
[51] Royal Commission on Trade Unions and Employers' Associations, Cmnd. 3623 (1965–8), para. 143.
[52] Department of Employment, 'Stoppages Caused by Industrial Disputes in 1982' (1983), 91, *Employment Gazette*, 297.
[53] Department of Employment (1990), 98, *Employment Gazette*, 343.
[54] Dickens et al., Dismissed, at p. 231.

affect more than marginally the levels of industrial action in response to disciplinary dismissals.[55]

LEGALISM

But if the law has not altered the practices of unions in protecting job security, has it affected the way in which grievances are presented? One possibility is that awareness of the legal principles applicable to dismissals has led to the presentation of claims in a form modelled on the reasoning developed by Industrial Tribunals.[56] Can we detect a move towards legalistic discourses in the conduct of industrial relations? The significance of such a shift would be that it might reveal an adoption by union officials of a more individualistic attitude towards dismissals, one which tended to discount a collective interest in joint regulation of the workplace.

Clark and Wedderburn, who raise this question of the 'juridification' of industrial relations,[57] by which they mean legalism in the conduct of industrial relations, seem to offer the equivocal answer that although management and unions must conduct themselves generally against the background of a more detailed legal framework than formerly, where strong union organization has been maintained, then legalism has not undermined the traditional union collective perspective on dismissals.[58] But evidence on this question remains scant since it requires interpretation of discourses rather than collecting statistics. The union's fear of legalism because it slowly poisons collective solidarity has yet to be proven unwarranted and finds some support in one survey.[59] But the more general worry that the existence of the legal right to claim unfair dismissal would have an adverse impact on levels of union membership seems to have been proved unfounded.

3. LABOUR MARKET

Under a crude neo-classical model of the labour market, we should expect regulation of employment to have the undesirable effects of reducing levels of employment and wages since the added cost of labour to employers should reduced demand. This model informs policies which seek to deregulate the

[55] Cf. similar findings in Italy: M. H. Lazerson, 'Labour Conflict within the Structure of the Law: Dismissals under the Italian Workers' Charter in Two Plants' (1988), 16, *International Journal of Sociology of Law*, 31.

[56] Royal Commission on Trade Unions and Employers' Associations, Cmnd. 3623 (1965–8), para. 535.

[57] J. Clark and Lord Wedderburn, 'Modern Labour Law: Problems, Functions, and Policies', in Lord Wedderburn, Roy Lewis, and Jon Clark (eds.), *Labour Law and Industrial Relations* (Oxford, 1983), at pp. 187–9. Cf. Steve D. Anderman, *Unfair Dismissal and the Law* (London, 1973), at pp. 11 ff.

[58] See also Dickens *et al.*, *Dismissed*, at pp. 252–3.

[59] Evans, Goodman, and Hargreaves, 'Unfair Dismissal Law and Changes in the Role of Trade Unions and Employers' Associations', at p. 96.

labour market in order to remove barriers to employment.[60] But can it be demonstrated empirically that the law of unfair dismissal has generated these undesirable side-effects? Has the price for increased job security for most workers been unemployment for a few?

EMPLOYMENT EFFECTS

This complex question has not been adequately tested, but the evidence so far suggests that nothing like this crude economic model of the labour market has operated. In a survey of employers in the mid-1970s, Daniel and Stilgoe found little sign that unfair dismissal legislation had inhibited the numbers employed.[61] In a study of small firms, though about one-quarter indicated that the legislation had affected the number of employees recruited, it was clear that another important factor in the employers' reluctance to take on new staff was the desire to improve productivity, so the effect of the legislation on small employers may in reality be much smaller.[62]

Rough econometric evidence also supports the view that the unfair dismissal legislation has had little effect, if any, on levels of unemployment.[63] This evidence supports the view that the legislation has contributed to an increase in the time taken by the unemployed to find jobs, thereby increasing levels of equilibrium unemployment, which results from more careful recruitment practices introduced by employers. On the other hand, the overall effect of the legislation seems from that evidence to reduce levels of unemployment, for the slow-down in hiring is more than offset by a reduction in the number of dismissals. For similar reasons, labour turnover seems to have been unaffected by the legislation.[64]

These conclusions which contradict the neo-classical theory should cause no surprise to those educated in the institutional qualities of the labour market.[65] In most large firms an internal administrative system which is substantially insulated from the impact of the external labour market determines the allocation of pay and jobs. In this context we should expect employers to respond to the legislation by closer governance of the internal

[60] e.g. Department of Employment, *Removing Barriers to Employment* (London, 1989), Cm. 655.

[61] Daniel and Stilgoe, *The Impact of Employment Protection Laws*, at p. 70.

[62] Clifton and Tatton-Brown, *Impact of Employment Legislation on Small Firms*, at pp. 16–17, 20–1.

[63] S. Nickell, 'The Determinants of Equilibrium Unemployment in Britain' (1982), 92, *Economic Journal*, 555. This study uses for the purpose of quantifying the variable of firing costs the number of formal claims for unfair dismissal. Obviously this must be an inexact proxy for the costs of termination of employment, for it ignores the mass of unlitigated claims, the different levels of compensation payable, and the employer's likelihood of successfully defending a claim.

[64] S. M. Burges and S. Nickell, 'Labour Turnover in UK Manufacturing' (1990), 57, *Economica*, 295. Labour turnover includes both dismissals and resignations.

[65] See Ch. 1 n. 25.

labour market of firms, by paying more attention to both the quality of recruits and the adequacy of criteria for promotion, and by pressing for more efficient use of labour through flexibility in manpower deployment. These are the normal responses for managers of an internal labour market seeking to reduce labour costs, and the survey evidence proves that these are precisely the measures which were adopted.[66]

LABOUR MARKET SEGMENTATION

Although the law of unfair dismissal seems not to have affected total levels of employment, it may have steered the labour market towards greater segmentation. The labour market segmentation theory suggests that certain phenomena such as differential levels of pay, levels of job security, and the length of periods of unemployment, may best be explained by drawing a distinction between two types of labour market present in the economy at once.[67] In the primary labour market, employees enjoy relatively good pay and considerable job security. The secondary labour market offers poorly paid jobs which tend to be temporary. This theory of segmentation of the labour market can be used to explain the persistence of low pay and different patterns of unemployment for social groups. For example, a skilled, white, male worker expects a job in the primary sector, so his jobs will normally be well paid and last for a considerable period of time. Following dismissal, he is likely to remain unemployed until he can obtain another job in the primary sector, which may be a lengthy period during a recession. In contrast, a female black worker usually has no expectation of good pay or permanent employment, so she may change low paid jobs frequently with scarcely any period of unemployment.

The question raised by the advent of the law of dismissal is whether the statute has tended to reinforce this segmentation of the labour market? For example, by requiring a qualifying period of continuous employment before the right to claim unfair dismissal was acquired, now set at two years,[68] the legislation tended to augment the security of tenure of jobs in the primary

[66] Daniel and Stilgoe, *The Impact of Employment Protection Laws*, at p. 74; Clifton and Tatton-Brown, *Impact of Employment Legislation on Small Firms*, at p. 17; Paul Davies and Mark Freedland, *Labour Law: Text and Materials* (London, 1984), at pp. 39–41.

[67] M. Reich, D. M. Gordon, and R. C. Edwards, 'A Theory of Labor Market Segmentation' (1973), 62, *American Economic Review*, 359; G. G. Cain, 'The Challenge of Segmented Labor Market Theories to Orthodox Theory: A Survey' (1976), 14, *Journal of Economic Literature*, 1215; J. I. Bulow and L. H. Summers, 'A Theory of Dual Labor Markets with Application to Industrial Policy, Discrimination, and Keynesian Unemployment' (1986), 4, *Journal of Labor Economics*, 376; W. T. Dickens and K. Lang, 'The Reemergence of Segmented Labor Market Theory' (1988), 78, *American Economic Review Proceedings*, 129; B. E. Kaufman, 'The Postwar View of Labor Markets and Wage Determination', in Bruce E. Kaufman, *How Labor Markets Work* (Lexington, Mass., 1988), ch. 5.

[68] EPCA 1978, s. 64, as amended by Unfair Dismissal (Variation of Qualifying Period) Order 1985, SI 1985, No. 782.

sector but to have no relevance to temporary jobs in the secondary labour market. Whereas the implicit contractual promise of a job for life in a large organization offering primary sector jobs could only be buttressed by legal guarantees, the marginal workers of the secondary sector had their disadvantage compounded by the peremptory denial of legal redress. This is a cause of concern, for it is precisely in these secondary sector jobs where the benefits of the legislation are needed most and where the Donovan Commission hoped that its proposed legislation would have its most significant impact. This need for the legislation by workers in the secondary labour market may be illustrated by the fact that most of the claimants for unfair dismissal come from workers on lower than average wages.[69] Other provisions of the legislation, such as the special treatment of small employers, also tend to exacerbate the disadvantage of workers in the secondary labour market.

But the social policies with regard to the segmentation of the labour market should be viewed in a broader context than the issue of job security. Using the crude neo-classical model of the labour market, which often applies fairly accurately to the secondary labour market, it has been argued that the absence of regulation of employment has served to facilitate the growth in levels of employment in this sector during the 1980s. At the same time, often these jobs offer more flexible hours creating better opportunities for women to enter paid employment. For example, the remarkable growth in part-time work during this period has certainly increased job opportunities for women and reduced overall levels of unemployment.[70] If it can be demonstrated that the absence of legal regulation, including the law of dismissal, has fostered this development,[71] then clearly we must engage in a difficult balancing of policies between promoting job security on the one hand, and spreading the opportunity to work on the other.

The precise causal connection between the absence of legal regulation and the growth of the secondary labour market cannot be determined, however, for it is possible to attribute the entire growth of this segment of the labour market to the lower rates of pay. A tell-tale sign of the relevance of the legislation would be the creation of jobs whose specifications fall just below the statutory minimum thresholds for qualifying for employment protection rights. Although this phenomenon occurs with respect to the tax threshold of national insurance payments,[72] it is far from clear that employment protection rights play a significant role in determining the types of jobs

[69] Stevens, 'Unfair Dismissal Cases in 1985–6', 651.

[70] C. Hakim, 'Trends in the Flexible Workforce' (1987), 95, *Employment Gazette*, 549, at p. 555.

[71] D. Blanchflower and D. Corry, *Part-Time Employment in Great Britain*, Department of Employment Research paper No. 57 (London, 1987).

[72] R. Disney and E. Szyszczak, 'Protective Legislation and Part-time Employment in Britain' (1984), 22, *British Journal of Industrial Relations*, 78.

created.[73] If so, then it may not be possible to attribute any role to the law of unfair dismissal in the intensification of labour market segmentation during the 1980s, though it remains true that the law tends to exacerbate the differences between the two sectors.

DISTRIBUTION OF UNEMPLOYMENT

We should also recall at this point that the redundancy payments legislation has had its own independent effects on the operation of the labour market. In Chapter 5, on economic dismissals, we noted that, because redundancy payments tend to increase with age (being tied to seniority), older workers may be more willing to accept dismissal as the level of payment is more substantial. In addition, this distribution of unemployment suits employers, who are prepared to foot the additional bill to preserve industrial harmony and to employ a younger, cheaper workforce. Since older workers normally experience longer periods of unemployment between jobs, the effect of the redundancy payment legislation must be to redistribute the experience of unemployment on to older workers. We accepted before the argument that this effect runs contrary to any worthwhile active manpower policy.[74]

But then we argued that in fact the redundancy payments legislation as a whole fails to serve any intelligible manpower policy. If we seek to improve general levels of employment and promote the efficient training and relocation of workers, the law seems again and again to provide exactly the wrong kind of cues to employers and workers. Far from assisting the adjustment of the labour force to a rapidly changing post-industrial society, the current legislation at best reduces the force of organized resistance to change, and at worst seriously impedes the process of transition.

4. THE ORGANIZATION OF CAPITAL

During the 1980s managers of large firms demonstrated a considerable interest in vertical disintegration. Instead of firms growing larger by integrating both backwards up the chain of supply towards the production of raw materials and forwards in the direction of distribution and retailing, there has been a pronounced shift towards the decomposition of capital into separate corporate entities. Many aspects of a business may not be conducted directly by a firm but rather arranged through subcontracting, franchising,

---

[73] C. Hakim, 'Employment Rights: A Comparison of Part-time and Full-time Employees' (1989), 18, *ILJ* 69; R. Disney and E. Szyszczak, 'Part-time Work: Reply to Catherine Hakim' (1989), 18, *ILJ* 223.
[74] W. W. Daniel, 'The United Kingdom', in Michael Cross (ed.) *Managing Workforce Reductions: An International Survey* (London, 1985), at p. 71.

concessions, and outsourcing.[75] The public sector has also adopted a similar strategy for organizing production as an aspect of the policy of privatization.[76] Can these developments in the organization of capital be attributed to any extent to the law of unfair dismissal?

These patterns of vertical disintegration probably result primarily from more immediate and substantial causes.[77] During periods of recession, large firms may respond to the uncertainty by using subcontracting as a buffer against market fluctuations. If demand falls, then the subcontractor bears the risk of going out of business and the waste of capital investment, because the core firm merely refrains from reordering the parts. But even in this example, the labour costs associated with economic dismissals may prove a significant consideration when determining the organization of capital. The device of subcontracting offers the core firm the flexibility of reduction of production without bearing the costs of lay-offs and redundancies.

Yet the pattern of vertical disintegration of production seems to have kept its momentum even after the recession of the early 1980s.[78] Large firms have discovered long-term advantages in diverting production to small firms. These peripheral contractors can offer flexible and specialized skills, can generate economies of scale within these narrow markets, and can achieve considerable innovation in production methods and products.[79] Is it possible to attribute some of this continuing momentum for vertical disintegration to the statutory law of dismissal?

Because employment protection laws limit their vesting of rights to employees who work a certain number of hours, with a continuous period of service for an employer at a particular place of work, one effect of vertical disintegration has often been to exclude or reduce the numbers of employees enjoying the benefits of legal protection. For example, a firm which makes a class of its professional staff redundant and then enters contractual arrangements with them periodically as freelance contractors achieves the position that it will no longer be liable for any claims for dismissal. The former employees will be regarded now as independent contractors, in business on

---

[75] National Economic Development Office, *Changing Working Patterns* (London, 1986), para. 1.36; D. Wood and P. Smith, *Employers' Labour Use Strategies*, Department of Employment Research Paper No. 63 (London, 1989), at pp. 35–7.

[76] Eric Batstone, *The Reform of Workplace Industrial Relations* (Oxford, 1988), at pp. 186–8.

[77] H. Collins, 'Independent Contractors and the Challenge of Vertical Disintegration to Employment Protection Laws' (1990), 10, *Oxford Journal of Legal Studies*, 353.

[78] Wood and Smith, *Employers' Labour Use Strategies*, at pp. 35–7. For doubts about these trends, see J. Rubery, 'Employers and the Labour Market', in Duncan Gallie (ed.), *Employment in Britain* (Oxford, 1988), 251, at pp. 264–8.

[79] S. Brusco, 'The Emilian Model: Productive Decentralisation and Social Integration' (1982), 6, *Cambridge Journal of Economics*, 93; M. Storper, 'The Transition to Flexible Specialisation in the US Film Industry: External Economies, the Division of Labour, and the Crossing of Industrial Divides' (1989), 13, *Cambridge Journal of Economics*, 273; but see M. H. Lazerson, 'An Outcome of Markets and Hierarchies?' (1988), 53, *American Sociological Review*, 330.

their own account, for whom employment protection rights are inappropriate and unavailable. The advantages to the firm of evading the statutory protection against dismissal seem striking and offer a plausible explanation of why vertical disintegration has become so prevalent.

In the light of the aims of the unfair dismissal legislation, such an explanation of the pattern of vertical disintegration appears alarming. In order to avoid judicial control over managerial disciplinary power, firms convert that power back into market power. They use their bargaining power in the market to determine the terms on which people work, substituting precise contractual measurements of performance backed by the sanction of discontinuance of commercial relations for the managerial discretion to direct and supervise labour. With labour in the form of independent contractors providing services once more, firms can treat it like any other commodity acquired through commercial relations. The employer no longer owes any duty to act fairly, to act reasonably, and with respect for the individual. Provided that they pay their debts, employers can terminate these commercial relations for any reason as an aspect of freedom of contract. The fear is therefore that the price for the improvement of job security achieved for many workers by the law of unfair dismissal has been a real diminution of job security for many others by the device of vertical disintegration.

Although the increased incidence of vertical disintegration does pose this threat to the success of the unfair dismissal legislation, it is far less clear that the legislation itself has been a contributory factor in shaping the organization of capital. I have little doubt that labour costs in general have played a major role in encouraging vertical disintegration,[80] but the dismissal legislation itself has probably played a minor part. Evidence from Italy[81] and France[82] supports the view that the costs of compliance with employment protection rights leads to a preference for forms of marginal work such as independent contracting, but surveys of British employers indicate that these costs do not figure significantly in their calculations.[83] Labour cost considerations which appear far more decisive consist in the opportunity afforded by vertical disintegration to avoid the high rates of pay in the internal labour market of a core firm and instead have the work performed at the lower cost of the external market, taking advantage perhaps of non-union rates, regional differences,

[80] Collins, 'Independent Contractors and the Challenge of Vertical Disintegration to Employment Protection Laws', at p. 360.

[81] Lazerson, 'An Outcome of Markets and Hierarchies?', at pp. 336–7; M. J. Piore, 'Perspectives on Labor Market Flexibility' (1986), 25, *Industrial Relations*, 146, at p. 153.

[82] F. Michon, 'Dualism and the French Labour Market: Business Strategy, Non-standard Job-forms and Secondary Jobs', in Frank Wilkinson (ed.), *The Dynamics of Labour Market Segmentation* (London, 1981).

[83] Daniel and Stilgoe, *The Impact of Employment Protection Laws*; P. Leighton, *Contractual Arrangements in Selected Industries*, Department of Employment Research Paper No. 39 (London, 1983); Wood and Smith, *Employers' Labour Use Strategies*.

and labour market segmentation.[84] At the same time vertical disintegration may also avoid or reduce the quasi-fixed costs associated with employment, such as hiring and training.[85] Although these more immediate and quantifiable savings in labour costs achieved through vertical disintegration have been crucial in the reorganization of capital, we should not forget that one underlying reason for the availability of cheaper labour in the secondary labour market is the absence of legal protection for employees, so that the unfair dismissal legislation may have indirectly contributed to the process.

Even though the role of the legislation in causing vertical disintegration is far from clear, the deleterious social effects are readily apparent. As well as the blunt attack on the interest in job security noted above, the pattern of vertical distintegration can undermine other aspects of the statutory dismissal law. We noted in our examination of economic dismissals in Chapter 5 that the separation of businesses into core firms and peripheral subcontractors could protect the core firm against the costs of redundancy payments and could avoid procedural duties to notify employees and consult with recognized trade unions. Although the core firm causes these economic dismissals by adjusting its orders to the subcontractor, it owes no legal duties to the employees concerned.

5. THE ROLE OF THE STATE

In Chapter 1, I argued that what was most striking and novel about the dismissal legislation was its abandonment of the labour law policy of industrial pluralism. Instead of regarding free collective bargaining as the best way of securing workplace justice, the State intervened by providing tribunals to control one aspect of managerial prerogative. I argued that this break with legislative policy also ran against the grain of the traditional ideology of the common law, which regarded the contract of employment as a private arrangement in which the manner of the exercise of managerial disciplinary power should not be judged or evaluated. To succeed in its goal of protecting an employee's interest in job security, the legislation would have to persuade the tribunals and courts to abandon their traditional attitude of abstentionism towards managerial prerogative and to embrace a new framework of legal rights for the governance of industrial relations.

THE PROBLEM OF JURIDIFICATION

My method of interpretation of the decisions of the courts and tribunals tried to present them in their best light, that is, to emphasize in my account

---

[84] C. Craig et al., *Labour Market Structure, Industrial Organisation, and Low Pay* (Cambridge 1982).

[85] W. Y. Oi, 'Labour as a Quasi-Fixed Factor' (1962), 70, *Journal of Political Economy*, 538; Arthur M. Okun, *Prices and Quantities* (Oxford, 1981), ch. 2.

of the law the extent to which these goals may have been realized. Even with this disposition to present such a favourable account of the interpretations of this legislation, it must be admitted that we have encountered considerable evidence that the courts and tribunals have been unwilling to transform substantially their attitudes to the role of the law in employment disputes. The 'range of reasonable responses' test of fairness seems to be the product of trying to reconcile the old ideology of abstentionism with the requirements of the modern legislation, but its effect is to preserve much of the traditional hesitancy of agencies of the State to interfere in the governance of the workplace. Both the unwillingness to use the remedy of reinstatement and to countenance challenges to employers' assessments of their manpower needs also reveal a disposition to preserve the traditional pattern of abstentionism. The courts seem to be at their most willing to intervene when the issue at stake is the protection rather than the control of managerial disciplinary power, as in the example of reduction of compensation for contributory fault where the courts actively engage in assessments of the behaviour of the parties.

These themes reveal that the legislation has not overcome what we called in Chapter 1 the problem of juridification. The boundary between public and private, between relations appropriate for careful regulation by the State and those civil and economic relations where privacy and autonomy should be respected, has been left largely unaltered. Despite the close analogy between public and private bureaucratic power, the latter, in the form of managerial disciplinary authority, retains its position as a largely unregulated sphere of conduct. What has happened instead is that the legislation has tended to reinforce those bureaucratic structures and the rationality of economic efficiency on which they operate.

TRIBUNAL OR ARBITRATION?

Whether or not some alternative institutional form for adjudication of disputes could overcome this problem of juridification is difficult to assess. Drawing on the North American experience of labour arbitration as an integral part of the collective bargaining relationship,[86] a pattern rarely imitated in Britain,[87] we might expect that an arbitrator who enjoys the confidence of the parties to the collective agreement could use the occasion provided by individual grievances to develop detailed rules for the exercise

---

[86] B. Aaron, 'Some Procedural Problems in Arbitration' (1957), 10, *Vanderbilt Law Review*, 733; I. Katz, 'Minimizing Disputes through the Adjustment of Grievances' (1947), 12, *Law and Contemporary Problems*, 249.

[87] Dickens *et al.*, *Dismissed*, at pp. 278–81; P. Lowry, *Employment Rights and the Third Party* (London, 1990), at pp. 130–4; Wedderburn and Davies, *Employment Grievances and Disputes Procedures in Britain*; P. L. Davies, 'Arbitration and the Role of Courts in the UK,' (1979), 3, *Comparative Labor Law*, 31.

of managerial disciplinary power in all its aspects including procedures and sanctions. In effect the arbitrator's decisions would elaborate the disciplinary code by setting standards which reflect an acceptable compromise between management and union.

Arbitration thus offers the potential for overcoming the abstentionism of the courts.[88] For this reason above all arbitration has been recommended as a replacement for Industrial Tribunals.[89] But the standards which arbitration imposes will not reflect some objective ideal of workplace justice. They will represent primarily a compromise of subjective interests set according to the relative bargaining power of the parties to the collective agreement.[90] In matters of procedure, for example, the arbitrator is likely to emphasize strict compliance with collectively agreed procedures at the expense of the individual's interest in natural justice.[91] This result should appeal to those who fear that the process of juridification expropriates conflict from the parties, because it alienates the problem of dismissal from the control of the immediate parties concerned, management and unions, and subjects the problem to an inappropriate and disfunctional set of legal institutions and rules.[92] For those industrial pluralists who retain a faith in the justice of the outcomes of collective bargaining, arbitration offers a better potential institutional solution to the problem of juridification than that provided by Industrial Tribunals, because it may restore control over the applicable norms to the parties to the conflict. Yet we should not expect labour arbitration to relinquish the shackles of legal rules and procedures entirely; for the experience in North America indicates that arbitrators, in order to establish their legitimacy and authority, often do succumb to legalism and intermittent observance of legal norms, especially general contractual principles.[93]

But for those who regard the individual interest in job security as too important to be left contingent upon the vicissitudes of bargaining strength in the market, labour arbitration cannot provide a satisfactory solution to the

[88] H. Collins, 'Capitalist Discipline and Corporatist Law' (1982), 11, *ILJ* 170; B. I. Mordsley and S. R. Wall, 'The Dismissal of Employees under the Unfair Dismissal Law in the United Kingdom and Labour Arbitration Proceedings in the United States: The Parameters of Reasonableness and Just Cause' (1983), 16, *Cornell International Law Journal*, 1.

[89] Dickens *et al.*, *Dismissed*, pp. 284–300; see, also, Justice, *Industrial Tribunals* (London, 1987); B. Hepple, 'Restructuring Employment Rights' (1986), 15, *ILJ* 69, at p. 83; R. W. Rideout, 'Unfair Dismissal—Tribunal or Arbitration: A Discussion Paper' (1986), 15, *ILJ* 84. Compare the debate in the USA: W. B. Gould, 'Stemming the Wrongful Discharge Tide: A case for Arbitration' (1987), 13, *Employee Relations Law Journal*, 404.

[90] J. G. Getman, 'Labor Arbitration and Dispute Resolution' (1979), 88, *Yale Law Journal*, 916; J. R. Bellace, 'A Right of Fair Dismissal: Enforcing a Statutory Guarantee' (1983), 16, *Journal of Law Reform*, 207, at p. 228.

[91] For similar points, see Rideout, 'Unfair Dismissal—Tribunal or Arbitration: A Discussion Paper', at pp. 89–91.

[92] See Teubner, 'Juridification: Concepts, Aspects, Limits, Solutions', at pp. 7–9.

[93] H. J. Glasbeek, 'The Utility of Model Building: Collins' Capitalist Discipline and Corporatist Law' (1984), 13, *ILJ* 133, at pp. 148–9.

adjudication of disputes over dismissals. It is true, of course, that Industrial Tribunals, like other courts, present a barrier to individual claimants to air their grievances. The absence of legal aid to support litigation before Industrial Tribunals and the charging of deposits against legal costs must significantly deter potential claimants.[94] Moreover the frequent practice of employers of using legal representation,[95] or similar professional advice from employers' associations,[96] presents claimants with the dilemma of either placing themselves at a disadvantage by presenting the claim in person,[97] or relinquishing control over the way the grievance is presented. The degree of disadvantage to applicants without legal representation is suggested by the relative success of applications before Industrial Tribunals. In a sample from the period 1985–6 applicants representing themselves won in 37 per cent of cases, but with legal representation they won 52 per cent of claims.[98] The claimant's chances of success appear at their lowest when he or she faces in person a legally represented defendant.[99]

Yet without the institution of an independent legal tribunal we must doubt whether the values of autonomy and dignity embedded in the legislation can be realized. A degree of legalism in the practice of Industrial Tribunals is the necessary price to be paid for the achievement of this fundamental goal of the legislation.[100] Unless the arbitration process is severed from control by the parties to the collective agreement, then the individual employee runs an equal risk of losing control over the presentation of his or her claim, a risk which can only be countered by an uncertain and vague legal duty of fair representation placed upon the union officials. But, above all, without a tribunal committed to the values of protecting individual interests against general welfare considerations, the subtle balance between these considerations sought by the law of unfair dismissal is likely to be upset in favour of collective interests in efficiency to the detriment of the individual interest in job security.

These reflections lead me to give broad support to the continuation of the Industrial Tribunal system for adjudicating disputes over dismissal. This

[94] EPCA 1978, Sched. 9, para. 1A(2), as amended by Employment Act 1989, s. 20. See S. Deakin, 'Equality Under a Market Order: The Employment Act 1989' (1990), 19, *ILJ* 1, at pp. 15–16.

[95] Employers have legal representation in slightly less than half of tribunal hearings: 'Special Feature' (1990), 98, *Employment Gazette*, 213, at p. 216; Banerji, Smart and Stevens, 'Unfair Dismissal Cases in 1985–86' at p. 550.

[96] Evans, Goodman, and Hargreaves, 'Unfair Dismissal Law and Changes in the Role of Trade Unions and Employers' Associations', at pp. 100–8; Banerji, Smart, and Stevens, 'Unfair Dismissal Cases in 1985–86' at p. 550.

[97] 'Special Feature' (1990), 98, *Employment Gazette*, 213, at p. 216.

[98] Banerji, Smart, and Stevens, 'Unfair Dismissal Cases in 1985–86', at p. 551.

[99] Hazel Genn and Yvette Genn, *The Effectiveness of Representation at Tribunals* (London, 1989), pp. 87–99; T. Mullen, 'Representation at Tribunals' (1990), 53, *Modern Law Review*, 230, at p. 232.

[100] For a good evaluation of the charge of legalism, see R. Munday, 'Tribunal Lore: Legalism and the Industrial Tribunals' (1981), 10, *ILJ* 146.

support must be qualified by two important reservations. If tribunals are to function effectively in supervising managerial disciplinary power, the many barriers raised by costs and technical requirements to access to justice for employees need to be removed. In addition, the composition of the tribunals also gives cause for concern. I believe that there is a danger that the lay element in the tribunals, that is, the wingmen drawn from both sides of industry, will tend to support the dispensation of popular justice rather than a kind of justice which pays strict attention to the legal rights of individuals. At the beginning of this book, we noted that the 'harsh but fair' dismissal of Mr Mathewson for being arrested during his lunch break in a park for possession of cannabis was approved by the lay members as reasonable but disapproved by the legally qualified chairman of the Industrial Tribunal. This difference in conclusion suggests the hypothesis that the lay members of the tribunals may be more willing than a lawyer to take a broad-brush approach to questions of dismissal, with their opinions suffused with popular ideals and prejudices, whereas the lawyer may be more concerned to take into account the more technical points in such a case, such as the unfairness of the procedure, the element of double punishment involved in both criminal prosecution and dismissal, and the absence of any adverse impact upon Mr Mathewson's work from the drugs. In other words, by their training lawyers may be better tuned to the defence of individual rights than laymen, and in so far as this legislation fits into the goals which I have ascribed to it, then individual rights represent its life-blood. On the other hand, the lay members undoubtedly have much to offer the system of adjudication from their wealth of experience of industrial relations practice in the workplace. The solution seems to lie in more rigorous legal training for the lay members, in order to make them more sensitive to issues of individual rights in their calculations of whether or not the employer acted reasonably.

Conclusion

AT some risk of oversimplification, we can describe the debates about the law of unfair dismissal canvassed in this book as representing an unceasing competition between two paradigms of the employment relation. A traditional paradigm receives its most articulate and authoritative exposition in the common law's conception of the contract of employment. I have attempted to use the law of unfair dismissal as the basis for constructing an alternative paradigm of the employment relation. But whereas the attributes of the traditional paradigm as evidenced by the common law can be clearly identified, the novel paradigm envisioned by the law of unfair dismissal has yet to be articulated fully. The interpretative methodology adopted in this book was intended in part to serve this purpose of constructing vital elements in a new paradigm of the employment relation, one which could fit into a broader scheme of justice in the workplace.

I hope to return one day to the task of elaborating a more comprehensive scheme of workplace justice. This scheme would provide an alternative to the two dominant themes of labour law policy in the twentieth century, the one which idolizes freedom of contract between individual worker and employer, and the other, industrial pluralism, which overstates the virtues and achievements of free collective bargaining. In their place, my scheme of workplace justice would reject both of these approaches to labour law policy on the principal ground that they inevitably render the position of the employee in the workplace contingent upon market forces. My view of the employment relation holds that this relation is too central to the quest to establish social and economic conditions under which individuals have the best chance to be the authors of their own lives to be left to be determined by market forces, which are, in the final analysis, no more than other people's choices.

In this book, however, my ambition has been narrower: to begin to construct a paradigm of the employment relation which fits such a scheme of workplace justice through an interpretation of the modern regulatory legislation of unfair dismissal. It must be admitted that starting at the back end, that is, the termination of the employment relation, is not ideal, but as well as reckoning that this tail wags the whole dog of the employment relation, the relative wealth of legal and social materials in this sphere of life in the workplace seems to offer the chance to make real progress in constructing a new paradigm of the employment relation. But what progress has been made?

Like other social institutions, the employment relation requires legitimacy in the eyes of its participants. For them to participate in the employment relation, to acknowledge and conform to its norms, they must accept its legitimacy, for, without this acceptance, short of brute coercion by the State, disruptive and subversive practices will prevent the social institution from achieving permanence and organizing force within a social order. The basis of this claim to legitimacy of the employment relation as a social institution then determines the shape and depth of its legal regulation. The law reinforces the normative structure of the social institution to the extent and in the manner contemplated in the source of the legitimacy of the social institution itself.

The traditional paradigm of the employment relation comprised in its essentials a market transaction between two private individuals. Its legitimacy as a social institution lay in its similar character to other private market transactions such as consumer purchases. It was an exchange transaction, freely chosen between equal citizens, which subsisted on the basis of the consent of the parties. In the light of this basis for legitimacy of the employment relation, the role of the law in reinforcing its normative structures had to be minimal. The law could ensure that the parties had freely entered into the agreement and could insist upon observance of its terms or require payment of damages instead, but it was beyond the legitimate scope of regulation for the law to impose terms upon the parties or to compel continuation of this private consensual relation. The guiding principles of the common law for regulation of the employment relation became those identified in Chapter 1, namely respect for the private autonomy of the parties through abstention from regulation of the content of the relation, the preservation of an even-handed neutrality between the parties by leaving it mainly to the parties to fix the terms of the agreement, and the protection of the formal equality of the parties by insisting upon the mutuality of rights such as the right to terminate the relation at will.

This traditional paradigm of the employment relation as simply another market contract still manages a considerable hold on popular perceptions of its nature and legitimacy. But I have sought to infer from and through an interpretation of the modern law of termination of employment that this new regulation presupposes a new source of legitimacy for the social institution of the employment relation, one which warrants the new scale and depth of legal regulation as evidenced in both legislation and recent developments in the common law. It is now time to piece together the elements of this new paradigm of the employment relation.

From both the substantive and procedural tests for fairness in the law of unfair dismissal, I think we may infer that the purely contractual image of the employment relation has ceased to be viable. In its place we find the image of a bureaucratic power structure, one which management uses to direct productive operations and to provide incentives for compliance with instructions and disciplinary sanctions to deter deviance. It makes sense within this framework to ask whether the disciplinary power has been exercised for a rational purpose, that is, one which avoids substantial harm to the business, and in a rational manner, that is, a way which is conducive to efficient decisions. In contrast, these questions make little sense within the framework of a freely chosen contractual relation, for it is the essence of this type of relation that it may be terminated at will, that is, for any reason and in any manner subject only to the terms of the agreement. We should infer therefore from the type of regulation countenanced in the law of unfair dismissal that the perception of employment as a simple market transaction has been replaced with a recognition of the bureaucratic framework of governance of the workplace.

Within this bureaucratic framework the ideals of autonomy and individual dignity take on a new resonance. Instead of these ideals being satisfied by the freedom of the parties to enter and terminate the relation on any terms they so wish, a new concern arises for the protection of autonomy and dignity against the potential for abuse of bureaucratic power. The regulation of employers' disciplinary practices through the law of unfair dismissal serves the goal of subjecting these discretionary powers to standards which constrain the rational pursuit of business objectives by the need to protect the individual employee's autonomy and dignity in the workplace.

This concern for the protection of individual rights in the workplace signals a further departure from the traditional paradigm. Instead of the workplace being a private sphere of social life where issues of the protection of individual rights and civil liberties have no place, the public–private distinction begins to collapse. We can infer both from the incipient category of public rights dismissals discerned in the legislative framework and from the increasingly fragile justifications for the exclusion of the public law notions of natural justice from employment relations that the perception of the employment relation as an exclusively private market relation has given way to a more complex perspective, which views the employment relation in terms of membership in an organization, an organization which embodies both public and private dimensions.

This in turn broadens the scope for public regulation of the employment relation. Dimensions of social policy hitherto regarded as only indirectly relevant to the regulation of the employment relation now become matters of central concern. The inept steps so far taken through the law of redundancy to regulate the termination of employment from the perspective of active manpower policies and the minimization of social cost nevertheless reveal a new perception of the employment relation, one where its very existence and the terms on which it is concluded become issues of public policy rather than matters for private agreement.

Summing up this new paradigm of the employment relation, we should highlight three central features. First, it envisages the employment relation as providing membership in an organization, which both implies a degree of continuity of membership and a say in how the organization is run. Secondly, it recognizes that the organization operates through bureaucratic power, a discretionary power which can only be legitimate if exercised for rational business purposes and without infringement of individual rights. Thirdly, the public interest in how these organizations are run and how membership is determined places the employment relation in a public domain in which considerations of public policy recognize no limits in principle to the scope of matters which might be the subject of legal regulation.

On reading this book, I hope that you will share with me both the sense that this new paradigm of the employment relation has been struggling to the surface of popular and legal consciousness, and at the same time the recognition that many of the controversies about the application of the legislation and developments in the common law can be explained in terms of an unceasing competition between the traditional and the modern paradigms of the employment relation. The range of reasonable responses test for fairness in the law of unfair dismissal, for instance, tries to forge a compromise between the traditional paradigm of the private autonomy of the parties and the modern paradigm that disciplinary power should be exercised by rational criteria. The emphasis upon the range of reasonable responses which are possible at the same time both confirms the need for rationality in the exercise of disciplinary power and simultaneously minimizes the degree of intervention by tolerating flexibility in procedural and substantive standards. Similarly, to take another example from the developments in the comon law, the increasing acceptance by the courts of the use by employees of injunctions to enforce disciplinary procedures springs from a notion that membership of an organization entitles the member to have the rules observed by those in positions of authority; but this development has been persistently obstructed by reversion to the private contractual framework in which the need for trust and confidence between the parties has been held up as essential to the continuation of the employment relation.

In so far as I have been critical of the legislation itself, or its application by the courts, then in the main my criticisms have pointed to occasions when the law has failed to grasp and endorse the modern paradigm of the employment relation. One persistent theme of my critical comments has been the failure to grasp the dimensions of public policy at stake in the law of termination of employment. The residual power of the traditional paradigm tends to insist upon a perspective in which the only interests at stake are those of employer and employee, without recognizing that the governance of the workplace raises broader issues of public policy. We can recall, for instance, the courts' willingness to abandon or at least qualify their concern for procedural justice in the exercise of disciplinary power by reference to the justice of the outcome between employer and employee, ignoring the possibility that the public policy which supports fair disciplinary procedures for the sake of respect for individual dignity, orderly collective industrial relations, and efficient manpower decisions should permit no exceptions to the demands of procedural fairness. In a similar vein I have argued that we should abandon the view that job security is essentially a private interest of employees, a kind of property right in the job, and begin to formulate principles which recognize that employers' manpower strategies must be fitted into broader public policies such as the minimization of social cost.

It is far from clear that this new paradigm of the employment relation has taken hold of popular perceptions of the employment relation. During the 1980s in Britain we have witnessed a formidable reassertion of the traditional contractual perception by government. Much of the success of this return to tradition in popular consciousness depends, I believe, upon the relative failure to articulate the alternative paradigm and its consequences for social practice. What I hope to have achieved in this book, if only in outline and at a level of intellectual reflection rather than shop-floor propaganda, is a contribution to the development of this alternative paradigm, so that it may be used as a resource in the future for the social and legal construction of a new perspective upon the employment relation, one which establishes firmer foundations for that vital element in workplace justice—justice in dismissal.

Index